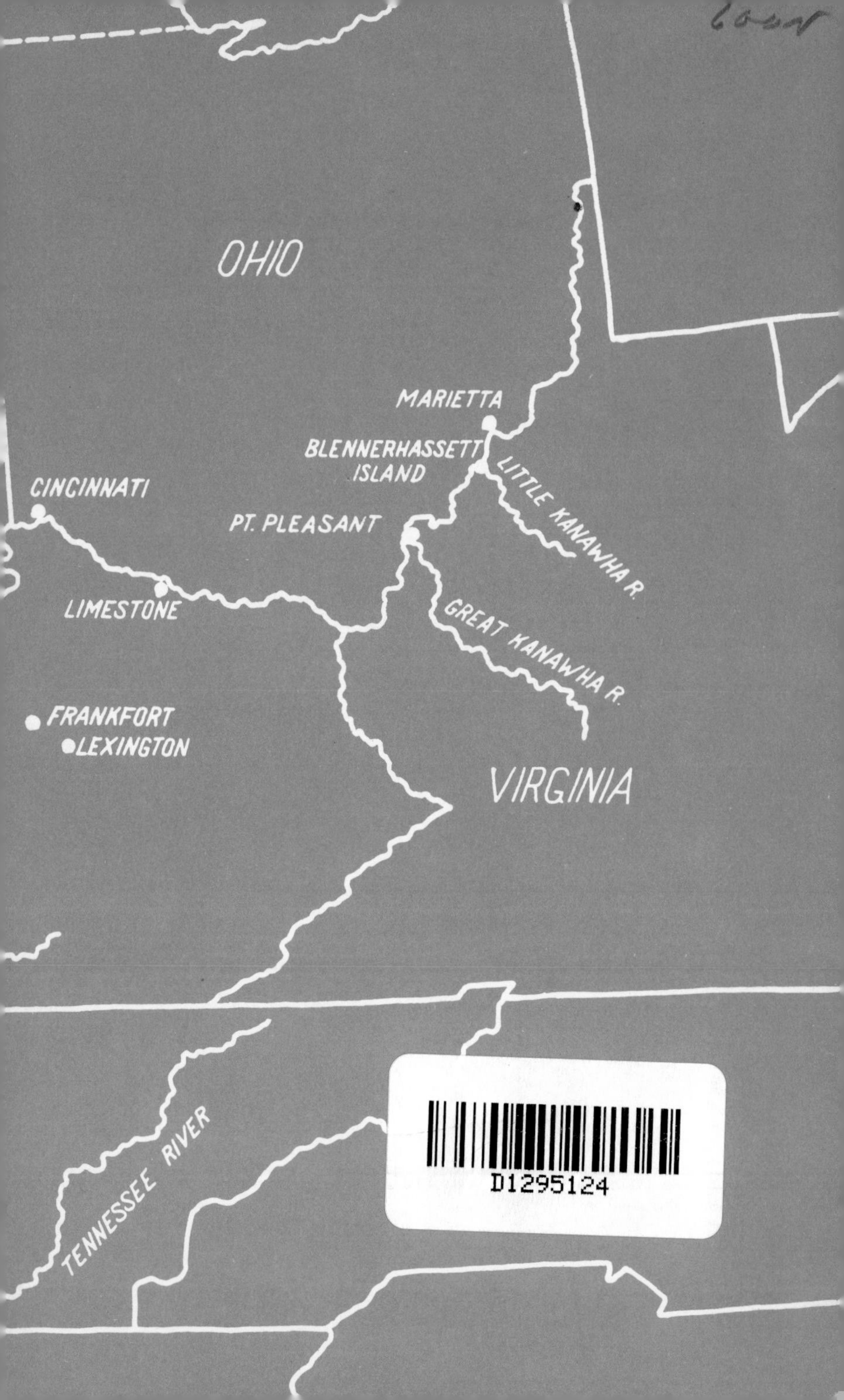
OHIO
MARIETTA
BLENNERHASSETT
ISLAND
LITTLE KANAWHA R.
CINCINNATI
PT. PLEASANT
LIMESTONE
GREAT KANAWHA R.
FRANKFORT
LEXINGTON
VIRGINIA
TENNESSEE RIVER

The Burr Conspiracy

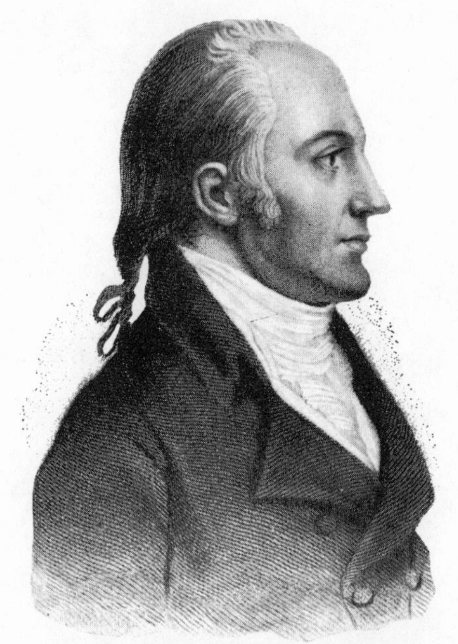

From James Parton's *Life of Aaron Burr*, published in 1858.

A. Burr

THE BURR CONSPIRACY

BY

Thomas Perkins Abernethy

GLOUCESTER, MASS.

PETER SMITH

1968

Library of Congress Catalogue Card Number: 54-6907

Reprinted, 1968 by Permission of
Oxford University Press

PRINTED IN THE UNITED STATES OF AMERICA

To the memory of

BLAKE ROBERTSON

The ocean was his home and
the wide world his alma mater.

PREFACE

In dealing with the first decades of our Union, it should be borne in mind that it takes time to weld a close-knit social and political order. There was no strong national spirit in the early Transmontane West; it was a period of tumult and separatist intrigues — the Spanish conspiracies, the Blount conspiracy, the Genet affair, and finally the Burr conspiracy. Disloyalty to the Union was not then looked on as the heinous crime it is today. It was still widely acknowledged that states which had voluntarily entered the compact could as easily withdraw from it. Even Washington feared that economic factors might bring about an eventual separation of the West from the East. Many men on 'the Western Waters' believed they were being sacrificed to the commercial East; they believed, too, that they had as much right to redress their own grievances as did the Colonies when they revolted against England. Indeed, numerous 'conspirators' were veterans of that struggle and were well aware that if it had failed, the Fathers, instead of founding our Republic, would have been lined up, listening with hard, uneasy faces to the sentence for treason.

The most interesting theme of this period of unrest is the conspiracy of Aaron Burr, who sought to further his overweening ambition by taking advantage of the explosive atmosphere in the West. The justification for a new study of so controversial a subject is to be found in the existence of a considerable body of materials which have been largely unexplored, notably Clarence E. Carter's *Territorial Papers*, Joseph Cabell's notes of evidence before the grand jury in Richmond, contemporary newspapers, and the Library of Congress photostats from the Archivo Histórico Nacional, Madrid.

In dealing with a clandestine operation such as the Burr conspiracy, it is extremely difficult to determine the value of evidence. The author has felt that he would be open to criticism if he undertook to pass upon each item, but he has tried to include, as free from prejudice as possible, all that seemed to be of value and to exclude that which was palpably worthless. Though there is much that cannot be taken at face value, the cumulative effect seems to be conclusive in many respects, especially in regard to Burr's ultimate objectives. It is hoped that the reader, regardless of the author's views, will be able to draw his own conclusions.

Many have assisted with the work. It is no perfunctory acknowledgment which I make to my wife, Ida Robertson Abernethy, the principal contributor, who claims that she has given the best years of her life to Aaron Burr. Lucretia Bishko has been an enthusiastic research assistant, who has gone far beyond the call of duty. John Wyllie, Francis Berkeley, and Louise Savage, of the staff of the Alderman Library, have been constant friends in time of need, and my colleague, Edward Younger, has read the manuscript and made helpful suggestions. To all others who have afforded sustaining aid and encouragement, I can give here only a sweeping expression of gratitude. The work would not have been possible except for the various grants made available by the University of Virginia Institute for Research in the Social Sciences, and one grant from the national Social Science Research Council.

THOMAS PERKINS ABERNETHY

University of Virginia
February 1954

CONTENTS

ABBREVIATIONS

Used in Footnotes

A.E., Cor. Pol., E.U. Archives du Ministère des Affaires Étrangères, Correspondance Politique, États Unis.
A.G.I. Archivo General de Indias.
A.G.N. Archivo de la Nación.
A.H.A. American Historical Association.
A.H.N. Archivo Histórico Nacional.
A.H.R. *American Historical Review.*
A.S.P. *American State Papers.*
Bacon, *Report: Report of the Committee Appointed to Inquire into the Conduct of General Wilkinson,* E. Bacon, Chairman.
Carter, *Territorial Papers:* Clarence Edwin Carter (ed.), *The Territorial Papers of the United States.*
Chillicothe Papers: Records of the United States Court for the Southern District of Ohio, Record group 21, Affidavits relating to the proposed trial of Aaron Burr, 1807. National Archives.
D.A.B. *Dictionary of American Biography.*
Est. Estado.
exp. *expediente.*
J.S.H. *Journal of Southern History.*
leg. *legajo.*
L. of C. Library of Congress.
M.V.H.R. *Mississippi Valley Historical Review.*
Plumer, *Memorandum:* Everett S. Brown (ed.), *William Plumer's Memorandum of Proceedings in the United States Senate, 1803–1807.*

The Burr Conspiracy

Chapter I

STAGE FOR CONSPIRACY

WHEN GEORGE WASHINGTON undertook to shape the destiny of the new government that called itself the United States, the states were united on paper only — even their territorial extent was open to question. By the treaty of 1783 Britain had agreed that the 31st parallel and the Mississippi River should be the southern and western boundaries, but Spain did not recognize the validity of this arrangement. She held all of Florida and Louisiana and claimed her territory included everything west of the Allegheny Mountains and south of the Tennessee River. She actually occupied Natchez, the most important settlement within the disputed region, and exercised a predominant influence over the Indians who were the most numerous and powerful inhabitants of the forests bordering the Gulf of Mexico.

The American position was stronger between the Tennessee and Ohio rivers. Such settlements as Louisville, Lexington, Frankfort, and Nashville had been able to hold their own against the hostile savages, but their inhabitants were not altogether happy in their isolation. Virginia and North Carolina had jurisdiction here, but neither these states nor the new Federal Government afforded much protection to the frontiersmen, who were still in constant danger outside the stockades of their primitive log forts. And if they wished to trade with the outside world, they had only their rivers which flowed into the Mississippi and down to Spanish New Orleans. The Father of Waters was truly their life line.

These hardy backwoodsmen who had made a home for themselves on the Western waters often had reason to feel that they were neglected by their compatriots of the Atlantic seaboard and were inclined to put their trust in their own resources. It is not surprising that Washington feared they might in time break away from the Union which he was trying to cement. Somewhat later Thomas Jefferson, writing about the Western settlers, said that 'if they see their interests in separation, why should we take sides with our Atlantic rather than our Mississippi descendants? God bless them both, and keep them in union, if it be for their good, but separate them, if it be better.' Still later he maintained that 'whether we remain in one confederacy, or form into Atlantic and Mississippi confederacies, I believe not very important to the happiness of either part. Those of the Western confederacy will be as much our children and descendants as those of the Eastern, and I feel myself as much identified with that country in future as with this.' In 1806 the Master of Monticello did not view a separation of the states quite so complacently.

In addition to the typical Westerner who fought Indians, grew corn, and distilled whiskey, the frontier attracted a miscellaneous lot of characters. Some were fugitives from justice and a few were fugitives from their wives; some were ambitious young lawyers hoping to turn a quick dollar from the litigation produced by conflicting land claims; and some were land speculators who hoped to make fortunes at the expense of brawny farmers seeking homesteads. Outstanding in this last group was James Wilkinson of Kentucky, founder of Frankfort and dreamer of strange dreams. Land speculation was only one of his varied interests.

Born in Maryland and married to the daughter of Clement Biddle of Philadelphia, Wilkinson had served during the Revolution as an officer of dubious reputation. Now pompous and domineering, now the fawning sycophant, his loyalty always went to the highest bidder. In 1784 he moved to Kentucky and went into the mercantile business, and later branched out into land speculation and politics. Taking the lead in a movement to establish Kentucky as a separate state, he went to New Orleans in 1787 and was introduced to the Spanish Governor, Esteban Miró, by a prominent merchant named Daniel Clark, who became his agent there. In the same year Wilkinson swore allegiance to the Spanish crown and was granted the exclusive privilege of selling Kentucky produce in the Louisiana metropolis. The next year he made a strenuous effort to separate Kentucky from Virginia, which district upon achieving statehood was not to join the Confederation but to be left free to make terms with her Spanish neighbors. Since he had himself monopolized the right to sell produce in New Orleans, leaving others no alternative except to transport their goods over the formidable mountain barrier to the Eastern cities, Wilkinson naturally found many malcontents ready to fall in with his scheme. Though supported by leading citizens, the plot failed because of opposition by the rank-and-file of sturdy pioneers. This incident is known as the 'Spanish Conspiracy,' though it might more fittingly have been named for Wilkinson, who was granted a pension of $2000 per year by the Spanish Government.

The creation of the new Federal Government in 1789 gave pause to Western secessionists and two years later Wilkinson decided to become a soldier again. He was commissioned a lieutenant-colonel in the regular army, and in 1792 he was promoted to the rank of brigadier-general. Two years later he fought under General Anthony Wayne at the battle of Fallen Timbers, where the Northern Indians were so decisively defeated, and in 1797 he became the ranking general of the United States Army, though the second star was not awarded him. Meanwhile the Spaniards had appropriated $16,000 for his nefarious use. His value to them went up with every promotion.

In 1795 the Spanish minister, Manuel de Godoy, negotiated with Thomas Pinckney the treaty of San Lorenzo whereby the 31st parallel was finally recognized as the boundary between Florida and the United States, and a place of deposit was established in New Orleans where American goods coming down the Mississippi could be unloaded for reshipment on ocean-going vessels. Thus the grievances of the West were largely removed. Peace was established with both the Northern and Southern Indians, and Western produce could move unmolested to the sea. Hordes of settlers flocked to Kentucky which had become a state in 1792, and to Tennessee, which was admitted to the Union in 1796.

But one problem was no sooner settled than another arose. The state of Georgia claimed that her western boundary extended to the Mississippi River, but the Federal Government asserted a right to that area which now lies within the states of Alabama and Mississippi; until 1795 Spain also laid claim to this territory. While the agreement with Spain was being negotiated, Georgia decided to settle the matter by taking possession of the land. Accordingly she granted fifty million acres of it to several companies of speculators who had shamefully bribed all but two members of the legislature. These 'Yazoo' grants created such a furor in the state that they were revoked the next year. In 1798 the United States, without consulting Georgia, created the Mississippi Territory and included in it the disputed lands, and it was not until 1802 that Georgia gave up her claim and turned over to the Federal Government the problem of dealing with the Yazoo speculators, who, meanwhile, had sold such rights as they possessed to investors who lived mostly in the commercial cities of the East. After several years the Supreme Court ruled that a land grant amounted to a contract and could not be revoked by a state, but still Congress made no provision for settling the dispute.

Thus there was created a considerable group of men of means who felt that the United States Government was denying their just claims to lands in the West. In addition to these Yazoo speculators, there were various other groups who claimed Western lands under cessions made by the Indians before and during the Revolution. Congress similarly refused to validate their dubious claims. There was conflict also over grants that the Spanish authorities had made in the territory they surrendered by the treaty of 1795; and later there were many small farmers who bought Federal lands for which they found themselves unable to pay. The patriotism of some of these men was liable to waver in case there was a movement to separate the West from the Union.

One of the Yazoo speculators was William Blount, senator from Tennessee, but his interest in this deal was small compared to the enormous claims he held in his own state. The value of lands depended on access to markets, and though Tennesseans could now send their produce down to New Orleans, the rivers flowing into Mobile Bay offered much shorter routes in case they could be developed. But the rivers flowing into the Gulf of Mexico through

West Florida were still closed to American commerce by the Spaniards. To make matters worse, Spain, in alliance with France, was now at war with Great Britain, and a rumor was circulated that Spain was going to cede Florida to her ally and again close the navigation of the Mississippi.

At this time Americans sharply divided their sympathies between France and England. Many, still thinking of their recent struggle for independence, believed that the French Revolution offered a new hope in the world — a world in which the common man would rule in the interest of liberty, equality, and fraternity. Thomas Jefferson was the leader of this element, whose partisans called themselves Republicans. But there were others who, despite recent differences, looked upon the British Government as the best in the world, and thought law and order, juridical and property rights, were being undermined by the French Jacobins. The term Federalist was applied to this pro-British element. Its strength lay in the Eastern cities and, fearing the loss of population and trade, it was consistently opposed to westward expansion.

Being a Federalist, Blount's sympathies were with the British and he believed France would be a more disagreeable neighbor than Spain. Consequently, in collaboration with Robert Liston, British minister to the United States, he concocted a scheme to bring down an expedition from Canada that would be joined by a legion of American frontiersmen, and as many of the Southern Indians as could be enlisted, for an attack on the Spaniards in Florida and Louisiana. Blount, of course, expected to get concessions for American trade in the event the British took over these provinces. An incautious letter found its way into print, and as a result the Tennessean was summarily expelled from his seat in the Senate. Federal officers were sent to his home state to arrest him but none of the local officers would execute the warrant. Furthermore, the president of the state senate resigned his place so that Blount might be chosen to occupy it. Thus it will be seen that the Westerners were inclined to view international relations in a light quite different from that which illumined the national councils.

It was not until 1801 that Napoleon succeeded in persuading Spain to retrocede Louisiana to France. Louisiana was not a profitable colony; it had never paid its way, and its chief value to Spain was as a buffer between the Americans and her rich Mexican empire. In 1802 Spain had not yet surrendered the province to France, and the Intendant, Don Juan Ventura Morales, withdrew the right of Americans to deposit and transship their produce at New Orleans. Thinking that France was responsible for this policy, the people throughout the West sent up a roar of rage. Kentucky threatened to move alone against New Orleans and West Florida if the Federal Government did not support her. Andrew Jackson wanted to take his backwoods militiamen and cut his way 'through the damned greasers to the City of Mexico.' The Federalists also demanded war. President Jefferson resisted this demand and instead sent James Monroe to Paris to assist Robert Livingston, our minister there, in purchasing New Orleans and West Florida. To their astonishment, Napoleon, who was having his troubles at home, offered to sell all Louisiana, and in 1803 one of the most amazing bargains in history was consummated. The Spanish were exceedingly wroth over the sale and Cevallos, the foreign minister, protested in strong terms, stating frankly that his king had consented to the retrocession of Louisiana to France only in order 'to interpose a strong dyke between the Spanish colonies and the American possessions.' Now, he continued bitterly, 'the doors to Mexico are to stay open to them.'

Arrangements were finally made for Spain to turn the province over to the French. For this formality, Napoleon sent Pierre Clement de Laussat to New Orleans as colonial prefect and Spain sent the Marquis of Casa Calvo as a special commissioner to act with Governor Juan Manuel de Salcedo. On 30 November 1803, these three officials met in the Cabildo at New Orleans and title to the vast region called Louisiana passed from Spain to France. Thus the last Spanish governor vanished from the picture. The Intendant, Morales, was presently transferred to the same office in West Florida, though he and Casa Calvo tarried for some time in New Orleans. It now remained only for de Laussat to transfer the jurisdiction of the province to the United States.

Such was the stage upon which a bizarre cast was soon to play out the drama of Burr's conspiracy: a motley population living in territory where land claims overlapped each other like shingles on a roof. Fortunate was the man who knew whether the tract of land on which he dwelt was actually his. These were staunch Americans whose first loyalty was to their own section rather than to the Federal Government and who did not question their right to leave the Union as easily as they had entered it; resourceful men who did not hesitate to redress their own grievances. Still threatened by the Indians, hemmed in by the great Appalachian wall on the east, at the mercy of inimical foreigners on the south who could sever at will their only artery of trade, the West, with little help forthcoming from the Federal Government, was seething with unrest. Into this explosive atmosphere Aaron Burr cast the inflammatory blandishments of his secessionist panacea. He was almost ready to lift his voice in an exultant *Te Deum* when James Wilkinson by his treachery, and the more level-headed frontiersmen by their common sense, pulled his house down around his ears.

Chapter II

BEGINNINGS OF THE CONSPIRACY

ON 20 DECEMBER 1803, the *Place d'Armes* of New Orleans was the scene of a little ceremony that represented the conclusion of one of history's significant transactions. It also represented the beginning of another series of events to be known as the Burr Conspiracy which were only a little less momentous than the acquisition of Louisiana by the United States. Governor William C. C. Claiborne of the Mississippi Territory and James Wilkinson, Commanding General of the United States Army, had come to the city to accept delivery of the province from the French Prefect, Pierre Clement de Laussat. After exchanging credentials and reading the treaty of cession in the Cabildo, these officials made their appearance on the balcony that overlooked the *Place d'Armes*. The buildings flanking this public square were much the same then as they are today, but instead of the rampant statue of Andrew Jackson in the center, there was a flagpole flying the colors of Republican France. Wilkinson's troops and the local militia faced each other across the square, and when the officials appeared on the balcony the French flag was lowered and the American banner went up. When they met at the center of the pole a signal gun was fired and this was answered immediately by salvos from the land batteries and the armed ships in the river.[1]

It was a fine morning and a large crowd had turned out to witness the ceremonies, but the French Creoles of New Orleans stood silent

[1] Charles Gayarré, *History of Louisiana* (New Orleans, 1885), III, 619–20.

during this historic spectacle. Only a small group of Americans standing at one corner of the square showed their patriotism by waving their hats and giving voice to a few cheers.[2] The people of Louisiana, nearly all of whom were French, had no great love for their late Spanish masters, but neither did they have any enthusiasm for the new Republic which was now to rule them.

General Wilkinson was not disturbed by the attitude of the Creoles, but he was keenly interested in that of the Spanish officials. The Marquis of Casa Calvo, still in New Orleans, had been joined by Don Vizente Folch, Governor of West Florida. Shortly after the ceremonies at the Cabildo, the American general got in touch with these officials and complained that his Spanish pension was in arrears to the extent of $20,000.[3] When they demurred at his demand for payment, he wrote to the Marquis on 12 March 1804, as follows:

> The Memorial which accompanies this Letter has its origin in the anxious solicitude which I feel for the prosperity of the two Powers, which I love equally . . . If your Excellency finds that these Reflections deserve consideration . . . I beg that they be sent to His Majesty's ministers, and if my agency be judged acceptable . . . I must ask that His Majesty deign to sanction the means, arrangements and observations following:
>
> My name, and whatever I shall write ought not to be disclosed, except to the first Minister of State [Godoy]; to Your Excellency, to Colonel Don Vincente Folch, Governor of West Florida, and in case of death or absence, to Don Gilberto Leonard, late Comptroller of Louisiana; to Don Andres Armesto, Secretary of the Boundary Commission . . . my name or condition shall never be written, and always shall be designated by the number 13.
>
> All our correspondence must be carried on in cypher; in general it shall be with Your Excellency alone, or in case that is impracticable, with Governor Folch . . . prepare me for addressing myself directly to the First Minister of State of Spain [Godoy] in case some sudden occurrence so demands.
>
> Don Gilberto Leonard will stay in this City, to receive, under a supposititious address, my information, or correspondence, with Your Excellency or with Governor Folch, in case of your absence . . . Don

[2] Ibid. 620.
[3] Ibid. 616.

Andres Armesto . . . should remain near Your Excellency to decipher, interpret, and facilitate our correspondence.

Wilkinson then asked to be paid immediately the arrears of his pension, amounting to $20,000, 'owed to me from the pension of 2000 which was granted to me during the governorship of Don Estaban Miro in the year 1788, and which has been withdrawn since 1793: the said pension having been raised to 4000 pesos at the beginning of this year, this being 2000 less than the salary which I now enjoy.' He considered the renewal of his pension to be a just recompense 'for the services which I shall render, and more particularly, to indemnify me for the eventual loss of the office which I hold, and which probably it will seem necessary for me to abandon in case of hostilities. This pension will be paid to me by the hand of Your Excellency or of Governor Folch . . .'

Yet this was not all the amiable General desired, and he continued:

So that I can extend my credit, attracting to our designs and interests certain individuals of influence in the national councils of the United States, I beg that it be permitted me further to propose that there be granted me the annual exportation of 16,000 barrels of flour from the said States to Havana for the space of four years, by which concession His Majesty will . . . aid me to form a corps of auxiliaries around the President made up of persons whom I know, and whose influence will be of irresistible weight.

Then, for the rest of his life, he wanted the right to export 5000 barrels annually to Havana, 'provided that the business which I propose should have the outcome which is expected . . . Spain recovering the right bank of the Mississippi.' Brigadier-General Wilkinson was also 'counting on effective precautions being taken, so that the correspondence may go safely, with the object of hiding my name . . . to which end I beg that this letter be destroyed after it is translated and certified: . . .' [4]

The General, after some dickering, accepted a cash payment of 12,000 pesos in lieu of the arrears of his pension, and promised to submit such information to the Spanish Government as he thought

[4] Wilkinson to Casa Calvo, 12 Mar. 1804, Archivo Histórico Nacional (Madrid, photostats in Library of Congress), Estado, legajo 5545, expediente 15, 463–70. (Cited hereafter as A.H.N.)

would be useful to it. In fulfillment of this stipulation, he drew up and presented a memorial in which he advised the Spanish authorities to fortify the Texas and Florida frontiers against American attack, to maintain control over the neighboring Indians, and to arrest the exploring expedition then operating under the command of Meriwether Lewis and William Clark. He stressed the aggressiveness of the Americans and insisted that Spain should work for the retrocession of the west bank of the Mississippi in order to forestall encroachments into Texas and the Interior Provinces.[5]

On 30 March, Casa Calvo forwarded a translation of Wilkinson's letter and memorial to Don Pedro Cevallos, the Spanish foreign minister, with the recommendation that Wilkinson's demands be granted but that Spain go beyond his proposals and seek to obtain the retrocession of the island of New Orleans in addition to the west bank of the Mississippi in exchange for commercial facilities in that city; the cession of East and West Florida, including Baton Rouge; and an unspecified monetary consideration. The Spanish Government approved the payment of the 12,000 pesos and the renewal of Wilkinson's pension. It also complimented Casa Calvo on the means he had adopted to keep the transaction secret from all but the few agents mentioned in Wilkinson's letter. The correspondence thus begun was continued for the next three years, and the Spanish minister to the United States, the Marquis of Casa Yrujo, also participated in it.[6]

Thus the General was making the most of the situation, but Louisiana was not the land of promise to all Americans. The Federalists of the Eastern states were bitter in their denunciation of the purchase, for the expanding West could be expected to draw off their population, rival their trade, and some day dominate the

[5] Isaac J. Cox, 'General Wilkinson and His Later Intrigues with the Spaniards,' *American Historical Review*, XIX (1913–14), 795–801 (cited hereafter as *A.H.R.*); *idem* 'The Louisiana-Texas Frontier,' Pt. II, 28–32, reprinted from *Southwestern Historical Quarterly*, XVII (1912–13), nos. 1–2; Nathan Schachner, *Aaron Burr* (New York, 1937), 293; Daniel Clark, *Proofs of the Corruption of Gen. James Wilkinson, and of His Connexion with Aaron Burr* (Philadelphia, 1809), 81–2; Philadelphia *Aurora*, 16 Jan. 1808.

[6] Casa Calvo to Cevallos, 30 Mar. 1804, A.H.N., Est., leg. 5545, exp. 15, 440–62, no. 1, 472–8, no. 3; Minute to Casa Calvo, 18 July 1804, ibid. 471, 479; Isaac J. Cox, 'The Louisiana-Texas Frontier,' loc. cit. 173–4.

Union. They felt this so strongly that four of New England's Federalist senators, led by Timothy Pickering, came to the conclusion that a dissolution of the Union was the only answer. Aaron Burr's brother-in-law, Tapping Reeve, wrote that he had seen many friends and all those whom he had consulted believed that the New England states must separate from the Union 'and that this is the favorable moment.' Roger Griswold of Connecticut was the leader of the secessionist forces in the House, and it was decided to bring New York into the plan by having Vice-President Burr elected governor of that state with the aid of the Federalist vote. The election was to take place 25 April 1804, and Burr decided to canvass although his term of office did not expire until March of the following year. Alexander Hamilton employed all his talents to defeat him, and so bitter were some of his invectives that a duel between the two ensued. When Hamilton was killed in the encounter at Weehawken on 11 July, feeling against Burr was strong and a warrant was sworn out for his arrest. He fled to Philadelphia and took refuge with his friend Charles Biddle, who was also a close friend of General Wilkinson.[7] Burr and Wilkinson had been friends since they were young officers together on the Quebec expedition during the Revolution. They often met at Biddle's home, and it was during this sojourn in Philadelphia that they concocted the first definite plans for the great conspiracy.[8] Aaron Burr, well-born, well-educated, a veteran of the Revolution, and a leading member of the New York bar, had been elected to the United States Senate at the age of 35. He and Thomas Jefferson had tied for the Presidency in 1800, and when the election was thrown into the House, Jefferson won by a single vote on the 36th ballot, and Burr became Vice-President. A dapper, elegant man of the world, Burr had innumerable affairs of gallantry; he was a hopeless spendthrift, being always head over heels in debt; he had a mania for education and turned his daughter into

[7] Charles Biddle, *Autobiography* (Philadelphia, 1883), 303–4; Albert J. Beveridge, *The Life of John Marshall* (Boston, 1916–19), III, 281–2; Francis Franklin, *The Rise of the American Nation*, 1789–1824 (New York, 1943), 149–50; Claude G. Bowers, *Jefferson in Power* (Boston, 1936), 216–17, 228, 246–7; Albert F. Simpson, 'The Political Significance of Slave Representation, 1787–1821,' *Journal of Southern History*, VII (1941), 327. (Cited hereafter as *J.S.H.*)

[8] Charles Biddle, *Autobiography*, 303–4.

one of the most learned women of her day; he captivated his friends by his charm and wit; the simpler sort of people he won by a kind of condescending bonhomie. Bold and ambitious, he was capable of planning high adventure, but he was loquacious and visionary and his dreams often ran away with his judgment. Now, at 48, the Colonel — he was usually called by his Revolutionary title — in the prime of life, was a financial and political bankrupt as well as a fugitive from justice. His career in the East was finished. But westward there were new worlds to conquer; he saw himself there at the head of a vast empire, larger and more powerful than the one he had lost by a *single* vote.

Burr and his friend James Wilkinson, with whom he was now conspiring in Philadelphia, were strangely contrasting figures. The Brigadier drank much and talked more, constantly prating of his sacred honor and his undying love for his country. Florid, robust, and swaggering, he lacked the appearance of subtlety but possessed it in marked degree. On the other hand, Burr, with his finely chiseled features and courtly, ingratiating manners, appeared to be the perfect diplomat but proved to be a bungler in intrigue. With all his charm and talent, he was no match for Wilkinson, the most skillful and unscrupulous plotter this country has ever produced.

On his return from New Orleans during the previous May, Wilkinson had spent the night with Burr at his stately 'Richmond Hill' estate overlooking the Hudson. Shortly afterward they met again in New York and discussed some scheme affecting our relations with Spain. During their sojourn in Philadelphia the two conspirators became associated with an Englishman named Charles Williamson, a friend of Henry Dundas, Lord Melville. Williamson now went to the British minister, Anthony Merry, and reported that Burr was prepared to assist the British Government in separating the Western states from the American Union. Merry recommended this proposal to his superiors and soon Williamson journeyed to London to advocate the plan.[9]

[9] James Wilkinson to Aaron Burr, 23 May 1804, W. C. Ford, 'Some Papers of Aaron Burr,' reprinted from *Proceedings of the American Antiquarian Society*, Apr. 1919 (Worcester, 1920), 82–3; I. J. Cox, 'Hispanic-American Phases of the Burr Conspiracy,' *Hispanic American Historical Review*, XII (May 1932), 145–50; *idem* 'Western Reaction to the Burr Conspiracy,' *Transactions of the Illinois State His-*

In the British capital he found Francisco de Miranda, a Venezuelan soldier of fortune, trying to induce the British Government to back an expedition to revolutionize South America. There was some hope of success with the Ministry, for war between England and Spain was threatening, and it actually broke out on 12 December 1804. Williamson served as an intermediary between Miranda and some of the ministers at the same time that he was backing the scheme of Burr and Merry.[10]

Shortly after Williamson's departure for London, Burr had started out for St. Augustine with a letter from the Spanish minister, the Marquis of Casa Yrujo. With young Samuel Swartwout of New York as his secretary, he went by boat from Philadelphia and reached St. Simon's Island, Georgia. Several members of the Swartwout family were important figures in the conspiracy. They proved to be unwavering friends throughout Burr's adversity, and thirty years later two of them helped to bear him to his Princeton grave. At St. Simon's an autumnal storm prevented the voyagers from proceeding to St. Augustine, and in returning northward Burr traveled nearly 200 miles in an open canoe to visit his beloved daughter Theodosia and his grandson, Aaron Burr Alston, in Charleston.[11] 'Gampy,' as the grandson was called, was to embark at the ripe age of two on a formidable program of education laid out for him by his grandfather.

While Burr and his henchmen were busy laying the groundwork of their intrigue, Upper Louisiana was, on 26 March 1804, incorporated as the District of Louisiana. At the same time all that part of the Louisiana Purchase lying south of the 33rd parallel was incorporated as the Territory of Orleans, and William C. C. Claiborne was appointed its governor. The American judicial system was in-

---

torical Society (Springfield, 1928), 74; Thomas Robson Hay, 'Charles Williamson and the Burr Conspiracy,' *J.S.H.*, II (1936), 181–3; Henry Adams, *History of the United States of America* (New York, 1890–91), II, 395; Edward Channing, *A History of the United States* (New York, 1916–26), IV, 336–9.

[10] William S. Robertson, *Life of Miranda* (Chapel Hill, 1929), I, 284, 293.

[11] Mark Van Doren (ed.), *Correspondence of Aaron Burr and His Daughter Theodosia* (New York, 1929), 177; *Raleigh Register and North Carolina State Gazette*, 10 Sept., 8, 29 Oct. 1804; *Georgia Republican and State Intelligencer* (Savannah), 16 Oct. 1804; *Louisiana Gazette* (New Orleans), 2 Nov. 1804; James Parton, *Life and Times of Aaron Burr* (New York, 1858), 371; I. J. Cox, 'Louisiana-Texas Frontier,' loc. cit. 274.

troduced, English became the official language, and the Creoles were required to prove their land titles and to pay taxes — things they had never been made to do under the Spanish regime.[12] They naturally objected to all this and also to the fact that under the first phase of territorial government they had no legislature or elected officials.[13]

The Creoles were inclined to be apathetic in political matters, and, though they had no love for the American regime, they would hardly have made any trouble if left to themselves. But refugees from revolutionary France had recently arrived, and Americans were pouring into the Territory. Among these elements were some men of restless tempers and political and economic ambitions. Their activities were first called to the attention of the Administration in a letter addressed by one John W. Gurley to Gideon Granger, the Postmaster General, 14 July 1804. He reported that some American adventurers had consorted with a few French inhabitants to cause trouble, and that Edward Livingston was the only man of talent among them, though General Wilkinson was accused of having taken a hand in the business before he left the city. The agitators, Gurley reported, had assembled about 200 French citizens, had themselves elected delegates to present their grievances to Congress, and Livingston had framed the memorial. This document protested the abolition of the slave trade and the division of Louisiana into two territories, demanded immediate statehood, and threatened resistance in case the demands were not met. The memorial had not been published when Gurley wrote to Granger about it, but he said that an appeal to Napoleon had been planned by the agitators.[14]

The most conspicuous leaders of this movement were Daniel Clark and Edward Livingston. The latter was the brother of Robert R. Livingston of New York, who, with James Monroe, had nego-

[12] Ben. Perley Poore, *The Federal and State Constitutions, Colonial Charters, and Other Organic Laws of the United States* (Washington, 1878), I, 691–5.

[13] Claiborne to Jefferson, 10 Dec. 1804, Clarence E. Carter (ed.), *The Territorial Papers of the United States* (Washington, 1940), IX, 348–9; Gayarré, *History of Louisiana*, IV, 1–7.

[14] *Memorial Presented by the Inhabitants of Louisiana to the Congress of the United States in Senate and House of Representatives Convened* (Washington, 1804); John W. Gurley to the Postmaster General, 14 July 1804, Carter, *Territorial Papers*, IX, 262–5.

tiated the Louisiana Purchase and who was to become Secretary of State in the Cabinet of Andrew Jackson. At the moment Edward was not doing so well. He had been educated at Princeton, had prepared himself for the practice of law, and had served several terms in the Federal House of Representatives. When that body was called upon in 1801 to decide between Aaron Burr and Thomas Jefferson for President, Livingston, though a personal friend of Burr, voted consistently for Jefferson. During the same year he was appointed mayor of New York City and also Federal district attorney. He accepted both offices, but in 1803 one of his agents defaulted and left him saddled with a debt to the Government of $43,666. His personal obligations at the same time amounted to an additional $195,000. As a consequence of this financial entanglement, he decided to start life over in New Orleans.[15] Daniel Clark was an Irishman who had come to the Crescent City from Sligo in 1786 to join his uncle of the same name who was one of the leading local merchants and the man who had befriended Wilkinson in 1787. For a time the junior Clark had worked as a clerk in the office of the Spanish governor and in this capacity he became acquainted with the intrigues which Wilkinson had initiated at that time.[16]

When the Mississippi Territory was organized in 1798, young Clark bought lands in the neighborhood of Natchez, became an American citizen, and renewed his acquaintance with Wilkinson, who by now had become a brigadier-general. In 1801 President Jefferson appointed Clark American consul at New Orleans and, though he never won Spanish recognition, he served unofficially until Spain surrendered Louisiana. On hearing that Spain had ceded the province to France, he hastened to Paris, probably with the idea of seeking political preferment. Nothing came of this journey, and in March 1803 he wrote to the Secretary of State, James Madison, to warn that Spain continued to hope that she might bring about a

[15] Richmond (Va.) *Enquirer*, 30 Aug. 1805; Allen Johnson and Dumas Malone (eds.), *Dictionary of American Biography* (New York, 1928–37), XI, 309–12. (Cited hereafter as *D.A.B.*)

[16] Ibid. IV, 125; Thomas P. Abernethy, *Western Lands and the American Revolution* (New York, 1937), 298, 327–8.

separation of the Western from the Eastern states of the Union. In the autumn of the same year he went even further and proposed that Governor Claiborne and General Wilkinson lead an American expedition to take New Orleans, for which purpose he promised to furnish, personally, $100,000.[17] For such service he hoped to be appointed governor of Orleans Territory, but when this aspiration was disappointed, he joined the opponents of the Administration. On 10 October 1804, he wrote to a friend:

> *I have encouraged, and will continue to encourage, the outcry and opposition to their* [the Government's] *measures; and if our grievances are not redressed, will infallably turn the popular odium against the advisers and promoters of them.* Our memorial, I presume, will trouble the digestion of *some folks*, who, since 1776, have *talked* so much about liberty . . . I have made the tour of the western parts of the country [Louisiana] . . . have every where pointed out to the people, who assembled at my call, in every parish, the disregard and violation of their rights; have read to them, and commented on, our memorial, which was universally approved of; and at the same time circulated universally for their information, copies of the address of Congress in 1774, to the Canadians . . . and the law for the government of Louisiana, that the people might compare the one with the other . . . You . . . may possibly conceive an idea of the success I have met with, and the effect produced by my journey. It will turn neither to the honor nor interest of those who have attempted to injure me . . . [who] might find it more prudent to soothe than attempt to irritate or prejudice me.

Clark went on to say that he had seen orders that the French Ministry of Marine and Colonies had given de Laussat before the treaty with the United States, orders that left the whole of Florida in the hands of Spain, and he stated that he believed we would never 'burn a priming' should Spain persist in retaining it. He then ended his letter with a flourish: 'Were they asleep when he [Jefferson] appointed that creature, Claiborne, to degrade the American government in the eyes of the inhabitants of Louisiana? . . . At the end of this month I shall go to Orleans to have an eye to the proceedings

[17] Clark to Madison, 8 Mar. 1803, Walter Lowrie and Walter S. Franklin (eds.), *American State Papers* (Washington, 1832–61), *Miscellaneous*, I, 713 (cited hereafter as *A.S.P.*); James Wilkinson, *Memoirs of my Own Times* (Philadelphia, 1816), II, app. 58.

of the legislature; and, in concert with a number more, well attached to their country, to point out to the people the consequences of all measures proposed, in order to prevent abuses.' [18]

In October an urgent letter from William Cooke of New York warned the Administration that a plot, presumably of French origin, was being directed against Louisiana. Another writer stated, however, that 'notwithstanding the plausible subtleties of a few ambitious schemers,' most of the thinking people of the Territory had never acquiesced in the demand for immediate statehood.[19]

At this juncture Burr was visiting in Georgia, and so far as we know there was no connection between his plans and the proceedings in New Orleans — that is, unless it is significant that his stepson, John B. Prevost, was one of the Territorial judges and an intimate of Livingston, and that the Territorial secretary, James Brown, brother to Senator John Brown of Kentucky, was a friend of the Vice-President. These appointments had been made on Burr's recommendation — in intrigue it is well to have friends in the seats of the mighty.[20]

Burr and Wilkinson spent the winter of 1804–5 in Washington and devoted much of their time to copying maps of East and West Florida, Orleans and Louisiana territories, and adjacent Spanish territory. The Baron von Humboldt had recently presented Jefferson with a copy of his map of Mexico, with the stipulation that it should not be duplicated. Wilkinson's request to be allowed to make a copy had been denied, but Burr somehow got access to it and had it reproduced.[21] On 10 December 1804, John Adair wrote the General that 'Mexico glitters in our eyes . . . the word is all we wait for,' but war with Spain was a prerequisite.[22] A month later

[18] Richmond *Enquirer*, 23 Feb. 1808, quoting Philadelphia *Aurora*.

[19] William Cooke to Secretary of State, 6 Oct. 1804, Carter, *Territorial Papers*, IX, 309–10; Jeremiah Brown, *A Short Letter to a Member of Congress Concerning the Territory of Orleans* (Washington 1806).

[20] Adams, *History of the United States*, III, 219.

[21] Isaac J. Cox, *The West Florida Controversy*, 1798–1813 (Baltimore, 1918), 188; Walter F. McCaleb, *The Conquest of the West* (New York, 1947), 33ff.; Joseph Wheaton's deposition, *Report of the Committee Appointed to Inquire into the Conduct of General Wilkinson*, E. Bacon, Chairman (Washington, 1811), 203–4 (cited hereafter as Bacon, *Report*); Memorandum by Genl. Henry Lee, *re* Humboldt map, Wilkinson MSS., Library of Congress; Parton, *Burr*, 384–7.

[22] James Riley Jacobs, *Tarnished Warrior, Major-General James Wilkinson* (New

Wilkinson wrote to Major James Bruff, commanding officer at St. Louis, and asked for information about Mexico, especially concerning the route to Santa Fe.[23] During February the New Orleans deputation, consisting of Messrs. Derbigny, Destréhan, and Sauve, arrived in Washington and presented Livingston's memorial to Congress. Wilkinson introduced them to Burr, whom he spoke of as 'the first gentleman of America,' saying that he was a man of the most eminent political and military talents, that he was certain to succeed in all that he undertook, and that, as soon as his term as Vice-President expired, he was going to Louisiana where he would undertake certain projects. The General asked Derbigny to give Burr all possible information about that part of the country, a request that, along with Wilkinson's line of conduct, quite mystified the gentlemen from New Orleans.[24] Congress did not see fit to grant statehood to the Territory of Orleans or to make any other major concession except to authorize the election of a Territorial assembly and a delegate to represent Orleans in Congress. Daniel Clark was presently chosen to fill this post.[25]

Naturally the commissioners were disgruntled and threatened to seek redress elsewhere, but Burr and Wilkinson saw no reason to complain. The unrest was a great asset to them. The same bill that gave Orleans Territory a legislature provided for the establishment of a regular Territorial government in that part of the Louisiana Purchase lying north of the 33rd parallel. This, when first incorporated as the District of Louisiana, had been put under the jurisdiction of the governor of Indiana Territory; but now Louisiana Territory, as it was called, was to have a governor of its own, and at Burr's request Wilkinson was appointed to fill the place — a queer union of civil and military duties for which President Jefferson was much criticized. This appointment, the Brigadier said ex-

---

York, 1938), 214; Isaac J. Cox, 'Western Reaction to the Burr Conspiracy,' loc. cit. 75.

[23] Bacon, *Report*, 226–7.

[24] Affidavit of Peter Derbigny, 27 Aug. 1807, Papers Relating to the Trial of Aaron Burr, United States District Court for the Southern District of Ohio, National Archives (cited hereafter as Chillicothe Papers); Everett S. Brown (ed.), *William Plumer's Memorandum of Proceedings in the United States Senate*, 1803–1807 (New York, 1923), 203–4. (Cited hereafter as Plumer, *Memorandum*.)

[25] Poore, *Federal and State Constitutions*, I, 696–7.

ultantly, would put him on the highroad to Mexico. His Territorial secretary was to be Dr. Joseph Browne, Burr's brother-in-law, and the Vice-President wrote jubilantly to Theodosia, 'Wilkinson and Browne will suit most admirably as eaters and laughers, and, I believe, in other particulars.' [26]

These appointments met the highest expectations of the conspirators in their efforts to entrench themselves in the West, but they had still other significant plans. On 17 January 1805, General Benjamin Hovey and associates petitioned Congress to grant them 25,000 acres of land for the purpose of digging a canal around the falls of the Ohio on the Indiana side. Burr was presiding over the Senate when this petition was presented, and a committee composed of Jonathan Dayton of New Jersey, John Brown of Kentucky, and John Smith of Ohio — all close friends of Burr — reported favorably on the project but failed to advise immediate action. Burr and Wilkinson were both active promoters of the canal, and when Congress failed to take action they appealed to the Indiana legislature, which granted them a charter with George Rogers Clark, Jonathan Dayton, John Brown, Davis Floyd, Benjamin Hovey, and Aaron Burr among its directors. Benjamin H. Latrobe, the distinguished architect, was invited to become chief engineer and to recruit 500 men for the project. He made some preliminary arrangements, but instead of digging a canal the promoters established a bank which had authority to issue paper money. This and the recruiting of laborers were the real objects of the scheme.[27] The same group pur-

[26] Jacobs, *Wilkinson*, 215; Adams, *History of the United States*, II, 401–2; Charles Biddle, *Autobiography*, 408; Mark Van Doren (ed.), *Correspondence of Aaron Burr and His Daughter Theodosia*, 203–4.

[27] Evidence of Benjamin H. Latrobe, Joseph C. Cabell, Notes of Evidence in the Case of Aaron Burr, MSS., Alderman Library, University of Virginia; Jefferson to George Hay, 19 June 1807, A. A. Lipscomb and A. E. Bergh (eds.), *The Writings of Thomas Jefferson* (Memorial ed., Washington, 1903–4), XI, 233–6; Joseph Hamilton Daviess, *A View of the President's Conduct Concerning the Conspiracy of 1806* (Frankfort, 1807), reprinted in *Quarterly Publications of the Historical and Philosophical Society of Ohio*, XII (1917), nos. 2 & 3, Isaac J. Cox and Helen A. Swineford (eds.), 66–8; Testimony of Major James Bruff, *Debates and Proceedings in the Congress of the United States*, 10th Cong., 1st Sess. (Washington, 1852), 599 (cited hereafter as *Annals of Congress*); Richmond *Enquirer*, 15 Oct. 1805, 3 Nov. 1807; Isaac J. Cox, 'The Burr Conspiracy in Indiana,' *Indiana Magazine of History*, XXV (Dec. 1929), 259–60; *D.A.B.*, XI, 23; *A.S.P.*, *Misc.*, I, 419; Deposition of Capt. George Peter, 9 Feb. 1811, Bacon, *Report*, 505; Jonathan Dayton to William

chased a large block of stock of the Kentucky Insurance Company, which also had the privilege of issuing paper notes, and Burr negotiated a loan of $25,000. After all, conspiracies had to be financed one way or another.[28]

But it was to England that Burr looked mainly for financial support, and during March he had a conference with Minister Merry. He said the Louisianians were determined to secure their independence, needing only the assistance of a foreign power and the American West. In support of this cause he wanted the British Government to furnish a half a million dollars and a naval force to co-operate with him at the mouth of the Mississippi and along the Gulf Coast. Merry was inclined to favor these proposals but Williamson did not seem to be making much headway in his London mission. Nevertheless, the Chief Conspirator's hopes were still high, and soon he was enthusiastically exploring other possibilities.[29]

Simms, 31 Mar., 2 June 1805, ibid. 496–9, 501–2; *Kentucky Gazette* (Lexington), 14 May, 1805; Nathan Schachner, *Aaron Burr*, 298–9; Beveridge, *Marshall*, III, 291.

[28] Yrujo to Cevallos, 16 Dec. 1806, A.H.N., Est., leg. 5546, apartado 1, 234–52, no. 787; Thomas D. Clark, *History of Kentucky*, 173.

[29] Walter F. McCaleb, *The Aaron Burr Conspiracy* (New York, 1936), 25–6; Schachner, *Burr*, 289–90; Adams, *History of the United States*, II, 403.

Chapter III

THREADS OF INTRIGUE

EARLY IN 1805 Burr had decided on a voyage down the Ohio and Mississippi rivers in order to consult with his friends and perfect his plans. He even asked the Spanish minister for a passport to visit Mexico, but this was refused.[1] On 9 March, Louis Marie Turreau, the French minister in Washington — the man who enlivened Capital gossip by beating his wife while his aide played the flute to drown out her screams — after talking with the delegation that had brought Livingston's petition from New Orleans, wrote to Talleyrand that 'Louisiana thus is going to be the seat of Mr. Burr's new intrigues; he is going there under the aegis of General Wilkinson. It is even asserted that he might find the means there already prepared by a certain Livingston whom the disruption of his business has driven from New York City and who is closely associated with Burr.' [2]

The significance of Burr's visit to the West at this time is emphasized by an incident that occurred the following spring. Lieutenant W. A. Murray, stationed at Fort Adams, a post located on the Mississippi between Natchez and Baton Rouge, received a call from Ensign W. C. Mead and Lieutenant Josiah Taylor, who had come up from New Orleans. The latter invited Murray to return to the city with him; the invitation was accepted and the three young officers on reaching New Orleans in May were invited to dine at

[1] McCaleb, *Burr Conspiracy*, 28.

[2] Turreau to Talleyrand, 9 Mar. 1805, Archives du Ministère des Affaires Étrangères, Paris, Correspondance Politique, États Unis, LVIII, 67. (Cited hereafter as A.E., Cor. Pol., E.U.)

the home of James Workman. Their host had formerly edited a newspaper in Charleston, had come to New Orleans penniless, and had been made judge of the County of Orleans by Governor Claiborne. Louis Kerr, an Irishman who had 'fled from Bengal for his virtuous deeds,' came in after dinner. He had more recently lived in Ohio and in Natchez, and was now brigadier-general of militia and sheriff of the city. These two had taken the lead in organizing the Mexican Association of New Orleans.[3]

We have little information about this group, numbering around 300 members. It was established soon after the American occupation of Louisiana, and was said to have been modeled on an earlier association in New York City. Daniel Clark and Edward Livingston were the leading spirits in it, and they and their cohorts carried on a vitriolic campaign in the newspapers against Governor Claiborne. Its avowed purpose was to bring about the conquest — or liberation, as they put it — of Mexico.[4] Workman and Kerr explained the program of the organization to Murray and Mead, informing them that Baton Rouge was to be seized. The Mexican standard then was to be raised, troops collected, and a British naval force from New Providence in the Bahamas assembled on Lake Ponchartrain. Arms were to be sent up to Fort Adams, a post that might be captured to serve as a base of operations — hence the importance of having Lieutenant Murray of that station brought in on the scheme. After the capture of Baton Rouge, the money in the banks and the shipping in the river at New Orleans were to be seized in order to organize an expedition to join Miranda by way of Mexico. Ensign Mead, brother to the secretary of Mississippi Territory, was concerned in the project, as were Lieutenant Taylor and several other young officers. When Lieutenant Murray told his close friend Daniel Clark about the proceedings at Judge Workman's home, Clark advised him to accept the offer made to him there.

[3] Extract from the examination of Lt. W. A. Murray (1807), Burr Conspiracy MSS., 1806–8, Library of Congress; Philadelphia *Aurora*, 20 Mar. 1807; Richmond *Enquirer*, 24 Mar. 1807.

[4] Isaac Briggs to Jefferson, 9 Feb. 1805, Carter, *Territorial Papers*, v, 382–3; Folch to Someruelos, 10 Feb. 1807, A.H.N., Est., leg. 5546, apartado 3, 648–55, no. 67; Adams, *History of the United States*, III, 223–4. Clark denied membership in the Mexican Association, yet he consistently worked with it.

Lieutenant Murray realized that the United States Government was not concerned, even clandestinely, in a move to seize property in American territory and under protection of Federal troops. Though General Wilkinson was not directly mentioned as backing the plot, his name was not absent from the discussions, and the fact that so many Army officers were involved is perhaps not without significance. Most interesting is the proposed co-operation with Miranda, for Burr was hostile to him, though many of his most important collaborators, including General Wilkinson and Senator Dayton, were interested in the plans of the Venezuelan adventurer. In fact, it was later alleged that 'the same men and their relations [notably the Ogdens] who furnished Miranda with ships and supplies, and upon whom Miranda had drafts from the British Government, were the counsellors and agents of Burr . . .' [5]

Lieutenant Murray's testimony is supported by that of Ensign Small, who said that Lieutenant Taylor and Lewis Kerr informed him that Livingston, Workman, Major Nott, the brothers Alexander, and some of the 'first characters of the United States' were involved in a scheme to seize Baton Rouge, erect the ancient Mexican standard, and collect forces there. Small further stated that vessels from New Providence would join them in the lakes and that they would then seize Mobile, where they expected to find $100,000. Afterward they would push on for the Province of Texas. The Ensign further averred that Miranda's expedition had been winked at by the Administration and that it had been supplied with arms from the public arsenal at New York. He deposed that he himself had employed John J. Connally of Baltimore to translate the laws of Mexico. Later Ensign Mead made a statement of his own connection with the plot.[6]

Eventually, on 10 April 1805, Burr set out for the West. He went by way of Pittsburgh where he was supposed to have met General Wilkinson, who was traveling to St. Louis to assume his new duties

[5] Extract from the examination of Lt. W. A. Murray (1807), Burr Conspiracy MSS., 1806–8, Library of Congress; Extract from deposition of Lt. J. R. N. Luckett, 11 Jan. 1807, ibid.; Philadelphia *Aurora,* 15 June 1807.

[6] Deposition of Ensign Small, *Virginia Gazette and General Advertiser* (Richmond), 28 Mar. 1807, reprinted from the Baltimore *American;* Statement of Ensign W. C. Mead, Philadelphia *Aurora,* 10 Feb. 1807; ibid. 20 Mar. 1807.

as governor of Upper Louisiana Territory. But the Brigadier did not arrive on time and just before leaving Pittsburgh on 30 April, Burr wrote to him saying that he hoped to meet him at Louisville, adding 'Make haste, for I have some things to say which cannot be written.' [7] The Colonel purchased an elegant flatboat which had four apartments with glass windows — a dining room, two bedrooms, and a kitchen with fireplace. The ark was 60 feet long, with a 14-foot beam, and cost $133. In this comfortable craft Burr set off, floating down the Ohio at the rate of eight miles an hour, traveling in company with Congressman Matthew Lyon of Kentucky as far as Marietta. A little lower down the river he stopped at Blennerhassett's Island, and, finding the master away, dined with the lady of the house. On 11 May he arrived at Cincinnati where he was entertained by his friend John Smith, Baptist preacher, storekeeper, land speculator, Army commissary, and United States Senator from Ohio. Undoubtedly the conversation of these two centered about the situation on the lower Mississippi. Jonathan Dayton, whose term as United States Senator had just expired, joined Burr and Smith and participated in the discussions.[8] He and Burr were fellow-Princetonians and had been lifelong friends. Soon after the visit of these Easterners to Cincinnati, rumors that the West would separate from the Union began to circulate in the neighborhood.[9]

Leaving his Cincinnati friend, Burr journeyed on down the river to Louisville where he took horse for Frankfort. There he was the guest of Senator John Brown, a former associate of Wilkinson in his early Spanish intrigues.[10] Burr did not tarry long here but pushed on to Lexington where he attended a concert and remained from the 22nd to the 24th of May. He then set out for Nashville, which he reached on the 29th.[11] In this neighborhood he spent four days

[7] Bacon, *Report*, 197.

[8] Cox, *West Florida Controversy*, 152; Stanley C. Arthur, *The Story of the West Florida Rebellion* (St. Francisville, La., 1935), *passim;* McCaleb, *Burr Conspiracy*, 29; Parton, *Burr*, 387.

[9] Deposition of George Williamson, 28 Oct. 1807, Papers in the defense of John Smith of Ohio, MSS. in collection of the Historical and Philosophical Society of Ohio, Cincinnati; Deposition of Samuel Hilditch, 20 Feb. 1808, in ibid.

[10] Aaron Burr to Theodosia, 30 Apr. 1805, Mark Van Doren (ed.), *Correspondence of Aaron Burr and His Daughter Theodosia*, 209; Thomas P. Abernethy, *Western Lands and the American Revolution*, 346–50.

[11] *Kentucky Gazette*, 28 May 1805.

at Andrew Jackson's 'Hermitage,' taking the occasion to assure his host that the Secretary of War, Henry Dearborn, was secretly in league with him. On 3 June he set off down the Cumberland in an open boat provided by Jackson. It took three days to reach Fort Massac on the Ohio, a short distance below the mouth of the Cumberland; navigation was slow and cautious because of the hazardous 'sawyers' in the river. At Fort Massac Burr finally made contact with Wilkinson, and the two were closeted together from the 6th until the 10th of June.[12]

The Brigadier had reached Cincinnati after Burr's departure, but he saw Smith and Dayton there. He had hoped his friend John Adair, soon to represent Kentucky in the Senate, would join them, but having failed in this he wrote to him: 'I was to have introduced my friend Burr to you; but in this I failed by accident. He understands your merits, and reckons on you. Prepare to visit me, and I will tell you all. We must have a peep at the unknown world beyond me.'[13]

At Fort Massac Wilkinson wrote three letters of introduction for Burr. One was addressed to Daniel Clark, and it closed with the statement that 'To him I refer you for many things improper to letter, and which he will not say to any other.'[14] The second was to the Marquis of Casa Calvo, still residing in New Orleans and taking a keen interest in political matters. To Gilbert Leonard, Wilkinson wrote on 9 June, another letter of introduction for Burr, saying 'he [Burr] will send your Idiot black guard W.C.C.C[laiborne] to the Devil.' On 7 June he addressed a mysterious letter to Major Bruff at St. Louis, advising him to cease his labors at that place.[15]

On 10 June Wilkinson furnished his friend with a handsome barge, manned by ten enlisted men and a sergeant, and Burr was

[12] James Parton, *Life of Andrew Jackson* (Boston, 1866), I, 309–11; Marquis James, *Andrew Jackson, The Border Captain* (Indianapolis, 1933), 110; *Kentucky Gazette*, 9 July 1805.

[13] McCaleb, *Burr Conspiracy*, 30.

[14] Wilkinson to Clark, 9 June 1805, Bacon, *Report*, 474.

[15] Wilkinson to [Gilbert Leonard], 9 June 1805, Archivo General de Indias (Seville) Papeles de Cuba, leg. 2375, no. 87 (cited hereafter as A.G.I.); Wilkinson to Casa Calvo, 18 Mar. 1805, ibid. leg. 2375, no. 87; same to Bruff, 7 June 1805, Bacon, *Report*, 228; Schachner, *Burr*, 301.

on his way to New Orleans. He was traveling in considerable style for a private citizen, for his term as Vice-President had expired on 4 March.[16] On 17 June he reached Natchez where he was visited by Governor Robert Williams of Mississippi Territory, and he must have tarried several days because he did not arrive at New Orleans until the 26th.[17]

Burr remained in New Orleans three weeks, where he enjoyed speaking French with the Creoles. He stayed with his friend Edward Livingston; was cordially received by Governor Claiborne; was lavishly entertained by Daniel Clark; paid marked attention to Juan Ventura Morales; snubbed the Marquis of Casa Calvo; and made contacts with the Mexican Association.[18] The Catholic Bishop of New Orleans agreed to participate in Burr's enterprise and designated three Jesuit priests to aid in the revolutionizing of Mexico. Sister Thérèse de St. Xavier Farjon, Mother Superior of the Ursuline Convent, was also sympathetic with the plan. A month earlier the Orleans *Gazette*, edited by James M. Bradford, had proclaimed that the hour had struck for dispatching an army of liberators to give the wretched subjects of despotic Spain the blessings of American republicanism.[19]

On 11 September, Daniel Clark set out on a specious commercial voyage to Vera Cruz, and remained there about two months. He made a second voyage in February 1806, and was reported to have held a conference with certain Spanish officials. On his return he brought back reports on the military and naval establishments in that vicinity and on the garrison towns between that port and Mexico City. He thought Mexico might be successfully invaded, but he wanted the expedition to be carried out by private individuals who would establish a new empire of their own and seek the sanc-

[16] Van Doren, *Correspondence of Aaron Burr and His Daughter Theodosia*, 210–15.

[17] *Louisiana Gazette*, 2 June 1805; Richmond *Enquirer*, 23 July 1805; Parton, *Burr*, 391.

[18] Wilkinson to Casa Calvo, 14 Sept. 1805, A.G.I., Papeles de Cuba, leg. 2375, no. 89; Claude G. Bowers, *Jefferson in Power* (Boston, 1936), 370; Gayarré, *History of Louisiana*, IV, 80–82; James, *Border Captain*, 110; Carter, *Territorial Papers*, IX, 489.

[19] Matthew L. Davis, *Memoirs of Aaron Burr with a Miscellaneous Selection from His Correspondence* (New York, 1852), II, 382; Beveridge, *Marshall*, III, 295; Bernard Mayo, *Henry Clay — Spokesman of the New West* (Boston, 1937), 228.

tion, but not the aid, of the American Government.[20] On 14 April he wrote to a friend, saying:

> I have been twice, since I last wrote you to *the Land of Promise*, but what is more surprising, I have got safe back from it after being represented to the Vice Roy, as a person dangerous to the Spanish Government . . . I knew all this before I undertook the last voyage, but was foolhardy enough to attempt it. I have made some money and acquired more *knowledge* of the *country* . . . and made those of our own Country better known to them than before. There is you know no harm in this interchange of useful information & at a future Day I shall communicate to you all I have picked up during my stay there.[21]

There can be no doubt that Burr and the Mexican Association were working together with the idea of invading Mexico. Lieutenant Murray's testimony shows that Fort Adams and New Orleans were to serve as bases for the conspirators, and that neither American soil nor property was to be respected by them. Such a coup could be carried out by a small force in case the local population was apathetic, and Clark and Livingston had been doing all they could to turn the Creoles against the Administration.

Burr left New Orleans on 14 July, letting it be known that he would be back the following October. He had two horses and a servant furnished by Daniel Clark, and after tarrying a week in Natchez, set out on the long 450-mile journey along the Natchez Trace to Nashville, where he again visited Andrew Jackson. From Nashville he went by way of Lexington and Frankfort, Louisville and Vincennes, to St. Louis, reaching the Brigadier's headquarters on 12 September.[22] Major Bruff, second in command at this post since the General's arrival, later gave testimony about what his superior was thinking at this time. Bruff had had several conversations with Wilkinson in the spring; he had seen Kentucky papers stating that the General and his associates had formerly had plans for separating the West from the Union, and doubted that they had

[20] Bacon, *Report*, 330–34; Clark, *Proofs*, 94–5; Parton, *Burr*, 396; Philadelphia *Aurora*, 16 Jan. 1808.

[21] Clark to Wilkinson, enclosed in Wilkinson to Folch, 16 Jan. 1808, A.G.I., Papeles de Cuba, leg. 2375, no. 113.

[22] Van Doren, *Correspondence of Aaron Burr and His Daughter Theodosia*, 210–15; Dunbar Rowland, *Official Letter Books of W. C. C. Claiborne*, 1801–1816 (Jackson, Miss., 1917), III, 127; Parton, *Burr*, 397.

been abandoned. He further testified that he had had a letter from Fort Massac, supported by information from Captain Amos Stoddard, that Burr and the General had been closeted there for several days. Naturally the Major's suspicions were aroused, and they were not allayed by the conversation of Wilkinson at this time.[23]

The General said the Democrats were planning a division of property and the honest and wise had united to save the Constitution. His policy favored the Creoles and Federalists, but he considered the former unfit for self-government and thought a military regime was needed. His methods appear to have been much like those of Livingston and Clark in New Orleans in that his object was to create dissatisfaction in the minds of the native French inhabitants. Bruff said that a condition approaching anarchy soon existed, with the Americans arming themselves with dirks and pistols and the Creoles lamenting the change of masters.[24]

On arrival at St. Louis, Burr inquired of Judge Rufus Easton if there were any officers of the garrison who could be trusted with the command of an expedition to Santa Fe. Easton indicated that Bruff would be the proper person. Wilkinson had previously asked Bruff for all available information regarding the route to Sante Fe, and had secretly told him that he was contemplating a 'grand scheme' which would make the fortunes of all concerned in it. He then asked the Major what he thought of 'General' William Eaton, formerly consul at Tripoli, for a distinguished command. Shortly after Burr left St. Louis, Wilkinson ordered Bruff to go down to Fort Adams and prepare ammunition for an attack on Baton Rouge.[25] Bruff said the General often told him that he considered a war with Spain highly probable.[26] Major Timothy Kibbey also was in St. Louis during Burr's visit, and later testified that Wilkinson said he had something very secret to tell him and wanted to know his mind before Burr left the next day. He wished information concerning the disposition of the people of St. Charles District, and asked whether Kibbey did not think the greater part of them

[23] Charleston (S.C.) *Courier*, 28 Oct. 1807.

[24] Philadelphia *Aurora*, 16 Jan. 1808; Bacon, *Report*, 205ff.; Adams, *History of the United States*, III, 222–3.

[25] Charleston *Courier*, 28 Oct. 1807; Bacon, *Report*, 212, 214, 217.

[26] Bacon, *Report*, 221.

would prefer a government separate from the United States. He said that he would presently be able to place Kibbey in affluent circumstances, and wanted him to meet Burr, whom he characterized as one of the most enterprising men in the country. Later Burr told Andrew Jackson that he and Wilkinson settled the plan for an attack on Mexico during this visit.[27]

Up to the time when Burr left St. Louis, there seems to have been close and perfect co-operation between him and the General. He devoted his main attention to the domestic situation while Wilkinson concerned himself primarily with the Mexican venture. It might appear that the General could not have been acting in good faith toward Burr because he was all the while in correspondence with Casa Calvo and Folch, but he could have revealed to them all he knew about plans to divide the Union without disturbing either them or his confederate in the least. In fact, both the Spanish and French ministers believed, or pretended to believe, almost until the end that a separation of the Western states and territories was the only object of the conspiracy.[28]

As for Wilkinson's plan to invade Mexico, that involved nothing more at the moment than the quiet collection of information regarding that country. The Spaniards apparently knew little of any such activities. In fact, it seems very likely that Wilkinson's correspondence with Casa Calvo and Folch threw them off guard, for they evidently trusted him, thinking that if he made a false move they could ruin him by betraying him to his own government. And his own government could hardly complain of a General who, expecting war with Spain, took thought to prepare for it in advance.

When Burr took leave of Wilkinson at St. Louis, their plans seemed to be maturing as well as could have been expected, but now things began to go wrong. On 2 August, while Burr was toiling up the Natchez Trace to Nashville, an article appeared in the *United States Gazette* of Philadelphia under the heading 'Queries.'

[27] Statement of Timothy Kibbey, 6 July 1807, *Quarterly Publications, Historical and Philosophical Society of Ohio*, IX (1914), 55–7; Evidence of Andrew Jackson, Joseph C. Cabell, Notes of Evidence in the Case of Aaron Burr, June–July 1807, 89, Alderman Library, University of Virginia.

[28] Nicia Luz, 'Spanish and French Views of the Burr Conspiracy' (MS. thesis, 1946, Alderman Library, University of Virginia), 62.

It asked whether Colonel Burr planned to revolutionize Louisiana and call an immediate convention of the states bordering on the Ohio and Mississippi rivers to form a separate government, taking possession of the public lands and offering them in *bounties* to entice inhabitants from the Atlantic states; and how soon, the article queried, would the forts and magazines at New Orleans and the military posts on the Mississippi be taken by Burr's party and be used for the reduction of Mexico and the appropriation of her treasures, aided by British ships and forces? [29]

On 9 August, Thomas Ritchie of the Richmond *Enquirer* noticed this article and commented that the project seemed to be little more than a revival of the Blount Conspiracy of 1797, of which he thought Burr was not 'wholly ignorant.' He believed Burr's intrigues might have received some stimulus from the Yazoo speculation which had recently been a topic of conversation among members of Congress. Ritchie said that one of the Yazoo men had told him that if Congress did not satisfy their claims, they would march a force into the country and take forcible possession of the disputed lands.[30] Later Ritchie stated that 'To the Yazoo, therefore, he [Burr] held out the realization of their speculations, — and behold they have not only deposited immense sums in the western country — but they have conveyed through British Canada, *brass field pieces to be ready for a great occasion.*' [31]

Editor Ritchie was not the only contemporary who believed that the Yazoo claimants were interested in Burr's scheme. Yrujo, the Spanish minister, thought so too.[32] But the Yazoo speculators were by no means the only people interested in Western land claims, including lands in West Florida which would appreciate in value in case that province was added to the territory of the United States or to a new Western empire. Burr's friend Senator John Smith had invested heavily in lands in the vicinity of Baton Rouge; and Daniel Clark and Edward Livingston were connected with the West

[29] *United States Gazette* (Philadelphia), 2 Aug. 1805.
[30] Richmond *Enquirer*, 9 Aug. 1805; *Georgia Republican*, 28 Nov. 1806, quoting *Virginia Argus.*
[31] Richmond *Enquirer*, 11 Dec. 1806.
[32] Yrujo to Cevallos, 29 Nov. 1806, A.H.N., Est., leg. 5546, apartado 1, 181–94, no. 773.

Florida Intendant, Morales, in large land speculations in that Spanish province.[33] After the cession of Louisiana to France, the Spanish authorities had continued to make many large land grants, which were still unconfirmed at the time the United States took possession. There was little chance that the Federal Government would validate these dubious claims, but Burr and his friends took great interest in them, especially in the enormous Bastrop grant on the Ouachita River in Orleans Territory, for a new jurisdiction would have a new land policy for this vast domain.[34] There can be no doubt that Burr's main support came from Eastern Federalists who objected to the Louisiana Purchase on both political and economic grounds, and from men who hoped to profit by a transfer of the fertile lands of the Mississippi Valley to a new jurisdiction.

Burr's friend, Anthony Merry the British minister, read the 'Queries' article and was much disturbed by it. He wrote home on 4 August that Burr had apparently been betrayed, 'for the object of his journey has now begun to be noticed in the public prints, where it is said that a convention is to be called immediately for the States bordering on the Ohio and Mississippi for the purpose of forming a separate government.'[35]

News of these disclosures must have reached New Orleans by early September, for on the 7th of that month Daniel Clark wrote to Wilkinson: 'Many absurd and wild reports are circulated here, and have reached the ears of the officers of the late Spanish government, respecting our ex-Vice-President . . . The tale is a horrid one, if well told. Kentucky, the State of Ohio, with part of Georgia and part of Carolina are to be bribed with the plunder of the Spanish countries west of us to separate from the Union.' Clark suspected that Stephen Minor of Natchez, a native American and an ex-Spanish official on whom Burr had called as he traveled northward from New Orleans, was responsible for the leak, but Burr later denied that he had confided in Minor, and the story could well have come from Philadelphia.[36] The Spanish officials were

[33] Claiborne to Jefferson, 10 Nov. 1804, Carter, *Territorial Papers*, IX, 333–4.
[34] Parton, *Burr*, 399–400; Thomas Rodney to Caesar A. Rodney, 8 Apr. 1806, *Pennsylvania Magazine of History and Biography*, XLIV (1920), 274.
[35] Adams, *History of the United States*, III, 226.
[36] McCaleb, *Burr Conspiracy*, 35.

apparently taking no chances, for in October 600 troops arrived in Pensacola from Havana and it was reported that Baton Rouge and Mobile were to be reinforced.[37] It was now that Wilkinson began to show a degree of coolness toward Burr. The 'Queries' article disturbed him, and, according to his own account, he wrote to the Secretary of the Navy, warning him to keep an eye on Burr. He began to talk about an expedition against Mexico which he himself would lead, and on 26 November 1805, wrote to the Secretary of War: 'Our situation at New Orleans is a defenceless one . . . I most ardently implore we may not be forced to War, because I seek repose and we are not indeed prepared for it, that is against European troops — yet if we must draw the Sword, the whole of the troops destined to operate West of the Mississippi should be mounted . . . If I do not reduce New Mexico, at least, in one Campaign, I will forfeit my Head.' A little later he wrote to Colonel John McKee asking whether he could raise a cavalry force to participate with him in a crusade to Mexico.[38]

As Burr traveled eastward from St. Louis, he stopped at Vincennes and presented a letter from General Wilkinson to Governor William Henry Harrison of Indiana Territory. Wilkinson asked Harrison 'for the sake of the Union' to have Burr sent to Congress as the Territorial delegate.[39] This letter has often been taken to indicate that Wilkinson was definitely preparing to drop Burr and wished to send him to Congress where he could do no harm. But Daniel Clark found Congress a congenial spot for a conspirator, and Wilkinson himself found no impediment in the Governor's chair. There had been an earlier plan to send Burr to Congress from Tennessee, and, in fact, official posts in the West were looked on as highly desirable for the purposes of the conspiracy. It is true, how-

[37] *Louisiana Gazette*, 25 Mar. 1805; Richmond *Enquirer*, 4 Jan. 1806; Parton, *Burr*, 399–400.

[38] Wilkinson to Dearborn, 26 Nov. 1805, Elliott Coues (ed.), *The Expeditions of Zebulon Montgomery Pike* (New York, 1895), II, 564fn.; Statement of Timothy Kibbey, 6 July 1807, *Quarterly Publications, Historical and Philosophical Society of Ohio* IX (1914), 55–7; Questions to be put to General Wilkinson by the Grand Jury, Cabell Papers, Burr Case, Alderman Library, University of Virginia; Isaac J. Cox, 'Western Reaction to the Burr Conspiracy,' loc. cit. 78; *Annals of Congress*, 10 Cong., 1 Sess., 643–4.

[39] Bacon, *Report*, 199; James A. Green, *William Henry Harrison, His Life and Times* (Richmond, 1941), 100–101.

ever, that from this time forward the General seemed to be trying to protect himself against any possible consequences of Burr's operations. He later testified that in October he wrote a high government official that the ex-Vice-President was up to something, but whether it related to internal or external affairs he could not discover.[40]

Though Burr's meeting with Harrison was pleasant, nothing came of the interview and he continued his way to Washington where he found trouble awaiting him. Arriving about the middle of November, he hastened to see Merry and find out what news there might be from London. There was no word from Williamson and the Colonel was deeply disappointed.[41] He told Merry he had found the West enthusiastic about his plans and he had agreed to return in March, though he did not actually plan to start operations before autumn. So impatient, said he, were the Louisianians under American rule that they were about to send a representation of their grievances to Paris, but he had persuaded them that independence under British protection was preferable.[42] The people of New Orleans, Burr said, were so resolved to separate themselves from the Union that he was sure the revolution there would be accomplished without the shedding of a drop of blood, for the American force in that part of the country, 'should it not, as he had good reason to believe, enlist with him,' was too weak to make any opposition.[43] All that was necessary was for Pitt to furnish him with £110,000 and a naval force consisting of two or three ships of the line and an equal number of frigates to cruise off the mouth of the Mississippi by 10 April, 'and to continue there until the commanding officer should receive information from him or from Mr. Daniel Clark of the country having declared itself independent.'[44]

Burr gave Merry clearly to understand that the heart of the plot was not in Kentucky, Tennessee, or the Ohio Valley, but at New Orleans. West Florida was to be included in the plan, for overtures

[40] Raleigh *Register*, 6 Mar. 1812; Parton, *Burr*, 384–7.
[41] I. J. Cox, *West Florida Controversy*, 190; McCaleb, *Burr Conspiracy*, 42–3.
[42] McCaleb, op. cit. 47.
[43] Ibid. 46.
[44] Schachner, *Burr*, 308–19; Adams, *History of the United States*, III, 230.

had been made to him by a person of greatest influence there.[45] But not a word was said about an invasion of Mexico. That, apparently, was primarily Wilkinson's affair.

Shortly after this discouraging conference with Merry, Burr called on President Jefferson, and when he left after a two-hour conference, his hopes were, for the time being, almost completely crushed. He and Wilkinson, it will be recalled, had always looked upon war with Spain as a necessary condition for the carrying out of their plans, and hitherto the chances for such a conflict had, since the purchase of Louisiana, seemed very bright. While failing to push a tenable claim that that province extended to the Rio Grande on the west, the United States Government steadfastly maintained, and wrongly so, that West Florida to the Perdido River was a part of Louisiana according to the treaty of cession. On 24 February 1804, Congress upheld this view by passing the Mobile Act which technically annexed the disputed territory by authorizing its incorporation as a customs district. On 13 May the Administration gave way in regard to the customs district, and later in the same year James Monroe was sent to Spain to negotiate for the cession of the Floridas and the recognition of the Colorado River as the western boundary of Louisiana. On 15 May 1805, Monroe's proposal was rejected by Cevallos, the Spanish minister of foreign affairs. Talleyrand, then French foreign minister, was responsible for the failure of these negotiations, for Napoleon was able to dominate the policy of his ally at that time. But by the autumn of 1805 Bonaparte had decided to bring pressure to bear on Spain in the matter of Florida if the United States would pay him for his services. His terms were transmitted through channels to Jefferson, who held two Cabinet meetings on the subject in November and sent two messages to Congress in December, the purport of which was, in plain language, that he wanted $2 million with which to bribe Napoleon to browbeat Spain into ceding West Florida to the United States. It was in the interval between the two Cabinet meetings and the transmission of the messages to Congress that Burr held his conference with

[45] Ibid. III, 231; McCaleb, op. cit. 44.

Jefferson and heard from the President that there was, after all, to be no war with Spain.[46]

Disheartened by this news, Burr set out for Philadelphia on 1 December, and on the same day President Jefferson received an anonymous letter saying:

> You admit him [Burr] at your table, and you held a long and private conference with him a few days ago *after dinner* at the very moment he is meditating the overthrow of your Administration . . . Yes, Sir, his abberations through the Western States *had no other object*. A foreign Agent, now at Washington knows since February last his plans and has seconded them beyond what you are aware of . . . Watch his connexions with Mr. M. . .y and you will find him a British pensioner and agent . . .[47]

In Philadelphia Burr for the first time met the colorful Francisco de Miranda, who had come to seek American aid in fitting out an expedition to Venezuela. The fastidious Burr was pleased with Miranda's social talents, but he made no secret of the fact that he looked upon him as a rival in Latin-American intrigue, whereas Dayton, John Swartwout, William S. Smith, Wilkinson, Williamson, Merry, Samuel G. Ogden, and most of Burr's backers either collaborated with the Venezuelan or showed an inclination to do so. Miranda later spoke of Burr as the detestable and infamous man who had betrayed his plans to Yrujo.[48] Yet on 5 December another anonymous letter was written to Jefferson announcing the arrival of Miranda at New York and adding, 'This event forms a link in Burr's manouevres. His instructions like those of Burr come from the same source. The same plans, or others similar in their tendency are to be offered to you . . . Although ostensibly directed against a foreign power, the destruction of our Government, your ruin

[46] Samuel Flagg Bemis, *A Diplomatic History of the United States* (New York, 1936), 185; Francis Franklin, *The Rise of the American Nation*, 1789–1824, 159; Samuel H. Wandell and Meade Minnigerode, *Aaron Burr* (New York, 1925), 59–60; Parton, *Burr*, 402; Adams, *History of the United States*, III, 106; Plumer, *Memorandum*, 360, 366–7; French E. Chadwick, *The Relations of the United States and Spain. Diplomacy* (New York, 1909), 68–9, 92–3; I. J. Cox, 'The Louisiana-Texas Frontier,' loc. cit. pt. 2, 185.

[47] Anon. to Jefferson, 1 Dec. 1805, Jefferson Papers, Library of Congress.

[48] John Rydjord, *Foreign Interest in the Independence of New Spain* (Durham, N.C., 1935), 232; William S. Robertson, *Life of Miranda*, I, 293–4; Claude G. Bowers, *Jefferson in Power*, 320–25; Adams, *History of the United States*, III, 189.

and the material injury of the Atlantic states are their true object.' [49]

When Burr reached Philadelphia, Dayton was already there and within a few days the ex-senator made a call on the Spanish minister. He told Yrujo that Burr had originally planned with Merry to revolutionize the Western states, and, with the aid of a British squadron, conquer West Florida; that Colonel Williamson had been sent to London to propose these plans to the British Ministry, which had, through the intercession of Lord Melville, shown itself favorable to the scheme. On visiting the West and talking with his friends in New Orleans, Burr had become convinced that an expedition against Mexico was also practicable, and Colonel Williamson had been advised to take this up with the ministers. But Melville was involved in difficulties, Dayton said, and negotiations had been delayed.

Yrujo realized that Dayton was speaking for Burr, and he was sure that these disclosures would not have been made to him if the conspirators had succeeded in getting British support. While he probably did not trust them implicitly, he dismissed the proposed Mexican expedition as ridiculous and chimerical, and even went so far as to suggest that the Spanish Government should encourage Dayton, yet not compromise itself.[50] The architect Latrobe said that at this time he often saw Dayton and Dr. Erich Bollman transacting business with Yrujo at Burr's lodgings in Richard Dell's tavern.[51]

Apparently having given up all hope of British aid, Dayton soon called again on Yrujo and proposed a plan which he said could be carried out without foreign assistance. Burr was to introduce his armed followers into Washington in a clandestine manner and carry out a *coup d'état*. They were to seize the President and Vice-President, the President of the Senate, and take possession of the Federal arsenal and the money in the Bank of the United States at Georgetown. Burr hoped then to be able to establish himself in the Capital City, but in case he did not succeed in this, he planned to

[49] Anon. to Jefferson, 5 Dec. 1805, Jefferson Papers, Library of Congress.

[50] Yrujo to Cevallos, 5 Dec. 1805, A.H.N., Est. leg. 5546, apartado 1, 22–45, no. 590; Bowers, *Jefferson in Power*, 372; Schachner, *Burr*, 310–11.

[51] Yrujo to Cevallos, 5 Dec. 1805, A.H.N., Est., leg. 5546, apartado 1, 35–8, 44–5; Evidence of Benjamin H. Latrobe, Cabell Papers, Burr Case, 88, Alderman Library, University of Virginia.

burn all the ships at the Navy Yard except the two or three that were ready for service and embark his followers and his treasure in them and sail for New Orleans. Once there, he would proclaim the independence of Louisiana and the Western states.[52]

This was the plan that the conspirators hoped the Spanish minister would be willing to recommend to his Government, but all they received was a gift of $1500, plus another thousand later. Yrujo said this money was paid partly because in the course of these conferences Dayton had revealed Miranda's plans to him.[53] Thus the year 1805 ended on a dismal note for the conspirators.

[52] Yrujo to Cevallos, 1 Jan. 1806, A.H.N., Est., leg. 5546, apartado 1, 47–59, no. 605.

[53] Robertson, *Miranda*, I, 296; Adams, *History of the United States*, III, 192–3; Wandell and Minnigerode, *Burr*, 63; McCaleb, *Burr Conspiracy*, 64.

Chapter IV
THE INTERLUDE

THE NEW YEAR found Burr still in Philadelphia, and not in the best of spirits. On 6 January he wrote to Wilkinson: 'You will know, long before this reaches you, that we are to have no Spanish war, except in ink and words. It is undoubtedly best so, for we are in poor condition to go to war, even with Spain. Tell Browne I shall write to him from Washington, where I shall be in a few days.' [1]

The writer was as good as his word this time, for he was soon in Washington, and so was 'General' William Eaton, who was there to collect $10,000 which he claimed the Government owed him on account of his spectacular Tripolitan campaign of 1804. While serving as consul in North Africa, he had led a motley detachment across the desert, captured the city of Derne, and was in a fair way to take Tripoli and bring the American-Tripolitan war to a victorious end. Peace was made and he was thus deprived of this triumph, but he assumed the title of General and came home in an unhappy state of mind.[2]

It was during this winter and probably at this very time that Burr conferred with the disgruntled Eaton and tried to interest him in his plans. Proceeding cautiously, as was his wont, he first stated that he was planning an expedition against the Spanish provinces on our Western frontier with the aim of invading Mexico, and he gave the impression — just as he did on so many other occasions —

[1] Bacon, *Report*, 200–202.
[2] *D.A.B.*, v, 613.

that these operations were approved by the Administration. But Eaton suspected there were other objectives and after some questioning, Burr admitted that he meant to revolutionize the Western states and create a new government with the Allegheny Mountains as its eastern limit, New Orleans as its capital, and the Hero of Weehawken as its chief of state. Going even further, he declared that if he 'could gain over the marine corps and secure to his interests the naval commanders Truxton, Preble, Decatur, and others, he would turn Congress neck and heels out of doors, get rid of the President, and declare himself the protector of an energetic government.' [3]

Eaton's testimony has been questioned, primarily on the grounds of his bibulous habits and his success in suddenly collecting his dubious claim against the Government after it had been hanging fire for several years, by all those writers who have interested themselves in proving that Burr had no treasonable intentions. If it had to stand alone, Eaton's testimony might be open to question, but the fact that it so closely parallels the proposals Dayton had made to Yrujo during the previous month would seem to accredit it without room for reasonable doubt. It is also supported by the testimony of Benjamin Stoddert who said that in the spring of 1806 he called on Burr and expressed dissatisfaction with Jefferson's Florida policy; that thus encouraged Burr said that with 500 men he could send Jefferson to Monticello and put himself at the head of the Government without bloodshed by operating on Congress. Burr assured Stoddert that 'men of property, energy and talents' were disgusted with the Administration, and that the mob could do nothing for want of leaders.[4]

'General' Eaton was not the only man who held a grievance against the Administration as a result of the Tripolitan War. Commodore Truxton had been appointed to command one of our Medi-

[3] Adams, *History of the United States*, III, 240; Evidence of General William Eaton, Cabell Papers, Burr Case, 7–17, Alderman Library, U. Va.; *Georgia Republican*, 17 Feb. 1807.

[4] Deposition of Benjamin Stoddert, 9 Oct. 1807, *Quarterly Publications, Historical and Philosophical Society of Ohio*, IX (1914), 7–9; Evidence of Benjamin Stoddert, Cabell Papers, Burr Case, 4–7, Alderman Library, U. Va.

terranean squadrons, but because he was not furnished with a captain for his flagship he resigned the command and the Administration interpreted this as a resignation from the service.[5] As a consequence, the Commodore was no friend of President Jefferson; but he was an old and intimate friend of Burr. It was to Truxton's home in Perth Amboy that Burr first went when he was fleeing to Philadelphia after the duel at Weehawken. Truxton had often met Wilkinson and Burr at the home of their mutual friend, Charles Biddle of Philadelphia. At some time during this winter Burr approached Truxton, for he needed ships to protect the mouth of the Mississippi if he took New Orleans, and to transport troops if he decided to attack Mexico. He informed Truxton that he planned to make this attack by way of Vera Cruz in case of a war between the United States and Spain. When the Commodore assured him that there would be no war — a fact with which Burr was already equally well acquainted — he said in that case he would settle the Ouachita lands which he was about to purchase and await developments with his colonists thus strategically located upon the frontier. When he had to admit to Truxton that the Government had not authorized such an expedition, the Commodore stated that he would not be interested, and the conversation ended.[6]

Another person approached by Burr during this winter of his discontent was Harman Blennerhassett. This visionary Irishman had migrated to the United States in 1796 and two years later had settled on an island in the Ohio River near Marietta. Here he built a rambling, weatherboarded mansion and furnished it with every luxury Europe afforded. In this manner he dissipated his fortune and wore out his enthusiasm for the rustic life.[7] It will be recalled that Burr had visited the island while on his way down the Ohio during the previous May, and finding the owner absent, had dined with Mrs. Blennerhassett, who was an attractive, talented woman. On his return to Washington in November the Colonel had written to his Gaelic friend and invited him to participate in his Mexican

[5] *D.A.B.*, XIX, 21–2.
[6] Evidence of Thomas Truxton, Cabell Papers, Burr Case, 1–4, Alderman Library, U. Va.; McCaleb, *Burr Conspiracy*, 285.
[7] *D.A.B.*, II, 367–8.

venture. On 21 December, Blennerhassett replied, accepting the invitation.[8] But so low were Burr's spirits by the time he received this letter that he did not answer until 15 April, and then he wrote: 'I had projected, and still meditate, a speculation, precisely of the character you have described . . . The business, however, depends, in some degree, on contingencies, not within my control, and will not be commenced before December or January, if ever . . . We shall have no war unless we should be actually invaded.' [9]

One of Blennerhassett's frontier neighbors was General Edward W. Tupper of Marietta. Burr had passed that way in October 1805, on his return from New Orleans and was introduced to Tupper by Return J. Meigs, Judge of Louisiana Territory. Toward the end of the year Tupper, thinking there would be war with Spain and hearing that Burr would command an army, wrote to him and offered his services. On 16 January 1806, Burr replied that he expected much talk but no real war. He promised, nevertheless, to call on Tupper in case a conflict should break out, and sent him a copy of *The Duty of a Soldier and Discipline of the Infantry as Now Practised in the French Army*. This work was delivered by Major Davis Floyd, of Jeffersonville, Indiana.

On 30 March 1806, Burr again wrote to Tupper saying: 'The object of Govt. seems to be to purchase the Floridas — Yet notwithstanding the pacific temper of the administration, it would not surprise me if Spain should commence hostilities against us on account of the expedition of General Miranda against the province of Caracas . . .' Burr then asked whether a full regiment could be raised promptly in eastern Ohio, and added, 'If you think so and will send me a list of the persons you would recommend for Officers from Ensign upwards, I will in the event of a call for troops, recommend your list to the department of War.' The Colonel also sent Tupper two documents concerning the question of the Barbary pirates and suggested that they be published in the local newspapers.[10]

It was during this period of gloom that Burr made a journey to Charleston, probably to visit his daughter and her husband Joseph

[8] Parton, *Burr*, 403–5.

[9] William Harrison Safford (ed.), *Blennerhassett Papers* (Cincinnati, 1861), 119–21.

[10] Deposition of Edward W. Tupper, 8 Sept. 1807, Chillicothe Papers.

Alston, who was one of the wealthiest men in South Carolina and the heaviest known contributor to the conspirator's treasure chest. Leaving Philadelphia at some time after 6 January, Burr journeyed first to Washington and, as stated, apparently held his fateful conference with Eaton there. On the 25th he arrived in Raleigh, North Carolina, on the same stage with Benjamin Hawkins, the well-known Federal agent to the Creek Indians. After visiting Charleston, he returned to Washington by way of Richmond,[11] and on 22 February he held another conference with President Jefferson. According to Jefferson's report of this interview — the only one available — Burr suggested that he could do the President much harm if he were so minded, but he would prefer to be appointed to some public office and remain on friendly terms. Jefferson, who had long disliked the man, defied his threats and refused the appointment on the ground that the public had withdrawn its confidence from the ex-Vice-President. This was the last meeting between these two.[12]

If this interview depressed the Colonel's spirits, he could hardly take comfort from the long silence of General Wilkinson. He had not heard from him since October 1805, when the General had called to his attention the rumors that Daniel Clark had reported to be current in New Orleans regarding the conspiracy. That this silence indicated something more than indifference is suggested by a letter John Adair wrote to Wilkinson on 27 January 1806. It may be recalled that the General had hoped to introduce Adair to Burr when the latter visited Cincinnati on his way to New Orleans the previous May. They failed to make connection there, but the two must have met when Burr passed through Kentucky, as the letter indicates. Adair wrote: 'You observe to me that I "have seen Col Burr and ask me what was his business in the west." Answer — Only to avoid a prosecution in New York. Now, sir, you will oblige me by answering a question in turn, for I know you can. Pray, how far is it, and what kind of way from St. Louis to Santa Fe, and from thence to Mexico?' [13] Wilkinson replied to the query concerning Santa Fe and Mexico, 'Do you not know I have reserved

[11] Raleigh (N.C.), *Minerva*, 3 Feb. 1806; Richmond *Enquirer*, 15 Feb. 1806; Plumer, *Memorandum*, 436.
[12] Ibid. 436; Schachner, *Burr*, 313.
[13] Bacon, *Report*, 343-4; Wilkinson, *Memoirs*, II, app. 77.

these places for my own, triumphant entry, that I have been reconnoitering & exploring the route for 16 years; and that I not only know the way but all the difficulties & how to surmount them. I wish we could get leave, Mexico would soon be ours.' The General was now, ostensibly, taking quite a proper attitude and viewing his old friend Burr with a suspicious eye.[14]

On 23 January William Pitt died and Charles James Fox became foreign minister of Britain. Thus faded the last hope of the conspirators for obtaining British aid in carrying out their plans — without the co-operation of naval vessels an invasion of Mexico by sea would have been difficult indeed. Wilkinson's frame of mind is reflected in a letter he wrote to Daniel Clark on 5 March, in which he said: 'What think you of the purchase of the Floridas by the U. S.? *Entre Nous*, I verily believe it is done. Something of *great importance* has been done in conclave, and that something is to perpetuate peace with Spain. Again, *entre nous*, I write in haste.'[15]

Late that month news reached St. Louis that the Senate had confirmed Wilkinson's appointment as governor of Louisiana Territory. The vote had been close and the confirmation was made possible by the Federalists, who supported the General unanimously; but Wilkinson was not downhearted by the close vote. When the messenger arrived about sunset, the bells of the town began to ring, a cannon was hauled to the governor's residence and commenced a 'federal' salute just at dark. A cord of wood with a barrel or two of tar was set afire, the band struck up a lively tune, and the crowd cheered and drank whiskey until midnight despite a storm which arose the instant they began to celebrate. Later a subscription dinner was tendered the martial governor at which one of the toasts proposed 'dollars to his friends, and lead to his enemies.'[16]

While Wilkinson was celebrating in St. Louis, Burr tarried in Washington, visiting little and seldom being seen; but Matthew Lyon was planning to resign his seat in Congress after the next election so that Burr might become a representative from Kentucky. On 24 March the Colonel wrote to Andrew Jackson that he thought

[14] Excerpt from the *New England Palladium*, 25 July 1807, Burr MSS., Library of Congress.
[15] Bacon, *Report*, 475–6.
[16] Ibid. 234–5; Plumer, *Memorandum*, 392–3.

there would be no war, though France and Spain might make trouble because Miranda was outfitted in the United States. He then asked the Tennessee general to make out a list of officers for one or two regiments, aside from the militia organization, and send it to him in case troops were called for, adding, 'I will send it to the Department of War & believe my advice would be listened to.' [17]

Peace with Spain was bad news for the conspirators, but out on the Texas frontier a situation was developing which was destined soon to revive the hopes of Burr and put General Wilkinson in a peculiar position. When France ceded Louisiana to the United States, she officially construed its boundaries to be the Iberville River on the east and the Rio Grande on the west. In other words, West Florida was not included but Texas was. Yet the Jefferson Administration, while making an unsuccessful effort to acquire West Florida, let Texas go by default.[18] The result was that Spanish forces occupied Texas without protest, placing the boundary at the Arroyo Hondo, a tributary of the Red River and therefore east of the Sabine. José de Iturrigaray, Viceroy of Mexico, ordered Simon de Herrera, Governor of the province of Nuevo Leon, to march to Texas with 1500 men and instructed him to attack the Americans if they crossed the Arroyo Hondo. Colonel Antonio Cordero was appointed governor of Texas and he proceeded to establish his headquarters at Nacogdoches, near the Sabine frontier. He was ordered to stop all intercourse with the United States in case of war, and all slaves escaping across the Sabine were to be set free. In October 1805, a Spanish force of 1300 men crossed the Sabine and occupied a post on Bayou Pierre, some 50 miles northwest of Natchitoches, the American outpost on the Red River. On 20 November, Secretary of War Dearborn ordered Major Moses Porter, the commanding officer at Natchitoches, to hold the Sabine line.[19]

[17] Parton, *Jackson*, I, 313–14; Plumer, *Memorandum*, 477.

[18] Isaac J. Cox, 'Louisiana-Texas Frontier,' loc. cit. pt. 2, 185; Chadwick, *Relations of the United States and Spain*, 69.

[19] Porter to Wilkinson, 29 Jan., 8 Feb. 1806, Wilkinson MSS., Library of Congress; Isaac J. Cox, 'Louisiana-Texas Frontier,' loc. cit. pt. 2, 179–80; Dr. John Sibley to Dearborn, 12 Mar. 1807, *Southwestern Historical Quarterly*, XV (1911–12), 296–7; Bacon, *Report*, 354–5; Dunbar Rowland, *History of Mississippi, the Heart of the South* (Chicago, 1925), I, 414–19; Vito Alessio Robles, *Coahuila y Texas, desde la*

On 5 February 1806, Captain Edward D. Turner with 60 men forced the Spaniards, numbering 29 men and one officer, to abandon Adais, a post about 14 miles west of the American headquarters at Natchitoches and on the road leading to the Spanish headquarters at Nacogdoches. Cordero reported this incident to his superior, Nemesio de Salcedo, brother to the last Spanish governor of Louisiana and Captain-General of the Interior Provinces, who in turn reported to Iturrigaray.[20]

When President Jefferson received news of the encounter, he sent a special message to Congress, dated 19 March, informing its members that:

> It was reasonably expected that while the limits between the territories of the United States and Spain were unsettled neither party would have innovated on the existing state of their respective positions. Some time since, however, we learnt that the Spanish authorities were advancing into the disputed country to occupy new posts and make new settlements. Unwilling to take any measures which might preclude a peaceable accommodation of differences, the officers of the United States were ordered to confine themselves within the country on this side of the Sabine River which, by delivery of its principal post, Natchitoches, was understood to have been itself delivered up by Spain, and at the same time to permit no adverse post to be taken nor armed men to remain within it. In consequence of these orders the commanding officer at Natchitoches, learning that a party of Spanish troops had crossed the Sabine River and were posting themselves on this side the Adais, sent a detachment of his force to require them to withdraw to the other side of the Sabine, which they accordingly did.
>
> I have thought it proper to communicate to Congress the letter detailing this incident, that they may fully understand the state of things in that quarter and be enabled to make such provisions for its security as in their wisdom, they shall deem sufficient.[21]

Thus Jefferson was determined to hold the Sabine line even at the cost of war, and the Spaniards were equally set upon pushing their frontier eastward to the Arroyo Hondo. Governor Cordero,

Consumación de la Independencia hasta el Tratado de Paz de Guadalupe Hidalgo (Mexico City, 1945–6), I, 37–40; Mattie Austin Hatcher, *The Opening of the Texas Frontier to Foreign Settlement*, 1810–1821 (Austin, 1927), 100.

[20] Salcedo to Iturrigaray, 23 Feb. 1806, A.H.N., leg. 5543, exp. 1, 21–3; *National Intelligencer* (Washington), 19 Feb., 28 Mar. 1806.

[21] James D. Richardson (ed.), *A Compilation of the Messages and Papers of the Presidents* (New York, 1897–1922), I, 388.

who commanded Spanish forces on this front, now ordered Colonel Herrera to reinforce the garrison at Nacogdoches with 600 men, and on 18 March, Spanish forces again occupied Adais. On the 8th of this month, Major Porter had reported to Secretary Dearborn that he had less than 200 men fit for duty, six guns, and a small, untenable stockade (Fort Clairborne at Natchitoches), and that the Spaniards were already east of the Sabine and refused to withdraw. Yet, in curious contradiction, Wilkinson wrote to the Secretary that Porter reported the status of his command was flattering and that the Spaniards were not really aggressive.[22]

Both Iturrigaray and Salcedo urged the bellicose Cordero to use caution and avoid becoming the aggressor in a conflict with the United States, especially at a time when Miranda was trying to stir up a revolution in Spanish America. Yrujo had already warned Iturrigaray that Burr might have designs on Mexico. He believed Jefferson was seeking war with Spain, not only because of his attitude on the Sabine question but because of the expulsion of Casa Calvo and Morales from Louisiana, the aid Miranda had received in New York, and the request for the recall of Yrujo, himself, as minister to the United States. He thought a clash on the Texas frontier was imminent since the American troops had orders to use force if necessary to prevent the Spaniards from recrossing the Sabine.[23]

The Jefferson Administration was firm in its stand. Dearborn now ordered Colonel Thomas H. Cushing to take command at Natchitoches, and Wilkinson was directed to reinforce that frontier.[24] Dearborn also wrote to Governor Claiborne regarding plans for the defense of New Orleans in case of attack.[25] Finally, on 6 May, he ordered Wilkinson to move his headquarters to New Or-

[22] Cordero to Calleja, 14 Feb. 1806, A.H.N., leg. 5543, exp. 1, 15–16; Calleja to Cordero, 1 Mar. 1806, ibid. 17–18; same to Iturrigaray, 1 Mar. 1806, ibid. 13–14; Porter to Dearborn, 8 Feb. 1806, Bacon, *Report*, 356–8; Wilkinson to Dearborn, 25 Apr. 1806, ibid. 363–4; J. F. H. Claiborne, *Mississippi as Province, Territory, and State* (Jackson, Miss., 1880), 264ff.; Carter, *Territorial Papers*, IX, 618; Schachner, *Burr*, 332.

[23] Yrujo to Cevallos, 14 May 1806, A.H.N., Est., leg. 5632, 104–6; Iturrigaray to Salcedo, 11 Mar. 1806, ibid. leg. 5543, exp. 1, 24–25; Yrujo to Cevallos, 28 Mar. 1806, ibid. leg. 5543, exp. 1, 47–50; ministerial notes, ibid. leg. 5543, exp. 1, 27–40; Yrujo to Cevallos, 14 May 1806, ibid. leg. 5543, exp. 1, 70–73; same to same, 19 Mar. 1806, ibid. 41–6.

[24] Dearborn to Wilkinson, 18 Mar. 1806, Bacon, *Report*, 360–61.

[25] Dearborn to Claiborne, Carter, *Territorial Papers*, IX, 627–8.

leans and to consult Claiborne about the necessity of resorting to hostilities to defend the Sabine line. Two days later Wilkinson ordered Cushing to avoid a clash with the Spanish forces on that front. On 19 April he had written Major Porter that he thought there would be no war. On the 30th he again wrote, saying that 'the departure of Casso Calvo is a strong indication the Dons don't mean to fight, — Yet I have received orders by the last mail to send Col. Cushing directly to you with the companies.' [26]

Early in April the Spaniards appeared to be taking a more pacific attitude and again withdrew their forces to the west bank of the Sabine,[27] but on 2 June, Colonel Constant Freeman arrived at Natchitoches with orders to explore the headwaters of the Red River. He had been appointed by the President in the spring of 1804 to undertake this expedition, but it was delayed by the fear of Spanish hostility. It finally got under way early in the summer of 1806, and Freeman indicated that he had hopes of reaching Santa Fe.[28] Leaving Natchitoches with a naturalist and a military escort of 40 men, he proceeded up the Red River to the Caddo Indian village in the neighborhood of the present Shreveport. These Indians accepted American jurisdiction and the American flag was hoisted in their village; but the Spanish authorities claimed that their boundary extended eastward of the Sabine River and that this place was within their territory. They accordingly sent a large party under Captain Don Francisco Viana in pursuit of Freeman. He had left the Caddo village when the Spaniards arrived, but they cut down the American flag and followed Freeman up the river.[29] Overtaking him near the present Texarkana, they forced him to retrace his steps.[30]

[26] Wilkinson to Porter, 19 Apr. 1806, Wilkinson MSS., Library of Congress; same to same, 30 Apr. 1806, ibid.; Dearborn to Wilkinson, 6 May 1806, Bacon, *Report*, 363–8; Wilkinson to Cushing, 8 May 1806, Wilkinson, *Memoirs*, II, app. 89.

[27] Porter to Wilkinson, 4 Apr. 1806, Wilkinson MSS., Library of Congress; same to same, 5 May 1806, ibid.; Porter to Dearborn, 7 June 1806, Bacon, *Report*, 368–9.

[28] Thomas Freeman to John McKee, (?) Nov. 1805, John McKee Papers, Library of Congress; *Louisiana Gazette*, 16 May 1811; Carter, *Territorial Papers*, IX, 450–53; *D.A.B.*, VII, 13–14.

[29] Yrujo to Cevallos, 17 July 1806, A.H.N., leg. 5543, exp. 1, 74–5; Claiborne to Herrera, 26 Aug. 1806, *Annals of Congress*, 9 Cong., 2 Sess. (1806–7), 919–20; Herrera to Claiborne, 28 Aug. 1806, ibid. 919–20; Cushing to Wilkinson, 31 July 1806, Bacon, *Report*, 370–73; Richmond *Enquirer*, 25 July 1806; Charleston *Courier*, 22 Sept. 1806.

[30] Yrujo to Cevallos, 12 Sept. 1806, A.H.N., leg. 5543, exp. 1, 76–83; Richmond

While these events were taking place, Herrera once more crossed the Sabine late in July with the Baron Bastrop and about 400 poorly equipped men. Bastrop visited Colonel Cushing and was told that the Americans would oppose the Spanish advance. Despite this warning, Herrera advanced to Bayou Pierre on 7 August. On the way he was met by Major Porter, whom Cushing had sent to demand that all territory east of the Sabine be evacuated. Nevertheless, on 10 August, Herrera sent a scouting party to within 17 miles of Natchitoches, where it remained until the 19th when it retired to Bayou Pierre. The situation was becoming so serious that Governor Cordero set out from Bexar on the 15th with 100 men to reinforce Herrera on the frontier.[31]

This aggressive move may be accounted for by the fact that Governor Cordero had received word from New Orleans that an expedition was being prepared in Kentucky to overrun Mexico. On 2 June, Inspector-General Viana made a similar report to him from Nacogdoches; and Intendant Morales at Pensacola stated that the Mexican Association was active in New Orleans.[32] Since Burr was not now planning a forward movement before December, it seems probable that Wilkinson circulated these reports through his agents in order to encourage the Spaniards to put up a bold front and thus lead Burr to expect a war and the fulfillment of his hopes.

Colonel Cushing was now in a difficult position. He had positive orders from the Secretary of War to push the Spanish forces back across the Sabine. Wilkinson, however, had ordered him to avoid hostilities. On 5 August, Cushing had demanded that Herrera with-

---

Enquirer, 19 Sept., 10 Oct. 1806; *D.A.B.*, VII, 13–14; Herrera to Cordero, 3 Aug. 1806, A.G.I., Seville, Audiencia de Guadalajara, 296, papeleta 98/3325, no. 56; Cordero to Salcedo, 10 Aug., ibid. papeleta 98/3326, no. 290.

31 Evidence of Benjamin H. Latrobe, June 1806, Cabell Papers, Burr Case, 88; Alderman Library, U. Va.; *Louisiana Gazette*, 26 Aug. 1806; Richmond *Enquirer*, 30 Sept. 1806; *National Intelligencer*, 8 Oct. 1806; Schachner, *Burr*, 333; Herrera to Cordero, 28 July 1806, A.G.I., Seville, Audiencia de Guadalajara, 296, papeleta 98/3323, no. 54; same to same, 31 July 1806, ibid. papeleta 98/3324, no. 55; Cushing to Porter, 5 Aug. 1806, ibid. papeleta 98/3330; Herrera to Cordero, 6 Aug. 1806, ibid. papeleta 98/3326, no. 290; same to same, 15 Aug. 1806, ibid. papeleta 98/3329, no. 293; Cordero to Commandant of Coahuila, 15 Aug. 1806, ibid. papeleta 98/3334; Wilkinson, *Memoirs*, II, app. 93.

32 McCaleb, *Burr Conspiracy*, 60–61; Hatcher, *The Opening of Texas to Foreign Settlement*, 116.

draw; the next day the Spanish Colonel refused to do so, and a clash appeared imminent. The governors of Orleans and Mississippi territories were notified of the critical situation and they met at Natchez on 17 August to decide upon a plan of action. At this time it was agreed that it was necessary to repel the Spaniards and that Governor Claiborne should raise a force of Orleans militia and march with it to the threatened frontier while Cowles Mead, acting Governor of Mississippi Territory, was to alert his militia, keep an eye on the situation in Orleans Territory during the absence of Claiborne, and be prepared to send troops there or to Natchitoches if necessary.[33] It is clear that the governors were not preparing for defensive measures.

Meanwhile Cushing had sent a Lieutenant Smith to Fort Adams with orders for Colonel Kingsbury to march his garrison to Natchitoches. Yet even with this reinforcement the entire force there did not exceed 500 men. A friend of Wilkinson by the name of W. Thorp, and Gilbert Leonard, whom the General used as a translator in his correspondence with Folch and Casa Calvo, got word of Lieutenant Smith's mission and relayed the information to Don Carlos de Grand Pré, Spanish commandant at Baton Rouge.[34]

Though Wilkinson had been ordered on 6 May to repair to New Orleans to take personal command of the troops and to repel any Spanish movement east of the Sabine, he still tarried in St. Louis.[35] Here he was by no means idle. One piece of business which occupied his attention was the dispatch, on 15 June, of Lieutenant Montgomery Pike — who had recently returned from an expedition to the headwaters of the Mississippi River — to explore the sources of the Red and Arkansas rivers. Wilkinson certainly knew that Constant Freeman was, at that very moment, undertaking to perform the same task, and he knew also, though his orders gave no hint of it, that Pike's real objective was not primarily to discover mountains which would bear his name but to reach the Spanish city of Santa

[33] Cushing to Herrera, 5 Aug., and Herrera to Cushing, 6 Aug. 1806, *A.S.P., Foreign Relations*, II, 801; Thomas Rodney to Caesar A. Rodney, 25 Aug., 6 Sept. 1806, *Pennsylvania Magazine of History and Biography*, XLIV (1920), 283–4, 289–91; Carter, *Territorial Papers*, IX, 696–7; Cox, 'Louisiana-Texas Frontier,' loc. cit. 283–4; McCaleb, *Burr Conspiracy*, 102–5.

[34] *Louisiana Gazette*, 10 June, 22 Aug. 1806.

[35] Richmond *Enquirer*, 3 Oct. 1806; McCaleb, *Burr Conspiracy*, 106.

Fe.[36] A letter written by Wilkinson on 2 August to Secretary of War Dearborn may shed a little light upon this mystery. In it he said: 'It is with deep regret I address you from this place instead of Ft. Adams, where I expected to have been three weeks ago. Circumstances [expected war with Spain] on which your orders were based, have ceased. Manuel Lisa, a native Spaniard, has formed some grand commercial or political speculation destined to Santa Fee. A party is formed at St. Louis for this purpose. I enclose a copy of Lt. Pike's instructions . . .' [37]

Such things, rather than war with Spain, appeared to be uppermost in the mind of the Commanding General of the United States Army at the very time when only the orders that he had given Colonel Cushing prevented a clash of arms on the Sabine. But the General was not really opening his mind to all his friends. On 17 June he had written to Senator John Smith that he intended to carry out his orders in regard to the Spaniards on the Sabine; and at about the same time he wrote to Burr, saying 'I shall be ready before you.' [38]

The question naturally arises why Wilkinson, who was so active a conspirator in 1805, had now not only failed to keep in touch with Burr but even appeared to be plotting against him. This question cannot be answered categorically, for only the General could have given an authoritative answer and he failed to do so. Yet circumstances do throw considerable light upon his motives, and these circumstances had changed drastically within the course of a year. War with Spain over the question of the Louisiana boundaries was expected in 1805, and Wilkinson could not have anticipated that the decision in the matter would be left in his own hands, as it actually was in 1806. If war had been declared, he would have been the leader of the American army, and it would have been necessary for him to attempt to invade Mexico by way of Santa Fe. He often said that he had long planned such an expedition. He knew that the Spaniards resented the domination of their country by Napoleon and that the colonies were ripe for revolt. All that they needed was

[36] Isaac J. Cox, 'Opening the Santa Fe Trail,' *Missouri Historical Review,* xxv (1930), 47–8; *Louisiana Gazette,* 15 May 1811.

[37] Bacon, *Report,* 374–8.

[38] McCaleb, *Burr Conspiracy,* 107.

leadership, and Miranda was planning to set the example in that field. An invading army might well find itself in the midst of a Mexican revolution, and in 1805 Burr and Wilkinson had taken pains to plant agents across the border.

What could Wilkinson's army do in such a case but assist in the establishment of Mexican independence? Of course the General could hardly set himself up as the head of a new state, but if Burr happened to be along as the leader of an independent force of volunteers, he would be the ideal man for the job. Burr's friends in New Orleans, who had prejudiced the Creoles against American rule, might hark back to 1776 and lead an independence movement in Louisiana, and they might add West Florida and possibly even the Mississippi Territory to their domain; but Wilkinson would be too far away to do anything about that, and no one would have reason to question his patriotism.

So things might have gone if war had broken out with Spain in 1805. But in 1806 the stage was set for a very different play. If independent governments were going to be set up at New Orleans and in Mexico, an American fleet at the mouth of the Mississippi might prove very embarrassing. That is where Commodore Truxton fitted into the picture, but neither Truxton nor any other American naval officers had been willing to listen to Burr. Of course the British navy might overcome this disadvantage, and since Miranda received British naval aid in the Caribbean, there was no reason to think that independence movements in Latin America would be viewed in an unfriendly light by the British Government. But Burr had failed to get any promises of aid and the American navy would certainly block the mouth of the Mississippi in case of a revolt in Louisiana.

Furthermore, Burr had talked too much. Rumors of conspiracy were flying from one end of the country to the other, and Wilkinson's name was always linked with that of the arrogant, ambitious little Colonel. If a war with Mexico should start now and Louisiana should revolt, Wilkinson would be branded as a traitor and his bridges would be burned behind him. The General was never one to jump from the frying pan into the fire, but it was too late to undo all that he had done. He could not tell Burr that he had changed his mind. He would let him go ahead with his plans for the invasion of Mexico and the revolutionizing of Louisiana, and, if at the last minute, the situation looked unfavorable, he might be able to call off the invasion and turn Burr in as a traitor. This would enable him to pose as the savior of two countries — and perhaps he might collect from both. He was, above all else, an opportunist.

Burr and his friends, of course, were not aware of what was going on in Wilkinson's mind, but when they finally heard of the situation that had developed on the Sabine, their hopes began to revive. In the beginning of February the Spanish forces had crossed that river and Major Porter had been ordered to see that they recrossed it. In March they advanced again and occupied Adais. Colonel Cushing was then ordered to take command at that post and Wilkinson was instructed to reinforce him. Governor Claiborne was anxious to attack, but was dissuaded by Cushing. News of these events reached New Orleans by the first of April,[39] but Burr could hardly have heard it when, on the 15th, he wrote to Wilkinson: 'The execution of our project is postponed till December: want of water in Ohio rendered movement impracticable; other reasons rendered delay expedient. The association is enlarged and comprises all that Wilkinson could wish. Confidence limited to a few . . . *Burr* wrote you a long letter last December replying to a short one deemed very silly. Nothing has been heard from Brigadier [Wilkinson] since October.' This refers to the letter in which Wilkinson relayed to Burr the report of Daniel Clark from New Orleans that rumors of a conspiracy were afloat and that the Colonel was suspected of having talked too freely to Stephen Minor in Natchez.[40] On the previous day Burr had written Blennerhassett that he expected no war with Spain, but hoped to revive his project in December. Wilkinson answered Burr's letter on 13 May, and the message must have incriminated both men, for they later conspired to prevent its publication.[41]

With the situation on the Sabine remaining critical and negotiations with Spain getting nowhere, Burr's hopes waxed brighter by the early part of May and he went back to see his old friend the

[39] Raleigh *Minerva*, 12 May 1806.
[40] Parton, *Burr*, 406; McCaleb, *Burr Conspiracy*, 60.
[41] Adams, *History of the United States*, III, 252.

Spanish minister, Yrujo. He again convinced him that his only object was the separation of the American West, and that this scheme was entirely practicable if circumstances were right. All that was needed was financial assistance from France and Spain, and agents from Kentucky, Louisiana, and Tennessee were to visit Spain during the next spring in order to promote the cause. Yrujo assured his Government that, when he returned home at that time, he would 'be the bearer of the whole plan, with the details that may be wanted.' [42]

But no additional aid was forthcoming from Yrujo and the next month Burr held his last conference with Anthony Merry, whom Fox had recalled during the previous March. Burr explained that since he had received no aid from Britain, he 'and the persons connected with him at New Orleans' would now, though reluctantly, be forced to appeal to France and Spain for assistance. 'He added, however,' Merry reported, 'that the disposition of the inhabitants of the Western country, and particularly Louisiana, to separate themselves from the American Union was so strong that the attempt might be made with every prospect of success without any foreign assistance whatever; and his last words to me were that, with or without such support, it certainly would be made very shortly.' [43]

At about the same time Jonathan Dayton made another call upon Yrujo. He pictured the new British Ministry as anxious to assist Burr, who, he said, was sending Dr. Bollman to London to cooperate with Williamson in soliciting aid. He warned that an attack on West Florida was contemplated. He said that he and Wilkinson opposed this design and suggested to the minister that Spain should reinforce Pensacola and Mobile.[44] This was a last desperate effort at deception, and it was the last conference either Dayton or Burr ever had with Yrujo. All hope of foreign aid had vanished.

It may be that Dayton, like Wilkinson, was really opposed to an attack on Spanish territory at this time, but he had not abandoned Burr's plan to bring about a separation of the West. The circumstances certainly did not appear too favorable. Not only had Burr

[42] Ibid. III, 247–8; Chadwick, *Relations of the United States and Spain*, 98.
[43] McCaleb, *Burr Conspiracy*, 65.
[44] Yrujo to Cevallos, 9 June 1806, A.H.N., Est., leg. 5546, apartado 1, 115–40, no. 690; Adams, *History of the United States*, III, 248–9.

been unable to secure foreign aid but since the autumn of 1805 he had had no assurance of the co-operation of General Wilkinson. He had, however, been able to collect various sums of money from his son-in-law, Joseph Alston, from Harman Blennerhassett, William S. Smith, and from Samuel G. Ogden. Both Smith and Ogden were New Yorkers and both were backers of Miranda's ill-fated expedition. Burr undoubtedly secured money from various other sources, for Blennerhassett later complained that he did not see how Burr could possibly have spent all that he collected.[45]

In June while he was rusticating at Falsington, Pennsylvania, with Theodosia and her family, he sent Dr. Justus Erich Bollman to call on Paul Henry Mallet Prevost of Huntington County, New Jersey. Bollman was a German who spoke French and English almost as fluently as he spoke his native tongue. He was an adventurer of no mean abilities. Born near Bremen, he had studied medicine and, after practicing at various European spas, he went to Paris and was there when the Revolution broke out. For a time he made himself useful to both sides, but later he went to Austria and settled at Olmutz in an attempt to liberate Lafayette from his prison there. Having failed in his feat of derring do, Bollman suffered imprisonment himself for eight months, and on his release migrated to the United States. As a friend of Lafayette he was warmly received and presently engaged in mercantile operations in New York. He failed in business, but became acquainted with Aaron Burr who decided he could use a man of the world who was so proficient in languages.[46] Now, Bollman told Prevost that he was going to Europe to raise money and asked him for letters of introduction but did not get them. Prevost and the Doctor then rode to Falsington and had dinner with Burr and his daughter. Afterward they went to Morrisville, near Trenton, to visit General Jean Victor Moreau, who had been evicted by Napoleon and who was now living in Morrisville in retirement. Next morning Prevost noticed on a table a manuscript map of the disputed Louisiana boundary. On being questioned, Burr said that the dispute could not be settled without war and that the Western people were anxious to co-operate with the

[45] McCaleb, *Burr Conspiracy*, 66.
[46] Bacon, *Report*, 310–18; Adams, *History of the United States*, III, 255.

United States Army as soon as hostilities should commence. Burr stated that the situation had led him to engage in Western land speculations, and he invited Prevost to visit him, which Prevost declined to do.[47]

During this sojourn at Morrisville, Burr saw General Moreau frequently and they undoubtedly discussed the prospects for an invasion of Mexico. The Colonel now made a brief trip to Philadelphia to broach the same subject to his good friend Charles Biddle. He told him that a number of important gentlemen in every part of the Union wished to establish a settlement of military men on the Mississippi; that the Mexicans were ripe for revolt and a rich reward awaited all those concerned in revolutionizing that country. Biddle commented that this would mean war with Spain, to which Burr replied that we would have such a war whether we invaded Mexico or not.[48]

By the latter part of July the arch conspirator was ready to begin operations. One matter of prime importance to Burr was to keep in close touch with the situation in New Orleans, and for that purpose Dr. Bollman, along with James Alexander, Lieutenant Robert T. Spence, and others, was dispatched by sea to that city. The letters that passed between Bollman and Burr were written partly in German and partly in cipher.[49] Burr had employed a German secretary, Charles Willie, to accompany him on his Western journey and to keep in touch with his agent in New Orleans. Dr. Bollman now carried a letter from Burr to Edward Livingston, dated 26 July, and a copy of a cipher letter to Wilkinson dated 29 July.[50]

In order to stimulate the reticent General, Dayton wrote him a letter on 24 July: 'It is now well ascertained that you are to be displaced in next session,' he said. 'Jefferson will affect to yield reluctantly to the public sentiment but yield he will. Prepare yourself, therefore, for it. You know the rest. You are not a man to despair, or even despond, especially when such prospects offer in another

[47] Affidavit of Paul Henry Mallet Prevost, 28 Sept. 1807, *Quarterly Publications, Historical and Philosophical Society of Ohio,* IX (1914), 28–30, also in Chillicothe Papers.

[48] Charles Biddle, *Autobiography*, 313–14.

[49] T. P. Abernethy, 'Aaron Burr in Mississippi,' *J.S.H.*, XV (1949), 17–18.

[50] Schachner, *Burr*, 370.

quarter. Are you ready? Are your numerous associates ready? Wealth and Glory! Louisiana and Mexico!' [51]

If Wilkinson was still hesitating about what his course would be, this letter must have decided him. He would play the hero: no President would have the hardihood to displace the savior of his country; instead of losing his high position as Commanding General of the Army and his snug pension from Spain, he would render inestimable service to each country which he 'loved equally well,' and each would reward him fittingly.

On the same day Dayton wrote to Wilkinson, Burr penned a letter to Blennerhassett and dispatched it, along with one to John Adair, by Samuel Swartwout, the younger brother of his friend Colonel John Swartwout, marshal of New York, and Peter V. Ogden, Dayton's nephew. They also carried Dayton's letter to Wilkinson and the one that Burr wrote in cipher to the General on 29 July.[52] The latter document is the most famous one relating to the conspiracy, for it furnishes the most concrete evidence we have about Burr's plans and expectations at this time. In it he said that he had obtained funds and commenced operations. Truxton was going to Jamaica to arrange with the British admiral on that station to meet the expedition on the Mississippi, and an American naval force was ready to co-operate. Burr would start westward on 1 August and move rapidly down to the Falls of the Ohio by the middle of November, bringing the first contingent of 500 or 1000 men with him in light boats which were already being built. He expected to meet Wilkinson in Natchez by the middle of December, 'there to determine whether it will be expedient in the first instance to seize on or pass by Baton Rouge. — The people of the country to which we are going are prepared to receive us; their agents, now with Burr, say that if we will protect their religion, and will not subject them to a foreign Power, that in three weeks all will be settled.' [53]

If Wilkinson was deceiving Burr, the latter was also trying to deceive him, for the Colonel knew he would not have the support of

[51] Safford, *Blennerhassett Papers*, 170–71; Adams, *History of the United States*, III, 252.

[52] Ibid. 252–5, 295; Safford, *Blennerhassett Papers*, 122–3.

[53] McCaleb, *Burr Conspiracy*, 68–9; MS. in collection of Everett D. Graff, 38 South Dearborn Street, Chicago. Here the document is dated 22 July.

either a British or an American naval force. Or perhaps in his visionary schemes, he was like the Duchess in *Alice:* 'If I say a thing three times, it is true.' But he did have some money and some boats were being built on the Western rivers, and he may well have had 1000 men enlisted in his cause. The statement relating to Baton Rouge is the most significant one in the letter, for it gives us a clue about the writer's real destination. Baton Rouge lies well to the south of the mouth of Red River, and if Burr had been planning to go directly to Natchitoches he would not have gone that way. If he planned to pass Baton Rouge, there were only two feasible destinations: New Orleans and Mobile. It is perhaps conceivable that he may have planned to launch a maritime invasion of Mexico from the tiny Spanish post at Mobile, but that would certainly be stretching the imagination. Furthermore, no good general, or even colonel, would have invaded foreign territory and left so important a post as Baton Rouge in his rear. The Spanish could easily have reinforced Baton Rouge by water and Burr's line of communication would have been completely severed.

The statement that 'the people of the country to which we are going are prepared to receive us' and 'that in three weeks all will be settled' is also significant. There is no evidence that there were any Mexican agents with Burr, but there may well have been agents from Louisiana. Though Burr had reason to believe that Mexico was ripe for revolt, it is not likely that he was so well posted on Mexican public opinion as to be able to say that the people were ready to receive him. But Clark and Livingston and their party had been fomenting unrest in New Orleans for two or three years, and Bollman was now going to represent Burr on the spot. And finally, is it likely that Burr expected to conquer Mexico and settle matters there in three weeks? Certainly Wilkinson could not make it to Natchitoches in that time, and considering that a fleet would have to be assembled, manned, and equipped in New Orleans — a fleet capable of transporting at least several hundred men — it hardly seems possible that even the visionary Colonel could have imagined such a thing. For these reasons, it appears that only one answer is possible. Burr was headed for New Orleans.

Chapter V

BURR ON THE OHIO

DURING THE FIRST WEEK in August 1806, Burr left Philadelphia and started for the West, giving it out that he was never to return. Theodosia with her infant son was at Bedford Springs in the Pennsylvania mountains for her health. Burr stopped here for a visit with her, and was soon joined by Colonel Julien De Pestre and Charles Willie. De Pestre was a French refugee who had served in both the French and the British armies, and he was now to act as Burr's chief-of-staff. This was a small retinue, but it was important that its movements should not attract undue attention. After a brief sojourn, the three took horse for Wheeling on the Ohio but Theodosia remained behind, intending to join them later in Kentucky.[1]

The adventurers passed through Chambersburg on 11 August and rode into Pittsburgh on the 21st.[2] Since this was to be a chief place of rendezvous for Burr's forces, he remained here several days while arranging for supplies and recruits. Making his headquarters at the tavern of James O'Hara, who was suspected of being a sympathizer, he got in touch with the 'aristocrats' and Federalists of the town, chief of whom was General Presley Neville. His son now enlisted for the expedition and was furnished by his father with a finely appointed boat. Another important recruit was young Thomas Butler, son of the Colonel of the same name whom General

[1] J. J. Combs (ed.), *The Trial of Aaron Burr for High Treason* (Washington, 1864), xvii; Evidence of Charles Willie, Cabell Papers, Burr Case, 28–9, Alderman Library, U. Va.

[2] *National Intelligencer*, 22 Aug. 1806.

Wilkinson had court-martialed for refusing to comply with an order of 1804 requiring all officers to crop their hair.[3] Incidentally, Colonel Butler defiantly wore his queue as long as he lived, and it is said that on his deathbed he gave instructions for an auger hole to be bored in his coffin, and for his queue to be tied with a blue ribbon and pulled through the hole.

The most important of Burr's associates at this juncture was Comfort Tyler of Herkimer, New York. Burr often said that a large group of 'choice spirits' from New York were to join him, and he had engaged Tyler to collect some of them. Tyler had served as county clerk, but falling upon evil days, had gone to New York City and had been arrested for vagrancy. Burr, who had known him in the New York Assembly, now rescued him from his distress. He was furnished with money and clothes and sent back to Herkimer to recruit for his benefactor.[4] Burr made a contract with him to deliver $40,000 worth of provisions on the Ohio in the following November. He also made a contract with John Wilkins, a Pittsburgh merchant, for 20,000 barrels of flour and 5000 barrels of pork to be delivered locally or to D. W. Elliot, a merchant at Natchez.[5] In Pittsburgh, Burr made contact with young Samuel Swartwout, who was on his way to the lower Mississippi to deliver the Colonel's cipher letter of 29 July to Wilkinson. At this time Wilkinson's letter of 13 August arrived. It was in cipher, but at the end in plain English was the statement, 'I am ready.' The Colonel answered in cipher that he and his friends would join the General in the expected war with Spain.[6]

Burr, accompanied by De Pestre, tarried in Pittsburgh a few days, and took the occasion to visit Colonel George Morgan, whom he had known while a student at Princeton. During the late colonial period, Morgan had been deeply interested, along with other leading

[3] Philadelphia *Aurora*, 8 Jan. 1807.

[4] *American Citizen* (New York), 23 Sept. 1806; Raleigh *Minerva*, 13 Oct. 1806, quoting *Farmers' Monitor*, Herkimer, N.Y.; Kentucky *Gazette*, 23 Oct. 1806, quoting same.

[5] Document marked 'confidential,' n.d., Burr MSS., Library of Congress; Dearborn to Wilkinson, 21 Jan. 1807, Bacon, *Report*, 410; *American Citizen*, 18 Nov. 1806; Richmond *Enquirer*, 18 Nov. 1806; *National Intelligencer*, 12 Nov. 1806; *Louisiana Gazette*, 23 Dec. 1806.

[6] Evidence of Samuel Swartwout, July 1806, Cabell Papers, Burr Case, 30, Alderman Library, U. Va.

mercantile and political characters, in certain land companies that secured Indian grants of huge tracts both north and south of the Ohio River. The British Government had failed to validate these grants, and so had the Continental Congress and the new Federal Government. For years Morgan had worked tirelessly to secure such a validation, but his efforts had been in vain and now the prospect was hopeless.[7] Only a separation of the West from the Union could have effected a change in land policy, and one of Burr's purposes in visiting his old acquaintance was to suggest just such an enticing possibility.

At this time Morgan was living with his two sons on an estate which he called 'Morganza,' near Cannonsburg about 15 miles from Pittsburgh. He seemed to have lost interest in land speculation and was devoting his time to growing grapes and engaging in other agricultural experiments, for he had a scientific turn of mind and had been elected to membership in the American Philosophical Society. He had also become a supporter of the Republican regime of President Jefferson.[8] Burr was evidently not aware of these changes in the status of his host when he and Colonel De Pestre dropped in for dinner on 22 August. The main object of this visit was to enlist the two sons of the house in his enterprise. Believing that he was in congenial company, Burr launched at once upon his business and declared that the West, because of its disadvantages in the Union, could be expected to separate within four or five years. He inquired particularly about the military strength of that part of the country; the number and organization of the militia; the leading military characters, and persons who had been concerned in the Whiskey Rebellion. He said that a wide field was sure to be opened to men of talents, particularly to military men. He spoke at length of the wickedness and pusillanimity of the Eastern states and went on to say — perhaps after the wine had been passed — that with 200 men he could drive the President and Congress into the Potomac, and that with 400 or 500 he could take New York City.[9]

[7] Max Savelle, *George Morgan, Colony Builder* (New York, 1932), 57–9, 64, 76–110; T. P. Abernethy, *Western Lands and the American Revolution*, see index, 'George Morgan.'

[8] *D.A.B.*, XIII, 169–70.

[9] Evidence of George Morgan, *Annals of Congress*, 10 Cong., 1 Sess., I, 425–8;

From the first statement it is clear that Burr had given up all hope that a separation of Kentucky and the Northwest could be effected at this time; but if the lower waters of the Mississippi could be controlled, the upper basin would presently find that its interests lay in that direction. About the threats against Washington and New York City, they hardly seem to be the product of a rational mind if they were uttered in earnest. But Burr did not say that he planned to make any such attacks; he was merely expressing his contempt for the President and the Government of which he was the head. There can scarcely be any reasonable doubt that he made these statements, for he repeated them on several other occasions.

Failing to get a favorable response from his dinner companions, Burr waited until the two young men had retired and again approached the father. He now asked him if he knew the Spaniard Vigo of Vincennes. Morgan replied that he knew him as a man who was deeply involved in the conspiracy of 1788, which, he added, was a nefarious scheme aimed at the division of the states. At this, Burr bade his host good night and the next morning he and De Pestre mounted their horses before breakfast and rode back to Pittsburgh.[10]

Disturbed by this interview, Morgan promptly sent an account of it to the President, and at about the same time, 2 September, he wrote to General Neville saying:

> With a view to the Development of a most nefarious Scheme against our Country, I invited Judge Roberts to breakfast with me yesterday, on his Road from Pittsburgh to Washington [Pennsylvania] & I authorized him in my Name to communicate to you, — the Information I gave him. — I did not recite to him all what I think our Government should be informed of, & which I wish to communicate to you, & to Chief Justice Tilghman, — I wish no other Persons than my own Sons, to be present at so important a Communication, & therefore I ask the favor of Mr. Tilghmans, & your Company, to dine with me at any Hour, next Sunday, which you & he may agree upon, — I wish Judge Roberts

---

Presley Neville and Samuel Roberts to James Madison, 7 Oct. 1806, Burr MSS., Library of Congress; Deposition of Julien De Pestre, 5(?) Oct. 1807, Everett D. Graff Collection.

[10] Evidence of George Morgan, *Annals of Congress*, 10 Cong., 1 Sess., 1, 427; Evidence of George Morgan, Aug. 1806, Cabell Papers, Burr Case, 37–8, Alderman Library, U. Va.

to be of the Party —. An unfortunate Accident disables me from riding, or I would not impose on you the task of coming here.[11]

The result of this letter was that on 20 September General Presley Neville, Chief Justice William Tilghman of Pennsylvania, and Judge Samuel Roberts dined with Colonel Morgan and his sons Thomas and John, the latter Adjutant-General of New Jersey militia. Neville was probably not surprised by what he heard, and he was in no hurry to make use of the information, but on 7 October, when news of Burr's activities was on every tongue, he and Judge Roberts wrote a joint letter to Secretary Madison and gave an account of their conference with the Morgans.[12]

By 18 November, Chief Justice Tilghman had returned to Philadelphia, and on that day he wrote an account of this interview. 'The Col.,' he said, 'was a good deal indisposed, & his disorder had considerably affected his brain — he talked much of Col. Burr, — & seemed deeply impressed with an Opinion that he had it in contemplation to effect a separation of the States.' He added that Burr asked John Morgan, the General, whether he would like to command a regiment. He also inquired about the most active and influential men in that part of the country, and who had been most active in the Whiskey Rebellion, remarking that 'if the Insurgents had been headed by a man of Talents, — not one of the troops sent against them, would ever have seen salt water again.' That evening Burr remarked to Colonel Morgan and his younger son that 'in the course of years there must, & would be a separation of the Western from the Eastern people.' 'It was,' said Tilghman, 'the expression of this Sentiment which shocked Col. Morgan, & seemed to predominate in his mind during his delerium.' The Chief Justice discussed the matter with Governor Thomas McKean, father-in-law of the Spanish agent, Yrujo, and 'The Governor thought there was no occasion for me to say anything to the Government of the United States —.'[13]

[11] George Morgan to Presley Neville, 2 Sept. 1806, Burr Papers, McGregor Library, U. Va.

[12] Presley Neville and Samuel Roberts to James Madison, 7 Oct. 1806, Burr MSS., Library of Congress, published in *The History of America in Documents* (The Rosenbach Co., Philadelphia, 1950), pt. 2, 82.

[13] Chief Justice Tilghman's Memorandum, Philadelphia, 18 Nov. 1806, Burr Papers, McGregor Library, U. Va.

Leaving Pittsburgh, Burr and De Pestre journeyed via Marietta to Blennerhassett's Island opposite the town of Belpré on the Ohio, where they arrived on 27 August. From Marietta they were accompanied by the son of Dudley Woodbridge, a merchant of that town with whom Blennerhassett had formed a business partnership.[14] The travelers found the master at home in his sprawling mansion with its handsome furnishings and fine library, and they lost no time in getting down to business. A contract was made with the senior Woodbridge for 100 barrels of pork; and Colonel J. Barker agreed to build 15 boats for them on the Muskingum a few miles above Marietta, and to deliver them on 9 December. These boats, like others built for Burr, were similar to those used on the Mohawk River and were larger and much more expensive than craft usually constructed for use on the Ohio. Ten were to be 40 feet by 10, and five were to be 50 feet long; they were fast row galleys of shallow draft and were intended for navigation upstream as well as down. Each would accommodate 40 or 50 men and their baggage, and one was especially fitted out for the accommodation of Blennerhassett's family.[15]

General Tupper of the Ohio militia asked Barker if he would take a Colonel's commission under Burr and go down the river in case of war with Spain. He understood that the expedition was sanctioned by the Government and showed Barker the copy of *The Duty of a Soldier and Discipline of the Infantry as now Practised in the French Army*, which Burr had sent him, asking if Barker would introduce some of the maneuvers in his regiment. Blennerhassett assured him they had no hostile intentions against the United States, which does not agree with other versions of the affair he was disseminating at this time. Burr, however, consistently gave men in the military service to understand that the Government approved of his project.

During the first few days of September the Island was humming

[14] Safford, *Blennerhassett Papers*, 124; Coombs, *Trial of Aaron Burr*, 191.

[15] Deposition of J. Barker, Sept. 1806, *Quarterly Publications, Historical and Philosophical Society of Ohio*, IX (1914), 62–3; Deposition of Edward W. Tupper, 8 Sept. 1807, ibid. 13–27; Coombs, *Trial of Aaron Burr*, 198; McCaleb, *Burr Conspiracy*, 72–3.

with excitement and activity. Corn was being ground and Mrs. Blennerhassett and her two small sons were busy packing their belongings for the final move down the Mississippi.[16] Burr spent much of his time with his host in order to inform him about his plans and intentions and to stir up his enthusiasm for the cause. This was not a difficult task, for the Irishman was in urgent need of recouping his fortune. Nevertheless, Blennerhassett was for the moment furnishing most of the funds with which Burr carried on his operations.[17]

The picture Burr painted for his host at this time was one to intrigue an adventurous spirit. The Spaniards had invaded American soil east of the Sabine, and Wilkinson would certainly use force to expel them, thus precipitating an undeclared war against Mexico to which Jefferson would not be averse. The people of Mississippi and Orleans territories were disaffected. There was a group of young men in New Orleans known as The Mexican Association who, during his recent visit there, had asked him to become their leader. Indeed, so disgusted were the people of that city that he expected to hear of their beginning a revolt, and of the seizure of all military stores, the banks, and the custom house, and the appropriation of the revenues and forces of the Territory. With the navigation of the Mississippi thus threatened, the West, already dissatisfied with a government under the control of Eastern commercial interests, would separate from the Union. This could be expected to happen within four or five years, and Burr was not sure whether the Allegheny Mountains or the South Branch of the Potomac River should be the eastern boundary of the Western Government. In any case, he thought he could defend any pass through the mountains with 300 men and three pieces of artillery. Burr said he had only a speculative interest in the independence of the West, but that people should be advised of the situation so they would not be taken by surprise. He also said that the question of a war with Spain did not concern him, but neither such a war nor the separation of the West would interrupt his enterprise, 'nor

[16] Evidence of Jacob Allbright, *Annals of Congress*, 10 Cong., 1 Sess., I, 428–31.
[17] Coombs, *Trial of Aaron Burr*, 197–9, evidence of Dudley Woodbridge.

would they be adverse to his own views, let them precede or follow his own undertaking.'[18]

On the 1st of September, Blennerhassett sat down to write a series of four articles, which, beginning 4 September, were published in the *Ohio Gazette* of Marietta under the heading 'Querist.' Burr had left the Island on the 28th, and therefore he did not have a direct hand in the composition of these papers, but the ideas they expressed were in complete accord with those he was now expressing. They undertook to explain how the Federal Government, under the control of the commercial East, was exploiting the agricultural West through its policies regarding taxation, land, and trade. A separation of the sections was proposed as the only practicable remedy.[19]

While thus sending up a trial balloon to explore the climate of Western opinion, the confederates proceeded with the recruitment of men for their enterprise. On 31 August, Blennerhassett sent a note to Captain Alexander Henderson, a prominent neighbor, saying that he would visit him within a few days to unfold an important plan. On the 8th the Irishman rode up with John G. Henderson, Alexander's brother. After dinner the three men walked in the meadow and Blennerhassett enjoined secrecy upon the brothers. He then told them that there was a plan under the auspices of Burr to divide the Union, and that it would be carried out within nine months. Louisiana was to be revolutionized, New Orleans was to be taken, the banks and public arms and stores were to be seized. If the Federal officials in Washington made trouble, they would be thrown into the Potomac. Blennerhassett acknowledged that he was involved in the plot, and said that John Graham, Secretary of Orleans Territory, was also concerned. During this conference, the visitor displayed the manuscript of the 'Querist' articles and confessed that he was the author of them.[20]

[18] Evidence of Alexander Henderson, 23 Sept. 1807, *A.S.P.*, *Misc.*, I, 525–8; Safford, *Blennerhassett Papers*, 124–6.

[19] James Taylor to James Madison, 13 Oct. 1806, James A. Padgett (ed.), 'Letters of James Taylor,' Kentucky State Historical Society, *Register*, XXXIV (1936), 113–16; Safford, *Blennerhassett Papers*, 132–40.

[20] Gayarré, *Louisiana*, IV, 179–80; Evidence of Alexander and John G. Anderson, Cabell Papers, Burr Case, 48–51, Alderman Library, U. Va.; James Taylor to Secre-

While great inducements were held out to such prospects as the Hendersons, the usual terms offered recruits were $12 per month, plus clothes and provisions, for six months' service, and a bonus of 150 acres of land at the end of that time. Burr also promised commissions to young men of talent, and thus made it clear that whatever his relations with General Wilkinson he intended to build up his own military force.[21]

Blennerhassett Island was to be the final rendezvous for Burr's Eastern forces, and he planned to start his expedition from that point; but having set the machinery in motion, he was soon ready to go on down the river in order to collect his cohorts in Kentucky and Tennessee. Accordingly, on 4 September, he presented himself to his friend Senator John Smith in Cincinnati. The Senator admitted that he knew more of Burr's plans than any man except one in Ohio, and he now told Elias Glover — who became a recruiting agent for the Colonel — that the plan was to revolutionize Mexico with the aid of the clergy, and that Burr said if he was resisted at Fort Adams, he would take the place; otherwise he would leave it alone.[22] Burr gave it out, said Smith, that he would be assisted by the British Navy and a part of the United States Navy — the same lie he told Wilkinson in his famous cipher letter. Glover had been brought to Smith's house to meet Colonel Burr by Judge William McFarland, an avowed proponent of Western secession. Smith, whose two sons were to join Burr, was building gunboats for the Government, but if they were not paid for, it was hinted that Burr might get them. During the next month Comfort Tyler visited Ohio with an English cartographer named Constable and engaged in recruiting.[23]

---

tary of State, 28 Dec. 1806, John Smith Papers, Historical and Philosophical Society of Ohio.

[21] Deposition of David Fisk, 27 Sept. 1807, *A.S.P., Misc.*, I, 524–5.

[22] Testimony of Elias Glover, *Quarterly Publications, Historical and Philosophical Society of Ohio*, IX (1914), 58–61; Leslie Henshaw, 'The Aaron Burr Conspiracy in the Ohio Valley,' *Ohio State Archaeological and Historical Quarterly*, XXIV (1915), 126; *D.A.B.*, XVII, 296–7.

[23] *American Citizen*, 19 Dec. 1806; Deposition of William McFarland, 15 Feb. 1808, John Smith Papers, Historical and Philosophical Society of Ohio; Deposition of Isaac Burnet, 29 Feb. 1808, ibid.; Statement by John Smith, 25 June 1808, ibid.; Deposition of Samuel Hilditch, 20 Feb. 1808, ibid.; Deposition of George Williamson, 28 Oct. 1807, ibid.

Burr's next stop was Frankfort, Kentucky, where he arrived shortly after sunset on 11 September. He had parted company with Colonel De Pestre at Chillicothe, and the Frenchman had reached Louisville on 8 September. From there he wrote on the 10th to Lewis de Mun of New Orleans, saying:

> I arrived here the day before yesterday after having rode 810 miles with a companion [Burr] whom I rejoined 150 mis. from Philadelphia, and who appeared to have friends & business in every corner of the back parts of Pennsylvania, Virginia and Ohio and Kentucky. I did not part with him until we reached Chillicothe when our common affairs (for I have become his associate) obliged us to take different routes to Louisville, where I expect him that I may take his letters to the merchants at St. Louis where I shall be charged with all the affairs of the company, while he will have the management on the Ohio. We will try to have our merchandise ready in October that it may be delivered at *New Orleans*, by the middle or end of *December*.[24]

In this connection it may be significant that Turreau, the French minister in Washington, wrote to his Government during November expressing the opinion that the Western states would be forced to separate from the Union because of the commercial disadvantages under which they labored; and he added, 'the first cause of disunion is so strongly perceived that a Company of traders, with a capital of one million dollars, is going to be financed in the West . . . to change the direction of a trade that is ruinous for their fellow countrymen . . . I have the program under my eyes — .' [25] The 'affairs of the company,' of course, involved much more than merchandise, and De Pestre was covertly informing his friend when the conspirators expected to strike in New Orleans. Andrew Jackson somewhat later warned Governor Claiborne to 'beware the month of December.'

From Louisville, De Pestre went to St. Louis for a visit with Wilkinson, who later said the Frenchman was the accredited agent of Burr, and that when he left St. Louis in October he bore a letter from Burr to a Mr. Provenchere, giving him assurances that a

[24] Translation of an extract of letter from J.D.P., Louisville, to Lewis de Mun, New Orleans, 10 Sept. 1806, Bacon, *Report*, 352; Kentucky *Gazette*, 11 Sept. 1806.

[25] Turreau to Talleyrand, (?) Nov. 1806, A.E., Cor. Pol., E.U., LIX, 292.

revolution of the Western states would take place on 15 November, and inviting him to join the scheme.[26]

After a brief visit with his friend Senator John Brown in Frankfort, Burr went on to Lexington where he lodged at Wilson's Tavern. After several busy days, he took the road leading southward and arrived at Nashville on 24 September. Riding out to the 'Hermitage,' he again visited General Andrew Jackson, commander of the militia of middle Tennessee. Nothing would have pleased the General more than to find some worthy occupation for his riflemen, and Burr had important business with him. Jackson was most hospitable to his distinguished visitor and the next evening introduced him at a reception which was held in his honor at Talbot's Hotel in the town.[27]

Sensing the qualities of his host, Burr did not confide in him as he had in Eaton and Blennerhassett. He told him that Spanish troops were encamped on American soil; that they had imprisoned five American citizens and had cut down and carried off the American flag in the Caddo nation. He said that war with Spain was imminent, and that he, Burr, would have a command in the army.[28] He requested Jackson's aid, and the Tennessean lost no time in issuing an order to his forces to be in readiness to take the field at a moment's notice.[29] Old Hickory then wrote a letter to President Jefferson saying that he had three regiments which would be ready to march whenever ordered to do so. This offer came as a distinct surprise to the President, who wrote the General requesting information about the circumstances on which it was based.[30] On 27 October, Burr wrote to Governor William Henry Harrison of Indiana Territory, sending him a copy of Jackson's order and asking him to issue a similar one.[31]

[26] Wilkinson to Jefferson, 3 Apr. 1807, Burr MSS., Library of Congress; Deposition of Julien De Pestre, 5(?) Oct. 1807, Everett D. Graff Collection.

[27] Marquis James, *Andrew Jackson, The Border Captain,* 127; Richmond *Enquirer,* 7 Oct. 1806, quoting *Western World,* 13 Sept.

[28] McCaleb, *Burr Conspiracy,* 75.

[29] *Kentucky Gazette,* 20 Oct. 1806.

[30] Plumer, *Memorandum,* 577–8.

[31] Henshaw, 'The Aaron Burr Conspiracy in the Ohio Valley,' loc. cit. 127; Richmond *Enquirer,* 27 Oct. 1807.

On 6 October, Burr quitted Nashville and rode back to Lexington, where he took lodgings with Judge John Jourdan. There he was joined by Blennerhassett, who was accompanied by Theodosia and her husband. The Alstons had come to the Island about the first of the month and then gone down the river with their host while their servants and horses traveled overland.[32] Now assembled under one roof, the conspirators busied themselves with preparations for their descent of the Mississippi. While Comfort Tyler was collecting recruits and supplies in the Pittsburgh area, Davis Floyd of Jeffersonville, Indiana, opposite Louisville on the Ohio, was employed to carry on similar activities in central Kentucky. In addition, Burr sent Andrew Jackson $3500 in Kentucky bank notes to pay for the construction of five large boats and for the purchase of supplies. The General's friend, Patton Anderson, was appointed recruiting agent in Tennessee, and he succeeded in enlisting 75 men, including Mrs. Jackson's nephew, Stockly Hays.[33] Burr was counting also on another militia General — Edward W. Tupper, of Ohio, to whom young Thomas Butler delivered a letter, dated 21 October. In this message, Burr assured the General that war with Spain now seemed inevitable, and he urged Tupper not to engage in any occupation which would prevent his taking part in the expected hostilities.[34]

Burr at this time experienced no great difficulty in raising funds. Blennerhassett advanced what he could, and Alston, who had recently suffered a financial loss because of poor crops, underwrote these loans. Burr received considerable sums from Kentucky merchants, and a $25,000 loan was negotiated with the Kentucky Insurance Company. Jackson was paid in the notes of this banking institution.[35] One purchasing agent reported on 22 October that Burr, with wealthy friends from New York, was moving mysteriously

[32] Testimony of Stephen Welch, Cabell Papers, Burr Case, 84–5, Alderman Library, U. Va.; Henshaw, 'The Aaron Burr Conspiracy in the Ohio Valley,' loc. cit. 127; Richmond *Enquirer*, 11 Nov. 1806; Deposition of Charles Fenton Mercer, 21 Sept. 1807, Chillicothe Papers.

[33] Parton, *Jackson*, I, 316–17; Adams, *History of the United States*, III, 276.

[34] Deposition of Edward W. Tupper, 8 Sept. 1807, Chillicothe Papers.

[35] Raleigh *Register*, 24 Nov. 1806; *National Intelligencer*, 7 Nov. 1806; Richmond *Enquirer*, 17 Mar. 1807.

about Kentucky, holding secret councils and buying enough supplies for an army of 25,000; that he was said to have spent $200,000 and to have drawn some bills on the firm of Ogden and Smith of New York — the same concern that had backed the Miranda expedition. The writer said that he himself was buying as much pork, beef, and flour as he could procure, and was paying for it in advance. He personally thought that the expedition was aimed at Santa Fe and Mexico, but others thought that a division of the Union was the object.[36] Other statements show that Ogden, who was a kinsman of Jonathan Dayton, was backing Burr financially, though he was not believed to possess extensive means.[37]

Shortly before this letter was written, Burr had added another string to his bow — the 'purchase' of the Bastrop lands. In 1795 Governor Carondelet of Louisiana made two large grants on the Ouachita River. One tract of 100,000 acres went to the Marquis de Maison Rouge, a French émigré. The other was an enormous tract of 1,200,000 acres which went to Felipe Neri, Baron de Bastrop, a Hollander and also a refugee. A condition of these grants was that Maison Rouge was to settle 30 families on his domain, and Bastrop was to settle 500, each family being entitled to a 400-acre homestead. These settlers were supposed to be brought from war-torn Europe, but before arrangements could be made for this purpose, the Intendant of Louisiana raised objections to the grants and the Governor was forced to suspend proceedings in 1797.[38]

With his plans thus thwarted, Bastrop, in 1799, sold his claims to one Abraham Morhouse, a New Yorker who had deserted his wife in that state and was currently living in Kentucky and operating as a land speculator. After various inconclusive transactions, and after the United States had taken possession of Louisiana, Morhouse transferred his claims to Edward Livingston of New Orleans and Charles Lynch of Shelby County, Kentucky, the former receiving four-tenths and the latter six-tenths of the whole, or about 700,000 acres. Meanwhile the Maison Rouge tract had passed into the hands

[36] Letter from a Gentleman in Shelbyville to his friend near Winchester, 22 Oct. 1806, Richmond *Enquirer*, 5 Dec. 1806.

[37] *American Citizen*, 29 Dec. 1806, quoting *Intelligencer*.

[38] Gayarré, *Louisiana*, III, 353-4.

of Daniel Clark, who had numerous ties with Livingston in New Orleans.[39]

Burr now purchased a half of Lynch's claim, amounting to about 350,000 acres, though he usually estimated it at 400,000. The consideration was $5000 in cash and the assumption of a debt of $30,000 which Lynch owed Livingston. The $5000 was paid by a draft on George M. Ogden of New York.[40]

The question naturally arises as to what Burr actually bought. The Spanish grant to Bastrop had been made on condition of settlement, and the condition had never been met. Furthermore, Carondelet had been forced to suspend proceedings and the King never validated the grant. Consequently no Spanish patent was ever issued and it was not the policy of the United States to validate such claims. Apparently aware of this, the grantees did not take the trouble to register their claims in the Louisiana land office after the United States came into possession nor did Burr ever register his purchase in Kentucky, and when claims were later filed under these grants, they were uniformly rejected by the commissioners of the Louisiana land office.[41]

Only one conclusion seems possible in view of these facts: Burr did not expect to make his claim good under the government of the United States. The purchase was a sheer speculation, the success of which was contingent upon the success of his other plans. Meanwhile, General Wilkinson had been careful to keep his name out of land transactions, and on 29 March he assured President Jefferson that he did not own an acre of ground in Louisiana Territory.[42] At St. Louis, however, he was assisting Daniel Clark with his speculations, and he informed his friend that most of his claims, registered

[39] J. O. Mitchell and R. D. Calhoun, 'The Maison Rouge and Bastrop Spanish Land "Grants,"' *Louisiana Historical Quarterly*, xx, no. 2 (Apr. 1937), 289–462, *passim;* Livingston to Madison, 15 Sept. 1804, Carter, *Territorial Papers*, IX, 294–5.

[40] Evidence of Col. Charles Lynch, *Annals of Congress*, 10 Cong., 1 Sess., 656–8; Evidence of Thomas Bodley, ibid. 655; M. L. Davis, *Burr*, II, 380; Richmond *Enquirer*, 11 Nov. 1806.

[41] Adam Seybert, *Statistical Annals of the United States* (Philadelphia, 1818), 356; Claiborne to Secretary of the Treasury, 11 Aug. 1806, Carter, *Territorial Papers*, IX, 479–80; *A.S.P., Public Lands*, II, 768, III, 53–4.

[42] Wilkinson to Jefferson, 29 Mar. 1806, Jefferson Papers, Library of Congress, Jacobs, *Wilkinson*, 219; Wilkinson to John Smith, 16 Mar. 1806, John Smith Papers, Historical and Philosophical Society of Ohio.

in the names of other persons, were doubtful. On his own account he had just arranged through John Forbes and Company of Pensacola to acquire Dauphin Island at the mouth of Mobile Bay, but this probably had nothing to do with Burr's prospects, as he told Clark that he thought the United States was about to purchase the Floridas.[43]

There were many allegations at this time that Burr was being backed by the Yazoo speculators, whose claims to millions of acres on the lower Mississippi had been rejected by Congress.[44] William Duane, of the Philadelphia *Aurora*, the best-informed editor on the conspiracy, wrote that:

> The designs of Burr, we are creditably informed, arose from an application made to him to favor the seizure and occupation of the Yazoo territory, under color of law, but by force of arms. At first Burr was not interested, but it was explained to him that the means to carry out the project could be had, both in the East and the West . . . the President is in possession of the facts . . . such a spirit of speculating rapacity throughout the nation has formed a *mass of corruption* in every state of the Union, which menaces the safety of the nation, and pointed out to the great conspirator the resources from which he was [to] draw the fund for that plan which Granger said would soon rise in the western country. In the new settled countries of the United States there are hundreds of persons who hold lands *for which they have not paid* . . . There are others whose titles to lands are bad, and some precarious. There are others whose ambition for high place has been disappointed. Burr appealed to such as these.[45]

Senators John Adair and John Smith, it will be recalled, were both Yazoo speculators,[46] and Smith had also invested heavily in West Florida lands.

Following the practice of the most successful speculators, Burr planned to back his Bastrop claim by actual settlement. Immediately after making his deal with Lynch, he sent young Thomas Butler to

[43] Wilkinson to Clark, 8 Mar. 1806, Clark, *Proofs*, 141–2; *A.S.P. Public Lands*, III, 14.

[44] *National Intelligencer*, 19 Nov. 1806; Raleigh *Minerva*, 13 Oct. 1806, quoting *Farmer's Monitor*, Herkimer, N.Y.; *Kentucky Gazette*, 23 Oct. 1806, quoting same; *American Citizen*, 8 Nov. 1806, quoting *Aurora; Georgia Republican*, 28 Nov. 1806, quoting *Virginia Argus*.

[45] Richmond *Enquirer*, 11 Dec. 1806, quoting *Aurora*.

[46] *A.S.P., Public Lands*, I, 231, 243.

confer with the merchant, William Wilkins of Pittsburgh, and his brother General Wilkins. Butler was to unfold Burr's plans to them and invite them to join in the speculation. The nature of these plans was not disclosed in the letter that Butler carried, but a map of the purchase was enclosed and this showed roads leading from the Mississippi River to the Ouachita tract and thence to Natchitoches near the Spanish border.[47] In the letter that Butler carried at the same time to General Tupper, and that was written the same day as the communication to the Wilkins brothers, Burr did not mention the Bastrop purchase, showing that this was not yet uppermost in his mind. But when, on 18 November, he again wrote Tupper, he tried to interest him in his plans for making a settlement there.[48]

On 26 October the Colonel gave more details in a letter that he wrote to Benjamin H. Latrobe. He said he was satisfied about the excellence of the soil and climate, and he was sending out forty or fifty men in a short time to clear the ground and to build cabins. He himself intended to go there with several friends during the course of the next year, and Latrobe was offered 10,000 acres if he would join them: 'I want your society, I want your advice in the establishments about to be made — in short you have become necessary to my settlement.' Burr said he would pass through Pittsburgh on his way to Philadelphia about the last of November, and he asked Latrobe to meet him there for a discussion of the proposal.[49]

From these letters we can form some estimate of Burr's intentions. A road of about thirty miles would be necessary to connect his tract with the Mississippi, and a somewhat longer one would reach Natchitoches. His pioneers were furnished with tools for clearing these roads, but they were not given either agricultural equipment or seeds; no women were allowed to accompany them. The settlement would be a valuable base for reinforcing the Sabine front, and since the boats which were being built for the expedition were con-

[47] Burr to Wilkins, 21 Oct. 1806, Burr MSS., New York Public Library.

[48] Deposition of Edward W. Tupper, 8 Sept. 1807, *Quarterly Publications, Historical and Philosophical Society of Ohio*, IX (1914), 13–27.

[49] Burr to Latrobe, 26 Oct. 1806, Burr MSS., New York Public Library; Evidence of Benjamin H. Latrobe, June 1807, Cabell Papers, Burr Case, 88, Alderman Library, U. Va.

structed so that they could ascend rivers, some of them must have been intended to reach Natchitoches. But Latrobe's talents as engineer and architect would not have been needed for establishing a mere military post, and Burr obviously was planning a permanent settlement after the objects of his present expedition had been accomplished. It is clear, however, that this was not a part of his original plan, nor was it now his main objective though he did offer land as an inducement to recruits and made it appear to some of them, especially after his motives became widely suspect, that settlement of this tract was his primary aim.

Up to this time Burr's plans had been carried out without any major obstruction. He still expected war with Spain and the Bastrop purchase was an offensive not a defensive move, but it soon came to serve a defensive purpose. The prospect of a war with Spain now began to appear doubtful; the press was alive with charges and counter-charges; and the countryside from Pittsburgh to New Orleans buzzed with excitement.[50]

Fearing that these reports might alarm the Spanish authorities, Burr decided it would be wise to reassure his friend, Yrujo. Therefore on 25 October, he wrote him a letter and dispatched it, along with the one to Latrobe and others to friends in the Eastern cities, by Colonel De Pestre, who had by this time returned from St. Louis.[51] De Pestre didn't reach his destination until 27 November, but Yrujo, who had sent Captain José Vidal to follow Burr on his journeying, had already received detailed information concerning the Colonel's plans. On 10 November he wrote his Government that some 500 men were being collected on the upper Ohio to move down the river in squads. The Colonel was to go with them under the pretext of settling them on the Bastrop tract. On passing Cincinnati they would raid the Federal arsenal and take possession of the 5000 stand of arms deposited there. The armed troops would then descend the Mississippi to Natchez, where Burr would wait until the Assembly met in New Orleans to declare the independence of the Western states [the Territory of Orleans] and to invite him

[50] Evidence of Col. De Pestre, July 1806, Cabell Papers, Burr Case, loc. cit.; Burr to Gov. William H. Harrison, 24 Oct. 1806, Richmond *Enquirer*, 27 Oct. 1807.
[51] Schachner, *Burr*, 330–31.

to place himself at the head of their government. Yrujo declared that Burr would accept this offer, and he understood that Burr had already written the declaration of independence, modeled on that of 1776. Burr had assured Yrujo that he had abandoned his plan to seize the Floridas, but the Marquis took the precaution of warning Governor Folch of the danger even though he thought that the Governor would already have been informed by means of his secret correspondence with Wilkinson.[52]

After De Pestre's arrival, Yrujo again wrote to his Government on 4 December. He said Burr had warned him through De Pestre that he would soon hear of his planning an attack on Mexico, but that his aim was limited to the emancipation of the Western states and that the other purpose was rumored merely for the sake of deception. Burr pictured Upper and Lower Louisiana, Tennessee, and Ohio as ripe for his purposes, but force would be required to control the situation in Kentucky.[53]

After De Pestre had gone to New York, he returned to Philadelphia and again reported to the Spanish minister. The Frenchman said that he had talked with Burr's friends in New York, especially to Colonel John Swartwout. He said he had also seen Dr. Erwin, Colonel William S. Smith, and Captain Lewis, brother to the commander of Miranda's ship, the *Leander*. They were informed that they should set out at once for New Orleans, and groups of young men were to be dispatched to Washington, Norfolk, and Charleston. Those in Washington were to watch the movements of the Federal Administration, those in Norfolk were to forward supplies, and those in Charleston were to act as officers of the recruits collected there by Alston, who was to return from the West to conduct them personally to New Orleans. Other recruits were to be sent from New York.[54]

The information given Yrujo about the prospects of a revolution in the West was certainly highly colored, yet it probably did not greatly exceed Burr's expectations. One statement is especially signif-

[52] Adams, *History of the United States,* III, 261.

[53] Ibid. 263; Yrujo to Cevallos, 4 Dec. 1806, A.H.N., Est., leg. 5546, apartado 1, 208–20, no. 776.

[54] Yrujo to Cevallos, 16 Dec. 1806, A.H.N., Est., leg. 5546, apartado 1, 234–52; Adams, *History of the United States,* III, 265.

icant because it is supported by much collateral evidence. This is the assertion that Burr would wait with his force in Natchez until he heard that a declaration of independence had been adopted by his supporters in New Orleans. It should be remembered he had written Wilkinson that he would meet him in Natchez, where they would decide whether to take or by-pass Baton Rouge.

Chapter VI

GATHERING CLOUDS

EXCITEMENT IN THE WEST increased as the crisp October days grew shorter. The publication of Blennerhassett's 'Querist' articles had not passed unnoticed, and his and Burr's recruiting activities attracted even more attention. Alexander Henderson was a prominent Federalist of Wood County, Virginia, of which Blennerhassett Island was a part, and the author of the 'Querist' papers had consulted him in regard to them. Henderson took no action at the moment, but subsequent events alarmed him and on 6 October he called a mass meeting of the people of the County. This body passed resolutions condemning the activities of the conspirators, avowing their support of the President, and providing for raising a corps of militia to be ready in case of emergency.[1]

Since the master of the Island had gone down the river with the Alstons, Mrs. Blennerhassett was left alone to make preparations for the long journey that lay ahead. News of the Wood County meeting and undoubtedly of other demonstrations of hostility alarmed her and she decided to send her gardener, Peter Taylor, to warn Burr of his danger and to summon her husband back to the Island. Since she did not know just where they might be found, she instructed Taylor to call on Senator John Smith at his grocery store in Cincinnati in order to get the address.[2]

By this time the Ohio Senator was becoming apprehensive and at first refused to give Taylor any information, but when the latter

[1] Henshaw, 'The Aaron Burr Conspiracy in the Ohio Valley,' loc. cit. 129; *Mississippi Messenger* (Natchez), 6 Jan. 1807.

[2] Safford, *Blennerhassett Papers,* 147–8; Adams, *History of the United States,* III, 275.

insisted, he gave him the desired address, and, with feigned innocence, wrote Burr a letter, dated 23 October, warning him that he was suspected and asking him to state his purposes. Proceeding on his journey, Taylor found Burr at Jourdan's tavern in Lexington, delivered Smith's letter, and informed the Colonel that the people would kill him if he returned to the Island.[3] Burr wrote an answer to Smith's communication, expressing surprise at his question; he stated that he had purchased the Bastrop lands and assured his friend that 'If there exists any design to separate the Western from the Eastern States, I am totally ignorant of it. I never harbored or expressed any such intention to any one, nor did any person ever intimate such a design to me.' To the end of his life Burr persisted in this assertion.[4]

Taylor then accompanied his employer back to the Island, and he later testified that on this journey Blennerhassett inquired at every tavern for young men who would go to settle the Bastrop lands, stipulating that they should supply themselves with rifles and blankets, but that they would be furnished with provisions and grog during the journey and for three months afterward, and would be given 100 acres of land as a bonus. Taylor offered to go and take his wife and family, but his master demurred at this. The gardener then asked what kind of seed they would need, and was told that they would need none because everything was to be furnished.

Finally Blennerhassett admitted that they were going to take Mexico, and that 2000 Catholic priests were enlisted to assist in the revolution. After the country was freed, Burr would be King and his daughter would succeed him as Queen. Taylor finally told his companion that the people thought the separation of the Union was the object of the expedition. Blennerhassett replied that he and Burr could not effect the separation themselves; they could only point out to the people the benefits that would accrue to the West from such a separation. He said the Westerners would do better to keep the $400,000 they paid in taxes and use it to build roads and to make other improvements.[5]

[3] Ibid. III, 276.
[4] Henshaw, op. cit. 129–30.
[5] Evidence of Peter Taylor, *A.S.P., Misc.*, I, 499–500.

Taylor later testified that about two weeks after reaching home, Blennerhassett sent him to see Dr. Bennett of Mason County, Virginia, to inquire whether he would sell the arms belonging to the militia; if the Doctor would not sell them, Taylor was to tell his master where they were so that he could capture them during the night. Taylor was to burn the letter after Dr. Bennett had read it, for, said Blennerhassett, 'it contained high treason.' Taylor carried out his instructions.[6]

On 13 October, James Taylor, a resident of Newport, Kentucky, to whom Blennerhassett had expressed secessionist views, wrote to inform Secretary Madison that he suspected a scheme to separate the West from the Atlantic states. He said he thought there was little doubt that Blennerhassett had written the 'Querist' articles, and he believed that the boats being built on the Muskingum were intended for Burr's expedition. He was surprised to find that the idea of separation met with so much approval, but he knew that designing, bad men could do much mischief in Kentucky, and they could accomplish even more in Ohio. The idea of seizing the public lands, he said, would be very attractive to some men.[7]

Such rumors as these were not confined to Kentucky. It was reported that shortly after Wilkinson went to St. Louis as governor of Louisiana Territory factions began to form and in some cases two officials were attempting to hold the same office. The report went on to say that in October a rumor was spread that Burr, at the head of a party in Kentucky, Indiana, and Louisiana, was preparing to convert the government of the Western country to that of France or Spain; that he had agents and spies in every quarter, that he was issuing proclamations and commissions, and that the standard of rebellion was to be raised on 15 November. Wilkinson was to ally himself, and all the troops that would follow him, with the Spaniards, and Burr was to join him with his recruits.[8] Such statements, of course, merely reflected the excitement of the times, but on 18 November, Major James Bruff, still stationed at St. Louis, wrote to J. H. Nichol-

[6] Ibid.

[7] James Taylor to James Madison, 13 Oct. 1806, Kentucky Historical Society *Register*, XXXIV (1936), 113–16; same to same, 8 Dec. 1806, John Smith Papers, Historical and Philosophical Society of Ohio.

[8] *Kentucky Gazette*, 11 Dec. 1806.

son that a separation of the Union was openly advocated there by some persons, and that most people agreed it would happen as a matter of course in a few years. 'I could relate,' said the Major, 'many curious and alarming circumstances respecting Burr, Wilkinson, and others of that party, but should not be believed.' [9]

Even from distant Detroit, alarming reports were received. Stanley Griswold, collector of that port and Secretary of Michigan Territory, wrote to Elijah Boardman of New Milford, Connecticut, that an attempt to set up a new government west of the Alleghenies was on foot. The plan was being backed, he said, by Western characters scattered from Michigan to New Orleans, together with many others in the Eastern states, but because of their regard for the President, they would not attempt to carry out their plot during his term of office. The Yazoo speculators, many of whom were New Englanders, were suspected of being involved along with Burr and Wilkinson. It pained Griswold to think that his own chief, Governor William Hull of Michigan Territory, was involved, for otherwise he was a good man. He thought the Governor and many civil officers in the West had been appointed by the united efforts of persons interested in the conspiracy, while officers of the local garrison were pro-British and cultivated close relations with their Canadian counterparts. He had seen the recent publications in the Kentucky and Chillicothe newspapers, and they deserved attention, but what had fallen under his own observation at Detroit was 'of too delicate a nature to be divulged' until special circumstances should require it. He went on to say, however, that a few months previously a bank had been established at Detroit with a capital of a million dollars, nearly the whole of which was owned 'by Yazoo men at Boston and elsewhere.' Governor Hull and Judge Woodward, a 'parfect Quid in politics,' were the patrons of this institution, but no honest man could understand the need of such a bank in a region where trade was carried on almost entirely by barter.[10]

Boardman apparently turned this letter over to William Duane, the *Aurora* editor, who sent an unsigned transcript to Jefferson.

[9] James Bruff to J. H. Nicholson, 18 Nov. 1806, Bacon, *Report*, 237–8.

[10] Stanley Griswold to Elijah Boardman, 10 Oct. 1806, New York Historical Society, Manuscript Collection.

Griswold had exaggerated the capital of the bank, which was fixed at only $400,000, and it has not been possible to trace any direct connection between the Yazoo speculators and this institution except that Governor Hull did own Yazoo stock. The charges were sufficiently serious, however, to cause the Administration to make an investigation, and the bank charter was disallowed by Congress in March 1807.[11]

Naturally the Administration was not ignorant of Burr's activities. Ever since 1 December 1805, Jefferson had been receiving messages warning him of the danger. The most persistent informant was Joseph Hamilton Daveiss, United States District Attorney for Kentucky, the first of whose numerous letters was written on 10 January 1806, but nothing was done as a result of these communications. On 10 August, Commodore Thomas Truxton sent the President a detailed plan for counteracting Burr's plot, and this also was laid aside.[12] It was not until news came that Burr was actually in the West making preparations for his expedition that Jefferson became apprehensive, and even then he did not think he could make any direct move against the Colonel until some illegal act should lay him liable to arrest.

The President later stated that his first definite information came in a letter which he received from Colonel George Morgan on 15 September. It was not until 7 October that Neville and Roberts wrote to Madison of their interview with Morgan, but their letter also reached its destination before any action was taken.[13] On 18 October, Jefferson received a letter from John Nicholson of New York giving an account of the activities of Comfort Tyler in that state and western Pennsylvania, and at about the same time Madison received similar information from a Mr. Williams, also of New York.[14] Additional information about Burr's movements came from Morris Belknap, a Marietta attorney who had formerly lived in Brimfield, Massachusetts, the home of 'General' William Eaton. On 11 Octo-

[11] Duane to Jefferson, 16 Nov. 1806, Jefferson Papers, Library of Congress.

[12] Truxton to Jefferson, 10 Aug. 1806, ibid.

[13] Presley Neville and Samuel Roberts to James Madison, 7 Oct. 1806, Burr MSS., Library of Congress.

[14] Jefferson to Gideon Granger, 9 Mar. 1814, Paul Leicester Ford (ed.), *The Writings of Thomas Jefferson* (New York, 1892–9), IX, 456.

ber, Belknap wrote to S. E. Danielson of Brimfield that 'Burr fever' had seized on the people of the West; the Colonel had offered commissions as army officers to several young men; boats were being built for him on the Muskingum; and the people of Wood County, Virginia, had formed an association to resist any insurrection. Joseph Alston, his lady, Theodosia, and suite had passed through Marietta the previous week, had stopped at Blennerhassett Island, and had gone on from there to Kentucky. Burr himself had revisited Cincinnati, and instead of staying with his friend Senator Smith, he had put up at a tavern, where a rabble collected with drum and fife and played the 'Rogue's March.' The host was enraged and was going to call the authorities to disperse the mob, but Burr dissuaded him, saying that he liked martial music and it would not trouble him if they played all night. Danielson showed this letter to Eaton, his stepfather, who, on 27 October, sent a copy to Madison.[15]

By this time the President had already taken action, and he did so as a direct result of information previously received from Eaton. The 'General' had told William Ely, Congressman from Massachusetts, of Burr's previous overtures to him, and on 14 October, Ely spent the evening with the Postmaster General at Springfield, taking the occasion to tell him of Eaton's disclosures. Granger took down the substance of this conversation, had it verified by both Ely and Eaton, and forwarded it to the President.[16] Jefferson later wrote to Granger, 'Your letter of October 16, conveying the communications of General Eaton to yourself and to Mr. Ely gave a specific view of the objects of this new conspiracy, and corroborating our previous information, I called the Cabinet together, on the 22d of October, when specific measures were adopted for meeting the dangers threatened in the various points in which they might occur.' [17] Granger's action on this occasion is interesting because he

[15] Louis B. Wright and Julia H. Macleod, 'William Eaton's Relations with Aaron Burr,' *Mississippi Valley Historical Review*, XXXI (Mar. 1945), 528 (cited hereafter as *M.V.H.R.*); Morris Belknap to S. E. Danielson, 11 Oct. 1806, Burr MSS., Library of Congress; Charles Prentiss, *The Life of the Late General William Eaton* (Brookfield, 1813), 396–400.

[16] Statement of Gideon Granger, 16 Oct. 1806, *Quarterly Publications, Historical and Philosophical Society of Ohio*, IX (1914), MS. in Everett D. Graff Collection.

[17] Ford (ed.), *Writings of Thomas Jefferson*, IX, 456.

was deeply involved in the Yazoo land speculations and it was widely suspected that he was also involved with Burr.[18]

At the Cabinet meeting Jefferson submitted his information to the department heads, and after consultation it was decided that confidential letters should be written to the governors of Ohio, Indiana, Mississippi, and Orleans, and to the district attorneys of Kentucky, Tennessee, and Louisiana Territory advising them to watch Burr and to have him arrested and tried if he committed any overt act. Gunboats were also to be sent up to Fort Adams to stop any suspicious craft that might try to pass that point on the Mississippi. And since Eaton had specifically stated that Wilkinson was concerned with Burr, and in view of the fact that the General had disobeyed the orders he had received at St. Louis on 11 June directing that he descend the river to New Orleans and take command at Natchitoches, the question was raised about what should be done with him. The meeting was then adjourned and the discussion was taken up again two days later.[19]

At this second conference it was decided to dispatch Captains Preble and Decatur to New Orleans to take command of the naval force there, which was to be strengthened by sending several additional gunboats from Eastern ports, if funds were available for this purpose. Governor Claiborne of Orleans Territory, the governor of Mississippi, and Colonel Constant Freeman, who commanded the garrison at New Orleans, were to be notified by post to be on their guard, but instead of writing to the other governors as previously decided, John Graham, Secretary of Orleans Territory, who happened to be in Washington, was to be sent through Kentucky on Burr's trail, 'with discretionary powers to consult confidentially with the Governors and to arrest Burr if he made himself liable.' Graham was to replace Wilkinson as governor of Louisiana Territory, and Dr. Joseph E. Browne, Burr's brother-in-law, was to be removed from his job as secretary; but other questions regarding the General were postponed until after Preble's departure.[20]

Another meeting of the Cabinet was held the next day, 25 Octo-

[18] *American Citizen*, 8 Nov. 1806, quoting *Aurora*.

[19] Lipscomb and Bergh (eds.), *Writings of Thomas Jefferson*, I, 459–61; Adams, *History of the United States*, III, 279–81.

[20] Lipscomb and Bergh (eds.), *Writings of Thomas Jefferson*, I, 461.

ber, and as 'A mail arrived yesterday from the westward, and not one word is heard from that quarter of any movements by Colonel Burr . . . We therefore rescind the determination to send Preble, Decatur, the Argus or the gunboats, and instead of them to send off the marines which are here to reinforce, or take the place of the garrison at New Orleans, with a view to Spanish operations . . .' [21] The only move which was actually taken against Burr was to send Graham on his track.

It is amazing that the failure of one day's mail to bring fresh news of the conspiracy should have caused Jefferson and his Cabinet to abandon practically all the defensive measures they had planned only the day before. It seems evident that something had happened to change the political situation, and, though we have no way of knowing what it was, it is probable that it concerned General Wilkinson. Jefferson later stated that he first became suspicious of him at the first Cabinet meeting on 22 October, and that measures to counteract any defection on the part of the General were taken two days later; but the Secretary of War Henry Dearborn was friendly to Wilkinson, and he may have been responsible for the change in policy.[22] Joseph Hamilton Daveiss had sent the President much information of the General's Spanish connection, but this had been ignored and nothing was done except to appoint Graham to succeed Wilkinson as governor at St. Louis. The General must have had powerful friends at court.

[21] Ibid. I, 462.
[22] Ibid. I, 458–61; J. H. Daveiss, *View of the President's Conduct Concerning the Conspiracy of 1806*, 77fn.

Chapter VII

TRIALS IN KENTUCKY

SINCE KENTUCKY was the heart of the American West, it was logical for Burr to fix his headquarters in Lexington while collecting recruits and supplies for his expedition. After Blennerhassett was called back to his Island, Theodosia and her husband were still with Burr, and he had many friends and associates in the Bluegrass Country. Davis Floyd, of Jeffersonville, was his principal agent in this region, but most of his friends were Kentuckians of high standing who had been associated with Wilkinson during the Spanish Conspiracy of 1786–8. Strangely enough, all of them were good Jeffersonian Republicans, whereas most of the Colonel's partisans in the Pittsburgh area and along the Atlantic seaboard were staunch Federalists.

His most active ally was United States Senator John Adair of Frankfort. He was a veteran of the Revolution and had served under St. Clair and Wilkinson in the Indian Campaign of 1791–2, being promoted from the rank of major to lieutenant-colonel.[1] Almost as important to Burr was John Brown, recently a member of the United States Senate. He lived in Frankfort and the Colonel stayed at his home when he visited the state capital. Brown, then a member of the old Congress, had been one of Wilkinson's collaborators during the Spanish attempt to separate Kentucky from the Union in 1787–8. We can only surmise the nature of the conversations which went on between these two in the fall of 1806.[2] Harry Innis, Judge of the Federal Court for the District of Kentucky, was

[1] *D.A.B.*, I, 34–5.
[2] Ibid. III, 130–31.

also one of Wilkinson's old allies and now a friend of Burr. He was a party leader, and on 3 July had written to his friend Preston Brown: 'The crisis of our state's political character has arrived, and it is now the duty of republicans to exert themselves in order to defeat the views and projects of the federalists . . . the present time is a trial of political principles and not of men's private character.' [3]

George Muter and Benjamin Sebastian, Chief Justice and Associate Justice respectively of the Kentucky Court of Appeals, were likewise old associates of Wilkinson. Sebastian had been the key figure in Spain's effort, through Thomas Power, to interest the General and his friends in attempts to revolutionize the West in 1795 and 1797–8. He had then made two visits to New Orleans to confer with the Spanish Governor, and was offered $100,000 to distribute for the good of the cause. Since that time he had been drawing a Spanish pension of $2000 a year. It is not known whether Burr had any direct dealings with either of the Justices at this time, but they were suspected because of their old associations.[4]

The people in general, thinking that Burr's object was merely to lead an expedition against the hated Dons, were enthusiastic supporters, and those who knew him were fascinated by his personality and flattered by his assiduous attentions. But the Colonel had his enemies in Kentucky, and they were not to be dismissed lightly. Chief among them were Humphrey Marshall and Joseph Hamilton Daveiss. The former had sat in the United States Senate; he was Kentucky's first historian, and was first cousin and brother-in-law to John Marshall, Chief Justice of the United States Supreme Court.[5] Daveiss, the Federal District Attorney for Kentucky, was young, handsome, and courageous, and he also was brother-in-law to the Chief Justice. Five years later he was killed at the battle of Tippecanoe, and a Kentucky county preserves his name. Naturally both these men were Federalists.[6]

[3] Harry Innes to Preston Brown, 3 July 1806, Harry Innes Papers, Library of Congress, vol. 18.

[4] Joseph Hamilton Daveiss, *A View of the President's Conduct Concerning the Conspiracy of* 1806, 81–3; Richmond *Enquirer*, 9 Sept. 1806; *D.A.B.*, XVI, 543–4.

[5] Ibid. XII, 309–10.

[6] Ibid. V, 80; Beveridge, *Marshall*, III, 315; Daveiss, *View*, 54–5.

As early as 1 December 1805, Jefferson had received an anonymous letter warning him against Burr, but Daveiss was the first to sound the alarm in the West. On 10 January 1806, he wrote to the President, saying: 'Spanish intrigues have been carried on among our people. — We have traitors among us. A separation of the union in favor of Spain is the object finally. A very exalted magistrate of this country [Sebastian] has lately drawn on Spain for his pension. — I am convinced Wilkinson has been for years and now is a pensioner of Spain.' Burr was not mentioned in this first letter, but on 10 February, Daveiss wrote again naming him as a chief conspirator and offering to make a personal investigation if the Government would pay his traveling expenses.[7]

It is not possible to determine the exact channels through which Daveiss acquired his information. Several of his Kentucky neighbors had firsthand information of the earlier Spanish intrigues, and, having been made administrator for the estate of his old law teacher, George Nicholas, who was implicated in the intrigues, he learned much from his papers. A little later he met and got information from Thomas Power, the Spanish agent who on several occasions had served as the contact man between Wilkinson and Sebastian and the Spanish governors at New Orleans. Burr's visit to Kentucky in 1805 had aroused suspicions, but it was not until near the end of that year that Daveiss was 'satisfactorily informed that several of our citizens were pensioners of Spain and that a revolutionary scheme in the west had been projected.' At this time he believed that the Spanish authorities were collaborating with the plotters, and therefore did not suspect that an invasion of Mexico was also planned.[8]

On receipt of Daveiss' first letter, Jefferson answered promptly. He said that he had shown the communication to Madison, Gallatin, and Dearborn, and he requested all possible information, especially the names of persons suspected of being implicated, and those who could give evidence. He pledged secrecy and hoped for a prompt reply.[9] The information was sent before it was requested, for on 13 February, Daveiss made out a list of the men whom he suspected

[7] Ibid. 68–71; Richmond *Enquirer*, 27 Jan. 1807, quoting *Atlantic World*.

[8] Humphrey Marshall, *History of Kentucky* (Frankfort, 1824), II, 400; Mayo, *Henry Clay*, 235ff.; Daveiss, *View*, 76–81.

[9] Ibid. 77; Mayo, *Henry Clay*, 233.

of complicity and sent it along with his letter of 10 February to the President. Here he named John Breckinridge, Wilkinson, Adair, John Smith, Sebastian, Innes, Henry Clay, Burr, and William Henry Harrison, Governor of Indiana Territory. He did not say that these men were guilty, but merely that he suspected them, and he later exonerated Clay and Breckinridge.[10]

During March and April, Daveiss wrote several additional letters to the President giving more information about the suspected Kentuckians, and in May, without having received the requested official authorization, he journeyed to St. Louis to try his hand at pumping General Wilkinson. At first the General showed no signs of suspicion; he spoke of Burr in the highest terms and commented on his 'impenetrable secrecy.' When Daveiss inquired about Pike's expedition, Wilkinson showed him a map of New Mexico and said, 'had Burr been President, we would have had all this country by now.'[11] Before the visitor could depart, however, the General received a letter from Frankfort warning him of the purpose of the call.[12]

Daveiss had also planned to make an on-the-spot investigation in New Orleans, but since he received no word from the President he abandoned the project, and he did not trouble to make any report on his visit to St. Louis.[13] By July 14, however, he thought he had secured important new information, and on that day he wrote again to Jefferson to report that the conspirators had changed their plans. Their present object was not merely to cause a separation of the Western country in favor of Spain, but 'To cause a revolt of the Spanish provinces, and a severance of all these Western States and territories from the union to coalesce & form one government. To purchase great quantities of land in the Spanish settlements to insure the desired influence when the Crisis comes —.'[14]

Daveiss waited a month and then wrote again, this time to Secretary Madison. He said that the conspirators considered a war with Spain inevitable, and that it was necessary to their purposes. When it came, the Mexican provinces including the Floridas were to be

[10] Daveiss, *View*, 75.
[11] Ibid. 89.
[12] Ibid. 89.
[13] Ibid. 77–81.
[14] Ibid. 91.

revolutionized and the American possessions on the Mississippi were to be taken over. A kingdom was to be set up here and the ruler was to be neither Wilkinson nor Burr, but the French émigré General Jean Victor Moreau, who, according to Daveiss' information, was to visit the West during the fall. 'When the war with Spain comes,' he said, 'the West will be called on for volunteers or drafted militia. These can be influenced into the proper course by their officers — So when they get their army right they can proceed to their ulterior purposes. The Western waters are counted on to fall in with the power possessing the mouths of its rivers. This is the best sketch of the affair I can collect.' He added that he daily found new evidence of the extensiveness of this scheme, especially among young men of parts.[15]

Finally, on 12 September, the President wrote to Daveiss. He curtly acknowledged his various letters, but offered no thanks for his pains, and no directions about future activities.[16] After having expressed such keen interest in his first letter, this treatment of the Kentucky attorney is surprising. Having asked for the names of suspected persons, Jefferson's curiosity flagged as soon as he received them. It is true that most of Daveiss' information was based upon hearsay and would not have been accepted in court, but his aim was to stop the expedition before it got under way, rather than to punish the conspirators. His actions seem to have been entirely patriotic and unselfish as far as any personal motives were concerned, but there was a partisan angle. He and his friends were Federalists and the men whom they were trying to discredit were all Republicans. Jefferson apparently did not overlook this pertinent fact.

The Federalist complexion of the agitation against Burr in Kentucky was brought more clearly into focus when, on 7 July 1806, John Wood and Joseph M. Street published in Frankfort the first number of a newspaper called the *Western World*. Wood was a Scot who had come from New York to Richmond and there assisted Nicholas Davis in editing a Federalist paper, the *Virginia Gazette*. He had previously written a scurrilous history of the administration

[15] Ibid. 92–5.
[16] Ibid. 95–6.

of John Adams, which Burr had had suppressed. This unprincipled political hack was described as being 'of most forbidding aspect' and of having undesirable personal habits. He formed what he admitted was an undue attachment for young Street, who had worked in Richmond as a clerk and had gained some notoriety by fighting a duel with a Mr. Gilmer.[17] As editors of the *Western World*, these two were under the patronage of Humphrey Marshall, who furnished them with their most important copy. It was rumored that Chief Justice John Marshall was back of this journalistic venture. There is no proof to substantiate this allegation, but the newspaper was definitely a Federalist enterprise.[18]

It has often been stated that Daveiss was the principal backer of the *Western World*, but he specifically denied this and said the editors did not get their information from him, inasmuch as some of it was incorrect.[19] The material furnished the paper by Humphrey Marshall was quite similar, however, to that which Daveiss sent to the President and it cannot be doubted that the two brothers-in-law worked in close collaboration. The first number of the paper undertook to show the connection between the old Spanish Conspiracy and the contemporary intrigues of Burr and Wilkinson. The fourth issue mentioned some who were suspected of complicity:

> The name of Jonathan Dayton will make a conspicuous figure near the close of our investigations, when the secrets of Aaron Burr, Edward Livingston, the Chief Justice Prevost of Louisiana, Gen. [Samuel] Smith of Baltimore, Col. [William S.] Smith of New York, etc. will be unfolded. At present it is only necessary to observe that Dayton and Wilkinson have been in close correspondence since the first dawn of the Spanish Association in Kentucky. That Dayton and John Brown, although they opposed each other in Congress, were inseparable friends in private life.[20]

Senator Brown was so touched by these remarks that on 25 July he wrote to Jefferson:

[17] Samuel Mordecai, *Richmond in By-gone Days* (Richmond, 1946), 231–4; Marshall, *Kentucky*, II, 375; *Kentucky Gazette*, 8, 15, 19 July 1806; Richmond *Enquirer*, 26 Aug., 5 Sept. 1806.

[18] Ibid. 5 Sept. 1806; Marshall, *Kentucky*, II, 385; Filson Club, *Publications*, no. 31 (Louisville, 1926), xcv.

[19] Daveiss, *View*, 92–5.

[20] Raleigh *Register*, 1 Sept. 1806.

The peace and tranquility of this State has lately been greatly disturbed by the establishment of a news paper at this place, entitled The Western World — The Editor is named John Wood — He has commenced a publication, the declared object of which is to prove that — all the Republicans of influence in this State, with a few exceptions, have been or are engaged in conspiracies against the Union & that many influential characters in the Atlantic States are connected with them. — It is said that Wood was sent out by John Marshall. He is patronized by his family in this country particularly by his three brothers-in-law, G. Brooks, Humphrey Marshall & Joseph H. Daviess, — The charges exhibited are false & without foundation.[21]

Naturally the publication of the *Western World* caused intense excitement in Kentucky and considerable interest in the rest of the country. On 5 September, Thomas Ritchie, editor of the Richmond *Enquirer*, stated that he had a poor opinion of the editor of the Kentucky sheet, but that he had a good target in General Wilkinson, whose

devotion to frivolous pomp; his obsequious court to every administration and to every party; his acknowledged hauteur towards his inferiors in office; are not the elements of which an unbending patriot is to be formed. That such a man should be appointed the Governor of Upper Louisiana, has affected with no little regret some of the sincerest friends of the present administration. His own character should have formed an almost insuperable bar to his elevation, his office as general-in-chief confirmed that objection.[22]

In October Humphrey Marshall made an attack on Judge Sebastian, charging him with being the recipient of a Spanish pension. Writing under the name of 'Observer,' he published his accusations in the form of a broadside and had it circulated among the people.[23] This caused the legislature to take notice of the matter. On 22 October that body resolved to make an inquiry, and a special committee, which began its work on 27 November, was appointed to sift the evidence. Sebastian at once resigned his seat on the bench, but the inquiry continued and Judge Innes was much embarrassed when called upon to give testimony. He did his best to exculpate his friend, but could not deny the facts. That Sebastian had been re-

[21] John Brown to Jefferson, 25 July 1806, Jefferson Papers, Library of Congress.
[22] Richmond *Enquirer*, 5 Sept. 1806.
[23] Marshall, *Kentucky*, II, 379.

ceiving a pension from the Spanish Government was proved beyond doubt and the House condemned the Judge by a unanimous vote.[24] Since George Muter, Chief Justice of the Kentucky Court of Appeals, had been involved in the same intrigue, he also resigned. Thomas Todd, a cousin and intimate friend of Innes, was appointed to take his place, and Felix Grundy succeeded Sebastian.[25]

So bitter were the feelings engendered by these developments that editor Street received many challenges to duels. They became so numerous that he declared he would merely file them and publish them in order.[26] He was finally shot and wounded by George Adams, a henchman of Innes and Burr. The assailant was brought into court with Henry Clay and John Allen acting as his counsel. The facts were not difficult to prove, but Adams escaped punishment because the prosecutor 'forgot' to charge intent to kill. This appears to have been a case of collusion.[27]

Late in September, Daveiss went to Louisville to check on Burr's preparations. There he found boats being built and cattle, pork, and flour being bought up in large quantities. Davis Floyd was in charge of operations here, and Daveiss wrote Madison that Burr's two chief lieutenants in Kentucky, Floyd and Adair, had told reliable witnesses that Mexico was their first object, the territories on the Mississippi the second, and the Ohio country was to complete the scheme. Burr and his friends were saying that a separation of the Union could be expected within a few years, and they gave the impression that the Administration was not opposed to their designs.[28]

So alarmed was the District Attorney that on 5 November he appeared before Judge Harry Innes in Frankfort and made an affidavit accusing Burr of preparing a military expedition against

[24] 'Report of the Select Committee . . . (which) charged Benjamin Sebastian . . . with having received a Pension from the Spanish Government' (Frankfort, Kentucky, 1806), in Innes Papers, vol. 18, Library of Congress; Deposition of George M. Bibb, ibid. vol. 22, pt. 1; *Georgia Republican*, 30 Jan. 1807, quoting Frankfort *Palladium*, extra, 6 Dec. 1806; *Kentucky Gazette*, 24 Nov., 1 Dec. 1806; Marshall, *Kentucky*, II, 380–82.

[25] Ibid. II, 415; *Kentucky Gazette*, 15 Dec. 1806; *Georgia Republican*, 20 Jan. 1807; Philadelphia *Aurora*, 8 Jan. 1807.

[26] *D.A.B.*, XVIII, 136–7.

[27] Marshall, *Kentucky*, II, 378.

[28] Daveiss, *View*, 98–101.

Mexico. He went on to say that he had equally valid information that Burr was also planning a separation of the states, but he could find no law that made this illegal though the President might call out the militia to prevent it. Daveiss moved the court to issue a warrant for Burr's arrest and to summon witnesses so that an indictment might be drawn, or Burr might be put under bond to restrain further activities. He said he preferred this procedure because it would be difficult to assemble all necessary witnesses at one time for a grand jury investigation. His main object was to prevent the expedition from getting under way.[29]

On the same day Innes wrote to Daveiss saying that the court could not conduct an inquiry previous to a trial, and the next day Daveiss answered with arguments in favor of his motion.[30] On the 8th Innes came into court and rendered his opinion denying Daveiss' motion, and Daveiss then requested that a grand jury be empaneled. This was done immediately, but the District Attorney asked that the jury be excused until he could collect his witnesses. The jury was accordingly dismissed, to assemble again on the 12th.[31] The witnesses were sent for and the jury convened again on the appointed day. Among those who appeared were John Jourdan, Burr's Lexington host, Charles Lynch, Benjamin Sebastian, John Brown, and John Adair — Davis Floyd was in Vincennes attending a meeting of the Indiana legislature. Daveiss thought he would be able to prove that supplies and recruits were being assembled for the expedition, but in order to establish that this activity was illegal, it was necessary to prove the purpose of the preparations. He did not believe that he could establish this essential point without Floyd's testimony, and accordingly asked that the jury be dismissed. The crowd, which had assembled to witness the proceedings, already in sympathy with Burr, was now vociferous in its ridicule of the District Attorney.[32]

Burr was in Lexington and about to set out on a return journey to

[29] Samuel M. Wilson (ed.), 'The Court Proceedings of 1806 in Kentucky against Aaron Burr and John Adair,' *Filson Club Historical Quarterly*, x (Jan. 1936), 31–40; *Louisiana Gazette*, 12 Dec. 1806; Daveiss, *View*, 96–7, 152–4.

[30] Innes to Daveiss, 5 Nov., and Daveiss to Innes, 6 Nov. 1806, Innes Papers, vol. 18, Library of Congress.

[31] Samuel M. Wilson, op. cit. 32–6.

[32] Ibid. 36; Kentucky *Gazette*, 17, 18 Nov. 1806.

Marietta when he received news of Daveiss' affidavit. He immediately changed his plans, hurried to Frankfort, and was in court, attended by Henry Clay as his attorney, during the proceedings of 8 and 12 November.[33] Because of his complicity with Burr, John Adair had just failed of re-election to the Senate and had immediately resigned his seat. Clay, only 29 years old, had been elected to fill the unexpired term.[34] Burr now returned to Lexington and on the 19th he mounted his horse to ride again to Cincinnati. He reached his destination by the 21st, and stayed as on his last visit at a tavern. It was reported that two travelers arrived in town the same evening and told of having passed two boats descending the Ohio. One was a large keelboat loaded with French muskets and the other seemed to be freighted with muskets and ordnance. The crew, who spoke nothing but French while the strangers were on board, said they had passed every town on the river at night, and that several large boats loaded with provisions would soon follow under command of Blennerhassett.[35]

Circling back to Louisville to make his final preparations there, Burr wrote to Governor Harrison on 27 November to assure him that he had no designs hostile to the Union, but was engaged in some speculations approved by high government officials, and by one especially. On the 30th the Colonel returned to Frankfort.[36]

Davis Floyd having returned to Kentucky, the District Attorney again, on 25 November, moved the Federal Court to summon a grand jury. Judge Innes complied and fixed 2 December as the day for the hearing.[37] Burr was anxious that Henry Clay should continue as his counsel, but the young attorney had heard so many rumors tending to incriminate his client that he asked him to state precisely the nature of his activities. On 1 December Burr answered from Frankfort, saying that he had no designs against the United States

[33] Deposition of Edward W. Tupper, 8 Sept. 1807, *Quarterly Publications of the Historical and Philosophical Society of Ohio*, IX (1914), 13–27; *Kentucky Gazette*, 30 Oct., 10 Nov. 1806.

[34] Willard Rouse Jillson, *Henry Clay's Defense of Aaron Burr in* 1806 (Pamphlet, 1943, in New York Public Library); *D.A.B.*, IV, 173–9.

[35] *American Citizen*, 22 Dec. 1806, quoting letter from Cincinnati dated 25 Nov. 1806; *Georgia Republican*, 6 Jan. 1807.

[36] Henshaw, 'The Burr Conspiracy in the Ohio Valley,' loc. cit. 131; McCaleb, *Burr Conspiracy*, 155–7.

[37] Samuel M. Wilson, op. cit. 36; Daveiss, *View*, 102–3.

and that the Government looked with complacency upon his acts. He also stated that he had issued no commissions and also that he did not own, nor did anyone own for him, any single article of military stores.[38] This disclaimer satisfied Clay and he appeared with Burr when the court opened in Frankfort next day. While the trial was in progress, Burr and Innes spent their evenings at the home of John Brown.[39]

On 2 December the grand jury assembled according to order and Judge Innes opened court, but John Adair, the principal witness, failed to appear and Daveiss asked for an adjournment until the next day. Adair appeared on the 3rd and the District Attorney preferred an indictment against him for having set on foot an expedition against Mexico. Daveiss asked to be allowed to appear before the jury to question witnesses, but Henry Clay and John Allen, Burr's counsel, opposed this and Innes ruled in their favor. Since there was not enough time to complete the hearing, the court adjourned until the next day.

On the 4th Daveiss renewed his request to be heard by the jury and this was again denied. He then read several questions he intended to put to Thomas Read, one of the witnesses. The purport of these questions was whether General Adair had, some months previously, in conversation with Read, informed him that an expedition of considerable magnitude was in agitation against Spain; that he (Adair) was acquainted with the leaders and advised Read to embark in it. Soon Read was brought into court and he inquired about the basis for these questions. Daveiss informed him that they were based upon a conversation which he (Daveiss) had had with Read in his home at Danville, when Read had made to him the statements attributed to him. Read replied that no such conversation had ever taken place, and that he considered Daveiss' statement a malicious fabrication. The grand jury returned 'no true bill' against Adair, and Daveiss immediately brought in a similar indictment against Burr, whereupon the court adjourned until the following day.[40]

On 5 December, Burr appeared to answer the charge of having

[38] Burr to Clay, 1 Dec. 1806, Richmond *Enquirer*, 20 Mar. 1807.

[39] *National Intelligencer*, 12 Jan. 1807, quoting *Western World*, 18 Dec. 1806.

[40] John Wood, *A Full Statement of the Trial and Acquittal of Aaron Burr, Esq.* (Alexandria, Va., 1807), 32–3; Samuel M. Wilson, 'Court Proceedings,' loc. cit. 37–9.

organized an expedition against Mexico. The jury sent for a file of the *Western World* and ordered its editors, Wood and Street, to attend. Street testified that he possessed no information relating to Burr that would amount to evidence. This was true because the articles that he had published were based upon the statements of Humphrey Marshall and perhaps others, and such information did not amount to evidence. Wood was called next and he made a statement similar to that of Street. But he went on to say that he had received a great deal of information with respect to this subject, and had made extensive inquiries concerning it. He stated that until very lately he had believed in the truth of the charges against Burr, but having recently received several explanations and seen some documents, he had changed his former opinion and now believed that 'the present designs of Colonel Burr is [*sic*] neither against the government or laws of the U. States.' [41]

The grand jury found 'no true bill' and then delivered a written report to the Court which stated:

> The Grand Jury are happy to inform the Court that no violent disturbance of the Public Tranquility or breach of the laws has come to their knowledge. We have no hesitation in declaring that having carefully examined and scrutinized all the testimony which has come before us, as well the charges against Aaron Burr, as those contained in the indictment preferred to us against John Adair, that there has been no testimony before us which does in the Smallest degree criminate the conduct of either of those persons, nor can we from all the inquiries and investigation of the Subject discover that anything improper or injurious to the interest of the Government of the United States or contrary to the laws thereof is designed or contemplated by either of them.[42]

Burr's friends were elated. The address of the jury was printed as a handbill and was given wide circulation among the people, and the hero of the occasion was feted that night at a grand ball in Frankfort which was attended by the families of Judge Innes and John Brown.[43] President Jefferson was so disappointed over the miscarriage of the trial that he removed Daveiss from office; [44] and Wood,

[41] John Wood, op. cit. 34; Mayo, *Clay*, 151–5.
[42] Wilson, op. cit. 39–40.
[43] *National Intelligencer*, 12 Jan. 1807, quoting *Western World*, 18 Dec. 1806; Marshall, *Kentucky*, II, 411.
[44] Daveiss, *View*, 58, 174fn.; McCaleb, *Burr Conspiracy*, 163.

having sold out to Burr, quarreled with Street and severed his connection with the *Western World*. He soon appeared in Washington where he established a paper which he called the *Atlantic World* and for a time devoted his talents to defending the man whom he had recently been attacking so viciously.[45] Street remained with the *Western World* and a number of libel suits were entered against him. Kentucky soon experienced a reaction against Burr and most of the suits were dropped for that reason, but Innes continued his case and finally won it in 1812. The editor was not able to pay the damage and was forced to leave Kentucky.[46] Burr and Adair remained in Frankfort a few days after the trial and then hurried together to Nashville for another visit with General Jackson.

Before leaving Kentucky, the Colonel had received a letter from his agent in New Orleans, Dr. Erich Bollman. This communication was delivered by Robert Spence, who had arrived in that city with Bollman and Alexander near the end of September. From Lexington, Burr sent Spence to Pittsburgh with a letter for Colonel Thomas Butler and a message assuring him that this was the proper time to join the army with a body of volunteers. From Pittsburgh, Spence returned to New Orleans in a boat which Senator John Smith was sending down with supplies presumably dispatched for the use of the army, but suspected by some of being intended for Burr's expedition.[47] Thus were Burr and his agents scurrying around in the Western country, trying to pick up the threads of their intrigue and knit them into proper co-ordination for the Great Adventure.

[45] J. Hughes to Harry Innes, 8 Feb. 1807, Innes Papers, vol. 19, Library of Congress; Mayo, *Clay*, 268–70.

[46] Richmond *Enquirer*, 25 Nov. 1806, 24 Mar. 1807; Raleigh *Register*, 12 Jan. 1807; *D.A.B.*, XVIII, 136–7.

[47] Evidence of Robert Spence, Cabell Papers, Burr Case, 40–41, Alderman Library, U. Va.

Chapter VIII

THE FLIGHT

WHILE BURR was making his preparations and undergoing his trials in Kentucky, Comfort Tyler was assembling supplies in the Pittsburgh area. He had several sub-agents to assist him in his commissary business: Joseph Davis and John Wilkins, Jr., of Pittsburgh, and a Mr. Weaver of Greensburgh, a town about thirty miles east of that city. Their practice was to ship beef, pork, flour, and whiskey in large canvas-covered keelboats to a Natchez merchant named Postelthwaite, who was also one of Burr's agents. This made the transaction appear to be a matter of normal business, and the civil authorities found themselves unable to interfere with it. Such shipments continued to be made for almost a month after the expedition was scheduled to get under way, and they were paid for by drafts on the New York firm of William S. Smith and Samuel G. Ogden.[1]

Ogden was the brother-in-law of Gouverneur Morris, and Smith, who was surveyor of the port of New York, was John Adams' son-in-law.[2] Earlier in the same year they had been prosecuted, though unsuccessfully, for complicity in the outfitting of General Miranda's ill-fated filibustering expedition to Venezuela; and they both were deeply involved in various land speculations.[3] It does not appear that

[1] *Georgia Republican*, 2 Jan. 1807, quoting Philadelphia *Aurora;* Richmond *Enquirer*, 27 Dec. 1806, 15 Jan. 1807, quoting communication from Pittsburgh, 31 Dec. 1806; Philadelphia *Aurora*, 8 Jan. 1807.

[2] *D.A.B.*, XIII, 642–3, XVII, 368–9.

[3] Thomas Lloyd (stenographer), *The Trials of William S. Smith and Samuel G. Ogden, for Misdemeanours, had in the Circuit Court of the United States for the New-York District, in July*, 1806 (New York, 1807).

they were possessed of very large capital, and it is likely, in the case of both Burr and Miranda, that they merely acted as agents for interested parties. Colonel De Pestre had conferred with Smith on his recent visit to New York, and the latter was scheduled to accompany a group of Burr's friends to New Orleans for the purpose of taking an active part in the conspiracy.

Recruiting was also being carried on in an energetic manner by Burr's agents. Tyler had fixed his rendezvous for 1 December at Beaver, Pennsylvania, downstream from Pittsburgh and near the Ohio line. Here he was building boats and collecting supplies. General Presley Neville and Joseph Davis of Pittsburgh, and Major Israel Smith of New York were all helping with the recruiting. Young men were being told that Mexico was the final objective, but that they would first ascend the Red River and establish a settlement on the Bastrop lands.[4]

There is no way of knowing just how many men were enlisted. When, on 4 or 5 December, Tyler set his four boats in motion for Blennerhassett's Island, he had a party of only thirty with him; but Burr's force was supposed to go down the river in detachments so as not to arouse public alarm. One interesting group which left Pittsburgh after the date of the rendezvous was made up of seven young men of good standing, including Thomas Butler and Morgan Neville, the latter carrying two military uniforms with blue coats, yellow facings, and gold epaulettes, which had been furnished by his father the General.[5]

It was said that amazing numbers of 'Yankees' were arriving at Pittsburgh by every stage and were inquiring for the rendezvous of Comfort Tyler. On 23 November, José Vidal, the Spanish agent sent out by the suspicious Yrujo to trail Burr to his destination, reported that he saw 100 men in the city under command of a colonel who declared openly that an attack on Mexico was their aim. Other information indicated that enlistments were being solicited in Meadville, Pennsylvania, and on 19 November a boat carrying 16 recruits from that place arrived at Pittsburgh and the next day went down

[4] Lancaster (Pa.) *Intelligencer*, 10 Dec. 1806, quoting letter from Beavertown; Philadelphia *Aurora*, 8 Jan. 1807; Report of James Knox of Meadsville, Pa., Burr MSS., Library of Congress.

[5] Richmond *Enquirer*, 27 Dec. 1806; Philadelphia *Aurora*, 3 Jan. 1807.

the river to Beaver. A full command was said to be setting out from Warren, Ohio, just beyond the Pennsylvania line, where Tyler had engaged the tavernkeeper and some others to recruit for him.[6] One Western informant reported that 300 young gentlemen descended the Ohio at this time and another said that on 24 December, two weeks after Blennerhassett left his Island, there were 1000 men on the river between Pittsburgh and Marietta.[7] A 'high authority' in Washington reported that between August and December 1806 more than 1000 young men had passed through New York and Pennsylvania on their way to join Burr on the Ohio. On 9 January, Yrujo stated that a large party of young men appeared suddenly in Pittsburgh the first of the year, and since they came by different roads from different directions, it was believed that that was the place and date of rendezvous. They behaved in a turbulent manner, abused the Government and President of the United States, and said they were going on Burr's expedition, with many others to follow them. They rendezvoused in the city and then went down the river in ordinary boats. On 12 January, James Ross wrote to James McHenry from Pittsburgh that many local young men had descended the Ohio to join Burr. Another report stated that the boats that had been and were being built up and down the length of the Ohio for the expedition would carry 40 to 60 men each, and were intended to ascend shallow rivers.[8] These statements are doubtless exaggerations, but since Burr planned to enlist 75 men in the small frontier settlement of Nashville, he must have expected a considerable force from New England, New York, and Pennsylvania. Judging by the quantity of supplies contracted for and the number of boats built, a total force of at least 1500 men must have been contemplated.

Contemporary comments make it clear that the leaders of Burr's Eastern cohorts were practically all Federalists — men who had

[6] Quoted in Yrujo to Cevallos, 4 Dec. 1806, A.H.N., Est., leg. 5546, 209–16; Report of James Knox, Burr MSS., Library of Congress; *Georgia Republican*, 2 Jan. 1807; Henshaw, 'Burr in the Ohio Valley,' loc. cit. 134–5.

[7] Philadelphia *Aurora*, 22 Jan. 1807, quoting *Virginia Gazette; Georgia Republican*, 6 Jan. 1807, quoting Bedford (Pa.) *Gazette*.

[8] Yrujo to Cevallos, 9 Jan. 1807, A.H.N., Est., leg. 5633, apartado 1, no. 795, 6–7; James Ross to James McHenry, 12 Jan. 1807, Edward Eberstadt and Sons, New York, *Catalogue No.* 129, 30; *Georgia Republican*, 20 Jan. 1807; Richmond *Enquirer*, 3 Jan. 1807.

opposed the Louisiana Purchase and dreaded the growing strength of the West. The Philadelphia *Aurora* named a number of his supporters in various communities and said that they were all Federalists, while the Pittsburgh *Commonwealth* stated that all local Burrites were Federalists and aristocrats, not a single Republican being involved.[9] Lieutenant Swearingen and the junior officers at Fort Lafayette were said to be sympathetic with the conspirators, and no attempt was made by either civil or military authorities to stop any of their preparations until the alarm had been sounded from Washington.[10]

John Graham, the sleuth whom President Jefferson had sent to trail Burr through the West, talked with Presley Neville in Pittsburgh, and reaching Marietta about the middle of November, was soon visited by that nearsighted and garrulous Irishman, Harman Blennerhassett. This gentleman had been told that Graham was one of Burr's supporters, and he therefore did not hesitate to discuss matters of supposedly mutual interest. He seemed surprised when Graham said he had not heard of the Mexican Association of New Orleans; and he was incredulous when informed that Charles Lynch had bought the Bastrop lands from Edward Livingston and that the latter had invalidated the contract in court. Blennerhassett now told Graham that he thought the Western states would benefit by withdrawing from the Union and that Burr agreed with him, but by means of the 'Querist' articles they had sounded out Western opinion and found that the people were not ripe for it. They thought that the separation would come in time, but they had no present interest in it. Graham had thought that the immediate object of the expedition, which Blennerhassett estimated at not less than 2000 men, was an attack on New Orleans, and this conversation strengthened his suspicion.[11]

Graham was told about the committee that had been organized in Wood County to oppose any illegal scheme that might be hatched

[9] Philadelphia *Aurora*, 8 Jan. 1807; *American Citizen*, 21 Nov. 1806; Lancaster (Pa.) *Intelligencer*, 10 Dec. 1806, quoting letter from Beavertown, Pa.; Philadelphia *Aurora*, 8 Jan. 1807, quoting Pittsburgh *Commonwealth:* Richmond *Enquirer*, 15 Jan. 1807, quoting same.

[10] Philadelphia *Aurora*, 8 Jan. 1807.

[11] Evidence of John Graham, 24 Sept. 1807, Cabell Papers, Burr Case, 32–4, Alderman Library, U. Va.; *A.S.P.*, *Misc.*, 1, 526–9; Safford, *Blennerhassett Papers*, 155.

within its jurisdiction, and on 21 November he met with that body at the Court House, now Parkersburg, situated at the mouth of the Little Kanawha just opposite Blennerhassett's Island. On the same day James Wilson, secretary of this meeting, wrote to James Madison that 1200 stand of arms had recently passed down the river; and Colonel Hugh Phelps, commander of the county militia, who dressed in frontier style but was a man of force and courtly manners, testified that Blennerhassett had urged him to join Burr's expedition, saying that General Jackson had promised to furnish 1000 or more men; that one gentleman in Kentucky had raised 500 and another, 300; that 200 or 300 were expected from Pittsburgh and some from other quarters. In addition, he stated that Burr had purchased an interest in the Bank of Kentucky and could draw to almost any amount on any bank in the United States.

Alexander Henderson also was present at this meeting of the committee which he had been instrumental in organizing. He now told Graham that he had had some confidential conversations with Blennerhassett, and that while he was not free to give any definite information, he considered it of the highest importance for the United States to send a strong force to New Orleans immediately.[12]

Having obtained this information, Graham hastened to Chillicothe, where he presented himself and his evidence to Governor Edward Tiffin on 1 December. The next day the governor sent a message to the legislature stating that Graham had informed him that Blennerhassett had proposed to two gentlemen of great respectability [Phelps and Henderson] to join him in an enterprise conceived by Burr, the object of which was to seize New Orleans and take possession of more than two million dollars deposited in the bank and the treasury there, also to seize the military stores of the United States and a fine park of brass cannon belonging to the French. This accomplished, a new government would be erected under the protection of a European power, and the rest of the Western country would then be induced or forced to throw in its lot with the power established at New Orleans and controlling the navigation of the

[12] James Wilson to James Madison, 21 Nov. 1806, Burr MSS., L. of C.; Evidence of John Graham, Cabell Papers, Burr Case, 32–4, U. Va.; Evidence of Alexander Henderson, 23 Sept. 1807, *A.S.P., Misc.*, I, 525–8.

Mississippi. The governor understood that a force of 1300 men had been collected on the Ohio, and that this was considered adequate to commence operations because of the disaffection of the people of Orleans Territory and because Wilkinson would have the American army concentrated on the Sabine to fight the Spanish. He had also been told that a foreign gentleman was prepared to furnish Burr with ample funds for carrying out his projects.

Governor Tiffin further reported that four days earlier he had received information from a general of the militia that two boats had passed down the Ohio loaded with artillery, muskets, and bayonets which were new and of French manufacture. The crew spoke the French language and the General wished to arrest them, but lacked legal authority to do so. The governor recommended legislation to authorize the seizure of the boats and stores on the Muskingum and the arrest of any of Burr's agents found within his jurisdiction or attempting to pass down the river. Such a bill was drafted by Lewis Cass and passed by the legislature on 5 December.[13] The next day Cass wrote to his wife:

> The plan of Col. Burr is finally and completely developed. We have received a private communication from the Governor informing us that Mr. Burr's plan is to collect about 1300 men, to rendezvous at the mouth of red river and to proceed from there to Orleans, to attack the city, to seize upon the bank and treasury, and upon the artillery and to form an independent government under the protection of Spain. This plan has been communicated to Mr. Harrison by Mr. Blennerhassett, and Mr. Harrison has proceeded to Washington, with the information.[14]

It thus appears that Governor Tiffin had received a warning from this gentleman as well as from Graham.

The Governor at once dispatched Generals Gano and Findley with Judge Nimmo to Cincinnati to mount one or two cannon and to watch the river at and above that point. They were to be supported by a sufficient force to meet the 300 men whom Blennerhassett and Tyler were expected to bring with them.

[13] *Supplementary Journal of Dec. 2, 5, 1806, 1–3,—the First Session of the Fifth General Assembly of the State of Ohio* (Photostats, U. Va., from Western Reserve Historical Society); *Georgia Republican*, 9 Jan. 1807.

[14] Cass Canfield (ed.), *General Lewis Cass* (Norwood, Mass., 1916), 9–11.

Judge Return J. Meigs and Major General Buell were sent to Marietta to seize the boats and arrest any conspirators who might show themselves in the area.[15] Having made their way to that town, they were setting out with a small escort of militia for the boatyard on the Muskingum when their movement was observed by the partner of Blennerhassett, Dudley Woodbridge, who started immediately for the Island to give the alarm. He soon met Blennerhassett accompanied by Comfort Tyler and a group of young men from Belpré who were on their way to take possession of the boats, which were due to be delivered to them that day. Woodbridge persuaded the party to return to the Island, and, after going to his counting house to arrange for final settlement with his business associate, he joined him at the Island.[16]

Buell and Meigs proceeded to carry out their orders. On 9 December they intercepted ten of the boats which were already headed down the river, and the rest were seized at the boatyard, four of them being unfinished. A hundred barrels of provisions were taken off the boats and another 100 barrels which had not been loaded were seized at the boatyard. The 11 finished boats cost $1200 or $1300, and these and the supplies had been paid for with a draft on Ogden of New York. This seizure marked the beginning of the end of Burr's conspiracy.[17]

Having left Beaver on 4 or 5 December with Major Israel Smith and about 30 genteel young men, Comfort Tyler had reached the Island two days before these events. Fearing an attack from Colonel Phelps and the Wood County militia, Tyler's men were kept busy running bullets and preparing their arms and supplies for an early descent of the river. Now that Blennerhassett's boats had been seized and it was to be expected that guards would be placed along the river, it was decided to get away that night in Tyler's four boats.[18]

[15] General Assembly of Ohio, *House Journal*, 1 sess., 5 Gen. Assembly, 15 Dec. 1806, 40–42; Henshaw, 'The Aaron Burr Conspiracy in the Ohio Valley,' loc. cit. 131–2.

[16] Evidence of Dudley Woodbridge, Coombs, *Trial of Aaron Burr*, 197–9.

[17] General Assembly of Ohio, *House Journal*, 1 sess., 5 Gen. Assembly, 15 Dec. 1806, 40–42; Letter of Return J. Meigs, 17 Dec. 1806, Philadelphia *Aurora*, 7 Jan. 1807.

[18] Evidence of Charles Lindsley, Cabell Papers, Burr Case, 81, Alderman Library,

The weather was exceedingly bad. There had been a recent snow, and now there were rain, mud, and ice to cope with. Fires were lighted along the shore and no one was allowed to approach the Island without giving the password. General Tupper, whom Burr long had been trying to interest in his enterprise, made a friendly visit and showed no inclination to interfere with the preparations which were being carried forward with so much haste.[19]

About dusk Woodbridge arrived at the Island to wind up his business with Blennerhassett. The Irishman had inherited an estate amounting to £20,000, but he had invested $40,000 or $50,000 in the Island which embraced about 180 acres, and its improvements. Six or eight years before he had paid $3000 for a half interest in Woodbridge's business, and was now given $6000 for his share of the profits. He also had some money invested in Philadelphia, so that he was currently possessed of about $17,000 and five slaves in addition to his island property. The Marietta merchant required about two hours to transact his business; then he went to bed around nine o'clock and was asleep when his host pushed off about one o'clock in the morning of 10 December with Comfort Tyler and his four boats containing about 30 men. Only Blennerhassett and one other man joined Tyler's party at the Island; Mrs. Blennerhassett was left to follow later.[20]

The departure was made in great haste because Colonel Phelps and his militia were expected to descend on the Island next day. They came as feared, but Phelps rode off at once to Point Pleasant at the mouth of the Great Kanawha in an attempt to intercept the fugitives. In this he failed, and it was said that his men were not on the alert because they had imbibed too freely of refreshments they

U. Va.; Evidence of James Knox, 4 Dec. 1806, Burr MSS., L. of C.; Evidence of same, 24 Nov. 1806, Coombs, *Trial of Aaron Burr,* 81; Evidence of Peter Taylor, 18 Aug. 1807, *A.S.P., Misc.*, I, 499–500.

[19] Deposition of Edward W. Tupper, 8 Sept. 1807, *Quarterly Publications of the Historical and Philosophical Society of Ohio,* IX (1914), 13–27; Testimony of William Love, Coombs, op. cit. 194–5; Evidence of Simeon Poole, ibid. 206–7.

[20] Testimony of Jacob Allbright, ibid. 185–6; Evidence of Dudley Woodbridge, ibid. 197–9. There is some difficulty about establishing the correct time of the departure from the Island. All accounts agree that it was made on 10 Dec., but the evening of that day is usually understood. The boats were seized late on the 9th and Woodbridge and Meigs agree that the party left the Island at an early hour the next morning.

found on the Island. Their comrades who remained there became boisterous and did some damage to the property despite the presence of the mistress of the house.[21]

The fugitives rowed all night and stopped only at daybreak, when they beached their boats and the men went ashore. Blennerhassett addressed them, saying that the Governor of Ohio had issued warrants for the arrest of himself and Tyler and that they must hurry down to the Falls. Without stopping again, they passed Cincinnati on the night of the 14th, and were not challenged by Governor Tiffin's guards. On the 16th they joined the boats of Davis Floyd at Jeffersonville. Floyd had about 40 muskets, some of which Tyler took on board.[22]

A few days after they left the Island a boat in charge of two sons of a Captain Dana passed down the river to join the squadron. Shortly afterward young Morgan Neville and Thomas Butler, Jr., arrived in a large boat handsomely fitted out with rooms and chimneys. Their company was mostly made up of young lawyers and other professional men from Pittsburgh. They were arrested and tried by the authorities on the Island, but were acquitted for lack of evidence. Mrs. Blennerhassett, who had failed to secure release of the boat that had been fitted out on the Muskingum for the use of her family, now found it necessary to accept the hospitality of Butler and Neville, and she went down the river with them to meet her husband.[23]

It was on the same day Blennerhassett and his party reached the Falls that the ever-persistent Joseph Hamilton Daveiss came down to Louisville to see what he could see. Arriving about two o'clock in the afternoon, he noticed that Davis Floyd was loading boxes that appeared to contain muskets and ammunition. But Anthony New, recently a Congressman from Virginia and now collector of the port of Louisville, was on board and it was clear that there would be no interference with the proceedings of Burr's friends; in fact, New's son was preparing to go down the river with them. Blenner-

[21] Safford, *Blennerhassett Papers*, 178, 193–7.

[22] Evidence of John Munholland [sp.?], Cabell Papers, Burr Case, 82–3, Alderman Library, U. Va.; Testimony of William Love, Coombs, *Trial of Aaron Burr*, 195.

[23] Philadelphia *Aurora*, 22 Jan. 1807, quoting letter dated Wood Court House, 28 Dec. 1806; Safford, *Blennerhassett Papers*, 193–7.

hassett had outrun John Graham and no official warning had been received here about the objects of the expedition. Before the day was over, all the boats passed over the rapids and headed for their rendezvous with Burr at the mouth of the Cumberland River. Daveiss returned to Frankfort and reported to Governor Christopher Greenup on the proceedings at the Falls.[24] The governor presented the matter to the legislature, and while that body was discussing it, John Graham arrived and was examined behind closed doors. On the 23rd an act similar to that previously passed by the Ohio legislature was voted and signed, and the governor at once sent a detachment of militia to the Falls, but a week had passed since the boats left that point.[25]

After Burr's trial in Frankfort ended on 5 December he had remained in the neighborhood for several days and during that time he went to call on Charles Lynch, with whom he had made the deal in regard to the Bastrop lands. He gave it out that he was anxious to hear of Wilkinson's success, and that if hostilities commenced he would go down and take all the men he could get to follow him, but if no fighting broke out on the Sabine front he would 'go to the southward.' One man with whom he talked said he knew that men were being enlisted for six months at ten dollars a month and a bonus of 100 or 150 acres of land.[26]

About the 10th of the month Burr and Adair mounted their horses and took the road leading southward to Nashville. They reached their destination by the 13th and called at the 'Hermitage' to see Andrew Jackson, who was building boats and collecting supplies for the expedition. This time the General was not at home, and Rachel was distinctly cool. Not being invited to stay, they took a common room in a neighboring tavern at Clover Bottom, and presently Jackson made a stiff and formal call.[27]

This coolness was caused by a Captain Fort, who had visited the

[24] J. H. Daveiss to Govr. Christopher Greenup, 16 Dec. 1806, Daveiss, *View*, 103–5; *Biographical Directory of the American Congress*, 1774–1927 (Washington, 1928), 1354.

[25] *National Intelligencer*, 2 Feb. 1807; Daveiss, *View*, 105, 123.

[26] *National Intelligencer*, 9 Jan. 1807, quoting Frankfort extract, 15 Dec. 1806.

[27] Thomas A. Claiborne to Wilkinson, 17 Mar. 1807, *Louisiana Gazette*, 10 Apr. 1807; Marquis James, *The Life of Andrew Jackson* (Indianapolis, 1938), 124; Parton, *Jackson*, I, 320; Philadelphia *Aurora*, 8 Jan. 1807.

'Hermitage' on 10 November while on his way from New York to join Burr in the South. He spent the night with the General and told him that the object of the expedition was to divide the Union 'by seizing New Orleans and the bank, shutting the port, conquering Mexico, and uniting the western part of the union to the conquered country.' He said this was to be accomplished with the aid of General Wilkinson and the troops under his command. When Jackson inquired about the source of this information, Fort replied that he hardly knew Burr, and that his informant was Colonel John Swartwout of New York, the brother of Burr's messenger.[28]

As soon as Captain Fort was gone, Jackson sat down to write a few passionate letters. To his friend Senator Daniel Smith of Tennessee he explained that the plot might be carried out, with Wilkinson's co-operation, by the junction of the Spanish force from the Sabine with Burr's force from the Ohio, and a descent upon New Orleans where the population was supposed to be largely sympathetic and where Governor Claiborne would be prevented by Wilkinson from using the militia to resist. The Senator was to tell the President to watch Wilkinson and to provide for the defense of New Orleans. Then Old Hickory wrote directly to Jefferson and offered the services of his command. He also wrote to Governor Claiborne, saying: '— I fear treachery has become the order of the day. — Put your town in a state of defense, — and defend your city as well against internal enemies as external — Keep a watchful eye upon our General [Wilkinson]. — You have enemies within your own city that may try to subvert your government and try to separate it from the Union. — Beware of the month of December. — I would delight to see Mexico reduced, but I will die in the last ditch before I would yield a foot to the Dons, or see the Union disunited.' [29]

When Jackson, accompanied by General John Coffee, called on Burr at the Clover Bottom tavern, he sternly asked for an explanation. The Colonel 'After much vehement denial — [assured him] *upon his honor* that his object — [had] the approbation of our govt & — pulled from his pocket a blank commission signed by Mr. Jefferson saying, "Gentlemen, I suppose this will satisfy

[28] James, *Jackson*, 121–2; Parton, *Jackson*, I, 317–18
[29] Rowland (ed.), *Letter Book of W. C. C. Claiborne*, IV, 53–4.

you.”’[30] Jackson appears to have been somewhat reassured, but suspicions had been aroused, as a consequence of which Patton Anderson failed to show up with his 75 recruits, and only a small quantity of provisions had been collected.[31]

Colonel Burr lingered in Nashville for over a week, probably trying in vain to collect his forces. On the 13th it was reported from that place that the Colonel was there and planned to set out for the mouth of the Cumberland River on the 20th.[32] On that day he dispatched a message to Blennerhassett by Stockly Hays, Mrs. Jackson's nephew, saying that he would meet him at the mouth of the Cumberland on the 28th.[33] Jackson had permitted the 17-year-old Hays to go with the idea of becoming private secretary to Governor Claiborne, to whom the General sent a letter. The lad was instructed to leave Burr in the event that he should become suspicious of his actions.[34]

Two days later Burr himself was afloat on the Cumberland with only two partially loaded flatboats, a few men, and some horses. Since unfavorable rumors had prevented the collection of men and supplies, three of the boats which had been built for him were left behind. Jackson consequently returned $1725.62 of the $3500 which Burr had sent him for the boats. Adair did not go down the river, but departed the same day and rode southward by a circuitous route toward New Orleans.[35] At the Falls, Blennerhassett had tarried only long enough to transfer from one of Tyler's boats to one that Floyd had prepared. Both parties then proceeded down the river to Shawneetown, Illinois, just below the mouth of the Wabash. This was a small village specializing in the shipment of locally made salt. Here the flotilla tarried four or five days. Articles of agreement were

[30] James, *Jackson*, 124.

[31] Ibid. 125, Parton, *Jackson*, I, 317.

[32] Deposition of Lt. George Peter, 19 Sept. 1807, *A.S.P., Misc.*, I, 566.

[33] Safford, *Blennerhassett Papers*, 185–6. Safford gives the date as the 23rd, but it would have been physically impossible for Burr to make the journey in that time. It seems probable that the editor of Blennerhassett's journal mistook an 8 for a 3. Philadelphia *Aurora*, 9 Jan. 1807, quoting Nashville communication dated 17 Dec. 1806.

[34] Parton, *Burr*, I, 321–2.

[35] Richmond *Enquirer*, 15, 20 Jan. 1807; *Louisiana Gazette*, 16 Jan. 1807, quoting Nashville communication, 27 Dec. 1806; Parton, *Jackson*, I, 322; Safford, *Blennerhassett Papers*, 187.

drawn up and signed by all the men; they provided for the settlement of the Bastrop lands and the military service of the settlers in case of war with Spain. The arrival of Burr was anxiously awaited, and finally Stockly Hays came with his message saying he would meet them at the mouth of the Cumberland.[36]

The flotilla now moved forward and on 26 December it reached an island opposite the mouth of the Cumberland. From there Blennerhassett wrote a letter to his wife, urging her to join him as soon as possible at the home of Judge Peter Bryan Bruin at Bayou Pierre. He hoped that Cushing, Fuller, and the others would bring along all friends even though they did not reach Natchez before the middle of April. He closed by saying that prospects were bright, an assurance his wife never received, for his letter was intercepted.[37]

The next day Burr arrived with his two boats, and the flotilla now consisted of ten craft including these and Tyler's four, Floyd's two, and two others, one of which was commanded by Blennerhassett. In addition, there was one boat loaded with supplies. It was stated that Burr had 103 men with him at this time, but other estimates place the number at about 60.[38] The boats could have carried a much larger number, to say nothing of the company which could have been transported by the 15 that had been left on the Muskingum and the three that Jackson had not delivered at Clover Bottom. With all 28 boats, between 1200 or 1500 men could have been transported.

Burr now lost no time. Having assembled his men on Cumberland Island, he told them that he could not then inform them of their destination, but would do so at a more convenient time. The presence of outsiders is supposed to have been responsible for his reticence, but most of the party thought that they were going to attack Spanish territory. Before the day ended, they pushed off for Fort Massac, and Burr notified Captain Daniel Bissell, who commanded there, that he was coming. It took less than two days to reach the fort, which stood on the north bank of the river, and as the flotilla

[36] Report of James Knox, Burr MSS., L. of C.; Journal of Blennerhassett's voyage down the river, 16 Dec.–29 Jan. 1806–7, Safford, *Blennerhassett Papers*, 184–92; Evidence of John Monholland [sp.?], Cabell Papers, Burr Case, 82–3, U. Va.; Evidence of James Kenney, ibid. 86.

[37] Richmond *Enquirer*, 17 Mar. 1807.

[38] Safford, *Blennerhassett Papers*, 179; Evidence of Charles Willie, Cabell Papers, Burr Case, 28–9, U. Va.

approached near the end of the day on the 29th, the Captain sent Sergeant Dunbaugh to greet Burr and offer assistance. The boats were beached a little below the fort, and the next morning Bissell came down to the shore to visit Burr and invite him to his quarters at the post.[39]

There Burr informed his host that he had heard, probably in Nashville, that Wilkinson had made a truce with the Spaniards on the Sabine and had occupied New Orleans.[40] This was indeed a serious blow to all the Conspirator's plans, for a war with Spain had all along been considered a necessary prelude to the operations he had intended to carry out. However, the Colonel did not seem to be unduly discouraged. He did not suspect the General of treachery, and thought his action was in response to instructions from the Administration in Washington. He still counted on Wilkinson for all possible co-operation, and Bissell must have held the same view, for he let Burr have a messenger to go to the lead mines in Missouri and gave Sergeant Dunbaugh a 20-day leave to accompany the Colonel down the river and instructed Dunbaugh never to leave him.[41] Both men knew that it would be impossible for the Sergeant to return to duty within that time; consequently he would soon be absent without leave and under the immediate command of Wilkinson. Obviously neither Burr nor Bissell had lost confidence in their General. Before the day was over the Colonel was again on his way down the river.

Two days later, 1 January 1807, John Graham reached Nashville from Frankfort, and Andrew Jackson's worst fears were now confirmed.[42] The next day he dispatched a messenger named John

[39] Henshaw, 'The Aaron Burr Conspiracy in the Ohio Valley,' loc. cit. 132–3; Safford, *Blennerhassett Papers*, 179–80; Evidence of Charles Willie, Cabell Papers, Burr Case, 28–9, U. Va.; Evidence of Charles Lindsley, ibid. 81.

[40] Schachner, *Burr*, 363.

[41] Safford, op. cit. 179–80; Dunbaugh to Bissell, 21 Apr. 1807, Everett D. Graff Collection.

[42] There is considerable confusion regarding the day on which the warning against Burr reached Nashville. Henry Adams says the President's proclamation reached there on 19 Dec., three days before Burr fled (*History of the United States*, III, 289), and he quotes Parton (*Life and Times of Aaron Burr*, 438) who says it reached the Governor of Tennessee on that date. But Knoxville was the capital of Tennessee at that time. In his *Life of Andrew Jackson* (I, 322–3), Parton says that Jackson was warned by the President on 1 Jan., and since the General took action the next day, this seems to be the proper date. However, it was probably John Graham, rather than

Murrell to ride to Fort Massac and warn Captain Bissell. Murrell arrived there on the 5th only to find that the Captain had received no word from Washington or elsewhere which aroused any suspicions about Burr's motives. When he returned to the mouth of the Cumberland he found that the Governor of Kentucky had stationed about 50 men there and he was told that three boats loaded with ammunition had been stopped at Louisville.[43]

Shortly after leaving Fort Massac, one of the men on Davis Floyd's boat, David Fisk by name, discovered a chest and a box containing some rifles, muskets, and other arms, which were within a few days distributed to the men. He later testified that at about this time he heard Floyd tell several of the party they were going to take Baton Rouge and Mexico. When Fisk asked how this could be done with so few men, Floyd replied that a large party was to join them at Natchez and that Wilkinson and his army would join them at the mouth of the Red River.[44]

As the old year died, the flotilla left the limpid waters of the Ohio and turned southward into the muddy stream of the Mississippi. On New Year's Day it stopped at New Madrid and three agents were sent ahead to do some recruiting. They succeeded in enlisting only a few men, who were to serve six months and receive $12.50 per month and 100 acres of land. They were given to understand that they were first to go to New Orleans to work on Burr's boats, and then to move to the Bastrop lands on the Ouachita.[45]

From New Madrid the flotilla passed on down the river, and on the night of the 4th Burr's boat touched ground under the guns of the fort at Chickasaw Bluffs, where the city of Memphis now stands. This post was commanded by Lieutenant Jacob Jackson, who was the only officer of the garrison. Burr asked him if he and his companions could spend the night and the request was granted. The party spent the whole of the following day, thus giving Burr ample

---

an express from Washington, who reached Nashville on that day. Philadelphia *Aurora*, 24 Jan. 1807; Marshall, *Kentucky*, II, 412–13.

[43] John Murrell to Andrew Jackson, 8 Jan. 1807, *Annals of Congress*, 9 Cong., 2 Sess., app. 1017; Daniel Bissell to Andrew Jackson, 5 Jan. 1807, ibid. 1017–18.

[44] Deposition of David Fisk, *A.S.P., Misc.*, I, 524–5.

[45] Testimony of Thomas Hartley, *A.S.P., Misc.*, I, 508; Henshaw, 'The Aaron Burr Conspiracy in the Ohio Valley,' loc. cit. 133.

time to talk with his young host. Lieutenant Jackson's brother, John George, was a member of Congress from Clarksburg, Virginia, and Burr, who had known his father George, evidently considered the young officer an especially desirable prospect.[46] The Colonel opened his conversation by explaining that although the leading officials in the Government did not wish to carry on open war with Spain they favored the campaign of liberation which he proposed to undertake. Jackson, understanding that an unofficial war would have official sanction, agreed to take part in it. Burr offered him a captain's commission and money to raise a company. He wished the Lieutenant to go with him or follow shortly with his men. Jackson refused, and then the Colonel asked that some men be allowed to accompany him down the river. Finally he requested that one man be given a 20-day furlough, saying that if he did not return, the Lieutenant could not be blamed. Sergeant Dunbaugh undoubtedly left Fort Massac under similar circumstances.

Burr was extremely anxious to send a messenger to see Colonel John McKee, former United States agent to the Choctaw Indians, and he asked Jackson how many men he thought McKee could raise among the tribe. He also asked to be supplied with arms and ammunition from the fort, saying that he had received some from another garrison and that the lieutenant would be justified in supplying them.[47] Burr was allowed to purchase 30 pounds of lead and three dozen tomahawks from the public stores, to have some of his arms repaired, and 500 musket balls run. Dunbaugh later testified that Burr had urged him to try to get ten or twelve soldiers of the garrison to desert and join him, and also to steal some muskets and rifles, requests which the Sergeant said he refused.[48]

Finally it was agreed that Jackson would resign his commission and return home to raise a company for the expedition. Burr said he was going down the river to set up his standard on Spanish soil where he would declare his further intentions. If Jackson did not receive word of this declaration before he left his post, he was to call on General Tupper at Marietta to whom it would be communi-

[46] *Biographical Directory of the American Congress* 1774–1927, 1143.
[47] Evidence of Lt. Jacob Jackson, *Annals of Congress,* 10 Cong., 1 Sess., 683–6.
[48] Beveridge, *Marshall,* III, 462–3.

cated, and he was given a letter addressed to the General. Burr said that many of the army were engaged with him, and he expected to get assistance from 'the present military force'; also that 'General' Eaton was coming around with the Navy and that he expected to receive soon 10,000 stand of arms. Before leaving the fort on the morning of 6 January, Burr gave the Lieutenant $150 in bills on the Kentucky Bank, and a draft for $500 more on his friend John Smith of Cincinnati. He also left a letter for Smith and one for McKee, which were dispatched the next day.[49]

The Lieutenant's testimony is supported by that of Thomas Peterkin, the Indian factor at the post. It is valuable information, for it gives us a clear picture of the workings of Burr's mind at this particular time. He believed the Administration was responsible for the truce made with the Spaniards on the Sabine, and he thought Wilkinson was still willing to render all possible assistance. If the General had gone to New Orleans, Burr reasoned that it could only be to raise the flag of secession there. By taking Baton Rouge with his own force, he would assure the success of the separatist movement in Louisiana.[50] Since Blennerhassett had failed to bring the expected recruits, he was trying by every means possible to make good the deficiency as he passed down the river. The Colonel was a man of sanguine temperament.

Proceeding down the Mississippi, Burr appointed officers, and the men who had muskets were drawn up on deck and drilled in the manual of arms. The flotilla, which had been followed all the way by the vigilant Spanish agent, José Vidal, made no more stops until it reached the settlement on Bayou Pierre, about 30 miles above Natchez in Mississippi Territory. Here Burr's boat, preceding the others, touched shore on Saturday morning, 10 January, and the Colonel went to call on his old acquaintance, Judge Bruin, at whose home he meant to stay several days while preparing for his further adventures. The Judge showed him a newspaper which was to leave him all but bankrupt in hope and fortune. It contained information

[49] Evidence of Lt. Jacob Jackson, 19 Oct. 1807, *Annals of Congress*, 10 Cong., 1 Sess., 683–6; Thomas Rodney to Caesar A. Rodney, 1 Mar. 1807, *Pennsylvania Magazine of History and Biography*, XLIV (1920), 302–3.

[50] *National Intelligencer*, 6 Feb. 1807, quoting letter from Nashville, 9 Jan. 1807.

that Wilkinson had betrayed him, that the President had issued a proclamation condemning the expedition, and that the acting governor of the Territory had ordered his arrest. These heavy blows apparently had been wholly unanticipated.[51]

[51] Evidence of James Kenney, Cabell Papers, Burr Case, 86, U. Va.; Evidence of Stephen Welch, ibid. 84–5; Henshaw, op. cit. 134–5; Safford, *Blennerhassett Papers*, 199–202; Adams, *History of the United States*, III, 325–6.

Chapter IX

PIKE'S PEEK

WHILE BURR was making his preparations along the Ohio, Wilkinson tarried in St. Louis. On 16 May orders had been sent from Washington requiring him to repair to New Orleans, and then take personal command on the Sabine front. Shortly after receiving these instructions he wrote, on 17 June, to Senator John Smith, who was commissary for the General's command, that it would be his duty to repel any encroachment that the Spanish troops might attempt. He said he would have a force of 1200 or 1500 men at his disposal, but, despite all indications to the contrary, he scoffed at the idea that this meant war, and assured his friend that it was actually the precursor of peace! He indicated that he meant to leave for his new post about the first of the month, but since his orders might be countermanded no mail was to be addressed to him on the lower Mississippi. He left no instructions about supplying the troops.[1]

Exactly one week after writing this letter, the General gave orders dispatching First Lieutenant Zebulon Montgomery Pike on an exploring expedition to Santa Fe. It is true that the orders did not read exactly this way. The Lieutenant was to ascend the Missouri and Osage rivers and return some Indian prisoners to their town of the Grand Osage. There he was to procure horses and proceed overland, cultivating the friendship of Indians along the route until he arrived at the country of the Comanches. At least a part of this

[1] Paper by John Smith, headed 'Adams' with sub-heading 'An Expose of the Disgraceful Intrigue,' n.d., John Smith Papers, Historical and Philosophical Society of Ohio.

nation lived within Spanish territory, but Pike was to call them to a conference in order to bring them under the influence of the United States, for Wilkinson was keenly interested in the Indian trade. In this connection, he wrote: 'As your Interview with the Commanches will probably lead you to the head branches of the Arkansas, and Red rivers you may find yourself approximated to the settlements of New Mexico, & therefore it will be necessary you should move with great circumspection, to keep clear of any Hunting or reconnoitring Parties from that Province, and to prevent alarm or offence, because the affairs of Spain & the United States appear to be on the point of amicable adjustment . . .' [2]

Thus the Lieutenant was given instructions to invade Spanish territory, but cautioned to be very careful not to give offense. Furthermore he had been entrusted by William Morrison, a merchant of Kaskaskia, with some papers authorizing the collection of a debt in Santa Fe, and at the last moment he was informed that his expedition would have Dr. John Hamilton Robinson as a volunteer. This personable and versatile young man of 27 was exactly the same age as Pike himself. Born in Virginia, he had studied medicine and migrated to St. Louis, where he practiced his profession and doubtless learned to speak the French language, which Pike also could speak. The Doctor was to pay for his passage by acting as surgeon to the expedition, but nobody has explained why he wished to make this long and arduous journey with no ostensible object in view except to see the country.[3]

As for Wilkinson's plans, they are hinted at in an affidavit of Judge Timothy Kibbey of St. Charles District in Upper Louisiana. The Judge stated that

> a few Days previous to the departure of Lt Pike . . . I asked the Genl. if Mr. Pike was sent by the Government of the United States. he replied no that it was his own Plan and if Mr. Pike suckseeded he the Genl. would be placed out of reach of his enemies and that in the course of eighteen months he would be in a situation (if the plan suckseeded) to call his

[2] Wilkinson to Pike, 24 June 1806, A.H.N., Est., leg. 5548, exp. 20, doc. 5, 453–6, in Elliott Coues (ed.), *The Expedition of Zebulon Montgomery Pike* (New York, 1895), II, 562–5.

[3] Harold A. Bierck, Jr., 'Dr. John Hamilton Robinson,' *Louisiana Historical Quarterly*, XXV (July 1942), 644–69.

> Damnd foes to an a/c for their Deeds. I asked the Genl. if he did not apprehend danger from the Spaniards, knowing their jealous disposition, on Mr. Pike's account with a party of American Soldiers at Santa fee. he answered that Mr. Pike and his party would have documents to shew which would make them as safe as in Philadelphia.

Wilkinson said that the expedition was of a secret nature, and that Pike himself was as yet ignorant of its real purpose.[4]

Before Pike set out upon his journey, word was sent by way of Natchez to Don Nemesio Salcedo, Captain-General of the Interior Provinces of Mexico, that the lieutenant was about to make an incursion into his domains; on 15 June, Lieutenant Don Facundo Melgares was sent from Santa Fe in search of his party. When Wilkinson was in New Orleans in 1804 to receive the surrender of Louisiana to the United States, he had known Salcedo's brother, the last Spanish governor of that province. He also knew Stephen Minor, the last Spanish commandant at Natchez, where he still lived and where the General was soon to visit him. Since the General was the only person who should have known of Pike's intended explorations, and since Minor still acted on occasion as a Spanish agent, it must have been Minor himself who, at Wilkinson's request, notified the Captain-General that Pike was being sent to Santa Fe.[5]

The motives of the Brigadier are not too difficult to fathom. He had lost confidence in Burr and had now definitely decided to make a hero of himself by turning traitor to his co-conspirator. Since he could not stop Burr if engaged in war on the Sabine, he had decided to make peace with the Spaniards. Pike was not let in on the secret; Dr. Robinson was to reveal Burr's plans to Salcedo and to inform him that Wilkinson wished to come to terms about the disputed boundary. But the General would avoid showing his hand by delaying his journey to the threatened frontier until the Colonel had had time to collect his forces and make his descent upon New Orleans. It was also necessary that he give Robinson time to deliver his message.

[4] Herbert E. Bolton, 'Papers of Zebulon M. Pike, 1806–1807,' *A.H.R.*, XIII (July 1908), 801–2; Statement of Timothy Kibbey, 6 July 1807, *Quarterly Publications, Historical and Philosophical Society of Ohio*, IX (1914), 55–7.

[5] Isaac J. Cox, 'Opening the Santa Fe Trail,' *Missouri Historical Review*, XXV (Oct. 1930), 51–2; Clarence E. Carter, *Territorial Papers of the United States*, V, *The Mississippi Territory*, 1798–1817, I, 309; Coues, *Pike*, II, 411, 562, 583.

Having moved his family to the cantonment at Bellefontaine on the Missouri River 14 miles above St. Louis, Lieutenant Pike, who had only recently returned from an exploration of the headwaters of the Mississippi, hastily prepared for his new expedition. His party consisted of 16 privates, nearly all of them veterans of the previous expedition, one corporal, two sergeants — Joseph Ballenger and William E. Meek — Lieutenant James B. Wilkinson, son of the General, and an interpreter, A. F. Baronet Vasquez of Upper Louisiana.[6]

By 15 July all was in readiness. Two large river boats had been stocked with provisions, including an abundant supply of coffee but little winter clothing. The 51 Osage and Pawnee Indian captives, including women and children, accompanied the party. The Indians marched stolidly along the banks of the river, while the soldiers warped, paddled, or poled their craft upstream. It was not a long journey to the mouth of the Osage and the boats presently entered its clear stream. Here cedars covered the bluffs and countless buffalo, elk, antelope, bear, and deer roamed the forests. The exploring party was well-fed, but navigating the boats against the current was difficult, and frequent rains caused some of the men to fall ill from exposure.[7]

By mid-August the party reached the Grand Osage village near the present Kansas-Missouri line and returned the Indian captives to their people. The villagers welcomed their visitors with joy and Pike received a letter from his General. This was in answer to one he had written Wilkinson on 22 July, saying that he was uncertain how to conduct himself toward the Spaniards. His visit to the Comanches would bring him into territory claimed by the Dons and if he should meet any of their parties from the neighborhood of Santa Fe, he would, he stated, explain to them that he was on his way to Natchitoches but, being uncertain of the geography of the region, had lost his way. He thought he should then visit Santa Fe if the commandant approved; if he did not, Pike thought that an

[6] Ibid. II, 357–8.

[7] Ibid. II, 370–86; W. Eugene Hollon, *The Lost Pathfinder, Zebulon Montgomery Pike* (Norman, Okla., 1949), 102–3.

unmolested retreat to Natchitoches would be allowed. If, however, the Spaniards should make them prisoners of war in time of peace, Pike trusted to 'the magnanimity of our Country for our liberation — and a due reward to their opposers for the insult, & indignity offered their National Honor — However unless they give us ample assurances of just and Honorable treatment, according to the custom of nations in like cases — I would resist, *even* if the inequality was as great as at the affair of Bender [a town in Russia], or of the Streights of Thermopole.' [8]

This message disturbed the General, for he did not intend to have the lieutenant starting any fights. He had already written on 19 July, 'be extreemly guarded with respect to the Spaniards — neither alarm nor offend them unnecessarily.' [9] Now on 6 August he wrote the reply that was received at the Osage village, and there was no mistaking his meaning. He said, in a letter bearing some internal evidence that he was either greatly perturbed or in his cups, 'In regard to your approximation to the Spanish Settlemen[t]s, should your route lead you near them, or should you fall in with any of their parties, your conduct must be marked by such circumspection and discretion as may prevent alarm or conflict, as you will be held responsible for consequences. On this subject I refer you to my orders.' In the same letter there was another interesting message: 'By the return of the bearer you may open your correspondence with the Secretary of War [General Dearborn], but I would caution you against anticipating a step *before you* for fear of deception or disappointment. To me you may and must w[r]ite fully and freely, not only giving a minute detail of every thing past worthy note, but also of your prospects and the conduct of the Indians . . . Should fortune favor you on your present excursion, your importance to our Country will I think make your future life Comfortable.' And he added, 'Miranda has botched his business.' [10] Thus it is clear that Wilkinson had designs that were not to be revealed to

[8] Pike to Wilkinson, 22 July 1806, A.H.N., leg. 5548, exp. 20, no. 11, 476–9, in Coues, *Pike*, II, 568–72.

[9] Wilkinson to Pike, 19 July 1806, A.H.N., leg. 5548, exp. 20, no. 7, 462–3.

[10] Wilkinson to Pike, 6 Aug. 1806, A.H.N., leg. 5548, exp. 20, no. 9, in Coues, *Pike*, II, 573–6.

his superior, the Secretary of War, and when Pike returned from his expedition, the General warned him not to give out any information that he had collected.[11]

On 1 September, Pike left the Grand Osage village, with 31 Indians, including one squaw, accompanying his party. Since his route now lay overland, he had disposed of his boats and had replaced them with 15 pack horses. A six-day march brought them to the dividing ridge between the waters of the Missouri and those of the Arkansas, and here they left the rolling prairie and passed into the great monotonous stretches of the High Plains, or the Great American Desert, as it was often called.[12]

On 25 September, after a tedious march of 375 miles, the expedition reached the Pawnee villages on the Republican River. Here, to his astonishment, Pike found that a party of approximately 300 Spanish troops, mounted on white horses and under the command of Lieutenant Melgares, had left the place not more than a month previously. This was the expedition consisting originally of 100 regular dragoons, 500 mounted militia, and 2075 horses and mules, which Captain-General Salcedo had sent out from Santa Fe to search for Pike after he received word from Natchez that the American expedition had been planned. The Spaniards had started for the Red River one month to the day before Pike began his journey up the Missouri![13] They thus jumped the gun and were too early for a meeting with the Americans. If they had captured the explorers and taken them to Santa Fe, it would have saved Pike an enormous amount of trouble.

Finding that the Pawnees were flying the Spanish flag in their village, Pike made a speech urging them to take it down and hoist the American flag in its place, saying: 'Your former Fathers the Spaniards have now no further Authority over you . . . after next year we will not permit Spanish Officers or soldiers, to come into this country . . .'[14] The natives gave up the flag reluctantly, but Pike, fearing that the Spaniards might return, finally relented and restored

[11] Wilkinson to Pike, 20 May 1807, Coues, *Pike*, II, 825–6.

[12] Ibid. II, 392–7.

[13] Hollon, *Pike*, 113–15; Coues, *Pike*, II, 409–14.

[14] Pike's speech to the Pawnee Indians, 29 Sept. 1806, A.H.N., leg. 5548, exp. 20, no. 17, 509; Coues, *Pike*, II, 414–15.

it to them. The American party remained two weeks in the Pawnee villages and it was here that Pike first learned from two French traders that Lewis and Clark had returned to St. Louis from the mouth of the Columbia River. This, too, had been a military reconnaissance.[15]

In his letter of 19 July, Wilkinson had urged Pike not only to send him detailed accounts of the country he traversed but to 'transmit me a sketch of your rout & of the Country before you agreeably to your information — This may be important in providing against a total loss by misfortune.' [16] Accordingly, the Lieutenant wrote on 2 October from the 'Pawnee Republic' as follows: 'Any number of men (which may reasonably be calculated on) would find no difficulty in marching by the rout we came, with Baggage Waggons, Field Artillery & all the usual appendages of a small Army, and in case of war was all the rout to Santa Fee of the same description I would pledge my life (& what is infinitely dearer my honor) for the successfull march of a reasonable Body into the Province of New Mexico.' [17] Though Wilkinson had decided to abandon Burr, he still envisioned a Mexican expedition at some later date.

The Pawnees became less friendly as Pike continued his stay with them, and finally their chief informed the explorer that he had promised the Spanish he would halt any American party attempting to cross the plains.[18] Ignoring this threat, the Lieutenant purchased some horses from the natives, assembled his party, and on 7 October marched southward. Of the 31 Indians who had left the Grand Osage village with him, only three warriors and the one squaw remained with the party. For several days the expedition followed in the tracks of the Spanish dragoons who had passed that way about a month earlier, this being the route which was known later as the Santa Fe Trail. They lost the trail, however, and Pike and Dr. Robinson left the party to search for it. The main body reached the

[15] Ibid. II, 415–19; Mary Adams, 'Jefferson's Reaction to the Treaty of San Ildefonso,' MS. thesis, U. Va. Library.

[16] Wilkinson to Pike, 19 July 1806, A.H.N., leg. 5548, exp. 20, no. 7, 462–3.

[17] Pike to Wilkinson, 2 Oct. 1806, A.H.N., leg. 5548, exp. 20, no. 21, 514, in Coues, *Pike*, II, 588.

[18] Ibid. II, 417.

Arkansas River on the 15th, but the lieutenant and the doctor got lost on the plain and it was not until three days later that they joined their men on the river where Larned, Kansas, now stands. From this point Pike and Robinson set out again in search of the trail of the Spanish dragoons which would lead them to Santa Fe. The fox was hunting the hounds; but Melgares was far in advance, having reached the New Mexican capital about 1 October.[19]

The plan was for Lieutenant Wilkinson to descend the Arkansas to the Mississippi while Pike went upstream to explore the headwaters of the river. On the 24th he wrote his final message to his General, saying: 'From this point we shall ascend the river until we strike the mountains, or find the Tetaus [Comanches]; thence bear more to the S. until we find the head of Red river where we shall be detained some time; after which nothing shall cause a halt until my arrival at Natchitoches.'[20] If Pike had with him Von Humboldt's 1804 map of Mexico, of which Wilkinson had made a copy,[21] he was led to believe that the Red River rose within a short distance of Santa Fe, and it was thus that he showed it on his own map of the Interior Provinces. Hence his statement that he was going in search of the sources of that river was not inconsistent with his desire to reach the New Mexican capital.

Two boats were now prepared for Lieutenant Wilkinson's descent of the Arkansas. One was made of buffalo and elk skins and the other of wood. They were stocked with provisions for 21 days for the party of eight, consisting of Lieutenant Wilkinson, Sergeant Ballenger, four privates, and the last remaining Osage Indian and his squaw. The boats were launched on 28 October 1806, and, in addition to various letters, the lieutenant carried a map that Pike had made of his route up to that point. Having watched his comrades float down the river, Pike and the remaining 15 men turned their faces toward the western mountains and traveled 14 miles before the sun set.[22]

[19] Ibid. III, 419–29; Alencaster to Salcedo, 8 Oct. 1806, Museum of New Mexico, Santa Fe, photostats, no. 2022.

[20] Pike to Wilkinson, 24 Oct. 1806, Coues, *Pike*, II, 592. The copy which Salcedo retained reads, 'where we shall be detained some time collecting,' and here a Spanish note says a page was purposely torn out. A.H.N., leg. 5548, exp. 20, no. 19.

[21] Jacobs, *Tarnished Warrior*, 212.

[22] Coues, *Pike*, II, 428–32.

For some days they ascended the river as it wound through the plains, and near the present site of Fort Dodge their eyes fell for the first time upon a herd of wild horses. After this they saw many such herds, some numbering several thousand animals. Soon they came upon herds of elk, deer, and buffalo; one herd of buffalo covered the plain as far as they could see. Their numbers so impressed Lieutenant Pike that he estimated 'there are buffalo, elk, and deer sufficient on the banks of the Arkansas alone, if used without waste, to feed all the savages in the United States territory one century.' [23]

As the party proceeded westward, November winds grew cold, forage grew thinner, and pack horses began to fall along the wayside. On the 9th they struck the Spanish trail again and estimated that the force must have consisted of 600 or 700 men. Two days later they passed another Spanish camp site. The face of the country was now becoming more rugged and on the 15th Pike recorded that 'At two o'clock in the afternoon I thought I could distinguish a mountain to our right, which appeared like a small blue cloud,' and when his companions caught sight of it 'they with one accord gave three cheers to the Mexican mountains,' for they thought these heights marked the boundary between American and Spanish territory.[24]

Still following what they supposed to be the Spanish trail, the party marched on. The weather was getting colder and more horses fell by the way, but buffalo were easily killed and the men feasted on their marrow bones and dried and packed 900 pounds of meat for future use. On the 22nd a party of 60 Pawnees gave them some anxious moments, but after the Americans prepared to fight, the Indians went their way with only such trophies as they had been able to beg or steal. Having arrived next day at the mouth of Fountain River, where Pueblo, Colorado, was to rise, Pike decided to establish a camp for his party. This done, he proceeded up the river with Dr. Robinson and two of the men with the idea of scaling the lofty peak he had sighted, thinking he could reach it in one day's march.[25]

[23] Ibid. 433–6; Hollon, *Pike,* 123.
[24] Coues, *Pike,* II, 444.
[25] Ibid. II, 451–4.

Setting off the 24th, they traveled for three days, and on the morning of the 27th reached the summit of Cheyenne Mountain. Here the snow was three feet deep, the temperature four degrees below zero — a hazardous situation for men who were clad only in light overalls with no stockings. But the sublimity of the view compensated somewhat for the extreme discomfort. 'The unbounded prairie was overhung with clouds, which appeared like the ocean in a storm, wave piled on wave and foaming, while the sky was perfectly clear where we were . . . The summit of the Grand Peak, which was entirely bare of vegetation and covered with snow, now appeared at the distance of 15 or 16 miles from us.' [26] His men had not eaten for two days, and Pike decided that in their condition it was impossible to go on. Reluctantly he turned his back upon the Peak which that other pathfinder, John C. Frémont, named for him a generation later.[27]

Within two days he reached his camp, and pressing on from here when snowstorms would permit, he reached the Royal Gorge of the Colorado on 5 December, and made camp near the present site of Canon City. From here he sent out several parties to look for the trail of the Spanish dragoons. When this quest proved unsuccessful, he decided to travel northward and on 13 December reached the South Platte River. Turning southward now, he came to a stream which he believed to be the Red River, and while he went in person to seek its source, he sent his main body downstream in the opposite direction. It was not long, however, before he realized that his object was impracticable, and retracing his steps, he rejoined the rest of his men on 24 December. He now decided to abandon his search for the Spanish trail and to return to the plains by following the river on which he was encamped. On 5 January he climbed a high mountain from which he could see the plains stretched out before him and the camp they had occupied at the Royal Gorge nearly a month previously. He knew then that he was back on the Arkansas River. The day was his twenty-eighth birthday.[28]

[26] Ibid. II, 458.
[27] Ibid. II, 479.
[28] Ibid. II, 484.

Remaining here for several days in order to reassemble his party, take his bearings, and kill some deer, Pike had to decide on his next move. Since his horses were no longer fit for service, he made up his mind to build a stockade, store part of his baggage, leaving his interpreter, Vasquez, and one of the men to guard it, and proceed southward on foot to search for the Red River. Having made his preparations, he started out on 14 January with Dr. Robinson and 12 soldiers, each carrying a total weight of about 70 pounds. Traveling southward up Grade Creek, the Wet Mountains lay to the east and the Sangre de Cristo range to the west of the explorers, 'through which we supposed lay the long-sought Red River.' On the night of the 17th, Pike's Réaumur thermometer read 18½ degrees below zero, or about 10 below, Fahrenheit, and the feet of nine of his men, including both the hunters, were frozen. The Lieutenant and the Doctor went out to forage for their helpless comrades and by great good fortune succeeded in killing a buffalo. By the 22nd all but two of the men were able to travel. Leaving food and ammunition for these two, the party again took up the southward trek.[29]

Pike had determined to cross the Sangre de Cristo mountains and on the 27th his party came to a stream running westward 'which we hailed with fervency as the waters of Red river.' [30] The next day, through his field glasses, the Lieutenant discovered a large river flowing southward. On the evening of the 30th the party reached the banks of the Rio Grande, but Pike called it the Red River.[31] Even his men knew that he was in Spanish territory when he crossed the Sangre de Cristo range,[32] and when he followed a stream that flowed westward to empty into a southward-flowing river, he certainly knew that it was not the Red. If he had Humboldt's map, he knew very well what river he was on. It is impossible to believe that when he was at the Royal Gorge he would have turned his back on the plains and the obvious route to the Red River to make this excruciating journey through the mountains to the Rio Grande

[29] Ibid. II, 484-7.
[30] Ibid. II, 490.
[31] Ibid. II, 493-4.
[32] Declaration of an American soldier, 1 Apr. 1807, A.H.N., leg. 5548, exp. 20, no. 35, 519-23; Coues, *Pike,* II, 504fn.

unless he had been secretly ordered by Wilkinson to do so. In calling the stream the Red River, he was merely laying ground for the fiction that he was 'lost.'

On the last day of January the party descended the river, looking for a suitable place to erect a stockade. After marching thirteen miles they came to a tributary, the Rio Conejos, flowing into the Rio Grande from the west, and five miles up this stream they decided to pitch their camp. Here the men spent a week hunting deer and laying the foundations of the blockhouse, which turned out to be a fairly elaborate affair. It was constructed of logs laid horizontally, and was 36 feet across and 12 feet high, but had no roof. It was provided with two bastions, loopholes, and a water-filled ditch surrounded the structure. Here Pike thought he could hold off 100 Spanish horse for a day or two until his party could make its escape by night.[33]

On 7 February, Dr. Robinson set out alone for Santa Fe with the ostensible purpose of collecting a debt from a Creole trader named Jean Baptiste Lalande, but with the real object of collecting information. Both he and Pike knew that they were near the New Mexican capital, and they knew that the collection business was merely a pretext, but it was supposed to protect Robinson from prosecution as a spy in case war had already broken out between the United States and Spain, which they considered probable, and for which reason the blockhouse was being built.[34]

On the same day Pike dispatched Corporal Jackson and four men to return to the Royal Gorge and bring in the baggage and the men who had been left along the route if they were able to travel. This left him with only four men at the blockhouse, two of whom had had their feet frozen. For the next eight days the lieutenant spent his time in directing work on the little fort, hunting, reading, and brushing up on his French grammar. But he did not build any boats to descend the river, as he had said he meant to do.[35]

On the 16th Pike went out hunting with one of his men, and when they were about six miles from the fort they were observed by a

[33] Ibid. 494–8.
[34] Ibid. II, 499–501; Hollon, *Pike*, 138; *Louisiana Gazette*, 15 May 1811.
[35] Coues, *Pike*, II, 502.

Spanish dragoon and a civilized Indian who accompanied him. The two parties approached each other with caution, but when they met the Spaniard informed Pike that Dr. Robinson had reached Santa Fe and had been received with great kindness by the governor. The Lieutenant now knew that he was indeed not far from Santa Fe, but he still pretended to believe that he was on the headwaters of the Red River, and the dragoon did not disabuse him. Pike took his visitors to the fort and told them he was preparing to descend the river to Natchitoches, but if Governor Alencaster would send out an officer who spoke French or English, he would account for his presence on the Spanish frontier. The visitors spent the night and left next morning, saying they could reach Santa Fe on the second day.[36]

That evening Corporal Jackson returned with three of his men and reported that the fourth soldier and one of those who had been left behind would come in next day, which they did. But two of the men who had been left with frozen feet were unable to travel. They had hailed the relief party 'with tears of joy, and were in despair when they again left them, with the chance of never seeing them more. They sent on to me some of the bones taken out of their feet, and conjured me, by all that was sacred, not to leave them to perish far from the civilized world.'[37] The next day Sergeant Meek was sent with Private Miller to return to the stockade at the Royal Gorge to bring in the two men left there with the horses and supplies, and on the way back to pick up and bring in the two with frozen feet.[38]

On the 26th the expected Spanish deputation arrived. It has usually been supposed that Pike had sent Robinson off with the intention that he should notify Governor Alencaster of his presence, hoping that the Governor would then have him conducted to Santa Fe. But there are reasons for doubting this interpretation. Pike certainly expected a visit from the Spaniards, but he was not sure whether the call would be a peaceable one. He was eager to complete his stockade and to collect all his men, and he was obviously not anxious to hurry the crisis.

[36] Ibid. II, 503–5.
[37] Ibid. II, 505.
[38] Ibid. II, 506.

Meanwhile Dr. Robinson had fallen in with two Ute Indians who conducted him to the Governor at Santa Fe after an eight-day journey. The Doctor announced that he was a French trader who had been abandoned by his companions. Doubting this statement, the Governor invited Robinson to dinner and dispatched a scouting party to try to locate his escort. The dragoon who later discovered the American camp gave every evidence of being surprised, however, when he came upon the intruders, and Alencaster got his first definite information from him.[39]

The Spanish party which visited Pike's fort was preceded by two Frenchmen who informed the Lieutenant that 50 dragoons were being sent by the governor to protect him from an expected attack by the Utah Indians. Soon the dragoons appeared with an equal number of mounted militia and two lieutenants. The officers were admitted to the stockade, having to crawl on their bellies to get in because of the small opening. They were served breakfast consisting of deer, meal, goose, and some biscuits that had been brought by the civilized Indian who had first visited the fort. Pike was then informed that the Governor, having heard he had missed his route, was prepared to furnish guides and transportation to conduct him and his party to the headwaters of the Red River; the Spanish officers stated that it was a journey of about eight days to the first navigable part of that stream. Pike expressed great surprise when told that he was on the Rio Grande, and at once had his flag hauled down. He was then told that the Governor had provided 100 mules and horses to take him and his party to Santa Fe. He knew that this was an order, but protested that he could not leave until Sergeant Meek, Private Miller, and the five other absentees had returned. It was finally agreed that he should go to meet the Governor, leaving two of his men at the fort to await Sergeant Meek, who had gone to bring in the four men who had been left behind. A Spanish lieutenant and 50 men remained to escort them, on their arrival, to Santa Fe.[40]

The ride to the New Mexican capital, a town of about 4500 inhabitants, proved pleasant and uneventful. The first signs of

[39] Ibid. II, 508; Salcedo to Wilkinson, 7 Apr. 1807, A.H.N., leg. 5548, exp. 20, no. 4, 450–52; Alencaster to Salcedo, 1 Apr. 1807, Coues, *Pike*, I, xlvi fn.

[40] Ibid. II, 508, 510, 595.

spring were already apparent in the valley, and the civilized Indians of the adobe villages through which the explorers passed showed them every possible attention. On 3 March they reached their destination and Pike was ushered into the presence of Governor Joachín Alencaster. The Governor asked Pike if he spoke French, and he replied that he did. Alencaster then asked if the Lieutenant knew Dr. Robinson. Pike said he did, but denied that the doctor was attached to his party. In his journal he explained this by saying he feared war might have been declared, and an admission of the truth might have placed Robinson in jeopardy.[41]

The next day the Governor examined the Lieutenant's papers and came to the conclusion that the object of the expedition was to claim all the territory drained by the tributaries of the Mississippi River and to attempt to get control over all the Indians living within this region. He then informed Pike that according to Salcedo's orders he must go to Chihuahua to see the Captain-General. Next, the Governor invited his captive to dinner, and, pitying him in his tattered, unkempt state, presented him with a new shirt and neckcloth for the occasion. The dinner proved to be an elegant affair and Don Joachín an affable host. The repast over, Alencaster ordered his coach, which was drawn by six mules, and accompanied the Americans on the first three miles of their journey to Chihuahua. On taking his leave, the Governor said to Pike, 'Remember Alencaster in peace and war.'[42]

Near Albuquerque, Pike made a visit to the commandant and there in his quarters, to his great surprise and joy, he found Dr. Robinson, who was technically held as a political prisoner but was allowed to practice his profession. This had given the Doctor some opportunity of 'examining the manners, customs, etc., of the people, to endeavor to ascertain their political and religious feelings, and to gain every other species of information which would be necessary to our country or ourselves.' At San Fernández, two villages farther on, Lieutenant Melgares — the man who had gone in search of Pike during the preceding summer — took command of the party and the American officer was allowed complete freedom to talk with

[41] Ibid. II, 608–9.
[42] Ibid. II, 610–13; Alencaster to Salcedo, 1 Apr. 1807, Coues, *Pike*, I, xlvifn.

the people and record his observations, though this had been prohibited when he left Santa Fe.[43]

On 21 March the party reached El Paso, and Pike considered it 'by far the most flourishing place we had been in.' He and his companions tarried here for three pleasant days. Melgares won considerable sums at cards and was lavish with his money. Pike noticed that he was quite popular with the Apache Indians who were there to make a treaty, and with the common people, to whom he was generous and friendly, while to his equals he was haughty and overbearing.[44] At the village of Carrizal, less than 50 miles from El Paso, Pike for the first time 'saw the gazettes of Mexico, which gave rumors of Colonel Burr's conspiracies, the movements of our troops, etc.; but which were stated in so vague and undefined a manner as only to create our anxiety without throwing any light on the subject.'[45]

Nine days and 230 miles after leaving El Paso the party reached its destination, Chihuahua, a town of about 7000 inhabitants and the capital of Don Nemesio Salcedo. On being ushered into the presence of the Captain-General, Pike found him to be a medium-sized man of about 55, and though his countenance was stern, he received the Lieutenant graciously and invited him to be seated. He then ordered the trunk containing Pike's papers to be brought in and sent for a Lieutenant Walker, a native of New Orleans of French and English parentage who had served under Andrew Ellicott during the survey of the Florida boundary in 1797–8. Since this gentleman spoke both French and English, he was directed to help with the examination of the papers.[46]

Pike was allowed to retain some of them on the plea that they were from 'a lady,' though he had heard from his wife only once since leaving home. The others were confiscated, but the Lieutenant had been able to secrete his journal before Governor Alencaster had taken possession of his trunk in Santa Fe. He also kept the notes which he had made on the march from that place. Though his

[43] Ibid. II, 625; Hollon, *Pike,* 149–50.
[44] Coues, *Pike,* II, 641–8.
[45] Ibid. 652; *Gazetas de Mexico,* 14 Jan. 32, 17 Jan. 35ff., L. of C.
[46] Ibid. 655–7.

maps and charts were seized, he was able to publish his journal with reconstructed maps after he returned to the United States. Thus Salcedo largely failed in his effort to deprive Pike of the record of his journey. In fact, it appears that only a half-hearted effort was made to do so.[47]

Pike remained in Chihuahua from the 2nd to the 28th of April; he and Dr. Robinson had their quarters with Lieutenant Walker, and were entertained by the Captain-General and many of the leading citizens of the town. Finally Lieutenant Melgares was ordered to conduct them to Natchitoches and Salcedo advanced Pike 1000 pesos toward his expenses on the journey.[48]

On 1 July, Pike, Robinson, and five of their men reached their destination and were thrilled to see the Stars and Stripes flying over Fort Claiborne.[49] Eight members of the original party had been left behind in Mexico. While Pike was in Chihuahua, Sergeant Meek was busy rounding up the unfortunates who had been left on the Arkansas and in the mountains, Corporal Jackson and Private Carter having been left at the fort on the Rio Conejos to await their coming.[50]

The whole group was finally collected and conducted to Santa Fe, which they reached early in April. One of the men who had been left behind now became disaffected and gave information to Governor Alencaster. He affirmed that Pike's men realized they were in Spanish territory when they crossed the Sierra Mountains in February and asked their commander where they were going. They were told that they were going to meet an American officer with a body of troops on the Red River. This statement may have referred to the expedition of Colonel Freeman, which had been turned back by Spanish forces on 29 July, as it was ascending that stream 430 miles above Natchitoches.[51]

He also informed the Governor that when Lieutenant Melgares arrived with his Spanish expedition in the Pawnee Republic in

[47] Ibid. 658; Pike to Wilkinson, 5 July 1807, ibid. II, 828–9.
[48] Madison to Foronda, 1 Sept. 1807, A.H.N., leg. 5548, exp. 20, no. 40, 543–4.
[49] Richmond *Enquirer*, 19 Sept. 1807, quoting letter from Natchitoches, 2 July 1807; Coues, *Pike*, II, 714–15.
[50] Ibid. II, 510fn., 855fn.
[51] Richmond *Enquirer*, 10 Oct. 1806; *A.H.R.*, XIII (1908), 804, 818fn. 52.

August, word reached St. Louis through some Indians that he was going to build a great fort there, and that Wilkinson immediately dispatched a courier with letters for Melgares, but that he arrived after the Spaniards had left the Pawnee towns. The informant then went on to give a detailed and apparently accurate account of Pike's dealings with the Pawnee chief.[52]

Though there are numerous inaccuracies in this story, Governor Alencaster reported that he had confirmed it all by means of evidence given by Private John Sparks to an American tailor named Nicholas Colle who had become a Catholic and taken up residence in the province. Colle also told the Governor that Pike had asked him whether the Mexicans were good fighters; whether they would fight the Americans; and whether they were satisfied with their government. Furthermore, he said that Pike and Robinson assured him that Wilkinson had long harbored a desire to conquer the Interior Provinces and had once been restrained by the President from attempting it.[53]

Governor Alencaster sent all this information to Salcedo by special messenger, and the American soldiers were also sent under guard to Chihuahua, but they were allowed to keep their arms. At the village of Carrizal, Sergeant Meek and Private Miller, both being somewhat under the influence of strong drink, fell into a quarrel and Meek killed Miller with his saber. He was arrested and sent to Chihuahua for trial, but the case dragged on until November 1808, when it was finally submitted to the Council of the Indies for adjudication. At the same time, a royal order directed that the other men be returned to the United States.[54] On 2 December 1809, the New Orleans *Courier* announced that they had returned to their native country during the previous month. Captain D. Hughes had conducted them on the journey, and the *Courier* went on to say that Sergeant Meek had been detained by the Spaniards 'for having nobly

[52] A.H.N., leg. 5548, exp. 20, no. 35, 518, 519ff.; ibid. 519.

[53] [Alencaster] to Salcedo, 7 Apr. 1807, ibid. 522.

[54] Record of trial, A.H.N., Est., leg. 5548, exp. 20, no. 69, 625–86; Minute of Royal order, 21 Nov. 1808, ibid. no. 1, 429; Royal order to Foronda, 24 Nov. 1808, ibid. no. 67, 622–3; Royal order to Governor of the Council of the Indies, 24 Nov. 1808, ibid. no. 66, 616–21; Royal order to Salcedo, ibid. 24 Nov. 1808, no. 68, 624; Hollon, *Pike*, 166–8.

taken the life of one of the party, who attempted by an insinuation to inculpate the motives of the expedition . . .' [55]

Pike had made himself famous but Robinson had arrived too late. The crisis on the Sabine had passed before he was able to deliver Wilkinson's message to Salcedo.

[55] Ibid. 168; Charleston *Courier*, 8 Jan. 1810.

Chapter X

WILKINSON ON THE SABINE

WILKINSON RECEIVED his orders to take command on the Sabine about the middle of June, but he dallied in St. Louis until August. On the fourth of that month he wrote to his friend, the army contractor and Senator, John Smith, that he would leave for his new post within a few days; but he averred that, despite the allegations being made in the *Western World*, he was neither going to fight the Spaniards nor join them.[1] As was his custom, he traveled slowly, but on 7 September he made his martial entry into the bustling river town of Natchez.

Pike had just reached the valley of the Arkansas and looked out for the first time over the lonely expanse of the Great Plains; Burr was visiting Senator Smith in Cincinnati; and a Spanish force was encamped at an old French village on Bayou Pierre, about 50 miles northwest of Natchitoches and 60 miles west of the Sabine. The General's orders required him to dislodge this force, and Governor Claiborne had already called out the militia of the western parishes of Orleans Territory in order to accomplish this purpose. President Jefferson looked upon war with Spain as a probability.[2]

On 8 September, Wilkinson wrote to Secretary of War Dearborn

[1] Wilkinson to Smith, 4 Aug. 1806, John Smith Papers, Historical and Philosophical Society of Ohio.

[2] Jefferson to John Langdon, 22 Dec. 1806, Jefferson Papers, Library of Congress, vol. CLXIII, no. 28617; Jefferson to Caesar Rodney, 5 Dec. 1806, Ford (ed.), *Writings of Thomas Jefferson*, VIII, 497; Coues, *Pike*, II, 397–8; McCaleb, *Burr Conspiracy*, 74.

that he would discourage the march of the militia until he had penetrated the designs of the Spaniards. He then went on to say that 'I shall drain the cup of conciliation to maintain the peace of our country . . . in opposition to the ardor which I think I discern in the executive officers of these territories . . .' [3] Contrary to these sentiments, the General on the same day instructed Cowles Mead to prepare his volunteers for a campaign, and he did not discourage the march of Governor Claiborne's men to Natchitoches. He also urged his friend Daniel Clark to meet him at Fort Adams. Clark declined to do this on the ground that he was preparing to go to Washington to take his seat as Territorial delegate in Congress, and he warned that a strong Spanish force in Pensacola might give serious trouble in case fighting broke out on the Sabine.[4]

The General had not heard from Pike and could not be sure that Salcedo would accede to his pacific overtures. Meanwhile, the attitude of the Spaniards on the border was defiant, and he decided to make tentative arrangements for an attack on Baton Rouge where Governor Grand Pré held a dilapidated fort with a weak garrison in the middle of a population made up largely of Americans. Wilkinson also made plans to send a force against Mobile from Fort Stoddert, whose commander was to be assisted by 200 Washington County militia under Colonel James Caller, and to make a feint against Pensacola to prevent Governor Folch from sending relief to the other posts.[5] Having completed these dispositions, he dropped down the river to Fort Adams, which was now garrisoned by only one company, the other three having been sent to Natchitoches. From here he continued his journey, ascending the Red River to the Rapids, where he met Governor Claiborne on 18 September.

At Natchitoches Colonel Thomas H. Cushing, under orders from Wilkinson, had prevented Claiborne from taking any offensive measures and therefore he must have been greatly surprised at the militant mood in which the commander greeted him. Wilkinson

[3] Bacon, *Report*, 378–83.
[4] Ibid. 478–9; Clark to Wilkinson, 27 Sept., 2 Oct. 1806, *Republican and Savannah Evening Ledger*, 11 Feb. 1808.
[5] Peter J. Hamilton, *Colonial Mobile* (Boston, 1897), 347; Cox, *West Florida*, 191–2; McCaleb, *Burr Conspiracy*, 108.

wanted the troops from New Orleans — a garrison of about 250 men — and all the available militia of Orleans County to rendezvous at Natchitoches on 3 October.[6] At the same time he wrote to acting Governor Mead, urging that the auxiliary forces required in his letter of 8 September be sent forward as soon as possible. This was necessary, he said, because:

> Governor Herrera with about fifteen hundred men [a great exaggeration, for his force never numbered more than 697] keeps post near the Bayou Pierre from whence his patrols are daily pushed forward, within eighteen miles of Natchitoches. These things will not be permitted with impunity, a single day after he shall refuse my requisition to withdraw his force to the Westward of the Sabine. I therefore shall await with impatience the arrival of your Militia, as I shall not attempt to enjoin before I am able to enforce.[7]

Claiborne promised to send 400 men, the rest to be kept in reserve to meet emergencies elsewhere. But recruiting in the western parishes proved to be so easy that 500 were actually sent under command of Colonel John Thompson in addition to 100 regulars from the New Orleans garrison. Mead also busied himself with preparations and the Mississippi battalion of 250 dragoons and mounted infantry was soon ready to march for Natchitoches under Major Ferdinand L. Claiborne, brother of the Louisiana governor. The American frontiersmen were eager to have a crack at the Dons, and even the Louisiana Creoles surprised everybody by espousing the cause.[8] Editor James M. Bradford of the *Orleans Gazette*, a zealous Burrite, waxed enthusiastic over the prospect of war and addressed his fellow citizens: 'Gallant Louisianians! now is the time to distinguish yourselves . . . Should the generous efforts of our Government to establish a free, independent republican empire in Mexico be successful, how fortunate, how enviable would be the situation in New Orleans! The deposit at once of the countless treasures of the South, and the inexhaustible fertility of the Western

[6] *American Citizen*, 31 Oct. 1806, quoting Natchez extracts of 30 Sept.; McCaleb, *Burr Conspiracy*, 108–9.

[7] Ibid. 102; Wilkinson to Mead, 19 Sept. 1806, Wilkinson Papers, Library of Congress.

[8] *Louisiana Gazette*, 7, 14 Oct. 1806; Claiborne, *Mississippi*, 266fn.; McCaleb, *Burr Conspiracy*, 111.

States, we would soon rival and outshine the most opulent cities of the world.' [9]

Before leaving the Rapids, Wilkinson wrote to Senator Smith that he thought it was inevitable that a clash of arms would occur within 12 days unless the Spaniards withdrew or his own orders were countermanded. He said he had called for 700 militia, which was all he could expect, and thought it was likely that hostilities on the Sabine would be instantly followed by an appeal to arms in West Florida.[10] The picture had changed considerably since his letter of 4 August. He still hoped to bluff the Spaniards by a show of force, but realized that he might have to fight however much he wished to avoid it.

Wilkinson reached Natchitoches on 22 September, and the next day he ordered Major Porter to equip 1500 infantry for a campaign.[11] On the 24th he addressed himself to Governor Cordero of Texas, who commanded the Spanish forces at Nacogdoches. He was, he said, reluctant to address him after the correspondence between Cushing, Claiborne, and Herrera; but he was commanded by the President of the United States to inform the Texas governor that the country east of the Sabine 'will be considered as fully within the limits . . . of the United States . . . and, therefore, any attempt on the part of His Catholic Majesty's officers to disturb the existing state of things' by holding territory east of the Sabine or west of West Florida would be considered an invasion of the United States and resisted accordingly. He demanded withdrawal of Spanish forces west of the Sabine, and warned, 'my orders are absolute, and my determination fixed, to . . . sustain the jurisdiction of the United States to the Sabine river against any force which may be opposed to me . . .' [12]

Three days later the General reported to the Secretary of War that the Spanish operations on the Sabine depended on the orders of

[9] Ibid. 109–10; *Louisiana Gazette*, 23 Sept. 1806.

[10] McCaleb, *Burr Conspiracy*, 112–13.

[11] Ibid. 109; Wilkinson to Porter, 23 Sept. 1806, Wilkinson Papers, Library of Congress.

[12] *Annals of Congress*, 9 Cong., 2 Sess., 922–3; *A.S.P., Foreign Relations*, 803–4; Bacon, *Report*, 384–7.

Captain-General Salcedo, who resided at Chihuahua, 600 leagues from Nacogdoches. 'Ignorant as I am,' the Brigadier continued, 'of the fate of the negotiation with Spain, & the consequent determination of Government; It remains with me barely to report the Information I may acquire, & to place before you my actual strength . . . I have no doubt of success in the object, & think I shall be able to drive our opponents before me & to take Nacogdoches . . .' but future prospects, he said, were not so good.

> You will observe I speak with assurance that Hostilities are to ensue, and I am confident nothing but the countermand of my own orders or those of my antagonist can prevent it; for he has no alternative but disgrace, or the assertion of the Spanish Jurisdiction to the Arroya fonda [Hondo], within seven miles of this post, where he yesterday had a patrole of Cavalry. The destructive consequences which would follow a discomfiture, will oblige me to pursue a line of great circumspection, for I must put nothing to hazard which can be avoided . . . Hence Sir my delay here, where I did not find on my Arrival, a piece of artillery ready to take the Field, or a Hoof or vehicle provided for the transport.

He wrote that he was making great exertions in order to advance within eight or ten days, and that his first position would be at Adais where he had strong reasons for believing that the Spaniards would meet and oppose him.[13]

While unburdening himself to the Secretary of War, Wilkinson wrote, on 26 and 28 September, to two of his principal supporters, but no word went to Burr. To Senator John Smith he said:

> I have made the last effort at conciliation in a solemn appeal to Governor Cordero, at Nacogdoches, who is in command on this frontier; Colonel Cushing bore my letter and is now with the don. I expect his return in four days, and then — I believe, my friend, I believe I shall be obliged to fight and flog them, for I shall advance into the contested tract the moment I have provided horses for four light pieces of artillery, our camp equipages, and a little provision. The orders of the Spaniards are, I know, peremptory to maintain the jurisdiction of the grounds to the sovereign; of consequence, they must make an attempt to oppose me; and I shall as surely push them over the Sabine and out of Nacogdoches as that you are alive, although they outnumber me three to one [!] . . . What may follow, I know, for I verily believe that preparations have been made in

[13] Wilkinson to Dearborn, 27 Sept. 1806, National Archives, Records of the Office of the Secty. of War (R.G., 107), letters received, W 190 (3).

the interior of the provinces, to bring forward to this frontier as many men as they may deem necessary, and commanding as they do a thousand or a million of mules and horses at their will, with a country covered with beef cattle, no difficulty can occur on the score of provisions. If therefore, this business should not be speedily terminated by negotiations you must speedily send me a force to support our pretensions, or we must yield them up, together with the Territory of Orleans. Five thousand mounted infantry to operate as dragoons, or fight on foot, may suffice to carry us forward as far as the Grand River [Rio Grande]; there we shall require five thousand more to conduct us to Monterey, the capital of the province of Neuvo Reino de Leon; after which, from twenty to thirty thousand will be necessary to carry our conquests to California, and the Isthmus of Darien. I write in haste, freely and confidentially.[14]

To John Adair, the aspiring imperialist said: 'The time long looked for by many & wished for by more has now arrived, for subverting the Spanish government in Mexico — be ready & join me; we will want little more than light armed troops . . . More will be done by marching than by fighting . . . Unless you fear to join a Spanish intriguer [Wilkinson] come immediately — without your aid I can do nothing.' [15]

The conspiracy, as far as Wilkinson was concerned, reached its climax when he wrote these letters, and they give as clear a glimpse as we can get of the workings of his mind at that crucial moment. Pike's mission had obviously failed and he now expected a fight, thus leaving the road to New Orleans open to Burr. Contrary to his statements, he could command a force that considerably outnumbered his opponents, but the Spanish contingent was made up largely of cavalry while Wilkinson had little beside infantry and dragoons, the four pieces of artillery apparently constituting the only exception. With this force he should have had no trouble in taking Nacogdoches, as he told Dearborn, but without cavalry or a supply train, how could he face the Spaniards on the plains of Texas with their unlimited supplies of horses and cattle? The prospects were 'not so good,' as he stated to the Secretary of War, unless indeed, as he said to Adair, he was 'a Spanish intriguer.' That he was actually an intriguer is made clear by his further statement to Adair that

[14] Wilkinson to Smith, 26 Sept. 1806, *Louisiana Gazette*, 11 Mar. 1808.
[15] Schachner, *Burr*, 334.

the time had now come for subverting the Spanish Government in Mexico and that more would be done by marching than by fighting.

He could not have been so sure of this unless he had known something of the mind of the commander on the other side, the Captain-General of the Interior Provinces, Nemesio Salcedo. Don Antonio Cordero, the governor of Texas who commanded at Nacogdoches, took orders from him, and Colonel Simon de Herrera took orders from Cordero. Salcedo was independent of José de Iturrigaray, the Viceroy of New Spain [Mexico], but they co-operated under orders from the home government. On 9 September, the Captain-General had written to Manuel de Godoy, and enclosed two packets of letters from Cordero. The Texas governor stated that American troops had been cleared from the area west of the Arroyo Hondo but that the American commander at Natchitoches had demanded that Spanish troops be withdrawn to the west bank of the Sabine, a demand which had, according to royal orders, been denied. Realizing that this refusal might bring on serious consequences, Cordero said that he was setting out for the front after having made arrangements for reinforcements to join him. Knowing that Cordero's force was quite weak in regard to both men and materiel, Salcedo at first ordered him to occupy no new positions and to confine himself to patrolling the disputed territory in order to prevent American encroachments. Now he reported to Godoy that he was, himself, soon setting out for Texas, that he had ordered Cordero to carry out whatever operations he thought advisable, and that he had, according to orders, sent this information to the Viceroy of New Spain and to Yrujo in Philadelphia.[16]

Thus the Spanish officials were determined to maintain a poorly founded claim to the paltry strip of land between the Sabine and the Arroyo Hondo, though they knew that Wilkinson had orders to hold it for the United States. They knew that this meant war, and that war might lead to revolution, but they apparently were prepared to face this contingency.

[16] Salcedo to Godoy, 9 Sept. 1806, A.G.I., Seville, Audiencia de Guadalajara, 296, papeleta 98/3322, no. 9; Cordero to Salcedo, 10 Aug. 1806, ibid. papeleta 98/3326, no. 290; same to same, 15 Aug. 1806, ibid. papeleta 98/3329, no. 293.

Iturrigaray was a partisan of Godoy who, in the hope of acquiring a crown for himself, was intriguing with Napoleon against King Carlos IV of Spain. The Viceroy was ambitious to become an independent ruler in Mexico, and a revolution would have been necessary for the attainment of this ambition. The Intendant Morales had written from Pensacola to warn him that the Mexican Association of New Orleans was plotting to bring about just such an upheaval in his domain. Because of his avariciousness and the economic crisis brought about by his disestablishment of the charitable foundations under orders from the home government, Iturrigaray was exceedingly unpopular, especially with the clergy and upper classes. He was later recalled by his government, tried for extortion and other crimes, and probably escaped the headman's axe only through a general amnesty.[17] One of Pike's duties was to feel the political pulse of the Mexicans, and he later reported that his guardian, Lieutenant Melgares, was one of the few officers of his acquaintance who was still loyal to the King of Spain. Thus it is clear that Wilkinson and Burr were correct in their opinion that Mexico was ripe for revolution, and Iturrigaray apparently was prepared to bring on the crisis.

But the crisis was not to come. On 25 August, Salcedo had been notified by Herrera that the American commander at Natchitoches had warned him that all Spanish troops would be expelled from the disputed area if they did not withdraw voluntarily. Herrera had refused to comply, but Salcedo, referring to the poor condition of his men, gave orders that he remain on the defensive and refrain from occupying advance posts, as had been intended.[18]

On 18 September, Salcedo wrote to Claiborne, saying that while he must defend the territory claimed by the King of Spain, his troops would make no new establishments in the disputed area, the fate of which was to be settled by negotiations then in progress. He thus hoped that no just cause for hostilities would occur. He later

[17] Rydjord, *Foreign Interest in the Independence of New Spain*, 210–11; Enrique Lafuente Ferrari, *El Virrey Iturrigaray y los Orígines de la Independencia de Méjico* (Madrid, 1941), 42–4; Antonio Ballesteros y Beretta, *Historia de España y su Influencia en la Historia Universal* (Barcelona, 1918), v, 362.

[18] Salcedo to Iturrigaray, 25 Aug. 1806, Archivo General de la Nación, Mexico, Provincias Internas, tomo 200, 155–8. (Cited hereafter as A.G.N.)

sent a copy of this letter to Godoy and explained, or rather justified, its contents.[19]

On 27 September, just as Wilkinson was writing his bellicose letters to Smith and Adair, Colonel Herrera, without orders from Cordero and on his own responsibility, evacuated his post at Bayou Pierre and pulled his forces back across the Sabine.[20] For a royal officer to disobey orders was a serious matter; he took his life in his hands and he knew it. He could not have taken so dangerous a step lightly, and he must have had good reasons for his decision. We may not be able to say just what these reasons were, but one or two things we do know of Herrera — he was loyal to his King, he had married an English wife, and he was friendly toward the United States, having visited this country and met General Washington. He preferred revolution to domination by Napoleon, and he evidently feared that the plans of his superiors would end in a Bonapartist regime.[21]

While Herrera was making his fateful move, Colonel Cushing was delivering Wilkinson's peremptory letter to Cordero at Nacogdoches. On 29 September, two days after Herrera's retreat, the Texas Governor replied that he had no power to act without orders from Salcedo, to whom he was transmitting the General's letter for consideration.[22] He did this the same day, and wrote a covering letter giving an account of Colonel Cushing's visit, but he made no mention of Herrera's withdrawal. On 4 October, Wilkinson notified Cordero that he would await Salcedo's reply, but meanwhile would move his forces forward to the Sabine.[23] A week later Cordero notified Wilkinson that Spain claimed to the Arroyo Hondo and that he would be forced to oppose an advance to the Sabine, and

[19] Salcedo to Godoy, 7 Oct. 1806, A.G.I., Audiencia de Guadalajara, 296, papeleta 98/3338, no. 10; *A.S.P.*, *Military Affairs*, I, 205–6; Richmond *Enquirer*, 4 Nov. 1806.

[20] Vito Alessio Robles, *Coahuila y Texas*, 41.

[21] Coues, *Pike*, II, 701–2.

[22] Cordero to Salcedo, 29 Sept. 1806, A.G.I., Audiencia de Guadalajara, 296, papeleta 98/3345, no. 315; Cordero to Wilkinson, 29 Sept. 1806, ibid. 296, papeleta 98/3344; *Annals of Congress*, 9 Cong., 2 Sess., 294; *A.S.P.*, *Foreign Relations*, 804ff.; Bacon, *Report*, 387–8.

[23] *Annals of Congress*, 9 Cong., 2 Sess., 924–5; *A.S.P.*, *Foreign Relations*, II, 804; Bacon, *Report*, 398.

'I leave your excellency the choice, after you receive this letter.'[24]

At the same time, 11 October, Cordero wrote to Salcedo, enclosing Wilkinson's letter and his reply. He then stated, erroneously, that the American general had more than forty cannon and numerous regular troops and militia stationed at Natchitoches. 'This indicates,' he said, 'a larger objective than merely to hold the Sabine line. I must insist that unless we receive assistance, this province and frontier are in danger. The epidemic fever has prostrated a large part of our troops and all the officers of this post and those I brought with me. I alone remain on foot. I have been able to send only fifty veteran soldiers and one sergeant today to reinforce Herrera, who is convalescing at a ranch nearby.' Still, there was no mention of Herrera's withdrawal.[25]

By 12 October, Salcedo had received Wilkinson's letter of 24 September to Cordero and replied, saying: 'On the 18th of September I wrote to the governor of Louisiana, Mr. William C. C. Claiborne, upon the same business' and sent orders to Lieutenant Colonel Don Simon de Herrera, 'this being all the answer that the letter of your excellency requires . . .'[26] Since he was under orders not to retreat, there was not much more that he could have said.

Thus Herrera's move brought about no change in the attitude of his superiors, but Wilkinson was not at first aware of this. After receiving Cordero's letter of 29 September, stating that he had no power to act but was sending the General's letter to Salcedo, he wrote to Dearborn on 4 October, saying: 'The varied style of this letter, when contrasted with those of Herrera to Colonel Cushing and Governor Claiborne, combined with the circumstance of the Spanish troops having recrossed the Sabine to a man, has induced me, on the ground of economy and expediency, also, to discharge the militia who had reached this place, and to countermand those under march, excepting about one hundred dragoons and mounted infantry, whom I shall retain in service (until I am apprised of the

[24] Wilkinson, *Memoirs*, II, app. 93; *A.S.P.*, *Military Affairs*, I, 205; Bacon, *Report*, 390.

[25] Cordero to Salcedo, 11 Oct. 1806, A.G.I., Audiencia de Guadalajara, 296, papeleta 98/3348, carpeta no. 317.

[26] Bacon, *Report*, 391–2.

determination of Captain Genl. Salcedo) to watch the movements of our neighbors.' [27] Evidently the General thought at the moment that Herrera's move had been authorized by his superiors and was later astonished when Cordero notified him that he would resist the movement to the Sabine.

Soon the Brigadier received another surprise, for on 8 October Samuel Swartwout appeared in camp with Burr's cipher letter of 29 July. He also brought the letter to Wilkinson from Jonathan Dayton saying that Jefferson would replace him as Commanding General of the Army at the next session of Congress.[28]

The General spent the night deciphering Burr's letter, and by the next morning he had made up his mind about the course he would pursue. Herrera's withdrawal had completely stalemated him. He could not cross the Sabine to attack, and if he remained idle in Natchitoches while Burr descended on New Orleans, he would get most of the blame and none of the booty. Only one other course was open to him — the one he had already contemplated: to play the part of the patriot and save New Orleans. Such a policy, as the astute schemer saw, would not be without its rewards. After a sleepless night, he announced his decision to Colonel Cushing on 9 October. He explained that Swartwout was the agent of Burr, who was at the head of a widespread conspiracy in the West; his purposes were inimical to the Government of the United States and he was supported by the Navy and by many men of wealth and talent. The General announced that he planned to march at once to the Sabine to make terms with the Spanish commander, and then to take what measures he thought the safety of the country demanded.[29] This was considerable information, yet it did not explain just what Burr was planning to do.

Swartwout remained in camp ten days, and during this time Wilkinson did nothing of consequence. He was trying to get what information he could out of his visitor while deceiving him about his own intentions. The pumping activities proved rewarding, for Swartwout asserted that Burr was raising 7000 men from New

[27] *A.S.P., Foreign Relations*, II, 803.
[28] Schachner, *Burr*, 321.
[29] Claiborne, *Mississippi*, 267–8; McCaleb, *Burr Conspiracy*, 121.

York and the Western states and territories, and that the main object was an expedition against Mexico. Five hundred men under Comfort Tyler and Colonel John Swartwout were to descend the Allegheny in light boats; Orleans Territory, 'where the people were ready to join them,' was to be revolutionized; and the money in the New Orleans banks would be seized in order to fit out the expedition, which would sail for Vera Cruz about 1 February. Swartwout further stated that they expected naval protection from the British, and that the officers of the American Navy were so disgusted with the Government that they were ready to join.[30]

Burr had made similar statements in his cipher letter, and his lies regarding the British and American navies seem to have deceived the General. Wilkinson, according to his own account, made return in kind by telling Swartwout that he admired the plan, and, while he was not free to join the expedition, 'the engagements which the Spaniards had prepared for me in my front might prevent my opposing it.'[31]

These were trying days for the Brigadier. Burr was making his final preparations in the Ohio Valley and Herrera remained poised on the west bank of the Sabine. Wilkinson had not yet had an answer to his letter of 4 October to Cordero saying that he planned to march to that stream to assert the jurisdiction of the United States, and he could not be sure that such an advance would not be resisted. With these problems weighing upon him, he wrote to Daniel Clark on the 13th: 'Never,' he said, 'was the ardent lover more impatient to embrace his mistress, than I have been to take you by the hand. The moment is certainly an eventful one, profoundly interesting to our common country, and therefore I have been deeply solicitous to avail myself of your counsel. Shall I be indulged?' He added that his advance was now west of the Adais — 'a blow once struck and away we go.'[32]

On the same day he wrote to Colonel Freeman, who commanded the garrison at New Orleans, that he was reinforcing Fort Stoddert and had ordered artillery to be sent to that post in preparation for

[30] Deposition of James Wilkinson, 26 Dec. 1806, *A.S.P.*, *Misc.*, I, 472–3.
[31] Ibid.
[32] Bacon, *Report*, 479–80.

an attack on the Spanish fort at Mobile. He then instructed the Colonel to proceed with construction of the blockhouse, since he himself had no prospect of visiting him.[33] We cannot say whether the preparations at Fort Stoddert were intended for offense against Mobile or defense against Burr. Wilkinson could not have been sure of that himself, but he was obviously not planning an immediate march to New Orleans.

Swartwout left camp on the 18th, and it must have been at about this time that Wilkinson received Cordero's letter of the 11th announcing that his orders required him to uphold his country's claim to territory west of the Sabine and to resist the proposed march to that river. This must have come as a shock, and it was now necessary for the General to make up his mind about his next move. On the 21st he wrote to the Secretary of War announcing his decision. He said the Governor's answer to his letter of 4 October made it clear that the Spaniards still claimed to the Arroyo Hondo, and that this 'confirms my determination to advance to the Sabine, for which point, my arrangements being completed, I shall march tomorrow morning, but agreeably to an idea expressed in a former letter, I intend to propose to the Spanish commander the withdrawal of our troops, respectively, to the points of occupancy at the period of the surrender of the province to the United States, and in case of his refusal I shall be governed by circumstances.' [34]

Wilkinson then wrote to Jefferson protesting against the charges which the *Western World* had made against him. Having assured the President that 'the Wealth & Power of the Wide World could not for a moment divert my course from the path of Honor . . .' he said he was enclosing a paper which had fallen into his hands. The louder the Brigadier talked of his honor, the faster President Jefferson should have counted his spoons, for the document enclosed was obviously written by Wilkinson himself. It stated that

> A numerous & powerful association, extending from New York through the Western States, to Territories bordering on the Mississippi, has been formed with the design to levy & rendezvous eight or ten thousand men

[33] *Quarterly Publications, Historical and Philosophical Society of Ohio*, IX (1914), 31.

[34] *Annals of Cong.*, 9 Cong., 2 Sess., 942; *A.S.P., Foreign Relations*, II, 804.

in New Orleans at a very near period, and from thence, with the co-operation of a Naval Arrangement, to carry an Expedition against Vera Cruz — Agents from Mexico, who were in Philadelphia the beginning of August, are engaged in this Enterprize; those Persons have given assurances that the landing of the proposed expedition will be seconded by so general an insurrection, as to insure the subversion of the present government . . . A body of the associates is to descend the Allegany River, & the first general Rendezvous will be held near the rapids of the Ohio, on or before the 20th. of next month, from which this Corps is to proceed in light boats . . . [to] the City of New Orleans under the expectation of being joined in the Route, by a Body of auxiliaries from the State of Tennessee & other Quarters. It is unknown under what auspices this Enterprize had been projected, from whence the means of its support are derived, or what may be the intentions of its Leaders, in relation to the Territory of Orleans; But it is believed, that the maritime cooperation, will depend on a British Squadron from the West Indies, under the ostensible command of American Masters . . . It is expected the Van will reach New Orleans in December; where the necessary Organization & Equipment, are to be completed with promptitude & it is proposed that the Expedition sail for Vera Cruz about the first of Feb. This information has recently reached the Reporter through several channels so direct & confidential, that He cannot doubt the Facts . . .

The document enclosed was dated 20 October 1806.[35]

Writing a second letter to the President the same day, the General offered a commentary on the enclosure in the first one:

My information appears too direct and circumstantial to be fictitious, yet the magnitude of the Enterprize staggers my belief — excites doubts of the reality against the conviction of my Senses . . . I have never in my whole life found myself . . . in such perplexity . . . for I am not only uninformed of the prime mover & ultimate objects of this daring enterprize, but am ignorant of the foundation on which it rests, of the means by which it is to be supported, and whether any immediate or Colateral *protection*, internal or external, is expected: Among other allurements proposed to me, I am informed you connive at the combination & that our Country will justify it, but when I examine my orders of the 6th of May, I am obliged to discredit these imputations . . . I have no doubt the revolt of this Territory, will be made an auxiliary Step to the main design of attacking Mexico, to give it a New Master in place of the promised liberty; could the fact be ascertained to me, I believe I should hazard my discretion, make the best compromise with Salcedo in my Power and throw myself with my little Band into New Orleans, to

[35] Burr MSS., Library of Congress.

> be ready to defend that capital against usurpation and violence . . . But Sir with my Instructions before me, & without evidence of the design, principle or support of the Corps of associates expected from the Ohio, I dare not turn my back on the Spaniards now in my front . . . to oppose the meditated movement from the Ohio, I would recommend . . . [that] the Troops from the bank of the Missouri, [and] from Vincennes . . . take post at the Iron Banks on the Mississippi, about fifteen miles below the mouth of the Ohio, with orders to prevent the passage of persons and property down that River . . . A squadron of Sloops of War & Gun Boats, should . . . take possession of the Mouth of the Mississippi. N.B. Should Spain be disposed to war seriously with us, might not some plan be adopted to correct the delerium of the associates . . . and to engage them in the Service of their Country? . . . I do believe that with competent authority I could accomplish the object.[36]

The next day, two weeks after Swartwout had appeared in camp, Lieutenant Thomas A. Smith was dispatched to Washington with these missives for the President. Wilkinson's delay was apparently due more to his uncertainty about what his 'neighbors,' the Spaniards, might do than to a desire to give Burr time to escape.

But the Brigadier was now in a hurry to bring matters to a head, and the day after Lieutenant Smith departed, he wrote to Colonel Freeman at New Orleans:

> Under my present views and impressions, I have not the least doubt, we shall soon be engaged in hostilities, and therefore, every preparation for defence should be made, which our humble means may enable. By buying up all the paper to be had in this country, I have made up about thirty-five rounds of musket cartridges for six hundred men — a handsome stock for a campaign, and when it may become immediately necessary to quadruple our force. I look with extreme solicitude at the French train [of artillery] near you . . . without a moment's delay . . . enter into a provisional contract for them . . . mount them as soon as possible . . . By employing the troops and hiring artificers and laborers . . . put Forts St. Charles and St. Louis, in best possible state of defence . . . Your place is to be completed by the 20th of December; and in those works, have all your artillery, arms, and military stores, and utensils secured. Should this operation excite inquiry, you are to say, the plan of fortification has been varied, and that the secretary of war has ordered the repairs of the old work. I cannot explain to you, at this time, the causes which prescribe this measure; but they are of a nature too imperious to be resisted,

[36] Ibid.

and too highly confidential to be whispered . . . Your silence, therefore, must be profound . . . The troops marched for the Sabine yesterday, and I shall follow them in a few hours. We go prepared to fight. But, I shall prefer to make a temporary compromise . . . and, in that case, you may expect to see me, with the troops from this [post], excepting one company. Under such equivocal circumstances, I have considered it most proper, to suffer your detachment to advance, because, should we come to action, they will be in season; and otherwise, they can be returned by water promptly. It is necessary, St. Charles and St. Louis, should be strongly endowed with artillery, arranged to command the river, and also the front of the city. The Fort at Placquemine, must also be strengthened and improved . . .[37]

This verbose letter is quite revealing, for Wilkinson was evidently perplexed and in earnest. He did not know whether the Spaniards would resist his march to the Sabine. If they did resist, the lower Mississippi would be undefended except for one company at Fort Adams below Natchez, the two dilapidated forts in New Orleans, and a small garrison at Fort Stoddert on Mobile River. These garrisons were capable of nothing more than defensive action, and with Wilkinson engaged with the Spanish army in Texas, Burr would probably have been able to muster enough strength to take them. That Wilkinson believed Burr's statements regarding the naval support expected is indicated by his order to strengthen the fort at Plaquemine. This was the first populated place above the mouth of the Mississippi and could have been useful only against a naval force coming up the river. The fate of the Southwest lay in the hands of the Spanish commanders and Wilkinson uneasily awaited their decision.

His concern would have been even greater if he could have seen the letter that Salcedo, while en route to Texas, wrote to Iturrigaray on 24 October, enclosing Cordero's plea for help, which had been written on the 11th. The Captain-General said, 'This will show Wilkinson's intentions. He has an estimated 7000 troops near Natchitoches, and the situation is so serious that I send this by express. Please decide upon the aid and number of troops you will send to Texas. Today I write the governors of Nuevo León and Nuevo Santander to direct to the proper destination, in accord with your

[37] Wilkinson, *Memoirs*, II, 2 app. 101.

orders, whatever troops they have prepared for the expedition.'[38]

The day before Salcedo wrote this letter, Wilkinson started his fateful march of about sixty miles to the east bank of the Sabine. He was accompanied by a new aide-de-camp, Walter Burling, who was a Mississippi planter living near Natchez. He was a friend of the General, and a volunteer private in Farrar's Mississippi dragoons. Wilkinson had repeatedly urged Daniel Clark to join him, and undoubtedly wished to use him in his confidential dealings with the Spaniards, since the New Orleans merchant had come to know something of them on his two voyages to Vera Cruz. But Clark would not come and Burling took his place, being made aide-de-camp with rank of captain.[39]

When it was discovered that the Spanish forces had completely evacuated the disputed territory, some of the officers urged that the expedition return to Natchitoches, but Wilkinson insisted on continuing the march.[40] On 29 October, when he had reached a point about 25 miles from the Sabine, he sent Burling with a letter to Cordero at Nacogdoches, a copy of which was to be left with Herrera at his camp on the west bank of the river. This letter contained the offer of a compromise that the General had previously outlined to the Secretary of War; the Americans were to return to Natchitoches and agree not to cross the Arroyo Hondo, while the Spanish forces were to agree not to cross the Sabine. The intervening territory was to remain as a 'neutral ground' until the boundary question should be settled by negotiations between the two countries.[41] Wilkinson wished to be free to go to New Orleans in order to take care of Burr, but he could not do this unless the Spanish agreed to remain on their side of the Sabine. Burling was doubtless instructed to make all this clear to Cordero.

The aide had barely set off on his mission when Salcedo's letter of 12 October was delivered to Wilkinson. The Spanish commander

[38] Salcedo to Iturrigaray, 24 Oct. 1806, A.G.I., Audiencia de Guadalajara, 296, papeleta 98/3349, carpeta no. 2.

[39] H. Yoakum, *History of Texas from its First Settlement in 1685 to its Annexation to the United States in 1846* (New York, 1855), 145; Claiborne, *Mississippi*, 268–70; *National Intelligencer*, 25 Nov. 1806.

[40] Deposition of Col. Walter Burling, 10 Sept. 1807, Claiborne, *Mississippi*, 269.

[41] Deposition of Walter Burling, 9 Nov. 1807, Bacon, *Report*, 259–65; ibid. 396–8.

refused to make any concessions, but Wilkinson sent word to Burling to continue on his journey and make his proposition to Cordero.[42] At the Sabine Burling found that Herrera had already erected barracks for 500 or 600 men and was busily building more.[43] He thought this augured no good for his mission but he proceeded and reached Nacogdoches on 1 November. Presenting Wilkinson's proposition to the governor of Texas, he informed him, at the same time, of Burr's projects. Cordero replied that he was bound by the orders of his superiors and could make no concessions without further instructions, which could not arrive in less than three weeks. Knowing how this would embarrass his General, Burling remained until next day to argue the point further, but this availed him nothing and he sadly retraced his steps to Herrera's camp.[44] Here, to his great surprise, the Spanish Colonel, after again receiving him cordially, told him that if he had known the contents of the letter to Cordero he could have saved him the trouble of the journey to Nacogdoches, and promised to send his second-in-command, Inspector-General Don Francisco Viana, to Wilkinson's camp next day to agree to his proposals.[45] This was accomplished on 5 November, and thus Herrera, on his sole responsibility, saved his country and the United States from war and revolution. He did not know it at the time, but as soon as Salcedo was informed of Herrera's original retreat across the Sabine, he sent orders to Cordero, dated 24 October, not to occupy the disputed territory or attack the Americans if they occupied it.[46] And when the Captain-General was informed of the 'neutral ground' agreement, he wrote to Iturrigaray that the utmost pretensions of Spain had been recognized.[47]

We cannot help wondering how it was that Herrera not only escaped punishment for his flagrant disobedience of orders but actually

[42] Wilkinson to Cordero, 30 Oct. 1806, Bacon, *Report*, 399.

[43] Deposition of Col. Water Burling, 10 Sept. 1807, Claiborne, *Mississippi*, 270.

[44] Cordero to Wilkinson, 1 Nov. 1806, Bacon, *Report*, 400–401; Deposition of Walter Burling, 9 Nov. 1807, ibid. 259–65.

[45] Wilkinson to Cordero, 4 Nov. 1806, Bacon, *Report*, 402; Herrera to Wilkinson, 5 Nov. 1806, ibid. 403–4; Claiborne, *Mississippi*, 270; Vito Alessio Robles, *Coahuila y Texas*, 41.

[46] McCaleb, *Burr Conspiracy*, 120.

[47] Salcedo to Iturrigaray, 3 Dec. 1806, A.G.N., Mexico, Provincias Internas, tomo 200, 119.

received commendation for his action. And why was it that Salcedo so quickly changed his mind as soon as he heard of Herrera's retreat? Pike got a firsthand account of the transaction when he dined with the two Spanish governors at San Antonio on 9 June 1807. Cordero proffered a toast to 'The President of the United States' and other toasts were drunk to General Wilkinson and to Pike's party. The Lieutenant reported that Cordero and Herrera agreed perfectly on one point — their hatred of tyranny of every kind, and a secret determination never to see that flourishing part of the New World subject to any European lord other 'than the King of Spain.' Pike stated that if Bonaparte should seize on European Spain, he risked nothing in

> asserting those two gentlemen would be the first to throw off the yoke, draw their swords, and assert the independence of their country . . . We owe it to Governor Herrera's prudence that we are not now engaged in a war with Spain. This will be explained by the following anecdote, which he related in the presence of his friend Cordero, and which was confirmed by him. When the difficulties commenced on the Sabine, the Commandant-General and the Viceroy consulted each other, and mutually determined to maintain inviolate what they deemed the dominions of their master. The Viceroy therefore ordered Herrera to join Cordero with 1300 men, and both the Viceroy and Salcedo ordered Cordero to cause troops to be attacked, should they pass the Rio Oude [Arroyo Hondo]. These orders were positively reiterated to Herrera, the actual commanding officer of the Spanish army on the frontiers, and gave rise to the many messages which he sent to General Wilkinson when he was advancing with our troops. Finding they were not attended to, he called a council of war on the question to attack or not,

and it recommended a predatory war at once, but no general engagement. Despite all this, Herrera 'had the firmness or temerity to enter into the agreement with General Wilkinson which at present exists relative to our boundaries on that frontier. On his return he was received with coolness by Cordero, and they both made their communications to their superiors.' Herrera feared the consequences, being conscious that he had served his country faithfully but at the same time he had violated every principle of military duty. At length the answer came, containing the thanks of the Viceroy and the Captain-General 'for having pointedly disobeyed their orders, with assurances that they would represent his services in exalted terms to the king. What could have produced this change of sentiment is to me unknown, but the letter was published to the army, and confidence again restored between the two chiefs and the troops.'[48]

The only possible explanation would seem to be that Herrera was aware of the revolutionary schemes of Iturrigaray and Godoy and had the courage to defeat them. If his superiors had persisted in their plans or undertaken to punish him, he doubtless could have ruined them by revealing the reasons why they wished to provoke a war with the United States over a very dubious claim to a very paltry bit of territory. It is hardly possible to conceive of any other circumstances under which a proud Spanish official would permit himself to be defied and his plans thwarted by a military subordinate.

The ink was hardly dry on the 'neutral ground' agreement when Wilkinson gave orders to Colonel Cushing to break camp and march the troops back to Natchitoches.[49] Hurrying forward with Burling, he reached that place next day and found several letters awaiting him. One of these was brought by a Frenchman from Dr. Erich Bollman in New Orleans, and it covered a message from Jonathan Dayton and a duplicate of Burr's cipher letter which Swartwout had already delivered.[50] In his note Bollman said, 'I have the honor to forward to your excellency the *enclosed letters* which I was charged to deliver to you by our mutual friend. I shall remain for some time at this place, and should be glad to learn when and where I may have the pleasure of an interview with you.'[51]

Dayton's letter read: 'Everything and even Heaven itself conspire to prepare the train for a grand explosion. Are you also ready? For I know you flinch not when a grand object is in view. Your present is more favorable than your late position, and as you can retain it without suspicion or alarm, you ought by no means to retire from it until your friends join you in December somewhere on the Mississippi River. Under the auspices of Burr and Wilkinson, I shall be

[48] Coues, *Pike*, II, 698, 702–3.
[49] Richmond *Enquirer*, 3 Jan. 1807.
[50] Wilkinson, statement, 14 Dec. 1806, Philadelphia *Aurora*, 26 Jan. 1807.
[51] Bollman to Wilkinson, 27 Sept. 1806, ibid. 25 Jan. 1807.

happy to engage & when the time arrives, you will find me near you.'[52]

Another letter came from James L. Donaldson of Natchez. He informed the General that a Mr. Michael Myers had come from St. Louis on his way to New Orleans and had declared that 'a plan to revolutionize the western country had been formed, matured, and is ready to explode — that Kentucky, Ohio, Tennessee, Orleans, and Indiana are combined, to declare themselves independent on the 15th November. That proposals have been made to some of the most influential characters at St. Louis, by an accredited agent of the conspiracy, to join the plan. That this person [Colonel De Pestre], whose name Myers refuses to reveal, is in a most respectable line of life, and had the most unquestionable vouchers of his mission in French and English.' He said that 'money might be commanded to any extent . . . but that the persons thus applied to at St. Louis altogether refused to concur in any plan of the kind . . .' and that 'there are only four persons in St. Louis, who are privy to the disclosure . . .'[53] Wilkinson said that he had not fully credited Swartwout's information, but 'this letter of Mr. Donaldson removed my doubts; and I lost not a moment, after the receipt of it, to put in operation all the means I commanded, for repelling the formidable force, which I now expected would soon be before New Orleans, to which capital my eyes were immediately directed.'[54]

Whatever else he may have believed, one thing is clear: Wilkinson was far more concerned about what might happen in New Orleans than he was about any force Burr might bring down the Mississippi, and he made all his dispositions accordingly. First, Major Porter was ordered to hasten down to the city with 100 men and all available artificers. He was to 'repair and mount every piece of ordnance you can lay hands on and work all hands double tides in fixing shot, shell, etc. Let your field pieces be all ready to take the field and let 6 or 8 battering cannon be mounted in Ft. Charles and Ft. Louis to bear on the river and the front and flanks of the city. Use every exertion

[52] Burr MSS., Library of Congress.
[53] Philadelphia *Aurora*, 6 Nov. 1807; Wilkinson, *Memoirs*, II, app. 98.
[54] *A.H.R.*, IX, 537fn.

to reach N.O. where you will find me on the 20th. Inst.' [55] Colonel Cushing was to follow Porter with all the remaining troops except one company which was to be left in Natchitoches.[56]

Lieutenant George Peter, in command at Fort Adams, was ordered to move all military supplies to New Orleans, but officers' families were to remain at the Fort because Wilkinson professed to believe that there would be an insurrection of blacks as well as whites to combat.[57] The Brigadier wrote to Colonel Freeman in New Orleans that, 'We must repair the old defences of the city; it is our only resort . . . we shall want, I expect, ten thousand pickets for palisades, fraisings, etc . . . Quarters for the troops from this place, (except Strong's company) those at Fort Adams, and Point Coupée, and one hundred from Fort Stoddert, must be provided and prepared.' [58]

Having made these dispositions, the General, accompanied by Captain Burling, took boat and reached Natchez on 11 November. Here he took up residence at 'Concord,' a rambling house which was then the home of Major Stephen Minor, and which survives to this day. Minor was a native of Philadelphia who had, it will be recalled, become a Spanish citizen and served as the local commandant before Natchez was turned over to the American forces under Wilkinson in 1798. Though he had now resumed his American citizenship, he still held a Spanish commission, and it was presumably he who, during the previous June, had relayed to Salcedo the news that had reached him from St. Louis of Pike's forthcoming expedition. Wilkinson probably thought that his staying with Minor at this time would encourage Burr.[59]

On the 12th Wilkinson wrote to Jefferson that the real design of the conspirators was 'to seize on New Orleans, revolutionize the territory, and carry an expedition against Mexico by Vera Cruz.' It would, he feared, 'receive strong support in New Orleans, from a quarter little suspected, from whence I have been recently ad-

[55] Wilkinson to Porter, 6 Nov. 1806, Wilkinson, *Memoirs*, II, app. 102.

[56] McCaleb, *Burr Conspiracy*, 135–6.

[57] Wilkinson to Cushing, 7 Nov. 1806, Wilkinson, *Memoirs*, II, app. 99; Deposition of Lt. George Peter, 19 Sept. 1807, *A.S.P.*, *Misc.*, I, 566.

[58] Wilkinson to Lt. Col. Freeman, 7 Nov. 1806, Wilkinson, *Memoirs*, II, app. 99.

[59] Coues, *Pike*, II, 699; Richmond *Enquirer*, 3 Jan. 1807; Deposition of Isaac Briggs, 1 June 1811, Bacon, *Report*, 265; Claiborne, *Mississippi*, 272.

dressed by a Gallo-American, formerly distinguished at Olmutz in a better cause [Bollman]. By masking my purposes and flattering his hopes, I expect to discover the extent and leading characters of the combination in that city; and, till this is effected, I shall carry an equivocal exterior to every person who may see me . . .' This letter was dispatched to Washington by Isaac Briggs, who delivered it to the President on 1 January 1807.[60]

On the same day the General wrote to Governor Claiborne:

> You are surrounded by dangers of which you dream not and the destruction of the American Union is seriously menaced. The Storm will probably burst in New Orleans, when I shall meet it & triumph or perish. The French train of light Artillery is indispensable to our defence. I therefore conjure you to aid Col: Freeman in getting or taking possession of it — assist him also in procuring Pickets to Stockade the town and strengthen the old fortifications — we shall have 1000 Regular Troops in the City in three weeks and I look for succour by Sea . . . You have spies on your every movement and disposition — and our safety and success depends *vitally* on the concealment of our intentions . . . do not breathe or even hint it . . .

After instructing Claiborne to suspend all measures until his arrival, Wilkinson continued: 'I shall leave this place the Day after tomorrow, but must dismantle fort Adams and remove every effective weapon from it. I fear our Government has been surprised . . . the plot . . . implicates thousands and among them some of your particular friends as well as my own . . . Inclosed to Col: Freeman to avoid suspicion and to be delivered by him in private.' [61]

In another letter the General told Freeman that he was writing Claiborne about 'the dangers which menace us imperiously, not from without, but from within,' and added, 'I have made up my mind to perish in the storm.' [62] From acting Governor Cowles Mead of Mississippi Territory he requested a force of 500 militiamen, but since he would not divulge the reasons for the request, it was denied.[63]

Before leaving Natchez the General took one other significant

[60] Wilkinson, *Memoirs*, II, app. 100; Deposition of Isaac Briggs, Bacon, *Report*, 265.

[61] Rowland, *Official Letter Books of W.C.C. Claiborne*, IV, 55–6.

[62] Wilkinson to Freeman, 12 Nov. 1806, Wilkinson, *Memoirs*, II, app. 101.

[63] Safford, *Blennerhassett Papers*, 146; Richmond *Enquirer*, 3 Jan. 1807; Claiborne, *Mississippi*, 273.

step. On 13 November he gave Captain Burling a passport addressed to 'all persons whom it may concern' authorizing him to visit the Viceroy Iturrigaray at Mexico City. He also gave him private instructions 'to avail yourself of the present alarm, produced by Col. Burr's project, to effect a visit to the City of Mexico by the interior and to return by water, in order to examine both routes, relatively to their practicability and the means of defence the Spaniards possess —I have long been in quest of this information . . .' he said.[64] Captain Burling carried a letter from the General to the Viceroy telling how he, on his own authority and at his own expense, was undertaking to defeat Burr's conspiracy and to prevent his landing at Vera Cruz with a force of 129 men who would attempt to revolutionize Mexico! Wilkinson indicated that this herculean effort had cost him a total of 121,000 pesos, and he asked that this sum be handed over to Burling! After having delivered this missive, Burling was to return by way of Vera Cruz and to collect all possible military information.[65]

When Burling arrived at Nacogdoches, he was announced as a public officer on important official business, and a detachment of cavalry was ordered to conduct him to San Antonio. Here he met Salcedo and informed him of Burr's intended invasion of the coast of Mexico in the neighborhood of Vera Cruz. The Captain-General immediately ordered Herrera to evacuate Nacogdoches and proceed to San Antonio,[66] while Burling made his way from that place to the Mexican capital.

Salcedo sent a messenger ahead of him, and shortly after this courier arrived, Iturrigaray received a warning from Yrujo in Philadelphia and gathered pertinent information from Louisiana newspapers. If either the Captain-General or the Viceroy had received previous information about the 'neutral ground' agreement, they had made no mention of it; but now, on 20 January 1807, Iturrigaray wrote to Cevallos that while he was expecting to hear of a clash of arms on the Sabine, Salcedo's messenger had informed him of this truce, and

[64] Wilkinson to Burling, 13 Nov. 1806, Burr MSS., L. of C.

[65] A.H.N., leg. 5545, exp. 15, 569–74, translated by William R. Shepherd in *A.H.R.*, IX (Apr. 1904), 534–7.

[66] John Sibley to Secty. Dearborn, 10 Jan. 1807, *Southwestern Historical Quarterly*, XXXV (1942), 292–5.

Yrujo gave news of the proclamation the President had issued against the conspirators after receiving the warning Wilkinson had sent from Natchitoches by Lieutenant Smith. The Spanish envoy thought the measures of the United States Government were entirely too weak to prevent the success of Burr's plan to separate the Western states, but the Viceroy assured his ministry that he was ready to chastise any enemies who should attempt to invade the dominions of the King.[67]

Burling arrived the same day this letter was written, and on the next, the Viceroy hastened to write to Wilkinson. He thanked the General for the information he had sent, but said that this was already available in the public press. In regard to the threatened invasion, he said he was prepared to repel a far larger force than the one mentioned, and he knew that Salcedo was fully able to defend Texas. He stated that he was not authorized to pay the sums requested and that there was no need to discuss the verbal messages Burling had delivered. He was, therefore, sending the courier back with the letter. The cynical Spaniard, cut on Wilkinson's own pattern, closed his communication by assuring the Brigadier of his earnest desire that all his honest intentions should be fulfilled.[68] Not until 12 March 1807 did Iturrigaray send Cevallos a copy of this letter, saying that in accordance with Wilkinson's request he had destroyed the original of his communication after having had it translated.[69] A month later Cevallos notified the Viceroy that the ministry had received his letter of 20 January and the King approved his conduct, but he was warned that Wilkinson was strongly suspected of being in league with Burr; that he should proceed with caution and report in detail on Burling's visit.[70]

Burling was escorted to Vera Cruz by a military guard and thence embarked for New Orleans, reaching that city on 20 February.[71] He brought with him all the information Wilkinson had required

[67] Iturrigaray to Cevallos, 20 Jan. 1807, A.H.N., leg. 5545, exp. 15, 531–6; Cevallos to Yrujo, 6 May 1807, ibid. leg. 5546, apartado no. 1, 398–9.

[68] Iturrigaray to Wilkinson, 21 Jan. 1807, ibid. leg. 5545, exp. 15, 575–7; Enrique Lafuente Ferrari, *El Virrey Iturrigaray*, 58–61.

[69] Iturrigaray to Cevallos, 12 Mar. 1807, A.H.N., leg. 5545, exp. 15, 565–8.

[70] Cevallos to Iturrigaray, 12 Apr. 1807, ibid. 560–62.

[71] Iturrigaray to Cevallos, 12 Mar. 1807, ibid. 565–9; Richmond *Enquirer*, 7 Apr. 1807.

regarding the routes to and military defenses of the capital of Mexico, and on 12 March the General wrote to Jefferson, saying:

> you can determine whether his [Burling's] Information, gives Him a Title to consideration or not; from another source which I deem confidential, I find the military of the havanna breathe the sentiments of their Brethren in Mexico. — Should your Estimate of the present times & particularly Bonapartes decree of the 21st. November, justify us in acting, or preparing to act, for the safety of our Independence, give me liberty with the means of expence, and I have at Command suitable agents, to foster the spirit demonstrated to Mr. Burling, & I have also the names of those with whom he conferred among the Mexican officers. But sir the apparent crisis in the affairs of the World, recalls to my mind your observations to me in 1804 respecting the Island of Cuba — Take that Island, Sir, & with the cooperation of a British Squadron, we can accomplish it in six months, from the Day we commence our operations; and by this single blow, we shall secure our own Western possessions, reduce the Floridas, & give Independence to Mexico. The fate of Prussia presents an awful lesson to the World, and you can best determine, whether the instance should affect our policies. But that Bonaparte aims at universal Domination appears unequivocal, and that our forbearance should awaken a sense of Justice in the Breast of a despot, who settles all questions by the sword, cannot . . . be reasonably expected.[72]

On the General's recommendation, Burling was paid $1500 to cover the expenses of his journey.[73] This seems modest enough, especially in view of the fact that Wilkinson failed to account for $16,882.12 which he drew from the Treasury in connection with the Sabine campaign.[74]

Back in Natchez, the Brigadier left his ailing wife at 'Concord' in the care of his good friend Stephen Minor and went down the river to Fort Adams, arriving at that post on 18 November 1806. Here he found Ogden and Swartwout. Ogden had returned from New Orleans where he had delivered letters to Burr's friends. Swartwout said that Lieutenant Spence had been sent from that city to Nashville with letters for Burr. Lieutenant Peter asked permission to arrest Swartwout, but the General refused because he had made the young man believe he would not oppose Burr, whom it was neces-

[72] Wilkinson to Jefferson, 12 Mar. 1807, Burr MSS., L. of C.

[73] Schachner, *Burr*, 342; Beveridge, *Marshall*, III, 330.

[74] Testimony of William Simmons, Dept. of War, 13 Apr. 1810, *Louisiana Gazette and New Orleans Advertiser*, 13 Sept. 1810.

sary to keep in the dark about the trap that was being set for him. Wilkinson informed the Lieutenant that he would assemble his whole force in New Orleans, but on the 19th he ordered Peter to proceed with what was left of his command to Natchez, where he was to watch for the approach of the party from the Ohio and give warning at the earliest possible moment.[75] From Fort Adams, Wilkinson proceeded to New Orleans, reaching that city on 25 November.

[75] Deposition of James Wilkinson, 26 Dec. 1806, *A.S.P.*, *Misc.*, I, 472–3; Deposition of Lt. George Peter, 19 Sept. 1807, ibid. 566; Rowland, *Claiborne*, IV, 149–55.

Chapter XI

WILKINSON IN NEW ORLEANS

BEFORE LEAVING NATCHITOCHES Wilkinson had decided to make his stand against Burr in the city of New Orleans, though Governor Claiborne and many others thought it would be better to meet him at some point up the river, before he had opportunity to assemble recruits in Natchez, to seize the military stores of the Spaniards at Baton Rouge, or enlist the slaves who greatly outnumbered the whites in the parishes above New Orleans.[1] With the two bomb ketches and four gunboats under Captain Shaw, and the force of about 800 regulars beside militia which the General could muster, there could have been little difficulty in stopping the 500 or 1000 men whom Burr said he could bring.[2] But there were other considerations which led to the decision to defend New Orleans. Burr had said that 'Naval protection of England is secured. Truxton is going to Jamaica to arrange with the admiral on that station. It [*sic*] will meet us at the Mississippi.' [3] We now know that this was pure fabrication, but Wilkinson believed it, and if a naval force had to be dealt with, it would have to be done at New Orleans or at the Plaquemine fort below the city.

Furthermore, Wilkinson knew that Burr was not planning to take the Territorial capital by storm but by means of a *coup d'état*. Today this may appear to have been an absurd idea, and historians

[1] Claiborne to Wilkinson, 4 Jan. 1807, Rowland, *Claiborne*, IV, 80; Claiborne to Captain Shaw, 4 Jan. 1807, ibid. IV, 79–80.

[2] Claiborne to Madison, 4 Dec. 1806, ibid. IV, 40–41.

[3] Adams, *History of the United States*, III, 253.

usually have treated it lightly, but Burr had good reason to think that it would succeed. New Orleans had experienced a wave of prosperity since it had become an American city. Business was booming and the population had increased rapidly and spread beyond the limits of the *Vieux Carré*. Most important among the newcomers were the American adventurers who had arrived since the change of government, and the French refugees from Santo Domingo. Many of the latter were men and women of charm and talent, and being more versatile than the native Creoles, they had given new tone to the life of the city. In 1806 the County of Orleans had a total population of 17,001, made up of 6311 whites, 8378 slaves, and 2312 free Negroes. In the city of New Orleans there were, beside the Creoles, about 230 Spaniards, 350 native American residents, 280 American soldiers, 100 to 150 sailors, and a large number of slaves and free Negroes.[4] These last were restive because the military organization which they had been allowed to maintain under the Spanish regime had been disbanded, and the racial prejudice of the new rulers was much greater than had been that of their Latin predecessors. Since relations between Spain and the United States were critical, the Spanish element in the city was considered dangerous by Governor Claiborne, and the loyalty of the Creoles to the American regime was often questioned.[5]

Yet it was not any of these groups, but the Americans themselves who gave the Governor the greatest cause for alarm. Daniel Clark and the lawyer Evan Jones were old residents who were friends of Burr and quite influential with the Creoles. They were both hostile to Claiborne, as was Edward Livingston, who by 1806 had established himself as the leader of the New Orleans bar with an income of not less than $35,000 per year. At first Governor Claiborne had consulted Livingston freely and had suffered politically as a consequence of taking his advice. Governor Williams of Mississippi Territory presently warned Claiborne of his mistake, and Livingston soon became a leading opponent of the Louisiana executive. James M. Bradford, brother to William Bradford of the *Ken-*

[4] John Graham to Madison, 2 Jan. 1806, Carter, *Territorial Papers*, IX, 552–6, 923.

[5] Statement of Stephen [a free Negro] to Governor Claiborne, 23 Jan. 1806, ibid. IX, 575–6; James Brown to Secretary of the Treasury, 7 Jan. 1806, ibid. IX, 558–60.

tucky Gazette, was editor of the *Louisiana Gazette*, the only English language newspaper published in the city, and mouthpiece of the opposition faction.[6] Judge James Workman of the Orleans County Court, an Englishman of three years' residence, was a leading member of the Mexican Association, the avowed object of which was to bring about an invasion of the neighboring Spanish province.[7] Judge John B. Prevost of the Superior Court of the Territory was Aaron Burr's stepson; James Brown, the District Attorney, and Dr. Samuel Brown were brothers of Burr's great friend, Senator John Brown of Kentucky.[8] All of these men formed a powerful Burr clique, bound by ties of blood and friendship as well as by mutual self-interest.

The Creoles found their new masters too crude and too arrogant to suit their tastes, and Governor Claiborne, though a conscientious and long-suffering administrator, lacked the urbanity that might have made him acceptable to the native population. Furthermore, there were many causes of friction which no governor could have eradicated. The old French inhabitants objected to the division of Louisiana into two Territories by the Congressional act of 1804, and they bitterly resented the prohibition of the slave trade. They also felt that they should have been given some voice in their own government instead of having all their officials appointed by the President of the United States or by the governor of the Territory.[9] But the new judicial system proved to be the greatest single cause of discontent.

The act of 1804 which created the Territory of Orleans provided for a Federal District Court to consist of one judge, and a Territorial Superior Court with three judges. The legislative power was entrusted to a Legislative Council to be made up of the Governor and 13 other members to be appointed annually by the President. Trial by jury was provided, and most Americans assumed that the

[6] Merrill Moores, 'Edward Livingston,' *Louisiana Historical Quarterly*, III (Oct. 1920), 486–97; Richmond *Enquirer*, 7 Oct. 1806; Adams, *History of the United States*, III, 300; Claiborne to Madison, 6 Aug. 1805, Carter, *Territorial Papers*, IX, 489, 753–4; *American Citizen*, 13 Oct. 1806, quoting extract from Natchez, 6 Sept.

[7] Statement of Lt. Col. Constant Freeman, 30 Dec. 1806, MS., New York Historical Society.

[8] *D.A.B.*, XI, 309; Adams, *History of the United States*, III, 296; Wilkinson statement, 6 Dec. 1806, unsigned, Burr MSS., L. of C.

[9] Grace King, *New Orleans, the Place and the People* (New York, 1899), 163–6.

common law was to be introduced in Louisiana; but the *émigré* lawyers from Santo Domingo had all been trained in the civil code of France, and they, aided and abetted by certain ambitious American lawyers, had other ideas.[10]

Dr. John Watkins, an American member of the Legislative Council, succeeded in having James Workman elected secretary of that body, though he was opposed by the governor. These two brought about the defeat of most of the legislation proposed by Claiborne, and had Edward Livingston and James Brown appointed to draft bills for the Council. Livingston and Brown, along with Workman and Watkins, framed most of the legislation which was actually passed, including a code of laws based upon what had been in use during the period of Spanish rule.[11] The resulting situation was that a population which spoke little but French had courts presided over by American judges; the Federal District Court used the common law, and the Territorial courts used Spanish law. Confusion could hardly have been more confounded.

In 1805 Congress provided that Orleans Territory was to have a General Assembly to be made up of an elected lower house and a small Legislative Council to be appointed by the President. At first the Creoles seemed to have been well pleased, for in 1806 they celebrated Washington's birthday with great éclat.[12] When the first session of the new legislature assembled at the end of March 1806, Creoles dominated both houses, Joseph Bellechasse, John Baptiste M'Carty, Jean Noël Destréhan, and Pierre Sauvé constituting the personnel of the upper chamber.[13]

Since the government was now organized under the terms of the Northwest Ordinance and this document called for the application of the common law in the Territorial courts, John B. Prevost, then the only judge of the Superior Court, appealed to the local bar for advice. Only Edward Livingston and Pierre Derbigny, a Santo

[10] Ben. Perley Poore, *Federal and State Constitutions*, I, 691–5.

[11] James Workman, *A Letter to the Respectable Citizens, Inhabitants of the County of Orleans, together with several letters to his Excellency Governor Claiborne, and other Documents relative to the Extraordinary Measures lately pursued in this Territory* (New Orleans, 1807), 7–12.

[12] Poore, *Federal and State Constitutions*, I, 696–7; *Louisiana Gazette*, 25 Feb. 1806.

[13] Ibid. 28 Feb. 1806.

Domingan refugee, favored the civil law; but the bar was directed by Judge Prevost to continue to use the code that had been drawn up by Workman and his friends.[14]

At the first session of the Assembly a bill was introduced to prescribe the legal works that were to be recognized as authoritative in courts of the Territory, and the list was composed of books on the French civil law. This was passed through both houses by large majorities, but the governor vetoed the measure. Then the majority chose James Brown and Moreau Lislet, another Santo Domingan refugee, to draft a civil code during the recess of the Assembly. When this was enacted, the governor applied his second veto and brought the wrath of the Assembly down upon his head. Two members of the Council, Sauvé and Destréhan, resigned in protest, and that body resolved that 'the General Assembly be immediately dissolved.'[15] The adjournment took place on 7 June, but before the members went home they took one more slap at the hapless governor; they elected Daniel Clark, his bitter enemy, to be the Territorial delegate in Congress.[16] A small group of French and American members even went so far as to concoct a secret scheme to depose Claiborne and install Wilkinson as military governor.[17]

Writing to a member of Congress to explain these events, one Jeremiah Brown said:

> Thus, my dear sir, this territory — appears to me at length on the eve of eternal alienation from the american union. — From the deliberations of all our public councils indeed one would suppose us rather in preparation to form a department of France than an american state. — And did but the general government know how high many a wayward pulse beats in this city at the present important moment they would not long hesitate to think with me that this is not the season when popular affection is to be conciliated by indulgence and concession.[18]

[14] Jeremiah Brown, *A Short Letter to a Member of Congress concerning the Territory of Orleans* (Washington, 1806), 1–12.

[15] Ibid. 19–22, 35–6; Gayarré, *Louisiana*, IV, 140–43; *Louisiana Gazette*, 5 June 1806, article translated from the *Telegraphe;* Claiborne to Jefferson, 4 June 1806, Carter, *Territorial Papers*, IX, 657–8; ibid. 641, 642, 650–57.

[16] Claiborne to Jefferson, 9 July 1806, ibid. IX, 670; *Louisiana Gazette*, 10 June 1806; Raleigh *Minerva*, 14 July 1806.

[17] Claiborne to Madison, 29 Jan. 1807, Burr MSS., L. of C.

[18] Jeremiah Brown, op. cit. 25–30.

The same writer described another incident which was not so important but more exciting at the moment than the matter of the civil code. Since there was, at the time, no Catholic bishop in New Orleans, supervision of the Church had been entrusted to the Reverend Patrick Walsh, an Irish-American, as Vicar-General. The Spanish Capuchin friar, Antonio de Sedella, had once been expelled from Louisiana by Governor Miró for trying to introduce the Inquisition, but he had returned and was now serving as curate of the parish of St. Louis, which included New Orleans. 'His little cabin cell, on the corner of St. Anthony's alley and Bourbon street, with its bare floor and pallet lying on a couple of planks, and rough table, crucifix, and chair, was the rock of spiritual authority in the city.' [19] One Sunday morning his congregation learned that he had been suspended from office by Father Walsh, and the faithful immediately foamed into fury. They voted Father Walsh out of office, 'elected' Père Antoine as parish priest, made the Cathedral of St. Louis the parish church, and chose churchwardens, with M. Jean Baptiste Castillon as 'President of the Fabrick of the Church of St. Louis.' Father Walsh appealed to the Superior Court of the Territory, but the new churchwardens objected to its authority. Castillon submitted the case to M. Portalis, minister of religious worship to the Emperor Napoleon, and on 5 June 1806 Portalis replied that the Pope had directed that the Bishop of Baltimore should administer the church at New Orleans pending the appointment of a local bishop, and that the Emperor had expressed his continuing interest in the inhabitants of Louisiana.[20] Governor Claiborne did not intervene except to require the Spanish friar to take the oath of allegiance to the United States, but Secretary of State Madison wrote him that the Catholics of New Orleans could not be allowed to have relations with the French Government and that the affair would be made the subject of conversations at Paris.[21] Father Walsh died shortly afterward as a result of the controversy, but Père Antoine, with white beard and venerable appearance, coarse brown cassock,

[19] Ibid. 26–8; Grace King, *New Orleans*, 176–7.

[20] Charleston *Courier*, 12 Jan. 1807; Richmond *Enquirer*, 7 Nov. 1806.

[21] Madison to Claiborne, 12 Nov. 1806, Carter, *Territorial Papers*, IX, 686; Gayarré, *Louisiana*, IV, 106–7.

rosary, sandaled feet, and broad-brimmed hat, remained the patron saint of the city until his death in 1829.[22]

Thus, with the Creoles perturbed and unhappy over their religious and legal situation, it is not surprising that Burr considered New Orleans the logical place to begin his revolution. His agent Dr. Erich Bollman later reported to Jefferson and Madison that the Colonel had divined Napoleon's project of absorbing Spain and her colonies and hoped to gain for himself a part of the crumbling empire.[23] In any such scheme, the strategic position of the city was crucial, and the political atmosphere of the place was inviting. Burr had told Anthony Merry that New Orleans was so resolved on separation 'and every way so completely prepared' that he was sure the revolution there would be accomplished without the shedding of blood, and it was there that the movement would commence.[24] The Conspirator thought he had gauged the situation accurately when he informed Merry that the disposition of the Westerners, and particularly the Louisianians, to separate themselves from the Union was so strong that an attempt at secession would doubtless succeed without any foreign help whatever.[25]

But before the movement could be set on foot in New Orleans, the conspirators suffered a serious defection there. The wealthy and influential Daniel Clark was one of Burr's most important followers. He had made two voyages to Vera Cruz to gather information about Mexico for Wilkinson and other friends. He was Burr's commercial agent in the city and the one to whom the stores for the expedition were to be consigned; and he was a heavy speculator in land claims derived from Spanish titles in Louisiana and Mississippi territories, and in West Florida.[26] On 16 June 1806, he wrote to Wilkinson: 'I have within these past 3 or 4 weeks found it necessary, in order to oppose Gov. Clabornes Creatures and schemes with success, to accept the appointment of Delegate from this Country to Congress.'

[22] King, *New Orleans*, 177.
[23] McCaleb, *Burr Conspiracy*, 62.
[24] Ibid. 46.
[25] Merry to Fox, 2 Nov. 1806, ibid. 65.
[26] Claiborne to Jefferson, 15 July 1806, Carter, *Territorial Papers*, IX, 172–4; Claiborne to Madison, 6 Aug. 1805, ibid., IX, 489; *National Intelligencer*, 16 Jan. 1807; William Dunbar to Clark, 14 Sept. 1806, MS., Louisiana Historical Museum; Gayarré, *Louisiana*, IV, 160; Philadelphia *Aurora*, 24 Jan. 1807.

He then went on to ask for information that might be useful in Washington, and promised that 'I shall shortly send you something respecting the Countries I have lately visited.' [27]

Yet later when the General stopped at Natchez on his way to take command at Natchitoches, Clark declined his invitation to visit him there, and paid no attention to his urgent appeals to join him on the Sabine front. This may be explained by the fact that about the middle of October, just as Clark was leaving for Congress, he called together his Creole friends, including Derbigny and Bellechasse, informed them of Burr's reputed designs, and urged them to take no part in the business but to support the Government. He strongly urged them and those members of the Legislature who were present, 'not to attend any call or meeting of either House, in case Colonel Burr should gain possession of the city, stating that such a measure would deservedly expose individuals concerned to punishment, and would occasion the ruin of the country.' [28]

This reveals something of Burr's plans but it throws no light upon the motives that produced the change in Clark's attitude. As Wilkinson also had decided to desert Burr, his and Clark's friendship was not interrupted, but there is no evidence that Clark had been able to anticipate the General's course. He appears to have made the decision independently, and it was not because he had lost any of his antipathy for Governor Claiborne. Only one explanation may be hazarded, and that is that Clark had always had political ambitions. He had been friendly toward the United States and had served as consul in New Orleans before the annexation of Louisiana, but when the new regime offered him no honorable post, his resentment was great and his hostility became active. Now that he was the Territorial Delegate in Congress, perhaps his ambition was satisfied and he was prepared to honor his oath of office.

On 27 September, Burr's agents, Dr. Bollman and James Alexander, arrived at New Orleans by sea from Philadelphia. Bollman hastened to send a special messenger to Natchitoches with the copy of Burr's cipher letter which had already been delivered by Swart-

[27] Clark to Wilkinson, 16 June 1806, Carter, *Territorial Papers*, IX, 660–61.

[28] Daniel Clark, *Proofs*, 142–50; Adams, *History of the United States*, III, 306–17; Claiborne to Madison, 5 Dec. 1806, Rowland, *Claiborne*, IV, 42–4.

wout. Wilkinson received this when he returned to Natchitoches on 6 November, after having made the 'neutral ground' agreement with Herrera, and on the same day he sent an answer to Bollman, but we do not know what message his letter conveyed.[29]

In New Orleans Alexander engaged in recruiting activities and predicted the separation of the Union; Bollman was busy preparing for the consummation of the plot, the object of which he later declared was to seize the French artillery in the city and take possession, by force if necessary, of the shipping in the river in order to convey Burr's expedition to Vera Cruz; then to revolutionize Mexico and set up a monarchy there.[30] Yet the arrival of the two agents caused no great stir, and it was not until Clark's disclosures to Bellechasse and others during October, and copies of the *Western World* came from Frankfort, that rumors began to multiply. When Colonel Freeman began repairing the defenses of the city, curiosity became rampant.[31]

The Spanish Governor Carondelet had originally constructed these defenses, which consisted of a wooden stockade enclosing the *Vieux Carré*, a fort at each corner of the square, a battery in the *Place d'Armes* [Jackson Square], and a fifth fort opposite it, just off Rampart Street. As soon as the Americans took possession, the stockade was torn down and used for firewood, and the forts were allowed to decay.[32] Now Freeman was repairing the two forts on the river and was undertaking to replace the stockade, which would enclose when completed only a part of the city, so greatly had it expanded. The military value of these repairs was seriously questioned at the time and it was suggested that they were intended to overawe the city rather than to protect it from attack.[33]

Governor Claiborne had returned to New Orleans from Natchi-

[29] Bollman to Wilkinson, 27 Sept. 1806, *A.S.P., Misc.*, I, 471; Statement of James Wilkinson, 18 Dec. 1806, ibid. I, 471; Adams, *History of the United States*, III, 295.

[30] Depositions of Dr. William Flood and John Nicholson, 26 Dec. 1806, Bacon, *Report*, 250–51; Deposition of M. Hooke and R. Davidson, 24 Dec. 1806, ibid. 349–50; *Letters and other Writings of James Madison* (Congress ed., 1865), II, 393–400.

[31] Adams, *History of the United States*, III, 307–8.

[32] Map of the *Vieux Carré* in G. William Nott, *A Tour of the Vieux Carré* (New Orleans, 1928).

[33] Dearborn to Constant Freeman, 27 Oct. 1806, Carter, *Territorial Papers*, IX, 683–4.

toches on 6 October and he at once began trying to recruit the local militia, but without much success. On 5 November, he wrote to President Jefferson: 'I observe in the Western Papers that Colo: Burr is in the Western States, and that a public Dinner was lately given him at Nashville; I know not the views of this Gentleman, but I fear they are political and of a kind the most injurious.' [34] His fears became more concrete when, on the 12th, he received the letter from General Wilkinson which began, 'you are surrounded by dangers of which you dream not, and the destruction of the American Union is seriously menaced . . .' [35] Claiborne at once transmitted this information to Secretary Madison and accused Daniel Clark of being one of the ring leaders, saying, 'he has often said that the Union could not last, and that had he Children he would impress early on their minds the expediency of a separation between the Atlantic and Western states. Dr. John Watkins and Mr. J. W. Gurley have heard these sentiments expressed by that Gentleman.' [36] Yet Cowles Mead suspected Wilkinson of complicity, and this suspicion was reinforced by Andrew Jackson's letter of 12 November, which Claiborne received on 5 December.[37]

The Governor's perturbation was not relieved when Wilkinson arrived on 25 November, for the General did not open his mind to him; and the people were more than ever mystified by the hurried repairs that were made on the fortifications of the city. The day after his arrival Wilkinson was visited by James Alexander, who brought Bollman's reply to the General's letter of 6 November, and offered to introduce that gentleman. Bollman had every reason to expect Wilkinson's co-operation, for the Brigadier had written that hostilities on the Sabine were unavoidable, and that his next dispatches would bring details of the first engagement. Edward Livingston called the same day and made the same offer, but both offers were declined. Claiborne also had a conference, and though he got no information, he was convinced that Wilkinson would co-operate with him in suppressing the threatened insurrection.

[34] Claiborne to Jefferson, 5 Nov. 1806, Rowland, *Claiborne*, IV, 33.

[35] Claiborne to Madison, 18 Nov. 1806, ibid. IV, 37.

[36] Claiborne to Madison, 18 Nov. 1806, ibid. IV, 36–7; Adams, *History of the United States*, III, 322.

[37] Claiborne to Jackson, 5 Dec. 1806, Carter, *Territorial Papers*, IX, 689–90.

Lowry Donaldson was another caller, and he was told that Burr harbored treasonable designs to dismember the Union; that New Orleans was in danger, and that the General had concluded a hasty compromise with the Spaniards in order to be able to withdraw his troops to defend the city. Wilkinson told Donaldson that Burr had many local agents 'who had already been assiduous in their visits and towards whom he was determined to act with cautious ambiguity' so as to gain possession of the whole plot. On the 27th, Dr. John Watkins, mayor of the city, called and informed the General that he would not be supported by the people of New Orleans if Burr came down. Meanwhile, the Brigadier went ahead with work on the fortifications while gathering all possible information from the conspirators.[38]

Finally, on 30 November, he called on Dr. Bollman in the hope of receiving news of Burr. He was informed that no dispatches had arrived though Bollman had sent Lieutenant Spence of the Navy with a letter for the Colonel, and he had heard of the arrival of the messenger at Nashville. The letter actually reached its destination at Lexington on 2 November. In answer to various questions, the agent said that Burr had gone too far to retreat; that he had written him about provisions and was expecting supplies from New York and Norfolk, where he had strong connections.[39] The next day the General disclosed his information about the conspiracy to Claiborne and Shaw, and on 4 December, he employed Silas Dinsmore, former agent to the Choctaw Indians, to go up the river and attempt to seize Burr, who was to be delivered to the President or to the governor of any state. Dinsmore was promised $5000 if he succeeded.[40]

The following day the General called again on Bollman, who now said that he had received a letter from Burr bearing the date of 30 October. In it the Colonel expressed great confidence in Wilkinson and said that he expected to reach Natchez on 20 December with

[38] Claiborne to Madison, 25 Nov. 1806, ibid. IX, 688–9; Deposition of James Wilkinson, 26 Dec. 1806, *A.S.P., Misc.* I, 472–3; ibid. 471; Philadelphia *Aurora*, 23 Feb., 16 July 1807; *Louisiana Gazette*, 20 Mar. 1807.

[39] *National Intelligencer*, 23 Jan. 1807; Philadelphia *Aurora*, 23 Feb. 1807; Deposition of James Wilkinson, *A.S.P., Misc.*, I, 469–70; Adams, *History of the United States*, III, 309.

[40] Claiborne to Shaw, 1 Dec. 1806, Rowland, *Claiborne*, IV, 38; McCaleb, *Burr Conspiracy*, 230.

2000 men, and that 4000 more were to follow. He would wait there until he heard from New Orleans, but he must visit the city in order to obtain shipping. Bollman suggested that the General might feign a defense in order to save face, whereupon Wilkinson told him that the conspirators would be opposed.[41]

This announcement closed the gates of information and marked the beginning of active operations on the part of the double-crossing General. His hand was now strengthened by the approach of the troops from Natchitoches. Eleven of the twelve companies stationed there had been ordered to New Orleans, where they arrived on 10 December; and a detachment called in from Fort Stoddert was expected to bring the number of available regulars up to 800, beside 180 in the battalion of New Orleans Volunteers. In addition, Wilkinson had made arrangements with the French consul to take over the brass cannon which the French Government still held in the city.[42] Governor Claiborne wished to call out the militia and march a force up the river to intercept Burr, but the General opposed the plan. On the other hand, he urged the governor to declare martial law, but the request was refused.[43] At the same time, 6 December, Wilkinson made an affidavit charging Swartwout and Ogden with treason and sent an officer to Fort Adams to arrest them.[44] Burr's cipher letter was used for this purpose, and now at last the General forwarded to Jefferson a translation of the document. He also sent his aide, Lieutenant Daniel Hughes, to arrest Lieutenant Jackson who commanded at Chickasaw Bluffs; and finished off his day's work by sending Governor Folch of West Florida an account of Burr's designs.[45]

[41] Statement of James Wilkinson, 14 Dec. 1807, *National Intelligencer*, 23 Jan. 1807, also in *A.S.P.*, *Misc.*, I, 469–70.

[42] Claiborne to Madison, 4 Dec. 1806, Rowland, *Claiborne*, IV, 40–41; same to same, 6 Dec. 1806, ibid. IV, 47–8; Dearborn to Wilkinson, 27 Nov. 1806, Bacon, *Report*, 408–9; Philadelphia *Aurora*, 12 Feb. 1807; *Writings of Thomas Jefferson* (Mem. ed.), III, 435.

[43] Wilkinson to Claiborne, 6 Dec. 1806, Rowland, *Claiborne*, IV, 46–7; same to same, 7 Dec. 1806, ibid. IV, 49.

[44] Henshaw, 'The Aaron Burr Conspiracy in the Ohio Valley,' loc. cit. 33; Affidavit of James Wilkinson (n.d.), printed pamphlet (incomplete), Chillicothe Papers, Record Group No. 21, National Archives; Adams, *History of the United States*, III, 320.

[45] Wilkinson to Folch and Morales, 6 Dec. 1806, A.G.I., Papeles de Cuba, leg. 2375, no. 93; Deposition of Daniel Hughes, 20 Jan. 1811, Bacon, *Report*, 303–18.

It seems strange that Wilkinson believed Burr's statement that he would have the co-operation of a British squadron and that Richard R. Keane had been sent to the West Indies to make the necessary arrangements. On 7 December, the General sent Lieutenant Swann of the Army to Jamaica with a letter addressed to Sir Eyre Coote. In it he said: 'having reason to believe — that — a British naval armament has been either promised or applied for to co-operate with and assist the insurgents — I deem it my official duty — to inform you that such a plan is contrary to the laws and constitution of these states — I shall, to the utmost of my ability, resist any foreign co-operation with the insurgents, either by land or sea.' Naturally, the Admiral was mystified.[46]

Two days later the members of the Chamber of Commerce were summoned to appear at the Governor's residence, which was the old house facing the levee near *Place d'Armes* where the Spanish governors had lived. They met at ten o'clock and were first addressed by the Governor, then by Wilkinson who informed them that Burr was planning to attack the city and that he would reach Natchez on the 20th with 2000 men out of the force of 7000 which he had raised. The merchants were asked to agree to a temporary embargo so that the seamen in port might be used, without resorting to an impressment, to man Captain Shaw's flotilla and the ships at the mouth of the river. This was readily agreed to and the merchants raised a fund to help defray the expense.[47]

This meeting represented a victory for Claiborne, for Wilkinson had desired an impressment. The merchants obviously appreciated the fact that they were taken into the confidence of the authorities, and though both the General and the Governor had previously harbored grave doubts regarding the loyalty of the Creoles, they now changed their minds and voiced their confidence in them.[48] It was

[46] Wilkinson to Sir Eyre Coote, 7 Dec. 1806, Bacon, *Report*, 416–17; Sir Eyre Coote to Wilkinson, 19 Jan. 1807, ibid. 418; Captain Shaw to Secretary of the Navy, 29 Nov. 1806, *American Citizen*, 3 Jan. 1807; *Louisiana Gazette*, 1 Sept. 1807; Charles Biddle, *Autobiography*, 411–12.

[47] Gayarré, *Louisiana*, IV, 166; Claiborne to Madison, 9 Dec. 1806, Rowland, *Claiborne*, IV, 52; Claiborne to Shaw, 9 Dec. 1806, ibid. IV, 67; Wilkinson to Jefferson, 14 Dec. 1806, Bacon, *Report*, 436–9; *Louisiana Gazette*, 12 Dec. 1806; Philadelphia *Aurora*, 14 Jan. 1807.

[48] Claiborne to Madison, 9 Dec. 1806, Rowland, *Claiborne*, IV, 50–52; McCaleb, *Burr Conspiracy*, 200.

probably because of this new attitude that the battalion of Orleans Volunteers was ordered to prepare for immediate service.[49] The day after the meeting, Wilkinson wrote to Daniel Clark, 'Thank God your advice to Bellechasse, if your character was not a sufficient guarantee, would vindicate you against any foul imputation.'[50] He was doubtless right in thinking that Clark's advice had helped to promote good relations, and it may have had something to do with the fact that not a single native Creole was involved in the conspiracy.[51] Wilkinson was so reassured that he now talked of marching his troops up the river to intercept Burr, and on 6 January it was announced at the Coffee House that all ship owners should have their vessels ready to put out into the stream at a moment's notice in order to intercept the conspirator should he reach Natchez, though the General did not think the move would actually be necessary. At the same time the governor called on the inhabitants above New Orleans to furnish one-tenth of their laboring Negroes to assist in the completion of the fortifications of the city.[52] But the excitement soon died down; work on the fortifications became perfunctory, and instead of devoting his time to military matters, the General became completely absorbed in an effort to capture the Colonel's agents who were within his reach.

Wilkinson had been urging Claiborne to suspend the writ of habeas corpus and declare martial law, but the Governor had steadfastly refused to do so.[53] This angered the General, and on 14 December he decided to take matters into his own hands and accordingly ordered the arrest of Dr. Bollman. The next day Bollman's associate, James Alexander, applied to Judge William Sprigg of the Superior Court for a writ of habeas corpus. Action was put off until the next day when Edward Livingston appeared in court with Alexander, and the writ was granted. Meanwhile Wilkinson had

[49] *Louisiana Gazette*, 9 Dec. 1806; Gayarré, *Louisiana*, IV, 166.

[50] Wilkinson to Clark, 10 Dec. 1806, Adams, *History of the United States*, III, 321.

[51] John P. Kennedy, *Memoirs of the Life of William Wirt* (Philadelphia, 1850), I, 151.

[52] Philadelphia *Aurora*, 26 Jan. 1807, quoting letter from New Orleans, 9 Dec. 1806; *Louisiana Gazette*, 6 Jan. 1807; Proclamation by Governor Claiborne, 6 Jan. 1807, Rowland, *Claiborne*, IV, 69; ibid. 94–5.

[53] Claiborne to Madison, 17 Dec. 1806, ibid. IV, 68; Claiborne to Wilkinson, 25 Dec. 1806, ibid. IV, 69; Gayarré, *Louisiana*, IV, 163–5.

removed his prisoner beyond the jurisdiction of the court and on the 18th made return that Bollman was arrested on a charge of misprision of treason and was being delivered to the President of the United States.[54]

By this time Swartwout and Ogden had been brought down to New Orleans, and on the 16th it was learned that the latter was confined on board the bomb ketch *Aetna* opposite the city. The Irish attorney, Lewis Kerr, now applied to Judge Workman for a writ of habeas corpus. This was granted and Ogden was accordingly released by Captain Shaw on advice of Governor Claiborne. Swartwout was confined on the same boat with Ogden, but when a writ was issued for his release, Wilkinson had him removed beyond the jurisdiction of the court.[55] Meanwhile, Alexander made the mistake of declaring that if Burr were a traitor, Wilkinson also was one. The General had him arrested on 19 December, and at the same time Ogden was again taken into custody. Writs were sworn out for them, and when Wilkinson failed to make sufficient return, an attachment against his person was applied for by Edward Livingston. Judge Workman applied to the governor to know whether he would enforce the order of the court, and when Claiborne declined to attempt the use of force against the Commanding General of the Army, Workman resigned his post.[56]

But before the Judge quitted the bench, he had more trouble with the General, who was busy collecting information against Burr's friends in New Orleans. Lieutenant William A. Murray gave evidence relating to the Mexican Association, and on 9 January, Wilkinson wrote to Jefferson that he had discovered that Workman 'had proposed to three persons of distinction, the idea of establishing the independence of this territory, and afterwards revolutionizing Mexico.' Wilkinson then assembled the individuals who had been named, and when he had confronted them with Murray's testimony, 'They not only confirmed the information I had received, — but declared that — they were ready to attest to the facts, when

[54] Ibid. IV, 170.

[55] Schachner, *Burr*, 368; Certificate of Captain Shaw, Rowland, *Claiborne*, IV, 69–70.

[56] James Workman, op. cit. 29; Wilkinson to Claiborne, 16 Dec. 1806, Rowland, *Claiborne*, IV, 62; Beveridge, *Marshall*, III, 335.

regularly called on in a court of justice.'[57] Claiborne made similar accusations against Workman, and on 12 January 1807, the Judge and Lewis Kerr, a justice of the peace for Orleans County, were presented by a grand jury to the Superior Court for having attempted, about twelve months previously, to engage army officers and citizens of the Territory in a plan to seize the banks in the city and the vessels in the harbor, then to capture Baton Rouge and march on Mobile, where a marine force was to join them in organizing an expedition to invade Mexico.[58] The legislature met on the same day and Wilkinson appeared before that body to demand a suspension of the writ of habeas corpus. The Assembly not only failed to adopt this measure but demanded an investigation of the Brigadier's conduct and, led by Dr. John Watkins and John Hughes, debated a memorial to Congress condemning his actions. Despite this rebuff, Wilkinson had Workman and Kerr arrested on the 14th, but both were soon released on the usual writ.[59]

Yet another and more sensational arrest was made the same day. Wilkinson's long-time friend, John Adair, who was to have been Burr's chief lieutenant in New Orleans, had left the Colonel in Nashville and had ridden with a servant through the Indian country in order to visit some of the leading men in the settlements above Mobile and Pascagoula bays. Though the Spaniards were allowed free access up the Mississippi to Baton Rouge, at Mobile they were obstructing access of the Americans to the sea; and those rough backwoodsmen would have been only too glad to take matters into their own hands.[60]

While spending several days at the home of a settler on Pascagoula River, Adair saw New Orleans papers which announced the

[57] Wilkinson to Jefferson, 9 Jan. 1807, Bacon, *Report*, 445.

[58] [Edward Livingston?] 'Faithful Picture of the Political Situation of New Orleans at the Close of the Last and the Beginning of the Present Year, 1807' (Boston, 1808, reprinted from the original New Orleans ed.), *Louisiana Historical Quarterly*, XI (July 1928), 410–13; Indictment by the Superior Court, 12 Jan. 1807, Rowland, *Claiborne*, IV, 170–73.

[59] [Livingston?] 'Faithful Picture,' loc. cit. 417–20; *Debate in the House of Representatives of the Territory of Orleans on a Memorial to Congress, Respecting the Illegal Conduct of General Wilkinson* (New Orleans, 1807); Gayarré, *Louisiana*, IV, 182; McCaleb, *Burr Conspiracy*, 142–3, 195–7; Beveridge, *Marshall*, III, 363–4.

[60] *National Intelligencer*, 24 July 1807, affidavits of William Bohannon and Henry Snellgrove; Bowers, *Jefferson in Power*, 391.

presence of Wilkinson in that city, and surmised that the General had taken possession with Spanish support. Traveling by canoe the rest of the way, the Kentuckian reached his destination about noon on 14 January, and took lodgings at Madame Fourage's boarding house. Here Judge Prevost called on him within the hour and told him that 'Col. Burr would be in town in Three days after him; and that it would soon be discovered if the constitution and justice would prevail, or that of the usurpation of power and tyranny manifested in the measures at present adopted.' Prevost then proceeded to the Coffee House where he met Captain Shaw and William Thorp and told them of his meeting with Adair. Shaw sent his servant to inform Wilkinson, who dispatched Colonel Kingsbury and 120 men to the boarding house where Adair was arrested just as he was sitting down to dinner about three o'clock.[61] The prisoner's baggage was immediately seized and sent to headquarters. How frantically the harried Brigadier must have searched through it for that incriminating letter he wrote from Natchitoches in which he labeled himself a 'Spanish intriguer'!

Adair was kept under guard until about two o'clock the next day when he was put aboard a schooner and taken 25 miles down the river. Here he was put ashore in the swamp and kept in a tent until the 22nd, when he was again put aboard ship and sent to Baltimore.[62] The General was taking no chances with the law in this case, and Swartwout was soon sent to the same city while Bollman was shipped off to Charleston. Adair later said that Wilkinson could not have arrested him if he had had 48 hours in New Orleans; and the General himself stated, 'if Adair had been permitted the liberty of the city for twenty-four hours . . . supported by 500 boatmen, and the mass of disaffection which infests this city, he would infallibly have produced an insurrection . . .'[63] John W. Gurley, the attorney general, told Wilkinson that Judge Workman had sounded

[61] Deposition of Captain Shaw and William Thorp, 16 Apr. 1807, Bacon, *Report*, 346–7; Address of John Adair, 1 Mar. 1807, Richmond *Enquirer*, 10 Mar. 1807; *Louisiana Gazette*, 26 Feb. 1808; Gayarré, *Louisiana*, IV, 174–8; Adams, *History of the United States*, III, 324.

[62] Claiborne to Madison, 15 Jan. 1807, Rowland, *Claiborne*, IV, 95–7; Beveridge, *Marshall*, III, 335ff.

[63] Wilkinson to Jefferson, 18 Jan. 1807, Bacon, *Report*, 446–7; Adams, *History of the United States*, III, 324.

him out on raising a force to depose the existing authorities, and in case of success to make John Brown governor.[64] But the General had scotched any such plans by his highhanded arrests.

Wilkinson was widely condemned for his conduct, and one New Orleans writer said that he had refused to take the advice of good citizens such as Benjamin Morgan and Mr. Saul [Soulé] of the United States Branch Bank; and instead of confining scores of Burr's confederates, who were numerous and to be found principally among the 'notables of the American circle . . . who would in any other country be decapitated, he has seized and sent off only a few of the best known, most active, decided partisans of the *arch-traitor* . . . The vociferators against these measures are the celebrated *Edward Livingston*, damned to everlasting fame, his protégé *P. L. Jones*, the attorney Ellery, John Smith the clerk of the Superior Court, and a man by the name of Parrot,' a member of the Louisiana House of Representatives.[65] This observer was quite correct: the most powerful and prominent of the local conspirators were permitted to escape the net of the chameleon Brigadier.

[64] *Louisiana Gazette*, 23 Feb. 1807, 26 Feb. 1808; Wilkinson to Jefferson, 18 Jan. 1807, Bacon, *Report*, 446–9.

[65] Philadelphia *Aurora*, 23 Feb. 1807.

Chapter XII

JEFFERSON AND BURR

NO PHASE of the Conspiracy is quite so puzzling as the manner in which President Jefferson chose to deal with it. Because of his delay in taking measures to put a stop to Burr's proceedings, he was often charged by his contemporaries with being a party to the plot. Yet there appears to be no reason to look upon these accusations in any other light than as partisan propaganda. It is true that the President loved the Spaniards as little as he loved Burr, and if he could have been sure that the Colonel was plotting only against them, he might well have been satisfied to please his Western constituents by keeping his hands off; but there never was a time when he could have been sure of this. His earliest warnings assured him that it was American territory which was threatened, and it was not until he received General Wilkinson's letter from the Sabine that the plot was pictured as being directed primarily against Spain. Whenever the danger to the American West was presented, the President discounted it by professing to place complete confidence in the patriotism of the transmontane population. This confidence was in the main justified by eventualities, and Jefferson was doubtless sincere in expressing it, but it does not furnish a complete explanation of the policy he pursued. In fact, no such explanation is possible, but in order to throw some light upon the means and motives of the President, it would seem well at this point to review the successive steps which he took in dealing with the Conspiracy.

As has already been stated, the first definite information which

Jefferson received concerning the Conspiracy was sent on 10 January 1806, by Joseph Hamilton Daveiss, District Attorney of Kentucky. At this time Daveiss thought that the separation of the American West was the only object of the plot, but by 14 July he had become convinced that an attack on the Spanish provinces was also planned. At first Jefferson was keenly interested and asked for all possible information, including the names of the conspirators; but when he learned that the situation in Kentucky was quite the reverse of that in all other sections of the country, that Burr's supporters were all Republicans and his opponents all Federalists, he at once lost interest in Daveiss' disclosures. When the District Attorney brought Burr and Adair before the grand jury, he was able to charge them only with planning an invasion of Mexico because there was no law making it illegal to plot insurrection against the United States. When Daveiss failed to get indictments, Jefferson condemned his proceedings as ill-advised and badly timed, and the Kentuckian was presently removed from his post. Apparently the President was not interested in preventive measures.[1]

By late summer information was coming in from sources that the Administration might be expected to take more seriously. On 10 August, Commodore Thomas Truxton, whom Burr had tried to enlist in his enterprise, sent Jefferson a detailed plan for counteracting the plot, but no attention was paid to this warning.[2] On 15 September, George Morgan's letter stating that the Colonel planned to separate the Western states from the Union was received. The President later said that this was the first news of the conspiracy which had reached him, but he considered it too vague and general to warrant action.[3] On 2 September, Yrujo wrote to Cevallos that the Kentucky newspaper called the *Western World* was clamoring about the revival of the old plan to separate the West with the aid of Spain, and he thought that if the report were true, the Federal Government would be unable to take any effective measures to counteract the movement. Turreau concurred in Yrujo's opinions,

[1] Daveiss, *View*, 58.

[2] Truxton to Jefferson, 10 Aug. 1806, Jefferson Papers, L. of C.

[3] Jefferson to George Morgan, 26 Mar. 1807, *The Writings of Thomas Jefferson*, (Mem. ed.), XI, 173–4; ibid. III, 428–9.

and they both professed to believe that there was no serious threat to Spanish territory.[4]

The complacency of the Administration ended, however, when Jefferson received Postmaster-General Gideon Granger's letter of 16 October, giving an account of the testimony of 'General' William Eaton, who indicated that Burr had the double objective of separating the West and invading Mexico and accused Wilkinson of being deeply implicated in the plot.[5] As a direct result of this communication, a meeting of the Cabinet was held on 22 October. Here it was announced to the heads of departments that the Spaniards had moved more than 1000 men to Bayou Pierre, and it was ordered that Mississippi and Orleans territories be called on to send 500 mounted volunteers to reinforce Wilkinson on the Sabine. This having been settled, the information from Eaton and others concerning Burr was brought up, and it was decided to write confidential letters to the Western governors or district attorneys directing them to have the Colonel watched and to arrest him in case he committed any overt act. Since Wilkinson had been accused by both Eaton and Burr, the Cabinet discussed the question about what should be done with him, but no action on the point was taken at this time or two days later when the matter was again discussed.[6] It was at this Cabinet meeting of the 24th, however, that it was decided to send John Graham to trail Burr through Kentucky and have him arrested in case he should lay himself liable. At the same time it was resolved that Captains Preble and Decatur be sent to New Orleans to take command of the naval forces there, the former to have great 'discretionary powers,' but on the next day, no further news of Burr's operations having been received, this latter order was countermanded.[7]

There is something passing strange about this action of the Cabinet. Wilkinson was believed to be, or about to be, at war with the

[4] Yrujo to Cevallos, 2 Sept. 1806, A.H.N., Est., leg. 5545, exp. 15, no. 715, 481–3; Turreau to Talleyrand, (?) Nov. 1806, A.E., Cor. Pol., E.U., LIX, 292.

[5] Jefferson to Granger, 9 Mar. 1814, *Writings of Thomas Jefferson* (Mem. ed.), XIV, 114–15.

[6] Ibid. I, 458–61; Dearborn to Col. Constant Freeman, 27 Oct. 1806, Carter, *Territorial Papers*, IX, 683–4.

[7] *Writings of Thomas Jefferson* (Mem. ed.), I, 461–2.

Spaniards on the Sabine, and there was strong evidence to the effect that he was in league with Burr who was stirring up trouble along the Ohio, yet the territories most threatened were required to send their militia to reinforce the General on the distant Sabine, and a single individual was sent out to stop Burr's operations. Making all due allowance for Jefferson's confidence in the loyalty of the Western people, it is still difficult to understand the weakness of the measures he took against Burr, or the confidence placed in General Wilkinson. It is clear, however, that he was anxious not to alarm the country before the Colonel had been given the opportunity to hang himself, and it is probable that he realized he would be powerless to handle Wilkinson in case the General should decide to play the role of traitor. The President knew that both men could become very dangerous if he should play the wrong card.

Within ten days after the Cabinet had made its decision, the Administration began to show signs of alarm. On 3 November, Jefferson wrote to Thomas Mann Randolph, his son-in-law, saying: 'In the quarter of Natchitoches I believe every thing will remain quiet. Burr is unquestionably very actively engaged in the westward in preparations to sever that from this part of the Union. We learn that he is actually building 10 or 15 boats able to take a large gun and fit for the navigation of those waters. We give him all the attention our situation admits; as yet we have no legal proof of any overt act which the law can lay hold of.' [8]

It is not improbable that the thinking of the Administration was influenced by William Duane, editor of the Philadelphia *Aurora*. For some time he had been insisting that the Spaniards were in league with Burr and at about this time he wrote:

> very probably he [Burr] may be at the head of the party which *Granger* said would go into the *Yazoo country* and occupy it by the force of arms, and that there may be an understanding through *Yrujo* with the Spanish movements as a diversion for the Yazoo, is not impossible. *Grandpré* [Spanish commandant of Baton Rouge] — very recently declared that the proceedings, of the Governor of *Texas* (on the Sabine) [Cordero who commanded] were wholly unauthorized by the court of Spain, and were taken only to cover some *private speculation* of the Spanish governor. It is well known that a very frequent and close intercourse was

[8] Ibid. XVIII, 249–50.

maintained between Mr. Burr when last in this city, and the Spanish Marquis *Yrujo*, and it is also very certain that it was through Dayton or Burr, that Yrujo obtained the intelligence of the secret proceedings of Congress.[9]

Duane did not believe that Spain would be capable of waging war in America after the defeat of the Spanish and French fleets by Nelson at the Battle of Trafalgar on 21 October 1805. His views were shared, at least in part, by D. M. Erskine, the British minister — Merry's successor — who wrote to Lord Howick on 6 January 1807, that 'Spain is said to be concerned in exciting these plots to endeavor to effectuate a division of the Western country from the Union.' [10] Three days earlier John Randolph wrote to George Hay that 'no man in his senses can doubt that the schemes of Burr are now carrying on in concert with the cabinet of Madrid and with Spanish money.' [11]

The Administration must have been thoroughly alarmed, for on 8 November it completely reversed its policy. The Cabinet then declared that 'The great probability of an amicable and early settlement of our difficulties with Spain at Paris has rendered the executive extremely desirous of avoiding hostilities,' which it is feared have begun. If so, it is ordered 'that hostilities shall be suspended — that the Sabine shall be accepted as the temporary boundary.' Neither side was to establish any new posts between Nacogdoches and Natchitoches, but the Spaniards were to be allowed to maintain their garrison at Bayou Pierre.[12] On the same day, Secretary of War Dearborn transmitted these orders to General Wilkinson, and wrote to Captain Thomas Swaine that,

If you have received any orders from the Genl. to act offensively against Mobile, or any other Spanish Post, East of Pearl River, you will on receipt of this, suspend any such act until further Orders, and remain at your Post, prepared only to act on the defensive. And if you shall have heard of any actual hostilities between the troops of the United States and those of his Catholic Majesty, westward of the Mississippi, you will, without delay, send a suitable Officer to Mobeile [*sic*], with an assur-

[9] Philadelphia *Aurora*, 5 Nov. 1806.
[10] McCaleb, *Burr Conspiracy*, 244.
[11] John Randolph to George Hay, 3 Jan. 1807, Leigh P. Williams MSS., Alderman Library, U. Va.
[12] Royal O. Shreve, *The Finished Scoundrel* (Indianapolis, 1933), 172.

ance that, the President of the United States has taken measures for preventing a continuance of such hostilities and for restoring harmony between the troops of the United States and his Catholic Majesty, and persuaded himself that the measures taken will have the desired affect, unless prevented by the indisposition of Spanish Officers to a friendly adjustment.[13]

The Cabinet was less than sincere in pretending that this reversal of policy had been brought about by the prospect of a diplomatic adjustment of our differences with Spain.[14] No such adjustment was in prospect and the retreat from the position that had been taken in regard to the Sabine boundary was due solely to the fear that Burr, possibly in alliance with Spanish colonial officials, might be able to succeed in his designs. The President had no reason to be sure that Wilkinson would obey orders, for he had previously disobeyed them, but he undoubtedly hoped that by compromising with Spain on the boundary question and thus depriving the General of an opportunity to invade Mexico, he might be induced to turn his forces against Burr.

In view of this drastic action, it is amazing to find Jefferson writing to editor Duane on 24 November to the effect that: 'in the Western quarter greater things have been meditated; but they will probably end in an attempt upon the public lands, & the question will be whether we have authority legally to oppose them by force.'[15] Duane had written him urging that he 'settle the public feeling on the subject' of the conspiracy;[16] that is, issue a proclamation condemning it, but the President was not yet ready to warn the public. He still wanted Burr to have the opportunity to commit an act of treason.

But tomorrow was another day, for then Lieutenant Thomas A. Smith galloped up to the President's mansion with Wilkinson's letter of 21 October, written from Natchitoches. The communication was verbose and vague; it conveyed no information which Jefferson

[13] Secretary of War to Thomas Swaine, 8 Nov. 1806, Carter, *Territorial Papers*, v, 485–6; same to Wilkinson, 8 Nov. 1806, Bacon, *Report*, 404–8; Schachner, *Burr*, 341.

[14] Cox, *West Florida Controversy*, 264–5.

[15] Jefferson to Duane, 24 Nov. 1806, Jefferson Papers, L. of C.

[16] McCaleb, *Burr Conspiracy*, 164.

did not already have — not nearly as much, in fact — but it created a new political situation.

When the General penned his missive, he stood in a very precarious situation. He was planning to march the next day to the Sabine and propose the terms of his 'neutral ground' agreement, but the Spanish commander had said that the march would be resisted. Therefore, peace and war hung in the balance and Wilkinson had told Colonel Freeman that he expected war.[17] He knew that Burr was making his final preparations on the Ohio, and it seems certain that he actually expected him to descend the river with a force of from 1000 to 1500 men and to be supported by a British naval force in the Mississippi. If the Spaniards should decide to fight, there would be no force available to check the progress of Burr's expedition, and Wilkinson knew that he would be charged with having cooperated with the conspirators. Therefore, in order to protect himself, he sent his warning message to the President. That assured him a certain degree of safety in any turn of events.[18]

Though Wilkinson's letter brought Jefferson no new information concerning the Conspiracy, it revealed the General's hand and made it impossible for the President to delay any longer taking a public stand. With a warning from the commander of the Army, he would now have to issue a proclamation and place himself on record before the people. Before the sun had set, he called the Cabinet together, but General Dearborn excused himself on the ground that he was unwell. The President then revealed to the other three heads of departments the contents of Wilkinson's communication, and it was agreed that a proclamation should be issued and orders sent to all posts on the Ohio and Mississippi from Pittsburgh to New Orleans, directing that all preparations for an expedition against Spanish territory be broken up with the aid of militia and that arrests be made where evidence warranted such action. It is surprising that Secretary Dearborn was directed 'to write to General [Andrew?] Jackson, supposed to be the General of the Brigade on the Virginia side of the [Ohio] river, to furnish any aid of militia which may be

[17] Wilkinson, *Memoirs*, II, app. 101.
[18] Burr MSS., L. of C.

necessary —.' At New Orleans, General Wilkinson was to 'direct the stations of the armed vessels, and if the arrangements with the Spaniards will permit him to withdraw, let him dispose of his force as he thinks best to prevent any such expedition, or any attempt on New Orleans, or any of the posts or military stores of the United States.'[19]

In compliance with these instructions, Dearborn wrote to Wilkinson two days later saying that he had agreed with the French minister to take over the brass cannon which the French still possessed in New Orleans, and ordering the General to direct the stationing of the armed vessels in the Mississippi and Lake Pontchartrain, and to withdraw part of his troops to New Orleans if arrangements with the Spaniards should permit. He was also to arrest all suspicious persons in or about his post, 'and if not amenable to military law, [they were] to be delivered over to the civil authority . . .' For the General's information, Dearborn went on to say that: 'Col Burr is generally considered the head, but his real object is doubtful. Your name has been very frequently associated with Burr, Dayton and others, and the new editions of the old stories lately published in Kentucky increased suspicions.'[20]

On the same day, 27 November, the President issued his proclamation, declaring that 'information has been received that sundry persons — are conspiring and confederating together to begin — a military expedition or enterprise against the dominions of Spain'; and 'warning and enjoining all faithful citizens who have been led without due knowledge or consideration to participate in the said unlawful enterprise to withdraw from the same without delay —'[21] No charge was made that the separation of the West was contemplated, and Burr was not even named!

That the public knew more than the President stated is indicated by the entries which Senator Plumer made in his journal during the next two days:

> Reports have for some time circulated from one end of the United States to the other, that Aaron Burr — with others, in the western States are

[19] *Writings of Thomas Jefferson* (Mem. ed.), I, 463–4.
[20] Dearborn to Wilkinson, 27 Nov. 1806, Bacon, *Report*, 408–9.
[21] James D. Richardson, *Messages and Papers of the Presidents*, I, 393–4.

> preparing gun boats, provisions, money, men, &c to make war upon the Spaniards in South America — that his intention is to establish a new empire in the western world & That he contemplates forming this Empire from South America & the western States of North America — Yesterday the President of the United States issued a proclamation, which is made public today. — There are many things reported agt Mr. Burr — some of them too foolish for him to be guilty of. Wm. Eaton has certified that Mr. Burr last winter desired him (Eaton) to accept of a commission under Burr — That Burr told Eaton that General Wilkinson was second in command — & under him, & that Eaton should be third. — At Philadelphia three things were stated to me — 1. That Burr had spent some time in that city — & had been observed frequently visiting in a private manner the Marquiss De Yrujo. 2d That a few of his confidential friends had given dinners to a particular class of young enterprizing men of good families — that Burr was present. 3d — That 2 or 3 young men presented an affidavit to the Chief Justice of Pennsylvania Tilghman stating that Burr had made overtures to them to engage in a secret expedition — But Tilghman declined swearing them —. This information was given me by Caesar Augustus Rodney, Esq. — [22]

Rodney, who was soon to be appointed attorney general, was the son of Judge Thomas Rodney of Mississippi Territory.

In view of reports of this kind, the proclamation appeared to be a very weak document, but the President had reasons for his moderation. There was no law against fomenting rebellion, and there was no reason to think that Burr had yet committed an overt act. But it was an offense to prepare a filibustering expedition and it seemed certain that such preparations had been made. The President had no desire to charge the Colonel with an offense that in all probability could not be proved against him, and thereby make a martyr of him. He ardently desired to trap his old rival in an act of treason, but since Wilkinson had forced the issue before this seemed possible, he had to make the best of the situation and confine his accusation to the lesser offense. Of course it was possible that Burr might yet lay himself liable to the graver charge.

In his annual message, delivered to Congress on 2 December, Jefferson referred to the situation on the Sabine, saying that Wilkinson had proposed that stream as the temporary boundary, and that the Spaniards had withdrawn their forces behind it, but that no

[22] Plumer, *Memorandum*, 515, 517.

answer to the General's proposition had yet been received. He then mentioned the Conspiracy almost casually, saying only that 'a great number of private individuals were combining together, arming and organizing themselves contrary to law, to carry on a military expedition against the territories of Spain, —.' Still nothing was said of Burr, or about a plan to divide the Union.[23]

In the face of the attitude of the Administration, it was becoming increasingly difficult for Yrujo to maintain that Burr's only object was the separation of the Western states and territories. He admitted that the Colonel had 'conceived the chimerical project of making an expedition against Mexico' because of its appeal to the Western Americans, but he still found it difficult to believe that so clever a man as Burr would seriously consider such a plan without being able to provide naval support.[24] By 4 December, De Pestre, whom the Marquis described as a French officer, had come with letters from Burr to reassure the Spanish agent, who was, by this time, apparently becoming suspicious.[25]

And so was the Administration. On 8 December, Duane gave Jefferson an account of a Mr. Gardette who had been a captain in the French army and who was now said to be an associate of Burr.[26] Somewhat later Madison received an anonymous letter charging that there was a close connection between Burr and Yrujo. Such evidence is not too convincing, but Madison was led to suggest that the Spanish Marquis was acting under the influence of France or the French party in the Spanish Government, and that he had agreed to a plan for making out of the Spanish possessions in America a subconfederate state for France with Burr at its head.[27] Whatever reasons the Secretary of State may have had for coming to this conclusion, it is difficult to explain in any other way the part which Yrujo played in this affair.

Six weeks went by and the air was thick with rumors and reports, but Congress had heard nothing from the President since his mes-

[23] Richardson, *Messages*, I, 349.

[24] Yrujo to Cevallos, 29 Nov. 1806, A.H.N., Est., leg. 5546, apartado I, no. 773, 181–92.

[25] Same to same, 4 Dec. 1806, ibid. no. 776, 208–16.

[26] Duane to Jefferson, 8 Dec. 1806, Jefferson Papers, L. of C.

[27] Anon. to Madison, received 5 Feb. 1807, ibid.

sage of 2 December. John Randolph was becoming increasingly impatient, and on 16 January 1807, he persuaded the House to pass a resolution calling on Jefferson to transmit all available information on the subject of the conspiracy.[28]

Six days later the President answered this request by a special message to Congress. He said that 'Some time in the latter part of September, I received intimations that designs were in agitation in the western country, unlawful and unfriendly to the peace of the Union; and that the prime mover in these was Aaron Burr, — It was not until the latter part of October, that the objects of the conspiracy began to be perceived, but still so blended and involved in mystery that nothing distinct could be singled out for pursuit.'[29] But at this time John Graham was sent to investigate. Thus Jefferson, according to his own statement, ignored the information sent him by Joseph Hamilton Daveiss, passed over that given him by George Morgan, and acted only when Gideon Granger sent 'General' William Eaton's testimony.

He then went on to say that 'on the 8th of November, instructions were forwarded to General Wilkinson to hasten an accommodation with the Spanish commander on the Sabine, and as soon as that was effected, to fall back with his principal force to the hither bank of the Mississippi,' but by his letter of 21 October, received on 25 November,

> we learn that a confidential agent of Aaron Burr had been deputed to him, with communications partly written in cypher and partly oral, explaining his designs, —. The general, with the honor of a soldier and fidelity of a good citizen, immediately despatched a trusty officer to me with information of what had passed, —. The general's letter, — and some other information received a few days earlier, when brought together, developed Burr's general designs, different parts of which only had been revealed to different informants. It appeared that he contemplated two distinct objects, which might be carried on either jointly or separately, and either the one or the other first, as circumstances should direct. One of these was the severance of the Union of these States by the Alleghany mountains; the other, an attack on Mexico.[30]

[28] John Randolph to George Hay, 3 Jan. 1807, Leigh P. Williams MSS., Alderman Library, U. Va.; Resolution of the House of Representatives, 16 Jan. 1807, Everett D. Graff Collection.

[29] *Writings of Thomas Jefferson* (Mem. ed.), III, 428–9.

[30] Ibid. 430–31.

It is noteworthy that the President gave Wilkinson credit for information sent by others and that he went out of his way to compliment that widely suspected character for having done considerably less than his duty. This attitude is difficult, if not impossible, to explain, and it helps to account for the bitterness felt toward Jefferson by John Randolph and many others in connection with this affair. Naturally the President was grateful for the assistance rendered, perhaps unexpectedly, by the General at this crucial moment, but when he spoke of his 'honor' and 'fidelity,' there were many men of high standing who knew that the preening and fawning Wilkinson was being misrepresented. Nearly a month before this message was sent to Congress, Senator Plumer had written: 'Governor Wilkinson — has long been in habits of intimacy with Burr, — I never had much confidence in the integrity of this same general. I do not know what offers may have been made him to betray his trust. But it is singular that the subtil [*sic*] cunning Burr should develope his treasonable designs to such men as James Wilkinson, Thomas Truxton & William Eaton. Three vainer men I never saw — Hasty, imprudent, unguarded men — incapable of retaining a secret.' [31] On 12 January 1807, he wrote: 'All parties & all classes of people who are informed, appear to distrust Genl Wilkinson the commander of our armies. — his friends, distrust him — Their confidence in him is not for his virtues — but they hope his *interest* will restrain him from committing treason.' [32] Even Dearborn wrote to Wilkinson himself that 'Your name was, on all occasions, placed next to Burr's, by himself and by many of his agents and abettors.' [33]

The Presidential message went on to inform Congress that Burr, having found the West firmly attached to the Union, 'determined to seize on New Orleans, plunder the bank there, possess himself of the military and naval stores, and proceed on his expedition to Mexico; and to this object all his means and preparations were now directed.' This, said the President, was the gist of his information when he issued his proclamation on 27 November; but John Graham

[31] Plumer, *Memorandum*, 542.
[32] Ibid. 569.
[33] Dearborn to Wilkinson, 21 Jan. 1807, Bacon, *Report*, 410–14.

and Governor Tiffin had brought about the seizure of Blennerhassett's boats before the proclamation reached Marietta. In spite of this, some boats escaped and passed over the Falls of the Ohio, and information had just been received that Burr had descended the Cumberland with two boats on 22 December. Whether any of these boats could be stopped was uncertain, but Jefferson did not think that so small a force could threaten serious danger to New Orleans.

Finally, the President stated that letters from General Wilkinson announced that he had arrested three of Burr's agents in New Orleans. One of them, Ogden, had been liberated on habeas corpus proceedings, but the other two, Bollman and Swartwout, were being sent on to Washington. The President probably did not know that these arrests had been made illegally, but he was too good a lawyer not to know that the accused parties had a right to be tried in the jurisdiction where their alleged offenses had been committed. This placed him in an embarrassing position, but Wilkinson had to be supported, and he put on the best face that he could muster. 'As soon as these persons shall arrive,' he said, 'they will be delivered to the custody of the law, and left to such course of trial, both as to place and process, as its functionaries shall direct.' He thought that circumstances 'render it equally desirable for the criminals as for the public, that being already removed from the place where they were first apprehended, the first regular arrest should take place here, and the course of proceedings receive here its proper direction.' What he meant by 'the first regular arrest' is not clear, but it is evident that Jefferson realized he could not make a good case for Wilkinson's actions in this matter.[34] Several years later he wrote that the General, expecting Burr and his followers from above, a British fleet from below, and a formidable conspiracy within the city of New Orleans, was justified in sending his prisoners to the seat of government, even though the written law gave them the right to a trial in the Territory.[35]

On 3 February, he wrote to Wilkinson: 'Your sending here Swartwout and Bollman, and adding to them Burr, Blennerhassett,

[34] *Writings of Thomas Jefferson* (Mem. ed.), III, 431–7.
[35] Jefferson to J. B. Colvin, 20 Sept. 1810, ibid. XII, 420–21.

and Tyler, should they fall into your hands, will be supported by public opinion. As to Alexander, who is arrived, and Ogden, expected, the evidence yet received will not be sufficient to commit them. I hope, however, you will not extend this deportation to persons against whom there is only suspicions, —. — be assured that you will be cordially supported in the line of your duties.' [36] On the same day the President wrote to Governor Claiborne: 'The Feds, and the little band of Quids [John Randolph's supporters], in opposition, will try to make something of the infringement of liberty by the military arrest and deportation of citizens, but if it does not go much beyond such offenders as Swartwout, Bollman, Burr, Blennerhasset, Tyler, etc., they will be supported by public approbation.' [37]

Wilkinson sent not only Swartwout, Ogden, and Bollman, but also Alexander and Adair to the East for trial. There was no chance of their conviction according to due process of law and therefore, on 23 January, the Senate passed a bill suspending the writ of habeas corpus for three months. Three days later the House, under the leadership of Jefferson's son-in-law, John Wayles Eppes, defeated the measure by the overwhelming vote of 113 to 19.[38] The cases were then left to be determined by customary legal procedure.

On 28 February, Chief Justice John Marshall heard the case of Swartwout and Bollman, and dismissed the defendants for lack of evidence. Other courts released the others on similar grounds, but the philosophical President was not too much perturbed. He later indicated that he would be willing to pardon any of them if he could only secure evidence that would make possible the conviction of Burr.[39] With the most important of the accomplices, he did have some success, for Bollman arrived in Washington on 22 January and the next day he proposed an interview. Jefferson and Madison promised him immunity, heard what he had to say, and made a memorandum of it.[40]

Bollman was interested in making the best possible case for him-

[36] Jefferson to Wilkinson, 3 Feb. 1807, ibid. XI, 149–50.
[37] Jefferson to Claiborne, 3 Feb. 1807, ibid. XI, 151.
[38] McCaleb, *Burr Conspiracy*, 246.
[39] Ibid. 248–9.
[40] *Letters and Other Writings of James Madison* (Cong. ed.), II, 393.

self and his principal, and admitted nothing but an intention to invade Spanish territory. He had worked with Burr in Philadelphia and his knowledge of French doubtless made him useful in dealing with Yrujo. His evidence in this connection is worth considering. According to him, Burr had duped the Marquis into believing that his object was to revolutionize Louisiana and separate the Western states, and the Spaniard entered eagerly and zealously into the plan; visiting the Colonel continually, he '*pestered* him with his advice and exhortations,' and offered him the use of 10,000 stand of arms, and money to any necessary amount. He was, said Bollman, so full of zeal that he would have gone to Spain to put his government in the course of effectual co-operation, but 'Burr despised the dirty character of Yrujo, and would never accept either money or any thing else from that quarter.' [41]

According to the German, Napoleon needed the wealth of Spanish-America in order to carry on his operations in Europe. He was therefore planning to take possession of these dominions, and, after having displaced King Carlos IV, put a member of his own house on the Spanish throne. Bollman maintained that the United States should support Burr's projected invasion of Mexico in order to save it from the grasp of Bonaparte. He said that Wilkinson's troops were not expected to join Burr's forces in a body, but some might do so individually, and the others were not expected to interfere. The Colonel's plan, according to him, was to proceed to New Orleans and, avoiding violence as far as possible, seize the French artillery deposited there; then, using only as much force as proved necessary, lay under requisition all the shipping in the river, which was expected to be sufficient to convey 6000 or 7000 men to Vera Cruz.[42]

We have no way of knowing just how much faith Jefferson put in this testimony, but the state of his mind is revealed by Plumer's notation of 27 January: 'Dined with the President of the United States — [he said] — he did not believe either France, Great Britain, or Spain was connected with Burr in this project, but he tho't the marquiss de Yrujo was — That he had advanced large sums of

[41] Ibid. II, 393–401.
[42] Ibid.

money to Mr. Burr — & his associates. But he believed Yrujo was duped by Burr. That last winter there was scarse a single night but that, at a very late hour, those two men met & held private consultations. I have since then ascertained the fact.' [43]

The next day the Marquis stated his version of the matter to Cevallos:

> According to appearances, Spain has saved the United States from the separation of the Union which menaced them. This would have taken place if Wilkinson had entered cordially into the views of Burr — which was to be expected, because Wilkinson detests this government, and the separation of the Western States has been his favorite plan. The evil has come from the foolish and pertinacious perseverance with which Burr has persisted in carrying out a wild project against Mexico. Wilkinson is entirely devoted to us. He enjoys a considerable pension from the King.[44]

On the very day that Yrujo wrote this letter, Jefferson sent a message to Congress saying: 'By the letters of Captain Bissel, who commands at Fort Massac, and of Mr. Murrell, to General Jackson, of Tennessee, copies of which are now communicated to Congress, it will be seen that Aaron Burr passed Fort Massac on the 31st December with about ten boats, navigated by about six hands each, without any military appearance, and that three boats with ammunition were said to have been arrested by the militia at Louisville.' [45] On 10 February he informed Congress that 'a letter from Cowles Mead, secretary of the Mississippi Territory, to the Secretary of War,' brought the information that 'Mr. Burr had reached that neighborhood on the 13th of January.' [46] Then on the 19th he was able to say that he was transmitting 'a letter from Cowles Mead, — informing us that Aaron Burr had surrendered himself to the civil authority of that Territory.' [47] This ended the period of uncertainty in Washington, and it is now necessary to trace the events that brought the adventurous Colonel to the end of the trail in distant Mississippi.

[43] Plumer, *Memorandum*, 543–4.
[44] Adams, *History of the United States*, III, 342; A.H.N., Est., leg. 5633, apartado I, no. 803, 22–47.
[45] Richardson (ed.), *Messages*, I, 405–6.
[46] Ibid. 407.
[47] Ibid. 409.

Chapter XIII

BURR IN MISSISSIPPI

AT THE TIME of the Conspiracy, the Mississippi Territory extended from the Spanish border at the 31st parallel to the southern boundary of the state of Tennessee, and from the Mississippi River to the Chattahoochee, which was the western boundary of Georgia. Most of this vast wilderness was inhabited only by Indians, with the Creeks toward the southeast, the Chickasaw in the northwest, and the Choctaw in the southwest. The two latter nations were traditionally peaceful, and the Creeks, under the able superintendency of Colonel Benjamin Hawkins, were temporarily so. Burr made no serious effort to interest any of them in his plans.

Only two areas in the Territory had been occupied by white settlers. The larger of these lay along the lower Mississippi with the town of Natchez as its focal point. It extended along the river from the location of the old Spanish Fort Nogales, or Walnut Hills, where Vicksburg grew up later, down to Fort Adams, just above the Spanish border. This area had been settled during the period of British control. It passed into Spanish hands in 1783, and the United States acquired it in 1795. Most of the inhabitants were native Americans who had come down the great river, or across from Georgia, during and after the Revolution, and they had prospered in their new homes. Tobacco was the original staple of the region, but since the invention of the cotton gin, planters had switched to the production of the new crop, and it had paid liberal rewards. Natchez had become something of a frontier metropolis and its leading citizens, familiar with the luxuries of New Orleans, lived in a style that was hardly eclipsed in the cities of the Atlantic seaboard.

About 175 miles east of Natchez lay a settlement of very different complexion. Along the Tombigbee River, above Spanish Mobile, there was a group of settlements which also dated back to British times. There was no real urban community in the region, but a village had grown up about the old Spanish fort of St. Stephens, and the small American Fort Stoddert, now under command of Lieutenant Edmund Pendleton Gaines, stood on guard just above the Spanish line. Midway between these two was the village of Wakefield, the seat of justice of Washington County, Mississippi Territory, which embraced all these Tombigbee settlements. Indian lands lay to the north and east, and the only contacts with civilization were down the river to Spanish Mobile, or west along McClarey's Path to Natchez.

The older inhabitants of this region, the most isolated in the United States, were known as Indian countrymen because they had long lived in close proximity to the Indians, had often cohabited with them, and had in some respects adopted their customs. Some of them were pack-horse traders who swapped tafia rum for furs and skins and hickory nut oil, but most of them were herdsmen. Cattle could live the year around on the cane and grass that grew in the marshes and along the numerous streams, and herds which numbered in the thousands roamed the woods at will. Some salt beef was shipped, but this was of poor quality and hides were the most valuable product.[1]

Since the invention of the cotton gin, some wealthier men had come in from the South Atlantic states and slave plantations had been established along the water courses. They exported their produce by way of Mobile, and by the same route they imported from New Orleans practically everything they consumed, often including the corn which was the standard food for man and beast. Even their clothing had to be imported, because they did not know

[1] Albert J. Pickett, *History of Alabama and Incidentally of Georgia and Mississippi*, 416–25; T. P. Abernethy, *The Formative Period in Alabama* (Montgomery, 1922), 9–19.

how to spin and weave their cotton, and of course they brought in iron and salt, and any luxuries they could afford. There were no woodsmen in this community. Hunting and trapping formed no part of the economy, and self-sustaining agriculture of the frontier type was not the rule. Thus the most isolated settlement in the United States was completely dependent upon an outside market for its produce, and had to import its supplies through a foreign port.[2]

The capital of the Territory was the pleasant little town of Washington, about six miles from Natchez. It stretched for almost a mile along a single street, and a number of wealthy planters lived in the vicinity.[3] Chief of the official circle that centered here was Governor Robert Williams. He was a North Carolinian, and during the early months of 1807 was visiting his home state on private business while the Territorial Secretary, Cowles Mead, served as acting governor. Next in rank were the three judges of the Superior Court of the Territory. One of these was Thomas Rodney, father of Caesar A. Rodney, Attorney General of the United States; and another was Peter Bryan Bruin who later resigned his office after the legislature had investigated his bibulous habits.[4] The third judge was Harry Toulmin, who lived at St. Stephens on the Tombigbee. He was an English Unitarian who had come to the United States with Joseph Priestly and Thomas Cooper, and had served as president of Transylvania Seminary and secretary of state for Kentucky. In 1804 he received his judicial appointment and moved from Kentucky to the primitive settlements above Mobile, where he did his best to lead his rather unruly neighbors in the paths of righteousness, but he found this a difficult task.[5] Other, and more typical, leaders of this community were the brothers John and James Caller, who had come from North Carolina and established themselves as cotton planters in the new country. James was colonel

[2] Richmond *Enquirer*, 18 July 1806.

[3] Letter dated Washington, M. T., 20 Jan. 1807, Richmond *Enquirer*, 17 Mar. 1807; *Mississippi Messenger*, 20 Jan. 1807.

[4] Resolutions of the Legislature of Mississippi Territory, 1 Mar. 1808, Carter, *Territorial Papers*, v, 615; ibid. 625–6, 650, 680.

[5] Marion Tinling and Godfrey Davies (eds.), *The Western Country in 1793, Reports on Kentucky, and Virginia by Harry Toulmin*, v–xx.

of the Washington County militia, and along with one Lemuel Henry, represented the county in the legislature. John, also a militia colonel, was presiding justice of the County Court.[6]

It has been mentioned that General Wilkinson, on his momentous journey from the Sabine to New Orleans, came by Natchez and tarried there from 11 November 1806 until the 20th of that month, making his headquarters with his friend Stephen Minor. The day after his arrival, he wrote alarming letters to Governor Claiborne and President Jefferson, saying to the latter that 'naught but an immediate peace in Europe can prevent an explosion which may desolate these settlements, — '[7] He ordered the garrisons of Fort Adams and Fort Stoddert down to New Orleans and dismantled the fortifications of the latter place.[8]

Naturally these events caused considerable excitement in the community and rumors flew thick and fast. The day after the General left for New Orleans, Judge Thomas Rodney wrote to his son Caesar that 'the existence of the plot was universally credited by all sorts of people,' and that

> The Design of the Conspiracy is said to be to unite Kentucky, Tennessee, Louisiana, The Floridas and part at least of Mexico into an Independent Empire — the Spanish Governors of those Provinces are to act in concert with the Conspirators of our Country to Effect this purpose under the Patronage and Protection of G. B. And that they Expect a British Fleet to aid them which is to arrive at the mouth of the Misisipi [*sic*] within two or three months at Farthest — Col: Burr, Genl. Wilkinson and D. Clarke — are said to be the Leaders — .[9]

The origin of such rumors is not certain, but Swartwout and Ogden were in the neighborhood at the time, and the mention of a British fleet — one of Burr's favorite fictions — indicates that they may have been doing much talking.

Two days later Secretary Mead wrote to Governor Claiborne:

[6] Thomas M. Owen, *History of Alabama and Dictionary of Alabama Biography* (Chicago, 1921), III, 291.

[7] McCaleb, *Burr Conspiracy*, 139.

[8] Letter from a gentleman in Natchez, Charleston *Courier*, 16 Jan. 1807; Thomas Rodney to Jefferson, 21 Nov. 1806, *Pennsylvania Magazine of History and Biography*, XLIV (1920), 294–6; *Kentucky Gazette*, 22 Dec. 1806.

[9] Thomas Rodney to Caesar A. Rodney, 21 Nov. 1806, *Pa. Mag. H. & B.*, XLIV (1920), 291–4; Philadelphia *Aurora*, 10 Jan. 1807.

Since my last communication to you I have obtained full and decisive information on the subject of the said association and have collected testimony which proves the thing beyond a doubt. The original plan makes your City the first place of attack — this is given me by a Gentleman of respectability and character, who has hitherto been thought by the conspirators to be friendly to their views — It is believed here that General Wilkinson is the soul of the conspiracy, —. Sir, you cannot be to [*sic*] much on your guard, your City is alive with those mischievous spirits & they are trained by the active and restless Daniel Clark — he is their head, father and promoter. — Your brother [Col. Ferdinand L. Claiborne] has promised to take charge of this communication —[10]

On 13 December, Major John W. Gurley, now aide-de-camp to Governor Claiborne, arrived in Natchez with a message warning Mead that Burr was about to descend the river. At once the Secretary dispatched Captain Joshua Baker with 25 militiamen to reoccupy Fort Adams and to guard the river at that point. The next day he wrote to Claiborne that 'my mind has long been prepared for the intelligence brought by Major Gurley, and you will find from his verbal communications that I have collected testimony of equal authenticity and weight on the same subject; which he has examined.'[11] On the 15th the Secretary sent a confidential message to the Territorial legislature informing it that he had received news of a conspiracy that aimed to separate the Territory from the Union, and he asked for authority to organize a battalion of 285 minutemen. A joint committee replied expressing confidence in Mead and saying that it would support any measures which he might see fit to adopt.[12]

Finally, on 20 December, a messenger arrived from Washington with the President's proclamation and orders from the Secretary of War.[13] On the 23rd the acting governor issued a proclamation saying that he had received information of the designs of an association to dismember the Union; that the conspiracy was 'directed by men [of] secret and profound intrigue for the aggrandizement of themselves and their minions, to the oppression of the great mass of the

[10] Mead to Claiborne, 23 Nov. 1806, Rowland, *Claiborne*, IV, 82–3.

[11] Same to same, 14 Dec. 1806, ibid. 65–6; Department of Archives and History of the State of Mississippi, *Third Annual Report* (1903–4), 43–4.

[12] Ibid. 40–42.

[13] Mead to Dearborn, 19 Jan. 1807, *A.S.P., Misc.*, I, 478.

people — ' He called on the soldiers and officers of the Territory to aid in detecting any agents of the conspirators and warned that any officers of the local government who had not taken the proper oaths of allegiance would be dismissed if they had not done so within 15 days.[14] The next day he wrote to Claiborne asking for a supply of arms and saying that his militia could be depended on to fight. He thought they could halt the expedition, but added 'if Burr passes this Territory with two thousand men, I have no doubt but that the General will be your worst enemy . . . Consider him a traitor, and act as if certain thereof. You may save yourself by it.'[15] The next day the militia of the Territory was ordered to muster, and shotguns and fowling pieces were purchased to make up the deficiency of arms.[16]

On 10 January a second express arrived from Washington with dispatches for the acting Governor, and at about noon on the same day Burr landed in Mississippi Territory. He had pushed ahead of the main party in a keelboat with 12 men and reached the home of his friend, Judge Peter Bryan Bruin, at Bayou Pierre above Natchez.[17] The convivial Judge was probably a bit dismayed by the arrival of his distinguished visitor, but the Colonel was even more shocked, for it was here, it will be recalled, that he was shown a copy of the Natchez *Mississippi Messenger*, dated the 6th, carrying the President's proclamation, the governor's proclamation, and his own cipher letter to Wilkinson. He was told also that the local militia was prepared to block his progress. Before leaving Nashville the Colonel had heard of the truce which Wilkinson had made with the Spaniards on the Sabine, but he did not suspect treachery and thought that the General had gone to New Orleans to prepare the ground for him there.[18] As he had stated to Lieutenant Jackson at the Chickasaw Bluffs and to others, his plan now was to take

[14] Miss. Dept. Arch. and Hist., *Third Annual Report*, 42–3; *Mississippi Messenger*, 6 Jan. 1807.

[15] Gayarré, *Louisiana*, IV, 169.

[16] Governor Holmes to Secretary of War, 7 Feb. 1810, Carter, *Territorial Papers*, VI, 45; Miss. Dept. Arch. and Hist., *Third Annual Report*, 44–5.

[17] *Mississippi Messenger*, 20 Jan. 1807; Safford, *Blennerhassett Papers*, 187.

[18] Deposition of Jacob Dunbaugh, *Quarterly Publications of the Historical and Philosophical Society of Ohio*, IX (1914), 66; John Smith to Jefferson, 2 Feb. 1807, Carter, *Territorial Papers*, V, 515; Adams, *History of the United States*, III, 325.

Baton Rouge, to raise the Mexican standard there, and to issue his proclamation. He would next attack Mobile, with Texas and Mexico reserved for later attention.[19] Now all his plans were thrown into confusion. The bold soldier of fortune must have spent a restless night under Bruin's roof.

The next morning Davis Floyd's boat, which had been sent ahead from New Madrid, arrived with Ralston and four or five men, and Blennerhassett and the rest of the party landed later in the day. There were nine boats and about 100 men in all.[20] As soon as Floyd and Ralston arrived, they were sent on to Natchez, but Burr then talked with Robert A. New, the son of a former Virginia congressman, who, as a result of the interview with his Chief, told the men that they were about to be opposed and asked whether they would stand by Burr or give up. New assured the men that what they had planned to do was legal and countenanced by the Federal Government. Burr's followers then agreed to stand together, and their leader posted sentinels, paraded his small force, and announced that he would take Baton Rouge and collect his forces there.[21] During the night, however, he moved his boats across the river to Thompson's Bayou on the Louisiana side, but fearing that the Mississippi militia might follow, the arms that had been brought in Floyd's boat were distributed and a guard was posted.[22]

Floyd and Ralston had left Burr before the announcement that the militia would oppose them had been made. After going to Natchez, they rode to the home of Dr. John Carmichael, who lived near Fort Adams. The Doctor was a former army officer who was now on the military staff of the governor of Mississippi Territory, and Burr looked upon him as a friend. The visitors spent the night of the 11th here and the next morning informed the Doctor that

[19] Affidavit of Dr. John F. Carmichael, Richmond *Enquirer*, 17 Mar. 1807; Deposition of David Fisk, *A.S.P.*, *Misc.*, I, 524–5; Letter from New Orleans, 17 Feb. 1807, Philadelphia *Aurora*, 20 Mar. 1807.

[20] Safford, *Blennerhassett Papers*, 187.

[21] Deposition of David Fisk, *A.S.P.*, *Misc.*, I, 524–5; Deposition of Jacob Dunbaugh, *Quart. Pubs. Hist. and Phil. Soc. of Ohio*, IX (1914), 66; Evidence of John Monholland, Cabell Papers, Burr Case, 82–3, Alderman Library, U. Va.

[22] John Graham to James Madison, 8 Feb. 1807, Burr MSS., L. of C.; Testimony of Samuel Moxley, Cabell Papers, Burr Case, 85–6, Alderman Library, U. Va.; Evidence of Stephen Welch, ibid. 84–5; Safford, *Blennerhassett Papers*, 187.

John Adair, whom Burr had dispatched from Nashville to ride through the Tombigbee and Pascagoula settlements and then confer with Wilkinson in New Orleans, was expected to meet them at his house. Their main business, they said, was to reconnoiter the defenses of the fort at Baton Rouge, to inform themselves of the situation at Fort Adams, and to find out who commanded the naval and marine forces in the neighborhood. On being informed that Captain Shaw commanded the naval forces, Ralston said that if he was one of the Mediterranean officers, a veteran of the Tripolitan war like Truxton and Decatur, he would be friendly to Burr's projects.

Ralston said that Burr was to be at Bayou Pierre on the 12th, where Adair was to join him. They were to wait there for reinforcements and receive information from Burr's agents who were circulating through the country at that time. When all preparations were complete, they were to proceed down the river, pass Natchez and Fort Adams in the night, and then take Baton Rouge by a *coup de main*. There Burr was to *raise his standard*, issue his proclamation disclosing his views, and make his communication to the Government of the United States respecting his future plans. Meanwhile he was to be joined by a body of men already engaged — as many as 10,000 if necessary. The agent said that the number then with Burr did not exceed 150, but that he had arranged for the reinforcements from Kentucky and Tennessee to join him in small parties so as not to alarm the Federal Government before Baton Rouge had been taken. He stated that it was not Burr's aim to divide the Union but to act against the Spanish Government and invade Mexico. He expressed great surprise at the conduct of General Wilkinson in arresting Swartwout, Ogden, Bollman, and Alexander, and repeatedly asked Dr. Carmichael whether he thought the General had deserted Burr or was only using this means to cover some greater objects.[23]

On the evening of the same day Floyd and Ralston visited Fort Adams and, after inspecting the fortifications, returned to Natchez. As soon as they had gone, Dr. Carmichael set out for New Orleans

[23] Deposition of Dr. John F. Carmichael, Bacon, *Report*, 347–9; Thomas Rodney to Caesar A. Rodney, 1 Mar. 1807, *Pa. Mag. Hist. and Biog.*, XLIV (1920), 302–3; Extract of a letter from New Orleans, 18 Jan. 1807, Philadelphia *Aurora*, 23 Feb. 1807.

and on the 17th relayed to General Wilkinson the information he had received from them. Adair had reached the city four days earlier and had been arrested immediately by the General.[24]

By 12 January, Mead felt sure that Burr's flotilla was approaching, and he believed it to be a large one. He prorogued the legislature until the 19th so that the members would be free to perform their military duty,[25] and placed a guard of 60 men on the banks of the river with orders to arrest Burr and search all boats attempting to pass. That night a craft did pass Natchez and fired on the guard which pursued it. The next day Mead received a letter from Colonel Thomas Fitzpatrick, who commanded the Jefferson County militia. It had been written the previous day and stated that: 'Coll. Scott — brings intelligence that Coll. Burr was this morning at Coll. Bruin's and that a detachment under the command of Captain Regan, with a civil warrant, went to take him prisoner.' [26] Of course the Captain did not find Burr, but he did find a letter which the Conspirator had addressed to Mead and left open with the idea that it should be read to the men of the assembled militia. It stated that the author had no hostile intentions toward the local or national governments; that he and his men were going to the Ouachita to settle the Bastrop lands; and that any attempt to obstruct them would be illegal and might provoke civil war.[27] At once Mead wrote to Colonel Fitzpatrick, saying: 'I recd. your Express with Col Burr's letter. — I should be proud to find him as innocent as he there professes himself — should the Colo. submit himself to civil authority, you will show him the respect due to his standing — if he has been vilified or injured by rumor or the Pensioned [Wilkinson] he shall receive all the benefits of my individual civility and the full and complete protection of the laws of the Territory.' [28]

The acting governor, however, did not believe that Burr would

[24] Wilkinson to Jefferson, 1 Mar. 1807, Burr MSS., L. of C.; Letter from New Orleans, 18 Jan. 1807, Philadelphia *Aurora,* 23 Feb. 1807.

[25] *Mississippi Messenger,* 20 Jan. 1807; Miss. Dept. Arch. Hist., *Third Annual Report,* 47–51.

[26] Ibid. 51; Mead to Dearborn, 13 Jan. 1807, *A.S.P., Misc.,* I, 477.

[27] Same to same, 13 Jan. 1807, Miss. Dept. Arch. and Hist., *Third Annual Report,* 52; Yrujo to Cevallos, 13 Feb. 1807, A.H.N., Est., leg. 5633, apartado 1, no. 809, 57–61; Safford, *Blennerhassett Papers,* 199–202.

[28] Miss. Dept. Arch. and Hist., *Third Annual Report,* 52–3.

submit peaceably to the civil authority. On the contrary, he thought that Burr commanded a large force which had come with hostile intentions and that he was even then reinforcing himself at Bayou Pierre. Mead accordingly sent a message to Captain Baker saying: 'Col. Burr was at Bayou Pierre yesterday morning — You will immediately Station your company on the bank of the Mississippi at or near Ft. Adams — intercept any boat that may pass — .' [29] Then Mead notified the Secretary of War of the receipt of Burr's letter and added, 'He will be apprehended if possible — . The want of arms and ammunition is the only ground on which we predicate a fear of his escape — Genl. Wilkinson left us perfectly bare of arms & ammunition,' and dismantled Fort Adams.[30] The busy and anxious young secretary did not neglect to send an express to New Orleans to notify the 'Pensioned' of Burr's arrival in Mississippi Territory. The next day he wrote to Captain Shaw, commanding the flotilla of gunboats at Pointe Coupee, 'Presuming that you have been stationed at Point Coupee for the purpose of intercepting Colo. Burr — have thought proper to advise you of his arrival at Bayou Pierre — ' [31]

After the hard day's work which he had put in on the 13th, Mead sat down at eight in the evening and wrote to Colonel Ferdinand Claiborne: 'Business of the first importance requires your presence at headquarters. Repair here at midnight. Let not suspicion even conjecture where you are bound. The fate of the country may depend on my movement.' [32] Claiborne was now put in charge of the preparations to oppose Burr, and on the 15th, with 300 men, moved by water from Natchez to establish headquarters at the house of Thomas Calvit at the mouth of Cole's Creek, about halfway between Bayou Pierre and Natchez.[33]

It was not until the 15th that Mead learned of Burr's removal to the Louisiana shore. He then received a letter which Colonel W. H.

[29] Ibid. 51; Claiborne, *Mississippi*, 286.

[30] Mead to Dearborn, 13 Jan. 1807, Miss. Dept. Arch. and Hist., *Third Annual Report*, 52.

[31] Mead to Capt. Shaw, 14 Jan. 1807, ibid. 56; Mead to Maj. Scott, 13 Jan. 1807, ibid. 53.

[32] Claiborne, *Mississippi*, 278.

[33] *Mississippi Messenger*, 20 Jan. 1807; Miss. Dept. Arch. and Hist., *Third Annual Report*, 55–6.

Wooldridge had written the previous day stating that he had arrived with 35 men at the mouth of Bayou Pierre on the morning of the 13th. Here he discovered that Burr had gone over to the opposite shore, but Burr, strangely enough, obligingly sent his skiff over for Wooldridge, who crossed with two of his officers and spent two or three hours with the fascinating adventurer. The meeting was a pleasant one on both sides, and Wooldridge reported that his party saw 55 or 60 men, four flatboats and five barges, that they saw no arms and Comfort Tyler assured them they had none.[34]

Major John Minor, who commanded the militia on the Louisiana side, was now notified that Burr had crossed over, and a copy of the President's proclamation was sent him. On the same day Mead wrote to Burr saying that he had ordered the militia to guard the Territory, but 'having heard thro Colo. Wooldridge that you profess perfect innocence . . . thought proper to send you a confidential Aide de Camp to receive from you such information on this subject as you may please to make —'[35]

The day after Wooldridge visited Burr, Colonel Fitzpatrick with about 60 dragoons paid him a call. He reported to Mead that the New York Colonel proposed to submit to the civil authority on condition that he should be tried in Mississippi Territory.[36] By this move Burr thought he could safeguard himself from a drumhead court-martial and the frantic rage which might possibly await him if he fell into Wilkinson's hands. Next day Secretary Mead wrote inviting Burr to come across the river and surrender, and promised him the full protection of the law. On the 16th he sent his aides, Major William B. Shields and George Poindexter, to visit Burr and offer him safe-conduct to a meeting at the house of Thomas Calvit on the following day. Burr accepted the invitation and met Mead as scheduled. After a lengthy conference it was agreed that Burr should surrender to the civil authorities of the Territory, that he should allow his boats to be searched and any military equipment seized. This was good news to the men of the militia, for a four-inch snow — the deepest ever seen in those parts — had fallen and they

[34] Ibid. 53–4, 58–9; Safford, *Blennerhassett Papers*, 188.
[35] Mead to Burr, 15 Jan. 1807, Miss. Dept. Arch. and Hist., *Third Annual Report*, 57–8.
[36] Ibid. 59–60; Safford, *Blennerhassett Papers*, 188.

had to sleep on the ground without tents to cover them. The next day Shields and Poindexter escorted Burr to the little town of Washington and he was placed under bond in the amount of $10,000 to appear before the next session of the Territorial Superior Court, which was to be held on 2 February.[37]

On the 19th Burr's boats were inspected by Colonel Fitzpatrick, who found no arms except the usual rifles. The Conspirator had taken the precaution of boring holes in the side of his own boat and suspending under water about 40 muskets with bayonets until the inspection was over.[38]

Young Thomas Butler presently arrived in his well-appointed boat with Mrs. Blennerhassett on board, and two militia officers reported that they had been informed of 12 or 13 boats, containing an unusual number of men as well as arms, ammunition, and supplies, which were within two days' sail up the river; and word came from Nashville that 2000 recruits for Burr were coming down.[39]

While awaiting trial, Burr did not find life altogether drab in the vicinity of Natchez, where several balls were given in his honor. The wealthier residents of the town were largely sympathetic Federalists, and they were reinforced by a group of army officers who had formerly been stationed at Fort Adams but were let out of the service when Jefferson reduced the military establishment. One of these was Colonel Benjamin Osmun, a staunch Federalist and a bachelor, who lived near Natchez and was one of Burr's bondsmen. They had been friends in former times, and now Osmun invited Burr to be his guest at 'Windy Hill Manor.'[40] There is a story that during this period Burr went to the home of one of Osmun's neighbors, the widow

[37] Mead to Dearborn, 19 Jan. 1807, *A.S.P., Misc.*, I, 478; same to Madison, 13 Apr. 1807, Carter, *Territorial Papers*, v, 544–6; *Mississippi Messenger*, 20 Jan. 1807; *Louisiana Gazette*, 6 Feb. 1807; Richmond *Enquirer*, 17 Mar. 1807; Claiborne, *Mississippi*, 280; Safford, *Blennerhassett Papers*, 188, 199–202; Agreement signed by Aaron Burr, George Poindexter, and W. B. Shields, 16 Jan. 1807, Everett D. Graff Collection.

[38] Safford, *Blennerhassett Papers*, 188, 198; Deposition of Jacob Dunbaugh, *Quart. Pubs. Hist. and Phil. Soc. of Ohio*, IX (1914), 66; Deposition of Stephen Welch, Cabell Papers, Burr Case, 84–5, Alderman Library, U. Va.

[39] Lt. John L. Patterson to Mead, 20 Jan. 1807, Miss. Dept. Arch. and Hist., *Third Annual Report*, 68; Claiborne, *Mississippi*, 282; Safford, *Blennerhassett Papers*, 189–91.

[40] Walter Leake to [W. C. Nicholas?], 15 Dec. 1807, Samuel Smith Papers, Alderman Library, U. Va.; George Poindexter to Dearborn, Jan. 1808, Carter, *Territorial Papers*, v, 604–10; Parton, *Burr*, 441.

Price, for a conference with the Abbé de Viel, a native of Louisiana who had spent much time in France; there the gay Conspirator, who made a career of women as well as intrigue, met Madeline, the beautiful daughter of Mrs. Price. The two are said to have fallen deeply in love and Burr urged Madeline to go with him on his subsequent flight. She refused but promised to be faithful until his return. She later rejected many suitors and did not marry until Burr had released her from her vow.[41]

Be this as it may, there is no question that Burr not only made many friends among the leading citizens of the community but also had the good will of the people in general. He was able to convince them, as he had apparently convinced most of his followers, that he planned no stroke against the Union, but intended only to attack Spanish territory. Most of the people of the Territory were thoroughly in sympathy with such an ambition, and they hated General Wilkinson for having thwarted it. This attitude is expressed in an article that appeared in the *Mississippi Messenger* of 20 January which asked:

> Is it not time, fellow citizens, for us to pause and reflect? We see Col Burr encountering the same attacks and persecutions from Pittsburgh to this place. We see the assertions and charges refuted by facts. We see him always submissive to law, and friendly to our Territories, and their inhabitants. We see a military despotism established in Orleans, our feelings were aroused, and our indignation burst forth.—In the case of Wilkinson, no man believes that he was acting under the orders, or by the sanction of the general government. In the case of Mead, from our experience of his discernment and moderation, no man believes that he has done, or suffered these things without that high authority, and we owe it perhaps to his moderation, that our citizens also have not been transported. Burr threatens to invade the Spanish colonies, and our citizens are armed against him. Our laws, our constitution, and the dearest principles of liberty are invaded, and we are silent and calm spectators. Let us pause and reflect.[42]

A week later the Territorial legislature passed a series of resolutions, introduced by James Caller of Washington County, which included the following:

[41] Claiborne, *Mississippi*, 287–8fn.

[42] *Mississippi Messenger*, 20 Jan. 1807, quoted in Miss. Dept. Arch. and Hist., *Third Annual Report*, 99.

Resolved unanimously that the continued obstructions by the spanish Officers of every navigable stream from Pearl River to Georgia the frequent denial of the use of the great high ways of nature to American Citizens residing on the Alabama, Tombigby, Mobile and Paspagola [*sic*], and ruinous exactions with which, when assuming the smiling Countenance of peace and conciliation they harrass the people of the Territory too severely to be longer tolerated, and that in the opinion of this Assembly the whole Country from Georgia to the Pearl River will be entirely abandoned to Indians and Spaniards, or that both the ties which bind Citizens to their Government and the dictates of Providence and society will be too feeble to restrain the Oppressed from making one last and desperate effort to rid themselves of their Oppressors.[43]

On 21 January, Mead wrote to Wilkinson that Burr was to be tried by the Superior Court of Mississippi Territory and asked that he send such testimony as would be necessary for his conviction. On the same day the General made an entry in the Coffee House book at New Orleans that he had been informed by messenger the previous night [actually he got the news on the 17th] that Burr was at Bayou Pierre.[44] He now knew also that Burr had been arrested, for he and Governor Claiborne wrote at the same time to Mead suggesting that the prisoner be sent to New Orleans for trial. In addition, they informed the Mississippi Secretary that Governor Folch of West Florida had gone to Baton Rouge with 400 [actually 300] men and warned him to watch the Spaniard.[45]

On that very day Folch had appeared with his troops at the head of Bayou St. John and asked permission to march through New Orleans on his way to Baton Rouge. This was a reasonable request since Wilkinson had advised him to reinforce that place and had promised to co-operate. But Governor Claiborne did not know of Wilkinson's correspondence with Folch and he was responsible for the rebuff to the Spanish governor. Being much embarrassed by the situation, the General hastily dispatched Lieutenant Hughes with a letter of apology and a private message for Folch. This did not alto-

[43] Resolutions of 27 Jan. 1807, Carter, *Territorial Papers*, v, 507–8.

[44] Miss. Dept. Arch. and Hist., *Third Annual Report*, 67; McCaleb, *Burr Conspiracy*, 221.

[45] Claiborne and Wilkinson to Mead, 21 Jan. 1807, Rowland, *Claiborne*, IV, 107–8; Letter from New Orleans, 18 Jan. 1807, Philadelphia *Aurora*, 23 Feb. 1807.

gether soothe the wounded feelings of the Don, who proceeded to his destination by land.[46]

Relations were not too much strained, however, for on 25 January Wilkinson addressed a letter to Folch saying: 'You have doubtless observed in the public prints of the United States, that my Name & Character have been Stigmatized & slandered, for a Criminal understanding imputed to me with the Spanish Governors of Louisiana, and that I am charged with holding a commission & drawing a pension from the Government of Spain.' Since Folch had been in Louisiana and West Florida ever since Wilkinson first visited New Orleans in 1787, the General asked him 'to declare upon the Honor of a Gentleman & an officer, whether such fact has ever come to your knowledge or whether you believe it has existence.' Folch obliged and on 10 February wrote Wilkinson, assuring him on his word of honor that 'there do not exist in the archives under my charge' any documents that would incriminate him.[47]

But this was not the only favor the General had to ask. As Folch was preparing to return from Baton Rouge to Pensacola, Wilkinson and Claiborne sent him a pressing invitation to go by way of New Orleans. The Spaniard declined this request because he had not been permitted to pass through the city on his way up, but after he had commenced his journey, he was met by a deputation from the American officials which urged that he change his mind and come to New Orleans. Accordingly he went, and at eight o'clock on the morning after his arrival the General sent a message asking for a conference at nine. At this meeting Wilkinson submitted to Folch numerous papers to show 'whether I have or have not been faithful to the cause of my country, and to the true interests of Spain.' Folch said, 'from all that I saw I was fully persuaded that he had acted conformably as suited the true interests of Spain, and so I assured him

[46] (Edward Livingston?), 'Faithful Picture of the Political Situation of New Orleans,' *Louisiana Historical Quarterly*, XI (July 1928), 422; Wilkinson to Folch, 21 Jan. 1807, A.G.I., Papeles de Cuba, leg. 2375, no. 101; Claiborne to Folch, 21 Jan. 1807, Rowland, *Claiborne*, IV, 106–7; Richmond *Enquirer*, 10 Mar. 1807; I. J. Cox, *West Florida*, 197–200; *idem* 'General Wilkinson and his later Intrigues with the Spaniards,' *A.H.R.*, XIX (July 1914), 803–6.

[47] Wilkinson to Folch, 25 Jan. 1807, A.G.I., Papeles de Cuba, leg. 2375, no. 102; Folch to Wilkinson, 10 Feb. 1807, ibid. no. 102.

for his satisfaction.' He further reported that 'during the disturbances of Burr the aforesaid general has, by means of a person in his confidence [Gilbert Leonard], constantly maintained a correspondence with me, in which he had laid before me not only the information which he acquired, but also his intentions for the various exigencies in which he might find himself.'

Having satisfied the West Florida Governor of his faithfulness to the interests of Spain, Wilkinson now explained that a memorial condemning himself and Governor Claiborne was being drawn up in the Legislative Council of Orleans Territory, and was being promoted by an association of New Orleans lawyers. This document was to be submitted to Congress, and Wilkinson asked Folch to use his influence with the members of the Council to have it defeated. Folch said later that he accomplished this, but that it required considerable effort. A few days afterward the General asked him to work for the passage of a memorial in his favor, which the Legislative Council was now considering. The Spanish Governor said that he also succeeded in this, and he commented, 'I thought that I ought to lend myself to it in order to show them that Spain could be useful to them even in their own country.' [48]

Back in the vicinity of Natchez the excitement had died down considerably, yet there was still some anxiety. It was reported that there was among Burr's boats one loaded with French muskets which was protected by 200 men. It was also stated that reinforcements were coming down the river and that a Mr. Butler from Kentucky had tried to buy arms for Burr, who, on 23 January, returned to his boats from the town of Washington.[49] Two days later, perhaps because of rumors about the approach of reinforcements, the boats dropped down the river from Petit Gulf to a point opposite the mouth of Cole's Creek. The next day Mead wrote to Secretary

[48] Wilkinson to Folch, n.d., ibid. nos. 95, 96; Folch to Someruelos, 25 June 1807, *A.H.R.*, x, 837–40; Livingston (?), 'Faithful Picture of the Political Situation of New Orleans,' loc. cit. 417–22; *Debate in the House of Representatives of the Territory of Orleans on a Memorial to Congress, respecting the illegal conduct of General Wilkinson* (New Orleans, 1807); Address from the Territorial House of Representatives, 26 Jan. 1807, Rowland, *Claiborne*, IV, 112–14.

[49] John A. Davidson to Mead, 20 Jan. 1807, Miss. Dept. Arch. and Hist., *Third Annual Report*, 67–8; *National Intelligencer*, 25 Feb. 1807; *Republican and Savannah Evening Ledger*, 19 Mar. 1807.

Dearborn that Burr's boats had been searched again and a few arms found, but that he believed others were hidden on shore and he would continue the search.[50] This was his last letter as acting governor, for Robert Williams returned on the 27th. The same day Blennerhassett heard of the return of the governor and that he was favorable to Burr, and on the 28th the Conspirator decided to call on Williams. Blennerhassett heard also that Captain Shaw was approaching Natchez with nine or ten gunboats in order to take him and his party into custody.[51] This, however, proved to be a false alarm.

The time for Burr's trial was nearing, and while he was in town awaiting it, his friend Robert A. New tried to sell Lemuel Henry, from the Tombigbee settlements, 40 or 50 muskets and bayonets at a third of their value.[52] When Burr first came to the Territorial capital Henry had been introduced to him by Colonel John McKee, the former Choctaw agent and friend of Wilkinson, to whom he had said, 'I had written a great deal about recruiting in Tennessee, — but *all our differences being settled with Spain* knocks all my Utopia to the devil.' [53] Burr had sent McKee a letter from the Chickasaw Bluffs directing him to join the expedition at Bayou Pierre, which he did. In a private conversation between Burr, McKee, Lemuel Henry, and James Caller, Caller had told Burr that if he had gone to the Tombigbee settlements and told the people that his enterprise was a secret one against Spain which had the sanction of the Government, he might have procured enough men to take Mobile, where he would have found sufficient arms and ammunition and armed vessels to convey his troops to whatever place he pleased. Burr replied that the Government had neglected these people and under the Constitution they had a right to erect a new government for themselves or to seek protection under another government. Burr stressed the 'constitutional right.' Henry quoted New as saying that no sensible man would believe that settlement of the Ouachita lands

[50] Mead to Dearborn, 26 Jan. 1807, Miss. Dept. Arch. and Hist., *Third Annual Report*, 70–71.

[51] Safford, *Blennerhassett Papers*, 191.

[52] Evidence of Lemuel Henry, *Annals of Congress*, 10 Cong., 1 Sess., 663–4; Claiborne, *Mississippi*, 281.

[53] Evidence of Col. John McKee, *A.S.P., Misc.* 1, 594; Safford, *Blennerhassett Papers*, 576–7.

was Burr's sole object; that this was only an excuse, but that it served a useful purpose.[54]

James Caller knew what he was talking about, for the Tombigbee people would have liked nothing better than a chance to take Mobile. In fact, as early as 1804 Governor Folch had accused Caller and his brother John of threatening to burn any Spanish boats that ventured above the line and throw their crews into the water. Spanish authorities had long permitted the trade of this region to be carried on upon the payment of a 12 per cent duty at Mobile, but in March 1806 the Intendant Morales put a stop to it. By closing New Orleans to Americans as a place of deposit, Morales had started the chain of events leading to the purchase of Louisiana by the United States. Since he was a large speculator in West Florida lands, making a deal with General Wilkinson at about this time for the sale to him of Dauphin Island in Mobile Bay, it seems probable that he was trying to bring about a similar transfer of West Florida. However, he was overruled by Governor Folch when Burr's movements began to cause anxiety, and the trade was reopened in September 1806.[55] In spite of this concession, the 'Bigbee' settlers were still bitter about the heavy duties that had to be paid, even on government supplies, at Mobile. Corn was said to be selling at five dollars a bushel, when obtainable at all, and it was predicted that the region would be abandoned to the wild beasts and the Indians unless the situation was remedied. It was this state of affairs which led the legislature to pass its resolution on 27 January, quoted above, and threaten to make 'one last and desperate effort to rid themselves of their Oppressors.' Burr could have seen an opportunity here.[56]

On 30 January, John Graham arrived at the town of Washington

[54] Thomas Rodney to Caesar A. Rodney, 1 Mar. 1807, *Pa. Mag. H. and B.*, XLIV (1920), 302–5; Evidence of Lemuel Henry, *Annals of Congress*, 10 Cong., 1 Sess., 662–4; Richmond *Enquirer*, 3 Nov. 1807; Claiborne, *Mississippi*, 288.

[55] A. P. Whitaker, *Documents Relating to the Commercial Policy of Spain in the Floridas* (De Land, Fla., 1931), Introduction, lvii; Folch to Someruelos, 8 Dec. 1804, A.H.N., Est., leg. 5542, exp. 13, 191; the King to Yrujo, 16 July 1805, ibid. 200–201; Carlos Howard to Folch and enclosure, 18 Sept. 1804, ibid. 191–7; Folch to Howard, 8 Oct. 1804, ibid. 198–9; Cox, *West Florida*, 183.

[56] Lt. E. P. Gaines to Dearborn, 17 Apr. 1807, Carter, *Territorial Papers*, V, 546–8; Claiborne to Madison, 21 Apr. 1807, Rowland, *Claiborne*, IV, 124–5; Richmond *Enquirer*, 2, 19 May 1807; Claiborne, *Mississippi*, 289.

and had a conference with Burr, who said it was absurd to think of separating the Union by physical rather than by moral means, but thought an attack on Mexico was feasible when they had a separate government. Graham next called on Governor Williams and gave him all the information he had been able to collect on the Ohio and in Kentucky and Tennessee; but, said he, 'no steps were taken by Judge Rodney in consequence of this information.' [57] Just a few days previously Blennerhassett had reported that 'Col. Burr also acquainted me with the indignation that Federal Judge Rodney had expressed at the exercise of the military law over Col. Burr and his friends, both in the Mississippi and Orleans Territories, the Judge assuring him, in opposition to the U. S. Attorney, Mr. Poindexter, that the civil authority of the Territory was competent to try him, adding — that if Wilkinson, or any other military force, should attempt to remove his person out of the Mississippi Territory, prior to his trial, he, the Judge, would again put on his old "76" and march out in support of Col. Burr and the Constitution.' [58]

It was in this atmosphere that Burr, with Lyman Harding and William B. Shields as counsel, appeared on 2 February before the Territorial Superior Court, which was presided over by Judges Thomas Rodney and Peter Bryan Bruin. Next day George Poindexter, the United States Attorney, declined to bring in an indictment because he held that the court, having only appellate jurisdiction, was not competent to sit on the case. He questioned also whether Burr had committed any offense cognizable within the Territory and thought that he should be transferred to some other jurisdiction where he might be tried legally. Governor Williams shared these views, but Judge Rodney did not.[59] He summoned a grand jury, said to have been packed with Federalists, which proceeded to take depositions, and on the 4th brought in a presentment

[57] Evidence of John Graham, Cabell Papers, Burr Case, 32–4, Alderman Library, U. Va.; same, *A.S.P.*, *Misc.*, I, 529–30; John Graham to Madison, 8 Feb. 1807, Burr MSS., L. of C.; McCaleb, *Burr Conspiracy*, 225–6.

[58] Safford, *Blennerhassett Papers*, 191.

[59] Thomas Rodney to Caesar A. Rodney, (?) Feb. 1807; *Pa. Mag. H. and B.*, XLIV (1920), 299–302; Gov. Williams to Madison, 23 Feb. 1807, Burr MSS., L. of C.; Harry Toulmin to Capt. P. P. Schuyler, 7 Feb. 1807, ibid.; *National Intelligencer*, 18 Mar. 1807; Richmond *Enquirer*, 17, 24 Mar. 1807.

that absolved Burr on all counts but condemned the Territorial administration for its treatment of the accused.[60] Judge Bruin now wished to release his friend, but Judge Rodney insisted on holding him to his recognizance. Burr protested against this, saying the agreement was that his bond should be valid only in case an indictment were brought against him.[61] He had insisted on a trial because he anticipated an acquittal, and he was disappointed that he had failed to obtain one.

While this farce was being enacted at the town of Washington, a melodrama was being produced at Natchez. Even before Burr reached Mississippi Territory, Wilkinson had sent John McKee and Silas Dinsmore up to capture him, but they had made no move in that direction. The General and Governor Claiborne had also appealed to Secretary Mead and Governor Williams to surrender their prisoner to them, but they had declined to do so.[62] Deciding finally that stronger measures were necessary, on 28 January Wilkinson dispatched Captain Moses Hook, with Lieutenants Mulford, Smith, and George Peter, and Doctors Davidson and Carmichael on a mission to capture Burr. They were dressed in civilian clothes and armed with pistols and dirks. On the day before the trial, this party arrived at the home of Captain Farrow in the neighborhood of Natchez. Their orders were to seize Burr and bring him to New Orleans on one of the armed boats. They had no civil warrants, and no crime was charged against Burr in their orders.

Doctor Carmichael, who was a medical officer on the staff of Governor Williams, along with Captain Farrow and Dr. Davidson, went to Washington to confer with the Governor, and Car-

[60] Presentment of Grand Jury, Superior Court of Mississippi Territory, Feb. 1807, copy enclosed in Gov'r. Williams to Jefferson, 23 Feb. 1807, Burr MSS., L. of C.; *Louisiana Gazette*, 20 Feb. 1807; *National Intelligencer*, 11 Mar. 1807; Richmond *Enquirer*, 17, 24 Mar. 1807; Philadelphia *Aurora*, 3 Apr. 1807; *Mississippi Messenger*, 26 Feb. 1807, in Miss. Dept. Arch. and Hist., *Third Annual Report*, 104–7.

[61] Harry Toulmin to Capt. P. P. Schuyler, 7 Feb. 1807, Burr MSS., L. of C.; Burr to Charles Biddle, 22 Feb. 1807, *Autobiography of Charles Biddle*, 315; Miss. Dept. of Arch. and Hist., *Third Annual Report*, 101–2.

[62] Testimony of James Wilkinson, *Quart. Pubs., Hist. and Phil. Soc. of Ohio*, IX (1914), 50; Wilkinson to Jefferson, 9 Dec. 1806, Bacon, Report, 431–4; Thomas Rodney to Caesar A. Rodney, (?) Feb. 1807, *Pa. Mag. H. and B.*, XLIV (1920), 299–302; Gov'r. Williams to Madison, 23 Feb. 1807, Burr MSS., L. of C.; Plumer, *Memorandum*, 616; McCaleb, *Burr Conspiracy*, 230.

michael returned the next morning, this being the day of the trial. He now informed the others of the party that the Governor had requested him, as his aide, to assure them that he would order Captain Farrow to parade his troop, and that he would furnish the Captain with orders to seize Burr, who would either be sent to Washington City or embarked on one of the armed vessels. On the evening of the same day Dr. Davidson and Captain Farrow returned with the news that no bill had been found against Burr. Farrow then stated that he was ordered to have his troop at Natchez the next day ready to execute an order from the Governor. On the morning of the 4th the group proceeded to Natchez and at 3:00 p. m. Captain Farrow paraded his troop. They waited until late that night but received no orders from the Governor. Fearful that Burr would make his escape, Captain Hook went to Washington and returned the next morning, saying that he had seen the Governor and had received assurance that Burr should not escape and that Farrow would be ordered to take him. Hook then returned to New Orleans, leaving Lieutenant Peter in command with orders to act in case the Governor did not. The troop remained throughout the day in Natchez, but received no orders. At about midnight Dinsmore arrived with the news that Burr had escaped and that the Governor had told him to get out handbills offering a reward of $2000 for the capture of the fugitive.[63]

Burr had disappeared from the town of Washington the day after the hearing, and on the 6th the Governor issued his proclamation accusing him of being a fugitive from justice.[64] The next day the court declared his bail forfeited. Meanwhile, the adventurer had taken refuge with his friend Dr. John Cummins of Bayou Pierre, and during this period he was once seen crossing the river with Major Robert Ashley of New Orleans, formerly one of Philip Nolan's men.[65] From the Cummins place, on the 10th of the month,

[63] Affidavit of George Peter, *Quart. Pubs., Hist. and Phil. Soc. of Ohio*, IX (1914), 35–9; Cross-examination of John Graham, *A.S.P., Misc.*, I, 530.

[64] Superior Court of Mississippi Territory, 7 Feb. 1807, Burr MSS., L. of C.; Copy of the Governor's proclamation, 6 Feb. 1807, ibid.; Miss. Dept. of Arch. and Hist., *Third Annual Report*, 73–4.

[65] Thomas Rodney to Caesar A. Rodney, *Pa. Mag. H. and B.*, XLIV (1920), 299–302; Extract of letter from Washington, M. T., 9 Feb. 1807, *National Intelligencer*, 27 Mar. 1807; Safford, *Blennerhassett Papers*, 205.

Burr wrote a note, which was unsigned and undated, to C(omfort) T(yler) and D(avis) F(loyd). It said: 'If you are yet together keep together and I will join you tomorrow night — in the mean time put *all* your arms in perfect order. Ask the bearer no questions but tell him all you may think I wish to know — He does not know that this is from me, nor where I am.' [66] This note was stitched in the cape of Burr's surtout, and a slave boy belonging to Dr. Cummins was dispatched on the Colonel's horse to deliver it. When he stopped at the house of William Fairbanks, who lived near the mouth of Cole's Creek, to inquire his way, his mount was recognized, he was searched, and the note was discovered. Fairbanks sent the boy to the Governor, who immediately placed guards on Burr's boats and on the roads leading to the neighborhood of Cummins' house. He also had Floyd, Tyler, Blennerhassett, Ralston, and about 40 members of Burr's party arrested and held for 24 hours. The next day they were all released except Floyd, Ralston, and Blennerhassett, who had been committed by Judge Rodney to the Superior Court of the Territory.[67]

Two days after the release of Burr's men, one of the Colonel's attorneys handed Governor Williams two notes from his client. One of these, dated the 12th, said: 'I have seen your proclamation — It is unworthy of you to lend the sanction of your name to a falsehood . . .' and then he went on to deny that the writer was a fugitive from justice on the ground that his recognizance was no longer in effect. The other note was undated and stated:

> The vindicative temper and unprincipled conduct of Judge Rodney have induced me to withdraw for the present from public view — I nevertheless continue in the disposition, which has been uniformly manifested, of submitting to civil authority so long as I can be assured that it will be exercised towards me within the limits prescribed for other citizens — It is proper however before again surrendering that I be informed of the cause or charge, if any, for which it is proposed to arrest me — whether bail will be received — the tenor of the recogni-

[66] Burr MSS., L. of C.; Evidence of Lemuel Henry, *Annals of Congress*, 10 Cong., 1 Sess., 664.

[67] Same, 662–4; Gov'r. Williams to Madison, 23 Feb. 1807, Burr MSS., L. of C.; Richmond *Enquirer*, 7 Apr. 1807; *Mississippi Messenger*, 17 Feb. 1807; Miss. Dept. Arch. and Hist., *Third Annual Report*, 103–4.

sance and the sum in which security will be required—I ask you further, your assurance that no attempt to send me out of the Territory shall be countenanced or permitted and that my person shall not be subjected to any military authority.[68]

The Governor had not previously been unfriendly to Burr; he believed him to be entitled to all the due processes of law which he claimed, and he had thwarted Wilkinson's agents in their attempt to seize him, but he did not believe that he should be tried in the Territory, and the captured note of the 10th had alarmed him. He was no longer inclined to be conciliatory, and accordingly answered at once: 'Your two notes, the one without date and the other under that of yesterday I have this moment received. You can only be considered a fugitive from justice. I can enter into no stipulations as to your surrender, but if you submit, the law will be applied to you as to any other.' [69]

There was now no hope but in flight, and David Fisk, one of the men who had come down the river in the boat with Davis Floyd, later testified that 'after the trial, Burr returned to the boats and remained one day. He made a long speech saying he was acquitted, but they were going to take him again and he was going to flee from oppression. He said his bills had been protested and he had nothing to give the men, but they might sell the property and go to the Ouachita lands if they liked.' Part of the stores was later sold and the money divided. Because the boats were of unusual construction and size, they brought $75 instead of the customary $25 or $30.[70] After the Governor's final note to him, it was six days before Burr was heard from again.

At about eleven o'clock on the night of 18 February, two strangers rode into the village of Wakefield. The moon was shining brightly but it had been raining hard and the streams were swollen. One of the men rode some 30 or 40 yards in front of the other on 'a small

[68] Burr to Gov'r. Williams, n.d., Burr MSS., L. of C.; same to same, 12 Feb. 1807, ibid.; Williams to Madison, 23 Feb. 1807, ibid.

[69] Williams to Burr, 13 Feb. 1807, Miss. Dept. Arch. and Hist., *Third Annual Report*, 75; F. L. Claiborne to Madison, 25 Oct. 1807, Carter, *Territorial Papers*, v, 563–7; George Poindexter to Dearborn, (?) Jan. 1808, ibid. 604–10.

[70] Deposition of David Fisk, *A.S.P. Misc.* I, 524–5; Deposition of Samuel Moxley, Cabell Papers, Burr Case, 85–6, Alderman Library, U. Va.

tackey of a horse'; his old saddle was covered with a bearskin, and he was disguised as a river boatman. A tattered blanket coat covered a homespun garb, a tin can was tied over one shoulder, a butcher's knife was stuck in his belt, and a dilapidated white hat flopped over his face and partly hid it. As the two wayfarers approached the office of Nicholas Perkins, registrar of the local land office, Perkins happened to be standing in the doorway. The first rider passed without looking up, but the second stopped and asked for directions to the home of Major John Hinson, whom Burr had seen at Natchez and with whom he planned to stay for a week. Perkins explained that swollen streams might make it impossible to reach Hinson's house, and added that the Major was away from home. Nevertheless, the strangers rode on in the direction indicated.[71]

It seemed unlikely to Perkins that honest men would be prowling through the woods at that time of night: robbers, probably, he decided — and then a startling thought came to him: could it be that one of the horsemen was the man named in Governor Williams' recent proclamation — the notorious Aaron Burr? On the strength of this suspicion, Perkins aroused the sheriff, Theodore Brightwell, and they rode together to Hinson's house. There they found the two men with Mrs. Hinson, and noticing that one of them spoke very little and seemed to wish to avoid being observed, Perkins decided that he was indeed Aaron Burr. Accordingly he slipped off quietly and rode to Fort Stoddert where he notified the commanding officer, Lieutenant Edmund Pendleton Gaines.[72] Setting out from the fort early the next morning with a sergeant and three men, Perkins and Gaines rode toward the Hinson house. Presently they met Burr and the sheriff coming toward them on their way to a ferry across the river, beyond which one road led to Pensacola and another passed through the Creek country to Georgia. When

[71] Safford, *Blennerhassett Papers,* 206, 216; Parton, *Burr,* 444; Claiborne, *Mississippi,* 288–9; Statement of Robert Ashley, *National Intelligencer,* 20 Apr. 1807; *Republican and Savannah Evening Ledger,* 24 Mar. 1807; Raleigh *Register,* 6 Apr. 1807; *The Examination of Col. Aaron Burr, before the Chief Justice of the United States, upon the charges of High Misdemeanor, and of Treason against the United States* (Richmond, 1807), 4.

[72] Richmond *Enquirer,* 31 Mar. 1807; Safford, *Blennerhassett Papers,* 217.

Burr was stopped, he protested that he was not subject to military arrest, but he offered no resistance and was taken to Fort Stoddert and placed under guard.[73]

Burr's companion on the previous night was Major Robert Ashley. He had left the Hinson farm before Burr's arrest, and the next day, in company with Thomas Malone, went to the home of Colonel John Caller, who during the previous year had tried to raise the militia in order to take Mobile. Ashley had gone to bed when Caller got home, but the next morning, still not knowing of Burr's arrest, undertook to interest his host in his plans. He said that he and Burr were to have met at a certain time at Baton Rouge and taken that place, but Wilkinson, because of 'some slight censure,' had deserted them, and now, knowing how anxious the settlers were to get the Spaniards out of Mobile, they were turning their attention entirely to the Tombigbee region. Ashley stated that Burr was going to the Federal capital, but he would soon return and join him; that he himself would bring down 1700 men, already enlisted, and with the help of Caller, Hinson, William Buford, and the local citizens, they would throw the Spaniards out of Florida, after which Great Britain would join forces with them. He denied that they had any hostile intentions toward the United States.[74]

That Burr was going to Washington or that Britain had promised any aid is not to be believed, but that an attack on Mobile was planned before Burr started for the Tombigbee seems highly probable. Colonel Caller stated to Ashley that he would be pleased to participate in such an undertaking, and Judge Toulmin, Lemuel Henry, and others in position to know, took this to be the temper of practically the entire population of the region.[75] Furthermore, Burr had friends within the Spanish Province. The Abbé de Viel and a Spanish officer from Pensacola had visited him at the town of Washington, and now the Spanish commander of an armed vessel came up from Mobile Bay and tried to see him at Fort Stoddert. Burr said he wished to send a message by him to Morales, but Gaines

[73] Letter from Lt. Gaines, 22 Feb. 1807, Richmond *Enquirer*, 17 Apr. 1807; ibid. 27 Mar., 31.

[74] Philadelphia *Aurora*, 5 Aug. 1807; Claiborne, *Mississippi*, 288–9.

[75] Ibid. 289; Philadelphia *Aurora*, 5 Aug. 1807; Richmond *Enquirer*, 24 Mar. 1807; Schachner, *Burr*, 385.

forbade the intended interview.[76] The second in command at Baton Rouge was reported to be involved with Burr, and Ashley told the sheriff that the Colonel had even more important friends in Florida, and planned to go to Mobile. A Spanish officer told Perkins that Morales was awaiting Burr there, where the local officials were expecting him. It is likely that an invasion coming down from the north would have met with very feeble resistance. Burr had asked the sheriff to point out the road to Pensacola, and it was in that direction he was traveling when he was accosted by Gaines. In fact, Yrujo said he expected Burr to try to escape by this route.[77]

A third member of the Colonel's party had failed to make contact with him at the Hinson farm. This was the young German, Charles Willie, the secretary whom Burr had employed in New York and whom, along with a servant, a young Negro slave, he had taken with him on his final expedition down the Mississippi. Willie had transcribed several letters which Burr wrote to Bollman, partly in cipher and partly in Willie's German translation. The young secretary had conferred with his chief at Dr. John Cummins' place, and had been entrusted with the delivery of Burr's luggage and his servant to the Hinson home; but the master was gone before the secretary arrived. Willie was arrested and questioned by Judge Toulmin, but he was able to give little information about the projects of his employer.[78] Dr. Cummins himself, who had studied medicine with Dr. Benjamin Rush and married the daughter of Judge Bruin, followed Burr with his papers, including maps of Mexico. He was stopped in the Creek country by Colonel Benjamin Hawkins, who broke open and examined his portmanteau. Proceeding to Richmond, Cummins was there during the trial, endorsed heavily for Burr and Blennerhassett, and lost about $65,000.[79]

[76] Elizabeth Brandon Stanton, *Colonel Aaron Burr* (n.p., 1939), 10ff.; *National Intelligencer*, 27 Mar. 1807; Richmond *Enquirer*, 17 Apr. 1807; Harry Toulmin to P. P. Schuyler, 7 Feb. 1807, Burr MSS., L. of C.

[77] Richmond *Enquirer*, 17 Apr. 1807; Philadelphia *Aurora*, 15 Apr. 1807; Safford, *Blennerhassett Papers*, 216; Pickett, *Alabama*, 492; Yrujo to Cevallos, 13 Feb. 1807, A.H.N. leg. 5633, apartado 1, no. 809, 57–61; same to same, 21 Feb. 1807, A.H.N., leg. 5633, apartado 1, no. 813, 62–5.

[78] Thomas W. Maury to Wilkinson, 29 Mar. 1807, Burr MSS., L. of C.; Toulmin to Jefferson, 7 Apr. 1807, ibid.; Richmond *Enquirer*, 6 Feb., 19 May 1807; *Georgia Republican*, 24 Feb. 1807; *Mississippi Messenger*, 14 Apr. 1807.

[79] Charleston *Courier*, 2 Nov. 1807; *Republican and Savannah Evening Ledger*,

Burr remained a prisoner at Fort Stoddert until 5 March. He played chess with Mrs. Gaines, who was a daughter of Judge Toulmin, and doubtless found other ways of amusing himself. But Lieutenant Gaines was not happy about the situation. He knew that Major Ashley, after being arrested, had escaped and made friends among the people of the district. He knew that Burr was intriguing with the guards in order to effect his escape, and he suspected that some of his Spanish friends might assist him. Furthermore, the people of the community, being favorable to the prisoner's West Florida plans, resented his arrest and might undertake to free him. Believing that he could not hold his famous captive much longer, he engaged Nicholas Perkins to conduct him through the Indian country to the national capital.[80]

With a guard of eight picked men, Perkins set out with his prisoner on 5 March. They traveled 30 miles the first day despite the fact that the Indian trace to Fort Wilkinson on the Oconee was narrow and rugged. They had only one tent, which Burr was allowed to use. He was also furnished with tea, coffee, wine, and brandy, though the party was without sufficient provisions for two or three days. The prisoner was even permitted to carry his pistols and a large knife. The horses were belled and hobbled at night so that they might feed on the cane while some of the guards slept near the campfire. With frequent rains and swollen streams, it was a hard journey for all until the party emerged from the Indian country at Fort Wilkinson and once again slept under a roof.[81]

At Chester, South Carolina, Burr attempted to escape. Jumping from his horse, he applied to some young men who were standing near by to take him before a magistrate; but the guard disarmed and remounted him and prohibited his speaking to anyone. Perkins

---

8 Oct. 1807; McCaleb, *Burr Conspiracy*, 77-8; Benjamin Hawkins to Dearborn, 14 Sept. 1807, Burr MSS., L. of C.; Reuben Gold Thwaites (ed.), *Early Western Travels*, IV, *Cuming's Tour to the Western Country*, 1807-1809 (Cleveland, 1904), 350fn.

[80] Communication to President Jefferson from citizens of Washington County, M.T., Charleston *Courier*, 10 Sept. 1807; *Mississippi Messenger*, 31 Mar. 1807; Philadelphia *Aurora*, 15 Apr. 1807; Richmond *Enquirer*, 17 Apr. 1807; Safford, *Blennerhassett Papers*, 219; James W. Silver, 'Edmund Pendleton Gaines and Frontier Problems, 1801-1849,' *J.S.H.*, I (1935), 323.

[81] Richmond *Enquirer*, 17 Apr. 1807; Pickett, *Alabama*, 485-502; Safford, *Blennerhassett Papers*, 220-26.

shortly placed him in a gig and proceeded to Fredericksburg, Virginia, where a messenger from Washington directed them to go to Richmond. During this last lap of the journey, the prisoner was provided with a seat in a stagecoach.[82]

[82] *Republican and Savannah Evening Ledger*, 24 Mar. 1807; Richmond *Enquirer*, 27 Mar. 1807.

Chapter XIV

TRIAL IN RICHMOND

BURR STARTED on his enforced journey eastward on 5 March 1807, but Wilkinson tarried in New Orleans until 20 May. Business was flourishing in the city even during the summer, but there was still considerable ferment among the people. Governor Claiborne dismissed Dr. Watkins, the mayor, because of his connection with Burr, and several lesser officers resigned in order to avoid dismissal. But the danger was past and the legislature of Orleans Territory, after having defeated a memorial to Congress condemning the General, hastened to declare its loyalty to the Union. Committees of citizens signed statements expressing their approval of Wilkinson's conduct, but his teeming mind was still occupied with many projects and problems.[1]

Though Wilkinson had sent Adair, Ogden, Alexander, Bollman, and Swartwout to Eastern cities for trial, there were numerous partisans of Burr still in New Orleans and Natchez. Various attempts were made to prosecute them, but Workman and Kerr were acquitted in New Orleans. No charges were brought against Burr's two chief henchmen in the Crescent City, Edward Livingston and Daniel Clark, for the latter was Wilkinson's friend and the former was too dangerous an enemy. Judge Toulmin of the Superior Court of Mississippi Territory committed Blennerhassett, Tyler, Floyd, and Ralston to be arraigned in the Territory and they were released

[1] Livingston (?), 'Faithful Picture of the Political Situation in New Orleans,' loc. cit. 430–35; Rowland, *Claiborne*, IV, 110–12; Claiborne to Jefferson, 3 May 1807, Carter, *Territorial Papers*, IX, 729–31; same to same, 19 May 1807, ibid. 734–6; ibid. 707, 743–4; Richmond *Enquirer*, 10 Apr. 1807, 1 May 1807.

on bail pending trial in May. Finally, after a hearing which lasted for two weeks, they were all discharged.[2] On 11 June, Blennerhassett set out for his Island in the Ohio, but on 14 July he was arrested in Lexington, Kentucky, and taken to Richmond to stand trial with Burr.[3]

No better success was had in the prosecution of those whom Wilkinson had sent to the East. Adair and Ogden were discharged by Judge Nicholson in Baltimore on the ground that they had committed no crime in that jurisdiction; Alexander was set at liberty by the Circuit Court of the District of Columbia on the same ground; and Bollman and Swartwout appeared before the Supreme Court of the United States on a writ of habeas corpus, with John Marshall presiding.[4]

This case had a direct and important bearing upon the later trial of Burr in Richmond, and it is therefore of especial interest. The only important evidence available was that sent by Wilkinson to Jefferson, which included Burr's cipher letter to the Brigadier. After deciding that it had jurisdiction and that Wilkinson's testimony was admissible, the court proceeded to enunciate several important principles regarding the crime of treason, of which the defendants were accused. Marshall declared,

> It is not the intention of the court to say, that no individual can be guilty of this crime, who has not appeared in arms against his country. On the contrary, if war be actually levied, that is, if a body of men be actually assembled, for the purpose of effecting by force a treasonable purpose, all those who perform any part, however minute, or however remote from the scene of action, and who are actually leagued in the general conspiracy are to be considered as traitors. But there must be an actual assembling of men, for the treasonable purpose, to constitute a levying of war.[5]

Continuing, the court said:

[2] *Republican and Savannah Evening Ledger*, 4 Apr. 1807, communication from New Orleans, dated 23 Feb. 1807.

[3] Burr MSS., L. of C.

[4] McCaleb, *Burr Conspiracy*, 254.

[5] William Cranch (ed.), *Reports of Cases Argued and Adjudicated in the Supreme Court of the United States, in the years 1807 and 1808* (New York, 1812), IV, 122; Prentiss, *Eaton*, 396–400.

> To complete the crime of levying war against the United States, there must be an actual assemblage of men for the purpose of executing a treasonable design. In the case now before the court, a design to overturn the government of the United States, in New Orleans, by force, would have been unquestionably a design which, if carried into execution, would have been treason, and the assemblage of a body of men for the purpose of carrying it into execution, would amount to levying of war against the United States , . .

Marshall then went on to explain that the mere enlisting of men for a treasonable purpose did not constitute treason, but if groups from different points were brought together to carry out a treasonable design, then treason had been committed. 'If the term levying, in this place, imports that they were assembled, then such fact would amount, if the intention be against the United States, to levying war.' [6]

It was finally stated that the plan to seize the banks in New Orleans would amount to robbery rather than an act of war. The Chief Justice then declared that, 'It is, therefore, the opinion of a majority of the court, that in the case of Samuel Swartwout there is not sufficient evidence of his levying war against the United States to justify his commitment on the charge of treason.' [7] In spite of the outcome, it seemed to have been decided that the assembling of groups of men with a treasonable object in view amounted to treason even though no actual force had been used, and anyone who had performed any part in bringing about such an assemblage, even though he was not actually present at the rendezvous, was as guilty as those who were there. This was the basis upon which the indictment of Burr was founded and upon which the prosecution based its case against him.[8]

At early candlelight in Richmond, Virginia, on the evening of 26 March 1807, a strange cavalcade of seven horsemen and a stagecoach made its way down Main Street to the Eagle Tavern, then the principal hostelry of the little city of about 6000 inhabitants. The tavern was a brick structure occupying an entire city block

[6] Cranch (ed.), *Reports of Cases* . . . IV, 126, 133.
[7] Ibid. 134.
[8] Safford, *Blennerhassett Papers*, 413, 433; Beveridge, *Marshall*, 466.

on the south side of Main Street between Twelfth and Thirteenth Streets, nearly opposite the capitol building which Jefferson had designed. Burr, who still wore the floppy white hat and the river boatman's costume in which he had been captured, rode in the coach, and he and his escort from the backwoods must have created a sensation as they entered the building.[9]

For four days the Colonel was kept under guard in his room, but on the 30th, John Marshall, Chief Justice of the Supreme Court and the leading citizen of Richmond, appeared with a warrant which he himself had drawn up. He was accompanied by Caesar Rodney, Attorney General of the United States, George Hay, United States Attorney for the Virginia District and son-in-law of James Monroe, Edmund Randolph and John Wickham, counsel for the prisoner, and Major Joseph Scott, Marshal of the Virginia District, who served the warrant.

Burr was now conducted to a secluded room in the tavern where Marshall awaited him, and the loiterers in the public room stood silent as the prisoner passed. The prosecution presented the record of the Bollman and Swartwout case, which included the affidavits of Eaton and Wilkinson, and Major Perkins was called on to give an account of the arrest of the prisoner. This having been finished, Hay submitted a motion that Burr be held on a charge of misdemeanor for having set on foot an expedition against the dominions of the King of Spain, and on a charge of treason for having assembled an armed force for the purpose of seizing the city of New Orleans, revolutionizing Orleans Territory, and separating the Western from the Atlantic states.[10]

Since it was apparent that this motion would lead to considerable discussion, it was agreed that the hearing should be removed next day to the capitol building, and there, in the hall of the House of

[9] Samuel Mordecai, *Richmond in By-gone Days*, 57; John P. Little, *History of Richmond* (Richmond, 1933), 103; William Cabell Bruce, *John Randolph of Roanoke*, 1773–1833 (New York, 1922), I, 300; Pickett, *Alabama*, 499; Richmond *Enquirer*, 27 Mar. 1807.

[10] William W. Hening and William Munford (eds.), *The Examination of Col. Aaron Burr before the Chief Justice of the United States upon the Charges of High Misdemeanor and of Treason Against the United States, Together with the Arguments of Counsel and Opinion of the Judge* (Richmond, 1807), 3; James Alston Cabell, *The Trial of Aaron Burr* (Albany, 1900), 1–9.

Delegates, all future proceedings in the trial were conducted.[11] Jefferson's capitol remains today much as it was then, except that wings have been added and the bricks have been covered with plaster, but the grounds have undergone a greater change. Instead of the present serpentine brick walks and shaded lawns, there was a gully-washed hillside, and winding stone steps led up its steep slope to the classical portico of the building. There was a horse-rack near each entrance, and goats nibbled among the weeds or lay in the shade of the trees. Such was the scene of the trial of Aaron Burr.[12]

For two days the argument on Hay's motion for commitment continued and a motley throng of curious citizens overflowed the hall of the House of Delegates. Finally on 1 April, John Marshall delivered his written opinion. He quoted Blackstone to the effect that a prisoner could be discharged only when it appeared that the suspicion against him was 'wholly groundless,' but that this did not mean that 'the hand of malignity may grasp any individual against whom its hate may be directed or whom it may capriciously seize, charge him with some secret crime and put him on the proof of his innocence.' But, said he, 'I ought to require, and I should require, that probable cause be shown; and I understand probable cause to be a case made out by proof furnishing good reason to believe that the crime alleged has been committed by the person charged with having committed it.' [13]

The Chief Justice stated that no proof had been adduced to show that Burr had assembled troops for a treasonable purpose, though 'Months have elapsed since the fact did occur, if it ever occurred. More than five weeks have elapsed since the . . . supreme court [in the Bollman and Swartwout case] has declared the necessity of proving the fact, if it exists.' He then concluded: 'I shall not therefore insert in the commitment the charge of high treason, since it will be entirely in the power of the Attorney-General to prefer an indictment against the prisoner for high treason should he be furnished with the necessary testimony.' Burr was then bailed in

[11] Hening and Munford (eds.), *The Examination of Aaron Burr*, 3–5.

[12] Mordecai, *Richmond*, 71–3.

[13] Joseph P. Brady, *The Trial of Aaron Burr* (New York, 1913), 12; Beveridge, *Marshall*, III, 376.

the sum of $10,000 to answer the charge of misdemeanor at the next term of the Circuit Court of the United States, which was to be held in Richmond on 22 May.[14]

When President Jefferson heard of Marshall's opinion, he was enraged and on 20 April wrote to Senator William B. Giles of Virginia referring to the 'tricks of the judges to force trials before it is possible to collect the evidence, dispersed through a line of two thousand miles from Maine to Orleans . . . In what terms of decency,' he asked, 'can we speak of this? As if an express could go to Natchez, or the mouth of Cumberland, and return in five weeks, to do which has never taken less than twelve.' He accused Marshall of having confused *probability* with *proof*, and the Federalists of having made Burr's cause their own.[15] Matching his actions with his words, he conferred for three days with the attorney general, and a Mr. Drew was commissioned to summon witnesses from all parts of the West.[16] Thus at the very beginning of the case, the President made himself a party to the prosecution, and the Chief Justice became a real, though not an avowed, partisan of the defense.

Within a week after his liberation, Burr dined with his chief counsel, John Wickham, and the Chief Justice sat at table with him. Wickham was the leading light of the Richmond bar and an important social figure in the Capital. He and Marshall were neighbors and they often played chess and dined together. It has been argued that the Chief Justice did not know Burr would be present on this occasion, and that politeness required him to remain even after he had discovered the presence of the man upon whom he was to sit in judgment. Be this as it may, the incident stirred up considerable comment in the Republican press.[17]

But Jefferson was no more correct than Marshall was in his attitude toward the accused. On 2 April, the day after Burr was committed, the President wrote to James Bowdoin, minister to Spain, saying, 'Although at first, he [Burr] proposed a separation

[14] Ibid. 378; Brady, *Trial of Aaron Burr*, 12–13.

[15] Jefferson to William B. Giles, *Writings of Thomas Jefferson* (Mem. ed.), XI, 187–91.

[16] Ibid. I, 467–8, 470; Daveiss, *View*, 106.

[17] Richmond *Enquirer*, 10 Apr. 1807.

of the western country, and on that ground received encouragement and aid from Yrujo . . . yet he very early saw that the fidelity of the western country was not to be shaken, and turned himself wholly towards Mexico. And so popular is an enterprise on that country in this, that we had only to lie still, and he would have had followers enough to have been in the City of Mexico in six weeks.'[18] This was what Jefferson wished the Spanish ministry to believe, but his real opinion was stated to Lafayette in a letter of 14 July: 'Burr's first enterprise was to have been to seize New Orleans, which would powerfully bridle the upper country and place him at the door of Mexico.'[19]

The President has been much criticized for his conduct in relation to Dr. Bollman. After that adventurer was released from custody by the Supreme Court, he made the statement in which he gave his version of the conspiracy to Jefferson and Madison. The next day the President requested the Doctor to write down the substance of his disclosures, giving him his word of honor that the information would never be used against him and that the paper would never go out of his hand.[20] In spite of this, Jefferson sent the document to Hay, but instructed him to show it to no one except his associate counsel. So anxious was he to have Bollman turn state's witness that he sent Hay a pardon for him in order that he might testify without incriminating himself. This was offered to him by Hay in open court, but the Doctor haughtily refused it.[21]

Seeing the Administration make itself a party to the case, the Court acted with equal partiality. Marshall allowed counsel for the defense to belabor the Executive in no uncertain terms, and on one occasion permitted himself to remark that the Government 'expected' Burr's conviction. Hay wrote to Jefferson that 'This expression produced a very strong and very general sensation. The friends of the Judge, both personal and political, Condemned it.

[18] *Writings of Thomas Jefferson* (Mem. ed.), XI, 185.

[19] Ibid. XI, 279.

[20] Philadelphia *Aurora*, 16 July 1807; Bowers, *Jefferson in Power*, 414; Beveridge, *Marshall*, III, 391.

[21] Bollman Pardon, 18 May 1807, Records of Burr Trial, Clerk's Office, United States District Court, Richmond, Va.; Coombs, *Trial of Aaron Burr*, 54; McCaleb, *Burr Conspiracy*, 281.

Alexr. McRae rose as he had finished, and in terms mild yet determined, demanded an explanation of it. The Judge actually blushed.'[22] A little later, when the crowd had thinned, Marshall acknowledged the impropriety of the expression and informed the defense counsel that he had erased it. After he had adjourned the court, he told Hay that he regretted the remark.[23]

Thus high did tempers rise, and the people in general, stirred up by the Republican press, were convinced that Burr was guilty of treason and should be condemned. Marshall was so impressed by the clamor that he declared 'it would be difficult or dangerous for a jury to venture to acquit Burr, however innocent they might think him.' But the Federalist aristocrats of Richmond were Burr's devoted partisans, and the ladies took the lead in paying him marked attention.[24] As the trial progressed, even the Republican majority was influenced by the success of the defense counsel in making the President appear as a vindictive prosecutor and Burr as the victim of persecution. So sensational was the trial — though it was not decided on the merits of the case — that it has tended to overshadow the conspiracy itself; even historians have been influenced by the spirit that pervaded it and have frequently seen Burr as a shining example of injured innocence.[25]

When the United States Circuit Court for the District of Virginia convened in the hall of the House of Delegates at 12:30 on 22 May 1807, with John Marshall presiding and Cyrus Griffin, district judge, later joining him on the bench, the chamber itself and the passages leading to it were thronged with curious spectators. There were laborers and artisans clad in honest homespun, and gentlemen wearing old-fashioned small clothes or the pantaloons of the sans-culottes. Some came merely to satisfy their craving for excitement; others had been summoned to serve on the grand jury or to act as witnesses. The emaciated and vitriolic John Randolph, now a bitter enemy of the Administration, was there, and so was Winfield Scott, then a fledgling lawyer just admitted to the bar. Andrew

[22] Beveridge, *Marshall*, III, 448–9; Cabell, *Trial of Aaron Burr*, 12.
[23] Beveridge, *Marshall*, III, 449.
[24] Ibid. 401; Safford, *Blennerhassett Papers*, 465–6; Bowers, *Jefferson in Power*, 403.
[25] Beveridge, *Marshall*, III, 450.

Jackson had come to testify for Burr, but he did not wear buckskins or a coonskin cap. Except for his harangue on the capitol steps in favor of Burr, his condemnation of the President, and his allegation that Wilkinson was a Spanish pensioner, no notice would have been taken of him, for he had not yet been heard of much beyond the neighborhood of Nashville. The tippling and flamboyant 'General' William Eaton and Colonel George Morgan and his two sons had come to bear witness against the accused; but Dr. Erich Bollman, Jonathan Dayton, and Colonel Julien De Pestre would be more friendly witnesses provided they were given a chance to testify. Washington Irving was a young attorney at the time, but he attended the trial as a friend of Burr and as a reporter for a New York newspaper. Benjamin Latrobe, the architect, along with many others, had been summoned as a witness.[26]

That this trial was supposed to be a full-dress affair is indicated by the caliber of the panel summoned to constitute the grand jury. Among prospective jurymen were William B. Giles, United States Senator from Virginia, Wilson Cary Nicholas, friend and neighbor of Jefferson and former United States Senator, Littleton W. Tazewell and James Pleasants, each afterward governor of Virginia and United States Senator, James Barbour, later to serve as governor, Senator, and Secretary of War under John Quincy Adams, and Joseph C. Cabell, one of the founders with Jefferson of the University of Virginia, who took and preserved notes on the proceedings.[27] Marshall granted Burr the unusual privilege of challenging grand jurors, and Giles and Nicholas were stricken from the list. Sixteen names were finally approved and Marshall appointed John Randolph, shrill-voiced and sharp-tongued leader of the anti-Administration Republicans in Congress, to serve as foreman.[28]

The jury was now duly sworn by the court clerk and the Chief Justice delivered his charge. It then retired and assembled again

[26] David Robertson (stenographer), *Report of the Trials of Colonel Aaron Burr* (New York, 1875), I, 396–7; Prentiss, *Eaton*, 408–9; Bruce, *Randolph*, I, 301; Bowers, *Jefferson in Power*, 403.

[27] Brady, *Trial of Aaron Burr*, 22–3; Joseph C. Cabell, Notes of evidence in the case of Aaron Burr, Indictment for Treason, Richmond, Va., 13 June 1807, Cabell Papers, Alderman Library, U. Va.

[28] Brady, *Trial of Aaron Burr*, 21; Beveridge, *Marshall*, III, 409–10.

the next day, but since General Wilkinson, the principal witness for the state, had not appeared, it was necessary for the jury to adjourn from day to day until he arrived. Fearing that Burr might forfeit his bond and disappear before the General came, District Attorney George Hay moved the court, just after the empaneling of the grand jury, that the Colonel be committed for treason, an offense which was not bailable.[29]

Marshall had previously ruled against such a commitment, but Hay thought that sufficient additional evidence was now available to warrant his motion. Counsel for the defense argued that the court could not commit while the grand jury was in session, but Marshall ruled against them. At the same time, however, he informed Hay that it would be necessary to prove an overt act of treason and that the submission of adequate evidence at this stage in the proceedings might prejudice the case. Hay then reluctantly called up several witnesses; they were examined, and the opposing counsel indulged in lengthy debates. Convinced that Hay meant to proceed, Marshall gave ground and declared that 'as very improper effects on the public mind' might be produced, and that the 'appearance of colonel Burr could be secured without . . . proceeding in this inquiry,' he wished that no opinion would be required of him previous to the action of the grand jury. Seeing the Judge embarrassed, Burr now relented from his former stand and agreed to give additional bail. Marshall eagerly accepted the offer, and four new sureties bound themselves in the amount of $10,000, bringing the total bail to $20,000.[30]

Among the sureties was Luther Martin, who put in his appearance as counsel for Burr on the very day the bond was signed. He was the most prominent member of the Maryland bar and one of the greatest tipplers of his day. It was said that he could not argue a case unless he was under the influence of ardent spirits, and that he always kept a bottle conveniently at hand while attending court.[31] He and Burr had become close friends during the im-

[29] Brady, *Trial of Aaron Burr*, 24–7.

[30] Cabell, *Trial of Aaron Burr*, 20; Beveridge, *Marshall*, III, 428–9.

[31] Wright and Macleod, 'William Eaton's Relations with Aaron Burr,' loc. cit. 532; Martin to Joseph Alston, 26 June 1805, Worthington C. Ford, 'Some Papers

peachment trial of Justice Samuel Chase, on which occasion Burr, then Vice-President, had presided over the Senate, while Martin served as chief counsel for the accused. Now he came to offer his services free of charge, and when Theodosia arrived he became quite enamoured of her. His language and manners were coarse, but he was a great lawyer and a staunch Federalist. His weight was soon felt on the side of the defense, for nothing pleased him more than an opportunity to attack the President. Years later Burr repaid the debt by taking Martin, then poverty-stricken and feeble in mind and body, into his own home and caring for him faithfully until the Marylander's death.[32]

While proceedings were still being held up because of the failure of Wilkinson to arrive, Burr arose in court on 9 June and stated that the letter which the General had addressed to the President on 21 October, Jefferson's reply to the same, and the orders issued to the Army and Navy for his apprehension, were material to his defense. He said that access to these papers had been denied to him and his counsel, and requested that a subpoena *duces tecum* be issued to the President, requiring him to appear personally before the court and produce the desired papers.[33]

Hay at once notified his chief of this move, and Jefferson replied: 'Reserving the necessary right of the President of the United States to decide, independently of all other authority, what papers, coming to him as President, the public interests permit to be communicated, and to whom, I assure you of my readiness under that restriction, voluntarily to furnish on all occasions, whatever the purposes of justice may require.' He said he had turned over the Wilkinson letter and all other documents relating to the trial to the attorney general and he would instruct that official to make them available.[34] At Wilkinson's request, however, he returned

of Aaron Burr,' reprinted from the *Proceedings of the American Antiquarian Society*, Apr. 1919 (Worcester, 1920), 83–4.

[32] Safford, *Blennerhassett Papers*, 375–9.

[33] Statement of Aaron Burr, 10 June 1807, Records of Burr Trial, U.S. District Court, Richmond, Va.; Richmond *Enquirer*, 13 June 1807; Cabell, *Trial of Aaron Burr*, 20–22.

[34] Jefferson to Hay, 12 June 1807, *Writings of Thomas Jefferson* (Mem. ed.), XI, 228.

to him a letter which the General had addressed to Jonathan Dayton. Both the President and the Secretary of War were unswerving in their support of the star witness for the prosecution throughout the trial.[35]

Burr's motion was the signal for an acrimonious debate between opposing counsel which lasted until 13 June. William Wirt charged that Burr's lawyers, on the slightest pretext, 'flew off at a tangent . . . to launch into declamations against the government, exhibiting the prisoner continually as a persecuted patriot: a Russell or a Sidney, bleeding under the scourge of a despot, and dying for virtue's sake!'[36] Marshall was embarrassed and, before adjourning court, stated that though he had not approved of the assertions of counsel made 'in the heat of Debate,' he had not interfered.[37]

The prosecution admitted that the court might subpoena the President as well as any other man, but maintained that he was not bound to disclose confidential communications. Marshall held otherwise and on the 13th handed down his opinion that, 'On a motion of Attorneys for reasons appearing to the Court, it is ordered that a subpoena *duces tecum* be awarded to summon the President of the United States, or such of the secretaries of the departments as may have the papers mentioned . . .'[38] But when the writ was drawn up, it contained the statement: 'The transmission to the Clerk of this Court of the original letter of General Wilkinson, and of copies duly authenticated of the other papers and documents described in the annexed process, will be admitted as sufficient observance of the process, without the personal attendance of any or either of the persons therein named.'[39] Thus Marshall did not issue the challenge to the President which he had indicated in court that he would issue, and consequently historians have been misled into believing that Jefferson defied the order of the Chief Justice.

While this debate was in progress, the laggard Wilkinson arrived

[35] Jefferson to Wilkinson, 21 June 1807, Bacon, *Report*, 463–4; Dearborn to Wilkinson, 22 June 1807, ibid. 414–15.

[36] Beveridge, *Marshall*, III, 438.

[37] Ibid. 439.

[38] Records of Burr Trial, U.S. District Court, Richmond, Va.; Beveridge, *Marshall*, III, 445.

[39] Document dated 13 June 1807, Records of Burr Trial, U.S. District Court, Richmond, Va.

in Norfolk with eight or nine witnesses in tow and reached Richmond on Saturday, 13 June, just as Marshall was delivering his opinion on the question of the subpoena.[40] On Monday, the General, portly and red-faced, decked out in full uniform, strode into court and, according to Washington Irving, 'stood for a moment swelling like a turkey cock.' Burr, now wearing black silk and a powdered wig, gave him a scornful glance, and Wilkinson, according to his own account, 'darted a flash of indignation at the little Traitor, — This Lyon hearted Eagle Eyed Hero, sinking under the weight of conscious guilt, with haggard Eye, made an Effort to meet the indignant salutation of outraged Honor, but it was in vain, his audacity failed Him, He averted his face, grew pale & affected passion to conceal his perturbation.' [41] Washington Irving gives a very different picture of the meeting.

Having been sworn, the General now appeared before the grand jury to present his evidence against Burr. Seeing that he was wearing his sword, John Randolph, the foreman, ordered the marshal to 'take that man out and disarm him. I will allow no attempt to intimidate the jury.' [42] Wilkinson was kept on the carpet for four days, and was forced to admit that in his version of Burr's cipher letter he had omitted the opening sentence, 'Your letter postmarked 13th May, is received,' and several other passages. He also admitted that the cipher was devised in 1794 instead of 1804, as he had originally sworn. A motion was then made to indict the General for misprision of treason, and it failed by the narrow margin of seven to nine votes only because of a technicality.[43] This so disgusted Randolph that he wrote: 'The mammoth of iniquity escaped, — not that any man pretended to think him innocent, but upon certain wire-drawn distinctions . . . Wilkinson is the only man that I ever

[40] John Graham to Madison, 11 May 1807, Burr MSS., L. of C.; Cabell, *Trial of Aaron Burr*, 23.

[41] Beveridge, *Marshall*, III, 408, 456–7.

[42] Cabell, *Trial of Aaron Burr*, 24.

[43] Bruce, *Randolph*, I, 303–5; Richmond *Enquirer*, 3 Nov. 1807; *Louisiana Gazette*, 26 Feb., 22 Mar., 13 May 1808; Clark, *Proofs*, app. 164–5; *Annals of Congress*, 10 Cong., 1 Sess., I, 630; Questions to be propounded to Genl. Wilkinson, Joseph C. Cabell, Notes of evidence in the case of Aaron Burr, Cabell Papers, Alderman Library, U. Va.; Copy of Burr's cipher letter indicating parts omitted by Wilkinson, ibid. 73–5.

saw who was from the bark to the very core a villain . . . Perhaps you never saw human nature in so degraded a situation as in the person of Wilkinson before the grand jury, and yet this man stands on the very summit and pinnacle of executive favor . . .' Four days earlier, on 21 June, Jefferson had written to comfort the General: 'Your enemies have filled the public ear with slanders and your mind with trouble on that account. The establishment of their guilt will let the world see what they ought to think of their clamors . . .'[44]

After having examined about 50 witnesses, including Andrew Jackson and William Eaton, the grand jury, on 24 June, brought in indictments against Burr and Blennerhassett for treason and for misdemeanor, and the next day Jonathan Dayton, John Smith, Comfort Tyler, Israel Smith, and Davis Floyd were also indicted, but no charges were made against such prominent friends of the former Vice-President as Bollman, Swartwout, Ogden, Adair, Clark, or Livingston.[45] Because treason was not a bailable offense, Burr spent one night in the city jail, but on the 26th his attorneys made oath that this confinement was endangering his health and interfering with their access to him. Accordingly Marshall ordered that he be removed to the house occupied by Luther Martin and there confined to the front room with the windows barred, the door padlocked, and a guard of seven men detailed to watch it.[46] When Yrujo heard of the indictment he came to the conclusion that the Colonel would be condemned to the gallows.[47]

The action against Burr could have afforded John Randolph little satisfaction, for he believed that a greater malefactor had escaped the toils of the law. Consequently, on the day after the Colonel was indicted, he asked him to submit to the grand jury the letter of 13 May, which he had said he received from the General. Burr now, in his best manner, drew the mantle of his righteousness about him and declared that he could not reveal a confidential communi-

[44] Bruce, *Randolph*, I, 303–4; Adams, *History of the United States*, III, 465; McCaleb, *Burr Conspiracy*, 277.

[45] List of witnesses before the Grand Jury, Burr Case, Cabell Papers, Alderman Library, U. Va.; Records of Burr Trial, U.S. District Court, Richmond, Va.; Bruce, *Randolph*, I, 303; Beveridge, *Marshall*, III, 465, 466fn.

[46] Ibid. 474; McCaleb, *Burr Conspiracy*, 276.

[47] A.H.N., Estado, leg. 3633, apartado I, no. 873, 184–8.

cation unless 'the extremity of circumstances' impelled him to such conduct or unless it was extorted from him by law. He could not even 'deliberate on the proposition to deliver up anything which had been confided' to his honor.[48]

That such confidential relations should have existed between Burr and Wilkinson at the time seems astounding, but there was something more than showed upon the surface. The General had denied that he knew anything of Burr's plans before receiving his cipher letter at Natchitoches,[49] but some time later he turned over to two of his friends four or five cipher letters which he had received from the Colonel while still at St. Louis and which had been written before the one Swartwout had delivered. Wilkinson said he had not examined them since he left St. Louis and did not remember their contents in detail, but 'having received them in confidence & knowing they blend personalities with Politicks, I have not permitted myself to reexamine them because I feel an insuperable repugnance to violate the trust of any man . . .'[50] Thus the General was as punctilious about his 'honor' as was the Colonel, who of course knew that if he surrendered Wilkinson's letter, the General would surrender those he had received. Wilkinson said later that if Burr would only produce his letter of 13 May and thus enable him to make the additional cipher letters public, the whole question regarding his conduct could be revealed in its true light. He even challenged Burr to produce the document, but the Colonel was not moved to change his mind.[51] It is unfortunate that these bitter enemies were forced to protect each other in this instance and thus deprive historians of evidence that probably would have avoided all the controversy arising in regard to the real nature of the conspiracy.

Although Burr's quarters at Luther Martin's house were barred and padlocked, Hay considered them a bit too cozy for a prisoner charged with treason and obtained permission of the state authori-

[48] Beveridge, *Marshall*, III, 466–7.

[49] Philadelphia *Aurora*, 6 June 1807, extract of letter from Richmond, 1 June 1807.

[50] Deposition of A. L. Duncan, 5 Sept. 1807, Chillicothe Papers; Charleston *Courier*, 30 Oct. 1807.

[51] Safford, *Blennerhassett Papers*, 438–9.

ties to have him removed to the penitentiary. Accordingly, on the last day of June, the Colonel was removed to three rooms on the top floor of that institution, which stood near the James River on the outskirts of Richmond, where the penitentiary, much enlarged, still stands. There were no other prisoners on the same floor, and Burr must have had considerable indulgence, for he was able to entertain a constant stream of guests. He was anxious that his daughter should not be perturbed because of his situation, and thinking that he might comfort her during the trial, sent for her to come to Richmond. She and her husband, Joseph Alston, soon to become governor of South Carolina, arrived on 4 August, the day after the treason trial opened, and took up their abode in the rooms that the Colonel had lately vacated at Luther Martin's house.[52]

Harman Blennerhassett, having been arrested in Kentucky while making his way to his island home, was brought to Richmond on the same day and was assigned quarters near Burr in the penitentiary. The Federalists of the city were almost as attentive to him as to his principal. Mrs. Brockenbrough, 'the nearest approach to a *savante* here,' took keen interest in the 'Querist' articles; Mrs. Carrington offered to send him jellies and soups, and General Henry (Light Horse Harry) Lee proffered any services that might be required.[53] Somewhat later Blennerhassett met Mrs. David Randolph, sister to Jefferson's son-in-law, Thomas Mann Randolph, and

> heard more pungent stricture upon Jefferson's head and heart, because they were better founded than any I had ever heard before, and she certainly uttered more treason than *my wife* ever dreamed of; for she ridiculed the experiment of a Republic in this country, which the vices and inconstancy of parties and the people had too long shown to be nothing more than annual series of essays to complete a work ill begun, and which appeared to be nearly worn out before it was half-finished . . . And as for treason, she cordially hoped whenever Burr, or any one else, again attempted to do anything, the Atlantic States would be comprised in the plan.[54]

[52] Theodosia Burr Alston to Mrs. H. Blennerhassett, 5 Aug. 1807, W. C. Ford (ed.), 'Some Papers of Aaron Burr,' loc. cit. 85; Dice R. Anderson, *William Branch Giles* (Menasha, Wis., 1914), 109–10; Cabell, *Trial of Aaron Burr*, 25.

[53] Safford, *Blennerhassett Papers*, 312, 425–6.

[54] Ibid. 457.

Relations between Blennerhassett and Burr, while not broken off entirely, were far from cordial at this time, the former saying he had known for nine months that he had been duped by the Colonel.[55] Burr was consorting mostly with Bollman and Alston while planning to dispose of some of the Ouachita lands and then go to England to carry on his imperialistic projects. Blennerhassett claimed to have lost $21,000 by endorsing notes for Burr, which he was trying to get Alston to make good, but the latter had lost $50,000 on his own account. The Colonel was making an effort to get both these men to take Ouachita lands in lieu of their claims, but Blennerhassett said that Comfort Tyler and Israel Smith 'who had once been very intent on settling there, had long ago abandoned the scheme, believing . . . Lynch's title was bad,' and refused to make any such deal, remarking that 'This may turn out to be another instance in which Burr may have reason to deprecate my knowledge of him.' [56] The islander appears to have been a bit jealous of Bollman's intimacy with Burr and remarked that the Doctor 'has possibly never heard from *authority* that I have been offered to choose him or Shaw for my private *secretary*, when I should name a diplomatic appointment for myself.' [57]

Burr's dignified deportment, the warm friendship that the local Federalists showed for him, and the skillful management of his counsel, gradually won a degree of recognition from the average citizen of Richmond, and Wilkinson's popularity declined proportionately.[58] One day young Swartwout — who accused Wilkinson of stealing his watch when he seized his baggage in New Orleans — met the General in public and shouldered him off the sidewalk into the middle of the street. The hero of the Sabine swallowed this insult, but the New Yorker was not satisfied and challenged him to a duel. Wilkinson refused to honor the challenge, declaring that he would have no dealings with traitors, upon which Swartwout published notices branding him a coward.[59] The General, however,

[55] Ibid. 372–3.
[56] Ibid. 254, 353.
[57] Ibid. 351.
[58] Beveridge, *Marshall*, III, 472.
[59] Ibid. 471–2; Cabell, *Trial of Aaron Burr*, 24; Bruce, *Randolph*, 305–6; Safford, *Blennerhassett Papers*, 459.

was determined to show his mettle and challenged Wickham for having called him a perjurer in open court. The attorney declined this encounter on the ground that perjury was an actionable offense and that the question should be settled legally.[60]

Finally, on 3 August, the famous trial of Aaron Burr for treason got under way as the oppressive heat of late summer settled over Richmond. It did not last quite a month and attracted as much attention as any trial that was ever held in the United States, but it turned out to be little more than a farce. The first business before the court was the selection of a jury, and this proved to be no easy matter. Two panels of 48 each were called up before 12 men could be selected, and some of these admitted a prejudice against the accused. It was not until 15 August that this business was completed and the jury sworn, Edward Carrington, brother-in-law of the Chief Justice, being made foreman.[61]

The prosecution had called 140 witnesses to back up its case, which was based, as was the indictment of the grand jury, upon Marshall's opinion in the Bollman and Swartwout case. Hay and his colleagues understood the Chief Justice to have said that an armed force that was assembled for a treasonable purpose was guilty of an act of treason, and that anyone who had helped to bring about such an assemblage, whether or not he was present in person, was a party to the crime.[62] But Hay was not sure he would succeed, and while the jury was being selected he wrote to Jefferson, 'There is but one chance for the accused, and that is a good one because it rests with the Chief Justice. It is already hinted, but not by himself [that] the decision of the Supreme Court [in the Bollman-Swartwout case] will no[t be] deemed binding. If the assembly of men on [Blennerhassett's is]land, can be pronounced "not an overt act" [it will] be so pronounced.'[63]

The forces concerned in the conviction of Burr spared no pains in their effort to collect evidence. Jefferson sent blank pardons to

[60] William Upshaw to Wilkinson, 29 Oct. 1807, John Wickham Papers (microfilm), Alderman Library, U. Va.; Wickham to Dr. Upshaw, 31 Oct. 1807, ibid.

[61] Cabell, *Trial of Aaron Burr*, 25.

[62] Beveridge, *Marshall*, III, 466, 484; William Cranch, *Reports of Cases Argued and Adjudicated in the Supreme Court of the United States*, IV, 126–7.

[63] Beveridge, *Marshall*, III, 484.

Hay in order that they might be offered to key witnesses inclined to turn state's evidence.[64] Colonel William Duane, editor of the Philadelphia *Aurora* and a strong Administration man, came down to Richmond, called on Blennerhassett, and intimated to him that if he would acknowledge the authorship of certain papers (the 'Querist' articles), the editor would intercede for him in Washington 'where nothing he should ask would be refused him.' [65] And, according to Blennerhassett, Colonel De Pestre, Burr's chief-of-staff, was approached with an offer to provide for him handsomely in the American Army 'if his principles or engagements were not adverse to the administration,' but the French Colonel declined.[66]

When the jury was finally sworn on 15 August, the trial proceeded and 11 witnesses were examined, including Eaton, Commodore Truxton, Colonel George Morgan, and his son General John Morgan. All the other witnesses were persons who could give testimony about what happened on Blennerhassett Island on the night of 10 December 1806. There being no further testimony regarding the events on the island, the defense moved that since no overt act of treason had been proved, collateral evidence about what had been said or done elsewhere and beyond the jurisdiction of the court should not be admitted.[67]

After Wickham and his colleagues had argued this point at length, the Chief Justice allowed the defense four days in which to prepare its answer. Alston told Blennerhassett that a friend of Marshall's asked him was not this against all precedent, and the Chief Justice answered that it was, but that if he should decide in favor of the defendant, he would be accused of not having been disposed to allow the prosecution an opportunity to answer. Blennerhassett had also heard that while playing chess with Wickham, Marshall had asked, 'Don't you think . . . you will be able to check-mate these fellows, and relieve us from being kept here three weeks more?' [68] This was a serious charge against a great jurist, and the story may have been manufactured out of whole cloth, but Blennerhassett

[64] McCaleb, *Burr Conspiracy*, 181.
[65] Safford, *Blennerhassett Papers*, 356.
[66] Schachner, *Burr*, 431.
[67] Beveridge, *Marshall*, III, 491.
[68] Safford, *Blennerhassett Papers*, 354–5.

wrote his journal only for the eyes of his wife, and it was not published during his lifetime. It reveals more rancor against Burr than against any other participant in the trial, and the author certainly had no reason to be prejudiced against Marshall. One good reason for accepting the evidence of the journal is that in it Blennerhassett never proclaimed his innocence, but frequently implied guilt, as when he admitted that the Hendersons were the most dangerous witnesses against him and blamed them for betraying his confidence to John Graham. He also censured Burr for having committed himself to Wilkinson and the Morgans.[69]

The day before the court handed down its opinion, Blennerhassett recorded that Mercer, a charming gentleman and in love with a relative of the Chief Justice, tried 'to discharge our apprehensions . . . that the Chief Justice would possess *all* the energy that would be necessary to reconcile the opinion he had delivered . . . in the case of Bollman and Swartwout, with such another as would be required of him to establish the most material of all the points now before him.' [70] Then a few days later the Irishman said that Bollman, Swartwout, and young Ogden were agents of Alston whose industry had enabled him 'to anticipate the opinion of the Chief Justice . . . long before any body else scarcely would venture an opinion, or conjecture about it.' [71] It also appears that some undercover work enabled Burr to obtain a complete transcript of the proceedings before the grand jury.[72]

Finally, on the last day of August, the Chief Justice was ready to hand down his momentous decision. He realized that his reasoning in the Bollman and Swartwout case required some explanation, and went to great lengths to explain it. Albert J. Beveridge, in *The Life of John Marshall*, says that 'The opinion of the Chief Justice was one of the longest ever rendered by him, and the only one in which an extensive examination of authorities is made. Indeed, a

[69] Blennerhassett to Mrs. Blennerhassett, 4 Aug. 1807, Safford, *Blennerhassett Papers*, 276; ibid. 309–10, 329, 347.
[70] Ibid. 375.
[71] Ibid. 388.
[72] Ibid. 417–19; Philadelphia *Aurora*, 15 Aug. 1807, notice from Richmond, 7 Aug. 1807.

greater number of decisions, treatises, and histories are referred to than in all the rest of Marshall's foremost Constitutional opinions.' [73]

The decision in this case depended upon two separate conclusions. In the first place, the jurist held that 'war could not be levied without the employment and exhibition of force . . . Intention to go to war may be proved by words,' but the actual going to war must 'be proved by open deeds.' If it was not 'a military assemblage in a condition to make war, it was not a levying of war.' He admitted that he had failed to state in his earlier ruling that the rendezvous must be in considerable force, but now held that no testimony regarding events that occurred after the assemblage on Blennerhassett Island could be admitted as relevant to prove Burr's intentions, and consequently no overt act of treason could be shown to have occurred there. This despite the fact that in the Bollman and Swartwout case he had indicated that it was only necessary to prove that the armed force *intended* to commit treason.[74]

In the second place, Marshall did not declare that the accused must necessarily have been present at the place where the treasonable assemblage was held. He might be adjudged guilty if he merely procured the assemblage, 'But the fact that he did procure the treasonable assemblage must be charged in the indictment and proved by two witnesses, precisely as must actual physical presence.' Yet he said that it was not treason merely to 'advise or procure treason.' Since Burr had not been charged with the procurement of the rendezvous on the island, and since no such procurement had been proved by even one witness, no overt act of treason had been established and no collateral testimony was admissible.[75]

It took the Chief Justice three hours to read his opinion, at the end of which he said: 'The jury have now heard the opinion of the court on the law of the case. They will apply that law to the facts, and will find a verdict of guilty or not guilty as their own consciences may direct.' [76] The next morning Hay announced that the prosecution had no further argument or evidence to submit,

[73] Beveridge, *Marshall*, III, 504.
[74] Ibid. 507–9; Cabell, *Trial of Aaron Burr*, 29–30.
[75] Beveridge, *Marshall*, III, 510, 512.
[76] Brady, *Trial of Aaron Burr*, 88.

and the jury retired. After a consultation which lasted only 25 minutes, the jurors returned and their foreman, Colonel Edward Carrington, reported, 'We of the jury say that Aaron Burr is not proved to be guilty under this indictment by any evidence submitted to us. We therefore find him not guilty.'[77] Burr's counsel at once objected that this was an irregular verdict and that the finding should be simply 'guilty' or 'not guilty.' Marshall compromised by directing that the verdict stand on the bill as the jury wished it, but the entry of 'not guilty' be made on the record. Thus ended the trial of Aaron Burr for treason, and with it fell the cases against Blennerhassett and other associates.[78] Blennerhassett said that Burr was in high spirits and was planning to renew operations, but it was his opinion that the Colonel always surrounded himself with an air of mystery and that no one really knew his mind.[79]

All the prisoners were now free men. We can be certain that between his daughter Theodosia and his numerous Richmond friends, Burr was not lacking for entertainment. Blennerhassett's wife had remained all the while in Natchez, but Blennerhassett also knew how to amuse himself. On 10 September he wrote: 'I went this evening to the Harmonic Society . . . The flutes were good, with four moderately good violins, two tenors, two bass players, one tolerably good and three excellent singers . . . The instrumental music was all old, and known to me.' A few weeks later he himself took part in a concert by the same society.[80]

On 3 September, Burr had been put under a $5000 bond to appear for trial on a charge of misdemeanor; that is, of having set on foot an expedition with the intention of invading the dominions of the King of Spain. The jury was empaneled on the 9th and the hearing got under way immediately, but Hay had no hope of a conviction and the proceedings dragged heavily. More than 50 witnesses were examined, but on the 15th the District Attorney moved to enter a nolle prosequi on the indictment. This was not permitted, and within a half an hour the jury brought in a verdict of 'not

[77] Beveridge, *Marshall*, III, 513.
[78] Cabell, *Trial of Aaron Burr*, 29.
[79] Safford, *Blennerhassett Papers*, 405, 442–3; Beveridge, *Marshall*, III, 518.
[80] Safford, *Blennerhassett Papers*, 399, 408.

guilty.'[81] Thus the trial which had begun with such fanfare ended on a falling note. It had lasted all summer and into the fall, and though it had made Burr something of a dark hero, it had hardly made shining ones of either the President or the Chief Justice.

[81] Beveridge, *Marshall,* III, 523-4; Cabell, *Trial of Aaron Burr,* 30; McCaleb, *Burr Conspiracy,* 296.

Chapter XV

WHITEWASH FOR WILKINSON

AFTER BURR'S ACQUITTAL, he and Blennerhassett were not long to enjoy their freedom, for on 16 September, they, with Major Israel Smith, of Cayuga, New York, a kinsman of the Swartwouts, were hailed before the court to show cause why they should not be held for trial in Ohio or Kentucky on a charge of having committed treason and misdemeanor when they assembled their forces on an island at the mouth of the Cumberland River. This hearing was continued until 20 October. Marshall admitted practically all the evidence offered; and though little new light was thrown upon Burr's activities, there was much that reflected upon the character and conduct of General Wilkinson.

That special attention was paid to the General was due to the plan of procedure adopted by Wickham and his associate counsel for the defense. In order to clear himself of the charge of treason, Burr had had to admit that he contemplated an expedition against Mexico, and this charge was now to be met by the argument that such a move had been planned in concert with Wilkinson on the assumption that the United States would be at war with Spain. But, far from engaging in war, the General, who could be proved to be a pensioner of that power, had undertaken, by concocting a charge of treason against the Colonel, to shield his benefactor from the blow which Burr intended.[1]

[1] *A.S.P., Misc.*, I, 608.

While the suave New Yorker was dealing out most of the punishment in court, some of his old friends were saying unkind things about him behind his back. Blennerhassett had several conversations with Major Smith and Colonel De Pestre and the latter assured him that if Burr had frankly disclosed his designs to Yrujo, and really projected a severance of the Union with no hostile intentions toward the Spanish provinces, he might have had easy access to the Spanish treasury and arsenals; he might even have had, last winter, the whole equipage of two French sloops of war, which offered to bring their small arms with them into his service.[2] Though De Pestre should have known much of Burr's foreign relations, he was now speaking of a discredited man, and his statements may be open to question.

Smith told Blennerhassett that Burr planned to set off for England immediately after his liberation in order to collect money for reorganizing his projects, 'which,' said the Irishman, 'I now have ascertained to be as baseless as the interests of the parties or persons to whom he discloses them are opposed or variant.' [3] He was jealous of his informants and remarked that he had had more of Burr's confidence than either of them, for the Colonel had insinuated to him that Smith was not disposed to fight when they landed on the lower Mississippi, whereas Blennerhassett had suspected Burr of not being inclined to do so. He accused the Colonel of lying about hiding his muskets while his boats were being searched, and about various other matters. His final judgment of his quondam chief was that his 'conduct may warrant the suspicions of Cowles Mead, and fully prove that there is at least *but method in his madness*.' [4] When Lieutenant Jackson put in his appearance and testified in court, Blennerhassett recorded that he added nothing to his affidavits which the prosecutors had published in the *Argus*, but 'he made out enough of treachery and perjury, probably, to swell the current of suspicion against Burr's treasonable designs.' [5]

One of the witnesses now introduced by Burr's counsel for the purpose of discrediting Wilkinson was Major James Bruff, who had told Secretary of War Dearborn that Wilkinson was a Spanish spy

[2] Safford, *Blennerhassett Papers*, 416–17.
[3] Ibid. 414–15.
[4] Ibid. 414–16, 435–6.
[5] Ibid. 459.

and a traitor. Luther Martin had met him in Baltimore and promised that if he would come to Richmond and testify, he would 'lash Wilkinson into tortures' by revealing the letter of 13 May which Burr said he had received from the General, but which he had so far refused to give up. The Major, seeing an opportunity for revenge against Wilkinson for having had him court-martialed, agreed to appear in court.[6]

Bruff had served with distinction as a young officer during the Revolution. He was wounded and captured at Camden, but was later exchanged and returned to active duty until the end of the war. In 1794 he again entered the service as a captain of artillerists and engineers, and was eventually sent to the frontier outpost of St. Louis. Here he was in command of the garrison, it will be recalled, when General Wilkinson arrived there as governor of Louisiana Territory in 1805. The Brigadier had at once attempted to interest him in some unnamed scheme which would make his fortune, and when Bruff took no interest in the proposal, the two became estranged and the court-martial followed. On 30 June 1807, Bruff resigned his commission.[7]

The Major was present during Burr's visit to St. Louis and he testified that there was a close relation between the General and the Colonel. He said that Wilkinson's measures as governor were such as to disgust the people with the American regime and prepare them for revolt, and that he cultivated the French element. He reported that Judge Easton of the Territorial Superior Court could prove that Wilkinson had projected the Miranda expedition, and that Easton, along with John Adair, Samuel Hammond, and Major Timothy Kibbey, could prove that Pike's Santa Fe expedition was connected with and a part of Burr's plan. He stated further that he had sent the Secretary of War a letter from St. Louis proving the latter fact, and added that none of the men whom he had named as able to prove the connection between Burr and Wilkinson had been summoned as witnesses. According to Bruff, Wilkinson had not withdrawn from the conspiracy until the country had be-

[6] Richmond *Enquirer*, 6 Nov. 1807; Adams, *History of the United States*, III, 454.
[7] Francis B. Heitman (ed.), *Historical Register and Dictionary of the United States Army* (Washington, 1903), I, 256; Carter, *Territorial Papers*, XIII, 16–17.

come alarmed over the Colonel's operations and the project appeared to be a desperate venture. But Secretary of War Dearborn had told Bruff that the President would support Wilkinson because of his energetic measures at New Orleans.[8]

Blennerhassett hastened to record in his journal that

> Burr and Martin made a considerable blunder to-day, by producing a Major Brough [*sic*], to the discredit of Wilkinson, as they thought. The Major it is true, told some curious stories to the court and to the General, as unexpected by the Judge, probably, as they were unpalatable to the Brigadier, but the effect only tended to show both Burr and Wilkinson equally rivals in treachery to the State, if not to themselves. Burr would gladly have pretermitted the exhibition of this scene, but it was too late; the curtain had risen, and 'Peacham' and 'Locket' stood confessed in every line of their characters, —.

As for Major Bruff, since Martin did not carry out his promise concerning Wilkinson's letter of 13 May, he regretted that he had agreed to testify.[9]

When Burr's counsel decided to make a determined attack upon Wilkinson, they sent James Alexander to New Orleans to get in touch with Edward Livingston and Judge John B. Prevost in order to collect evidence against the General. There they had no difficulty in getting pertinent statements from three residents of the city. John Mercier, a clerk in the office of the Spanish governor from 1792 to 1801, deposed that in 1795–6, Governor Carondelet carried on a secret correspondence in cipher with some person in the American West, presumably General Wilkinson, regarding a dismemberment of the Union, and that toward the end of 1795, Thomas Power, an agent employed by the Spanish authorities for secret negotiations, was entrusted with about $9000 delivered to him in the office of the governor in the presence of the deponent.[10]

Peter Derbigny, now a New Orleans attorney, testified that while

[8] Charleston *Courier*, 28 Oct. 1807; Richmond *Enquirer*, 6 Nov. 1807; *Annals of Congress*, 10 Cong., 1 Sess., 591–8, 600–602; Adams, *History of the United States*, III, 454–5.

[9] Richmond *Enquirer*, 6 Nov. 1807; Safford, *Blennerhassett Papers*, 444.

[10] Ibid. 429–30fn.; Deposition of John Mercier, Jr., 31 Aug. 1807, Chillicothe Papers; *A Plain Tale Supported by Authentic Documents Justifying the Character of General James Wilkinson*, 'by a Kentuckian' (New York, 1807), 5.

he was a resident of New Madrid in 1796, Power came to that place and received about $9000 from Dr. Thomas Portell, Spanish commandant there. Power concealed this money in barrels of coffee and sugar bought from the deponent and departed with it for Cincinnati. On his return, Derbigny was informed that the money had been delivered to Wilkinson. The deponent further stated that shortly after the surrender of Louisiana to the United States he had heard of Wilkinson's shipment of sugar paid for in Spanish dollars, lately coined and contained in bags that had not been opened since leaving the Spanish mint. Having lately become an American citizen, Derbigny felt it his duty to inform Governor Claiborne of this incident, whom he authorized to transmit the information to the President. Derbigny also stated that during the winter of 1804–5 he was in Washington as one of the agents sent to Congress by the government of Orleans Territory. On this occasion Wilkinson introduced him and his colleagues to Vice-President Burr, and advised them to cultivate his acquaintance.[11]

John McDonough, Jr., a commission merchant of New Orleans, deposed that in March 1804 Wilkinson had bought 107 hogsheads of sugar for shipment to New York, and paid him $9045.35 in Spanish dollars, part of which was contained in Mexican bags such as those that came from Vera Cruz. Edward Livingston sent these depositions to Burr, and had subpoenas issued to Daniel Clark and Thomas Power in order that they might be sent to Richmond to testify as to Wilkinson's Spanish pension.[12]

It is strange that Burr's supporters should have expected these two to give evidence against the General, for they had been his intimate friends. Just before he set out for Richmond, Wilkinson had written Clark, 'I deeply regret not seeing you before leaving New Orleans. I did earnestly desire a reconciliation between yourself and Gov. Claiborne.' Clark, arriving in New Orleans at the end of May, was honored at dinner by his Burrite friends, and was challenged to a duel by Governor Claiborne because of accusations made by Clark in the House of Representatives. The duel was

[11] Affidavit of Peter Derbigny, 27 Aug. 1807, Chillicothe Papers; Safford, *Blennerhassett Papers*, 431–2fn.

[12] Deposition of John McDonough, Chillicothe Papers; Safford, *Blennerhassett Papers*, 430–31fn.

fought near Manchac on 8 June, and Claiborne received Clark's ball through the right thigh, but the wound was not serious.[13]

During the previous March, Power had asked Wilkinson for a loan of $500, and on 16 May 1807, he had given the General a written statement to the effect that: 'I have at no time carried or delivered to General James Wilkinson, from the government of Spain, or from any person in the service of said government, cash, bills or property of any species. — said Wilkinson, to the best of my knowledge and belief, had no participation, and was a perfect stranger to the mission on which I visited Kentucky in the year 1797, —.'[14] Livingston and Prevost apologized profusely to Clark for putting him in an embarrassing position, and Power protested bitterly against the subpoena, but about the first of September they both sailed for Philadelphia on Clark's ship, the *Comet*, and by 11 October they had arrived in Richmond.[15]

When Wilkinson first heard the news of their coming, he was filled with consternation and wrote a long letter to Clark, which was both cajoling and threatening. Among other things, he said:

> Hitherto your name has not been mentioned, as I understand, in Burr's Trial. I have received several letters from New Orleans lately, which have occasioned me some surprise. They import, that you were coming round with capt. Power, to do me all the injury you were able, and that to induce Power to come, you had accommodated him with the means, and had agreed to support his family. This I could give no credit to, after the justice you had repeatedly rendered me, —. I have labored assiduously to avoid the violation of private correspondence, whilest Mr. Burr, in the true character of a depraved villain, had adverted to a letter said to be received from me [postmarked 13 May], in terms calculated to excite suspicions injurious to me, yet to my reiterated demands refuses either to bring forward that letter, or to give me leave to bring forward his private letters which I received at St. Louis, one of which relates to your communication received from New Orleans, in which you mention Power and Minor, and the report of a meditated Mexican expedition,

[13] Wilkinson to Clark, 24 May 1807, Clark, *Proofs*, app. 153; Claiborne to Clark, 23 May 1807, Carter, *Territorial Papers*, IX, 738; same to Jefferson, 1 June 1807, ibid. 742–74; *Louisiana Gazette*, 12 June 1807.

[14] Power to Wilkinson, 8 Mar., 16 May 1807, Bacon, *Report*, 118, 119–20.

[15] Bruce, *Randolph*, I, 304–5; Safford, *Blennerhassett Papers*, 450; James M. Bradford to Harry Innes, 4 Sept. 1807, Innes Papers, XXII, pt. 1, L. of C.; Edmund Randolph to Cary Nicholas, 19 Oct. 1807, ibid.; Edward Livingston to Daniel Clark, 17 Aug. 1807, Bacon, *Report*, 472; J. B. Prevost to Daniel Clark, 17 Aug. 1807, ibid. 473–4.

and the revolt of the western states, etc. etc. I had mislaid this letter, when I wrote you from Washington, but have since found it. —. Much pains were taken by Bollman to induce me to believe you were concerned. Swartwout assured me Ogden had gone to New Orleans, with despatches for you from Burr, and that you were to furnish provisions, etc. Many other names were mentioned to me, which I have not exposed, nor will I ever expose them, unless compelled by self defence, —. Among other documents handed to me in New Orleans, is a bill on you from G. D. Ogden in favor of P. V. Ogden — drawn, as he says, on account of the land purchase. This I have never uttered. Things of this nature, and the correspondence of twenty years, torn up before a court of justice in the hour of distrust and suspicion, may effect irreparable injuries to the innocent. Burr has said in court, that he expected testimony from New Orleans, to prove that himself and the country had both been sold. I shall be happy to hear from you.[16]

When Power arrived in Richmond, he called on Wilkinson, who, according to Power, locked his door, 'and with the emotions of agony and despair, raising his head and hands toward heaven, exclaimed, "What, Power, are you come here to do? And what evidence do you intend giving before the court? Can't you go out of the way?" ' Power assured him he would tell nothing that would implicate his own [the Spanish] Government, and Wilkinson exclaimed: 'If so, I am safe, give me your hand and promise this.' Power promised.[17]

When Clark put in his appearance, Wilkinson rushed to attorney Hay and, 'terrified beyond description, declared that Clark could ruin him.' It was Burr who saved him from this ordeal. The Colonel sent a message to Clark saying that he would like a conference with him, but the New Orleans merchant answered that he would speak with neither him nor Wilkinson until after he had given his testimony. Burr then informed him that he had not sent for him and did not wish him to appear as a witness. Clark left for Philadelphia without having been called into court.[18]

Power was not so fortunate. On 17 October he was put on the stand and Burr stated, 'This witness is to be examined for two purposes: first, to verify certain papers; secondly, to prove that

[16] Wilkinson to Clark, 5 Oct. 1807, ibid. 481–2.
[17] Deposition of Daniel W. Coxe, *Louisiana Gazette,* 19 July 1808.
[18] Deposition of Daniel W. Coxe, Bacon, *Report,* 465–71.

General Wilkinson was at a certain period in the pay of the Spanish Government; and then, by other witnesses, we shall prove that his pay has continued, and that he has frequently been in the habit of receiving large sums of Spanish silver. The object is to impeach his credibility, by proving the falsehood of his declaration that he had not corresponded with the Baron de Carondelet.' [19]

There was some argument between opposing counsel about whether such testimony could be admitted, and then Burr showed Power the affidavits of Derbigny and Mercier and asked him if he could identify the signatures attached to them. He said that he could. Burr then asked him, 'Do you know of any correspondence in cipher by General Wilkinson with the Baron Carondelet?' Power refused to answer this question on the ground that he was a Spanish subject and could not honorably give any testimony that might operate against the interests of his King. Burr's counsel insisted that he be compelled to do so and Power steadfastly refused. Marshall finally stated that the evidence would not, in any case, have any bearing upon his decision, and then ruled that Power must answer questions regarding the existence of the correspondence, but not about its nature. Power now admitted that for some time Wilkinson and Carondelet had communicated by means of a complicated cipher,[20] but the depositions of Derbigny and Mercier were not read in court. At about this time George Hay wrote to Jefferson that his confidence in Wilkinson had been 'shaken, if not destroyed.' [21]

Another witness summoned to Richmond by Burr's counsel was Judge Thomas Todd of Kentucky, an old friend of Harry Innes and others who had been involved in Wilkinson's earlier Spanish intrigues. When the General heard of this he was disturbed and wrote a note to the Judge asking for a statement testifying to his good character. Todd refused to comply with this request, saying that he preferred to present his evidence in court. When the Judge was put on the stand on 3 October, he was only questioned in detail about Burr's title to the Bastrop land, and his opinion was that it

[19] *Louisiana Gazette*, 17 Nov. 1807; *Annals of Congress*, 10 Cong., 1 Sess., I, 677-8.
[20] Ibid. 683.
[21] Hay to Jefferson, 15 Oct. 1807, Adams, *History of the United States*, III, 471.

was not valid.[22] A week earlier Todd had written a significant letter to Harry Innes in which he said: 'Public opinion has within a few days, changed very much to the prejudice of Burr & his party. The connection between Burr & Blennerhassett has been already proved & the declarations made by the latter, that it was intended to sever the Union, seize on New Orleans & revolutionize Mexico, have also been proved — Altho it may yet be doubted whether *Treason* has been committed, no doubt seems to exist as to Intention & that their plans were most diabolical —.' [23]

A similar line of reasoning was followed by William Wirt when he summarized the evidence for the prosecution. The statements Burr had made to Eaton and the Morgans were in substantial agreement with those Blennerhassett had made to the Hendersons and in the 'Querist' articles. They proposed a separation of the Union at the Alleghenies, an invasion of Mexico, and the establishment of a Western empire with New Orleans as its capital and Burr as its emperor. Wirt said that not only Eaton but also Silas Dinsmore and Captain Shaw had testified that the Burr party was so strong in New Orleans that the city might have been taken without striking a blow, and that by holding this strategic point the conspirators expected to force the Western states to join them. All this and more, said Wirt, could be established without relying upon the testimony of General Wilkinson — the case being strong enough to stand without it.[24]

On 20 October the Chief Justice handed down his final opinion on the motion to commit Burr, Blennerhassett, and Smith for trial on charges of treason and misdemeanor alleged to have been committed when their men assembled on the island at the mouth of the Cumberland River. He said that,

> The conversations of Mr. Blennerhasset evince dispositions unfriendly to the Union, and his writings are obviously intended to disaffect the Western people, and to excite in their bosoms strong prejudices against their

[22] James Wilkinson to Judge Thomas Todd, 15 Sept. 1807, Autograph Collection, Pennsylvania Historical Society.

[23] Thomas Todd to Harry Innes, 27 Sept. 1807, Innes Papers, XVIII, no. 12, L. of C.

[24] William Wirt, *The Two Principal Arguments of William Wirt, Esquire, on the Trial of Aaron Burr for High Treason and on the Motion to Commit Aaron Burr and Others for Trial in Kentucky* (Richmond, 1808), 104–218.

Atlantic brethren. That the object of these writings was to prepare the Western States for dismemberment, is apparent on the face of them, and was frequently avowed by himself. In a conversation with the Messrs. Henderson, which derives additional importance from the solemnity with which his communications were made, he laid open a plan for dismembering the Union under the auspices of Mr. Burr. To others, at subsequent times, he spoke of the invasion of Mexico, as the particular object to which the preparations then making were directed. In all those whom he sought to engage in the expedition, the idea was excited that, though the Washita [Ouachita] was its avowed object, it covered something more splendid; and the allusions to Mexico, when not directed, were scarcely to be misunderstood.

But, said Marshall, the charges of treason applied only to Burr and Blennerhassett. No such designs were communicated to the men on Cumberland Island. 'On comparing the testimony adduced by the United States with itself,' the Chief Justice continued,

this is observable. That which relates to treason indicates the general design, while that which relates to the misdemeanor points to the particular expedition which was actually commenced. Weighing the whole of this testimony, it appears to me to preponderate in favor of the opinion that the enterprise was really designed against Mexico. But there is strong reason to suppose that the embarcation was to be made at New Orleans, and this, it is said, could not take place without subverting for a time the Government of the Territory, which it is alleged would be treason.

Marshall admitted that violence and even treason might result from such an attempt, 'but this treason would arise incidentally, and would not be the direct object for which the men originally assembled.' As the result of this line of reasoning, he decided that no charge had been proved against Israel Smith, but that Burr and Blennerhassett should be held for trial on the charge of misdemeanor. Their bail was fixed in the amount of $3000.[25]

Blennerhassett's reflections on Marshall's pronouncement are significant. On the very day of the decision, he recorded that 'Mr. Marshall, at last, has delivered an elaborate opinion, purporting that he cannot commit any of us for treason; not because we had none in our hearts, but because we did none with our hands.' And two days afterward he wrote his wife that the final order of the

[25] *Annals of Congress*, 10 Cong., 1 Sess., I, 773-5, 778.

court was that he and Burr should be tried for misdemeanor in Chillicothe on the first Monday in January, though it was generally understood that the Government would drop all further proceedings. He said the Judge found no ground to entertain a suspicion of an overt act having been committed, though he thought proof enough had been exhibited of a *Treasonable design*. 'All friends of the Chief Justice here,' he added, 'are as much dissatisfied with his opinion yesterday [*sic*] as Government has been with all his former decisions. He is a good man, and an able lawyer, but timid and yielding under the fear of the multitude, —.' [26]

In January of the next year, Burr and Blennerhassett were indicted in the United States District Court at Chillicothe, Ohio, for conspiracy against the dominion of Spain, and some documents were sent from the files of the court in Richmond to be used in the trial, but the charges were never pressed.[27] The accused were at last free men, although Burr was not entirely clear of legal entanglements. Blennerhassett said that civil suits amounting to $36,000 were instituted against Burr in Richmond, and he added: 'It is quite unaccountable how he has disposed of all the cash he raised in Kentucky last year. Jourdan has convinced me that he, Burr, actually received through his hands, at Lexington, not less than $40,000, of which he never advanced more than $15,000 to all his agents and associates, to say nothing of all the property he procured upon his drafts. He could since have spent but little money, having received much from the United States, and having been in custody until very lately.' [28]

Blennerhassett, Martin, and Dr. Cummins went by stage to Baltimore, and were soon followed by Burr. While they tarried here, a handbill announced the intended execution that afternoon of Marshall, Martin, Burr, and Blennerhassett. Burr hurriedly left town and the mayor called out two troops of cavalry and sent a guard to protect Blennerhassett. But the Irishman, taking no chances, retired to the garret of his tavern and from this vantage point observed the

[26] Safford, *Blennerhassett Papers*, 300–301, 460–61.
[27] Chillicothe Papers, memo. dated 1808; Richmond *Enquirer*, 11 Feb. 1808.
[28] Safford, *Blennerhassett Papers*, 466–7.

mob of nearly 1500 men who appeared about five o'clock with carts bearing effigies of the purported victims of their displeasure, which were later hanged and burned. Before dispersing, the mob went to Luther Martin's house and played the 'Rogue's March' for Burr's benefit, but no damage was done and no violence committed; and the demonstration ended around seven o'clock in the evening.[29]

From Baltimore the travelers went to Philadelphia, where the families of the Federalist merchants paid them marked attention. There was much excitement over the crisis that the affair of the *Chesapeake* and the *Leopard* had brought on with Britain, but the social amenities were not forgotten. Burr stayed with his friend George Pollock; and Blennerhassett put up at the Mansion House, lately known as Bingham's, which was kept by an Englishman 'in the best style I ever saw in America.' The Irishman now met Bollman for the first time, and attended a party given by Burr for his host and Charles Biddle, Dr. Cummins, David Randolph, and young Tom Butler, who had accompanied Mrs. Blennerhassett down the Mississippi. Here, too, he met the famous merchant, Vincent Nolte, who had often seen Wilkinson at parties in New Orleans. Nolte presented him with a caricature of the General, à la Falstaff, which, however, was considered inferior to the one the merchant had done of Edward Livingston as Lawyer Greyhound. The Islander supped with Joseph Lewis, who had befriended him in Richmond, and at a dinner party he saw General Jean Victor Moreau who was leaving by stage the next day for New Orleans by way of Pittsburgh. Dr. Erich Bollman was to be his sole companion on this long journey.[30]

Soon Blennerhassett too was on his way westward. On 12 December he passed Wheeling en route to Marietta and he must have stopped to take a nostalgic look at his deserted island as he floated down the Ohio. On 5 January he arrived at the Falls and was arrested in Jeffersonville on suspicion that he was a fugitive from justice. He was quickly released, however, and his journey ended when he joined his wife at Washington, the village capital of Mississippi Ter-

[29] Ibid. 462, 464, 476–82; Beveridge, *Marshall*, III, 475–6, 517; *National Intelligencer*, 22 Nov. 1807.

[30] Safford, op. cit. 482–6, 491–2, 499, 501–2.

ritory. Near this scene of his former adventures he took up his residence in a dilapidated cabin, and with his wife and his library as solace, resigned himself to peaceful obscurity.[31]

While Burr was enjoying his new freedom in Philadelphia, his friend Senator John Smith of Ohio was having his troubles in Washington. Smith, in association with the Kemper brothers, had become interested in large land speculations in the neighborhood of Baton Rouge, and at the end of May he went to New Orleans and thence to West Florida to attend to his property. While there he heard that he had been indicted in Richmond, and offered to surrender himself to Governor Williams. This official furnished him with a guard which conducted him to the scene of the trial in a style befitting a Senator.[32] The case against him was quashed when Burr was acquitted and he proceeded to Washington to attend the session of Congress which convened late in October. On 23 November the President transmitted to Congress the record of the Burr trial and on the 27th the Senate resolved to appoint a committee to inquire into the connection which Senator Smith was alleged to have had with the conspiracy. John Quincy Adams was appointed chairman of this committee, and on the 30th it reported a resolution calling upon the President to submit any papers in his possession which might throw light upon the relations between Smith and Burr. On 2 December Jefferson complied by sending the affidavit of Elias Glover, saying that he had no other pertinent information. On the 9th the committee questioned Smith, and introduced Glover's testimony to the effect that the Senator built boats for Burr and shipped large quantities of supplies down the Ohio for his use; and that Smith and two of his sons had planned to join the expedition.[33]

[31] Richmond *Enquirer*, 2 Jan., 11 Feb. 1808; Reuben Gold Thwaites (ed.), *Early Western Travels*, 1748–1846, IV, *Cuming's Tour to the Western Country*, 1807–1809 (Cleveland, 1904), 320.

[32] Gov. Williams to John Smith, 24 Aug. 1807, Miss. Dept. of Arch. and Hist., *Third Annual Report*, 80–81; Proclamation by Gov. Williams, 22 Sept. 1807, ibid., 85–6; John Smith to George Gordon, 13 Aug. 1807, Burr MSS., L. of C.; Carter, *Territorial Papers*, V, 510fn.; Cox, *West Florida*, 208.

[33] *Queries Addressed by the Committee, 9 December, 1807, to Mr. Smith, with his Answers, as Finally Given*, 31 Dec. 1807, printed by order of the Senate, Senate Documents, 10 Cong., 1 Sess. (Rare Book Room, L. of C.); Jefferson to the Senate, 2 Dec. 1807, *Annals of Congress*, 10 Cong., 1 Sess., I, 53; James Taylor to Harry Innes, 29 Dec. 1807, Innes Papers, XIX, L. of C.

It was not until 31 December that the committee was ready to report, and then Adams introduced a resolution to the effect that, 'John Smith, a Senator from the State of Ohio, by his participation in the conspiracy of Aaron Burr against the *peace*, *union*, and *liberties*, of the people of the United States, has been guilty of conduct incompatible with his duty and station as a Senator of the United States. And that he therefor, and hereby is, expelled from the Senate of the United States.' [34] For more than three months this resolution was, from time to time, discussed by the Senate, with Francis Scott Key and Robert Goodloe Harper acting as counsel for the accused. At last on 9 April the vote was taken and it stood 19 for expulsion and 10 opposed. This failed of the necessary two-thirds by one vote, but on 25 April the Senator, in a letter to the governor of Ohio, resigned his seat and retired from public life.[35]

In Indiana, Davis Floyd fared better. A local court convicted him of high misdemeanor because of his connection with Burr and he was sentenced to pay a fine of ten dollars and to stand committed for three hours! A little later he was appointed clerk of the Territorial Legislature.[36]

Burr was never to face another investigation connected with the conspiracy, but Wilkinson was not so fortunate. Shortly after leaving Richmond, he aroused the enmity of two of his oldest and most intimate friends, and they stirred up a hornet's nest for his discomfiture. Before he left New Orleans, the General had secured from Thomas Power the statement of 16 May absolving him from the charge that he was a Spanish agent. This was given on condition that it would be shown only to President Jefferson and would never be published.[37]

On 17 October, as has been stated, Power was forced against his will to testify that there had been a secret correspondence carried on between Wilkinson and Carondelet, the Spanish governor of Louisi-

[34] *Report of the Committee appointed to inquire into the facts relating to the conduct of John Smith, a Senator of the United States from the State of Ohio, as an alleged associate of Aaron Burr* (Washington, 31 Dec. 1807); *Annals of Congress*, 10 Cong., 1 Sess., I, 62.

[35] Ibid. 324; *Louisiana Gazette*, 13 May, 5 Aug. 1808.

[36] Charleston *Courier*, 6 Nov. 1807.

[37] Power to Wilkinson, 16 May 1807, Bacon, *Report*, 119.

ana, and ten days later the General — who loved his 'sacred honor infinitely more than life itself' — published Power's statement denying his knowledge of any such intrigue. This naturally turned a former friend into a bitter enemy — an enemy who had the means to take revenge.[38]

It is harder to say why Daniel Clark turned against Wilkinson. He had gone to Richmond prepared to testify, but since neither the General nor the Colonel wished him to do so, he had not been put on the stand. From the Virginia capital he went to Philadelphia and at first showed no open animosity toward the General, but said he was through with Burr. His attitude toward Wilkinson soon changed, however, and according to the General it was because in Baltimore he had questioned Clark's financial credit, and the Louisiana merchant had heard of it. Since Clark was, and continued throughout life to be, one of the richest men in New Orleans, it is hard to see what Wilkinson's motives may have been, but it is not hard to understand Clark's purported reaction.[39] Clark himself gave no indication that he had ever heard of such an incident, but soon after reaching Philadelphia, he told his friend, Daniel W. Coxe, that Wilkinson had denounced him and many others in a secret letter to the President.[40]

Be this as it may, the stage was set for a sardonic little drama in Washington. On his way up from Richmond, Power had dined with Robert Goodloe Harper in Baltimore and showed him certain papers in his possession. Harper had advised him to publish them, but Power — a Spanish subject — did not feel free to do so without the consent of the Spanish agent, Yrujo. In Philadelphia he applied to Yrujo, who refused permission, but then, before returning to New Orleans, Power turned over the papers to Clark and authorized him to use them at his discretion. This degree of confidence is not surprising since Power had acted, on occasion, as agent for Clark and was presumably under obligation to him. Harper suggested to Clark that he

[38] Shreve, *The Finished Scoundrel*, 237ff.; *Annals of Congress*, 10 Cong., 1 Sess., I, 1258–60.

[39] Wilkinson, *Memoirs*, II, 7–9; Shreve, *Finished Scoundrel*, 242–3; Safford, *Blennerhassett Papers*, 499–500.

[40] Deposition of Daniel W. Coxe, *Louisiana Gazette*, 19 July 1808; Wilkinson, *Memoirs*, II, 185; Clark, *Proofs*, app. 128.

turn the papers over to John Randolph of Roanoke, who lost no time in putting them to use.[41]

Because of some charges that Randolph had made against Wilkinson before the grand jury in Richmond, the General, on 24 December, challenged the Congressman to a duel. The next day Randolph replied that 'Whatever may have been the expressions used by me in regard to your character, they were the result of deliberate opinion, founded upon the most authentic evidence, — ' adding that if he accepted the challenge, he would be obliged to treat Colonel Burr and Sergeant Dunbaugh also as his equals; that many, perhaps a majority, of the citizens felt toward the General just as he himself did, and that he could not condescend to his level. Early on the morning of 31 December a screaming notice was posted in various parts of Washington. It was headed '*Hector Unmasked*,' and proclaimed that 'In justice to his character, I denounce John Randolph, M.C. to the world as a prevaricating, base, calumniating scoundrel, poltroon and coward.' [42] It is not difficult to imagine the contemptuous, mocking smile with which the Virginian greeted Wilkinson's handbill.

Later that day Randolph arose in the House and read two of the letters which Power had turned over to Clark. One of them, dated 20 January 1796, was from the Baron de Carondelet to Captain Thomas Portell, commandant at New Madrid. It stated that he was sending Portell $9640, which was to be delivered to the order of the American General Wilkinson. Actually this money was packed in two sugar barrels and delivered by Portell to Power, who transported it up the river to Cincinnati. There it was turned over to Philip Nolan, who in turn delivered it to Wilkinson. Randolph next called on Daniel Clark — who still represented Orleans Territory in the House — for further information, but, 'for the sake of appearance,' Clark declined to testify unless compelled by the House to do so. Randolph then presented a resolution calling on the President to institute an investigation of the conduct of General Wilkinson.[43]

[41] Ibid. app. 121–3; Wilkinson, *Memoirs*, II, 55–6.

[42] Richmond *Enquirer*, 7, 9 Jan. 1808; Savannah *Republican*, 19 Jan. 1808; Bruce, *Randolph*, I, 313–15.

[43] Philadelphia *Aurora*, 4 Jan. 1808; Richmond *Enquirer*, 9 Jan. 1808; *Louisiana*

Randolph's resolution was tabled, but Wilkinson now requested the President to grant him a hearing, and on 2 January 1808, Dearborn appointed the officers who were to constitute the court-martial. Dearborn, like Jefferson, had consistently supported Wilkinson and was even charged by Timothy Pickering with having approved the General's improper financial claims against the Government.[44] Since the officers who made up the court were subordinates of the General, they could not have been expected to be too severe in their judgment of him. Obviously, this was not to be the kind of investigation that Randolph had in mind.

The House was apparently unaware of the President's move and, urged on by Randolph, continued to debate the Wilkinson affair. On 7 January it requested Clark to submit a full statement of his information, and on the 11th he complied in writing, accusing Wilkinson of having intrigued with the Spanish for the purpose of separating the American West from the Union and of having received a pension for his services.[45] Two days later the House took up the question again; Clark's statement was read, and Randolph moved that the President be requested to institute an inquiry into the charge that Wilkinson had 'corruptly received money from the Government of Spain, or its agents.' This was passed and then John Wayles Eppes moved that the President be called upon to submit to the House any papers in his possession which might relate to the case. This was also passed and a motion was adopted providing that the House should transmit to the President copies of the papers that had been submitted to it relative to the charges against Wilkinson.[46]

On 20 January the President made reply saying:

Gazette, 29 Jan. 1808; Wilkinson, *Memoirs*, II, 10; *Annals of Congress*, 10 Cong., I Sess., I, 1257.

[44] Ibid. 1258–60, II, 2729; Wilkinson, *Memoirs*, II, 11; Richmond *Enquirer*, 9, 21 Jan. 1808; Charleston *Courier*, 16 Feb. 1809.

[45] 'Statement of Daniel Clark, Washington City, Jan. 11, 1808, in Obedience to Resolutions of the House of Representatives,' *Republican and Savannah Evening Ledger*, 4 Feb. 1808.

[46] 'House of Representatives, Jan. 13, Statement of Daniel Clark,' Richmond *Enquirer*, 21 Jan. 1818; ibid. 19 Jan. 1808; *Annals of Congress*, 10 Cong. I Sess., II, 1445, 1458–61; *Louisiana Gazette*, 22 Mar. 1818.

Some days previous to your resolutions of the 13 instant, a court of inquiry had been instituted at the request of General Wilkinson, — To the Judge Advocate of that court the papers and information on that subject, transmitted to me by the House of Representatives, have been delivered to be used according to the rules and powers of that court —. In the course of the communications made to me on the subject of the conspiracy of Aaron Burr, I sometimes received letters, some of them anonymous, some under names, true or false, expressing suspicions and insinuations against General Wilkinson. But only one of them, and that anonymous, specified any particular fact, and that fact was one of those which had been already communicated to a former Administration. No other information within the purview of the request of the House is known to have been received by any department of the Government from the establishment of the present Federal Government. That which has been recently communicated to the House of Representatives, and by them to me, is the first direct testimony ever made known to me, charging General Wilkinson with a corrupt receipt of money: —.[47]

The President's attitude had amazed Andrew Ellicott, the surveyor of the Florida boundary line, who became acquainted with Wilkinson while on that service. On 14 January this gentleman wrote to Clark, 'To my knowledge, the present administration has been minutely informed of the conduct of General Wilkinson; and why he has been supported and patronised, after this information, is to me an inexplicable paradox. All the information I was able to obtain on the subject of those intrigues was faithfully detailed both to the former and the present administration.' A week later he wrote to Wilkinson telling him what information he had received and when he had communicated it to the Executive.[48]

Dearborn's military court was organized on 11 January at Morin's tavern, and it did not conclude its business until 28 June 1808. Clark refused to testify before it, but his business partner, Daniel W. Coxe of Philadelphia, did so. He said he knew that Clark considered Burr and Wilkinson united in the plan to sever the Union. He stated also that he had gone to Lancaster in order to get Ellicott to appear before the court of inquiry, and this gentleman then told

[47] Jefferson to the House of Representatives, 20 Jan. 1818, *Annals of Congress*, 10 Cong., 1 Sess., II, 2726–8.

[48] Andrew Ellicott to Daniel Clark, 14 Jan. 1808, Wilkinson, *Memoirs*, II, 161; Ellicott to Wilkinson, 21 Jan. 1808, Charleston *Courier*, 20 May 1808.

him that in June 1801, he had personally communicated to the President the exact sum of money sent Wilkinson by Don Thomas Portell, and that this payment was not on account of tobacco, but on account of Wilkinson's pension. Coxe also said that he had seen a Spanish letter from Yrujo to Cevallos, dated Philadelphia, 18 December 1806, expressing the confident conviction that Wilkinson, 'well known & designated in the correspondence of State under the name of No. 13, was united with Burr' in the plan to sever the Western country from the Union, and that there was nothing to fear from their views, which were directed not against the Spanish possessions but against their own country. On 23 July 1808, Valentín de Foronda, the Spanish chargé, wrote Cevallos that Coxe had testified that his friend Yrujo had insinuated to him jestingly that Clark, an intimate friend of Burr, was going to Vera Cruz. Yrujo had hastened to mention this to Clark, who replied that he had not known Burr until he came to New Orleans in 1805, and that he was not so crazy that he could adhere to a man of such desperate fortune.[49]

John Graham, late Secretary of Orleans Territory and now chief clerk in the State Department, was called to the stand and was asked if he had ever had any conversations with Daniel Clark concerning an expedition to Mexico or Burr's Conspiracy. He replied that he first became acquainted with Clark during the winter of 1805–6, when a gentleman of New Orleans informed him that Clark had some information he wished to relay to the Federal Government but did not wish to send it through Governor Claiborne. The great merchant had just returned from his voyage to Vera Cruz and he now turned over to Graham some papers which were copied and sent to the Secretary of State. Among them were estimates of the military force of Mexico, both regulars and militia, giving particular attention to the garrison towns between Vera Cruz and New Mexico. There were also a statement of the naval force at Vera Cruz and a copy of Baron Humboldt's statistical tables in the Spanish language. Clark indicated to Graham that he would

[49] Wilkinson, *Memoirs*, II, 12; Richmond *Enquirer*, 12, 21 Jan. 1808; Deposition of Daniel W. Coxe, *Louisiana Gazette*, 19 July 1808; Daniel Clark to W. Jones, 15 Jan. 1808, *Republican and Savannah Evening Ledger*, 9 Feb. 1808; Foronda to Cevallos, 23 July 1808, A.H.N., leg. 5545, exp. 15, 592–4.

be unwilling to take part in an expedition to Mexico sponsored by the Federal Government, but would participate in a free-lance expedition undertaken with the sanction, but not the aid, of the United States. The object would be to set up an independent empire, severing all connection with the country they had left. Clark then remarked to Graham, 'suppose such a person as yourself joined such an expedition, he might be made a duke.' Graham replied that he would not be interested in any expedition not sanctioned by his Government.[50]

Graham said he did not take Clark seriously until he heard in Lexington that Burr was authorized to draw on Clark for vast sums of money. Clark cross-examined Graham and asked him when he had first heard that Wilkinson was a pensioner of Spain. Graham replied that during his youth in Mason County, Kentucky, he had frequently heard Wilkinson's connection with the Spanish Government through the agency of Power discussed, but that he was young and the rumors made no lasting impression. When he was appointed Secretary of Orleans Territory, however, he had access to all of Governor Claiborne's correspondence, and there he found that the General was being charged with having received a large sum of money in a private manner from the Marquis of Casa Calvo. He immediately communicated this information to the Secretary of State.[51]

In his attempt to discredit Clark, Wilkinson brought in the testimony of Lieutenants W. A. Murray and J. R. Luckett. They agreed in stating that in the spring of 1806 Lieutenant Josiah Taylor and Ensign Mead visited Fort Adams and persuaded Murray to accompany them to New Orleans. In that city during May the three men dined with Judge James Workman, and after dinner they were joined by Lewis Kerr. There they were told of the existence of the Mexican Association of New Orleans and of its plan to seize Baton Rouge, Pensacola, and Mobile, and to send two expeditions to Mexico, one by way of Vera Cruz and the other by way of Natchitoches, which were later to join forces with Miranda. In order to fit out their expeditions the conspirators planned to seize the ship-

[50] Testimony of John Graham, *Louisiana Gazette*, 1 July 1808.
[51] Ibid. 5 July 1808.

ping at New Orleans and the money in the banks there. Lieutenant Murray demurred at this, but when he asked the advice of his good friend, Daniel Clark, this gentleman advised him to participate. Murray was still not persuaded, but Mead agreed to take part in the enterprise.[52]

After Wilkinson had turned against Burr and moved his forces from the Sabine to New Orleans, Luckett saw Mead again and the young man was much distressed. He said he had taken an oath in a private house in New Orleans to take part in a movement that 'would extend devastation from one extreme part of our country to the other' and that it had some connection with Miranda's expedition. Mead indicated that the military were implicated and that his brother, Cowles Mead, had taken depositions against Wilkinson 'as being instrumental in improperly and illegally endeavoring to affect the laws of his Country.'[53]

Another witness called up by the General was Lieutenant Robert T. Spence, who testified that he had sailed from Philadelphia to New Orleans on the ship with Bollman, Alexander, and a Madame D'Auvergne, alias Nora Haskel. He said he carried a letter of recommendation from Burr to Clark, and in New Orleans he had dined with Clark in company with Bollman. He then left the city with letters from Bollman and Madame D'Auvergne to Burr, whom he expected to find in Nashville, but actually met in Lexington.[54]

Since William Eaton had been one of the principal witnesses against Burr, Wilkinson also turned to him for aid. On 23 January 1808, he wrote him, 'The conspiracy formed for my destruction in New Orleans last spring, of which I was fully apprised at Richmond, at the time I was sounding Powers [*sic*] and Clark as to their object in coming there, has burst forth in consequence of my exposition of the turpitude of John Randolph, and Clark — [who] was an associate of the Mexican combination, and labored to promote Burr's *views*.'[55] Eaton replied on 6 February, 'Do you remember, sir, having showed me a confidential letter from Mr. Clark,

[52] Extract of deposition of Lt. W. A. Murray, Burr MSS., L. of C.; Extract of deposition of Lt. J. R. Luckett, 11 Jan. 1807, ibid.

[53] Ibid.

[54] Richmond *Enquirer*, 1 Mar. 1808.

[55] Wilkinson to Eaton, 23 Jan 1808, Prentiss, *Eaton*, 403–4.

which talked of *Dukedoms* and Principalities . . .' This letter, Eaton said, gave him the impression that 'at one period you [Wilkinson] must have thought of a *Western Empire*,' but that mature deliberation determined your adherence to duty and 'the Union.' Eaton said that Wilkinson's explanation of the manner of his receiving $20,000 from a Spanish officer, as due on a tobacco trade, smuggled through his connivance, was satisfactory to him; the conduct was lawful to any American citizen, but 'Mr. Clark swears *there was no tobacco speculation* in the case; this testimony must be invalidated, or *my opinion must suspend*. I really wait with great solicitude the result of the important inquiry; —' [56]

Some time later, in a public address, Eaton said

> I have jeopardized my life and reputation to preserve the integrity of the Union; and (I hope to be forgiven,) to this vigilance and fidelity, rather than to movements on the Sabine or at New Orleans, our hero of Carter's mountain owes his political if not personal existence: for, it was not until my public exposure had alarmed Gen. Wilkinson in his camp, that he, though more than two years acquainted with the treasonable plot, thought of *betraying* his *fellow traitor*, and *becoming a patriot by turning states evidence*.[57]

There was not much comfort in this for the doughty Brigadier.

While Wilkinson was thus busy, Clark was not idle and addressed two letters, dated 2 and 9 January 1808, to Power, who was now back in New Orleans. In the first of these he said that it was a well-known fact that Wilkinson had made no tobacco shipments since the year 1791. This could be proved by the books of a certain Spanish official, namely Don Matías Alfuente, inspector of tobacco since 1792. He wanted Power to collect evidence and urged him to call on (Richard) Relf (of the Firm of Chew and Relf) for assistance and write to Minor for information, and if Bradford or the Browns could be of any service, now was the time for them to come forward, for Wilkinson had accused them all.[58] In his second letter he urged Power to prevent Nicolas María Vidal, Gayoso's former secretary who was now Spanish consul in New Orleans,

[56] Eaton to Wilkinson, 6 Feb. 1808, ibid. 404.
[57] Ibid. 405.
[58] Clark to Power, 2 Jan. 1808, Wilkinson, *Memoirs*, II, 59–60.

from giving any certificates to clear Wilkinson, adding 'you *might* get from him many important things . . .' He also suggested that Power 'Write to Minor that he may not be entrapped, and see Watkins to inform him of what is going on.' [59]

The General also bethought himself of New Orleans and on 2 February addressed an open letter to the citizens of that city saying that his denunciations were confined to 'that diabolical band, which has meditated your destruction, under the title "*Mexican Association*," which is ready at this moment to cooperate in *any* plan to promote their illicit enterprize, and of which I shall prove Daniel Clark himself was a member.' This was published in the *Louisiana Gazette* on 8 March, and the Creoles appear to have accepted his view of the matter. Bollman, Workman, Kerr, and Alexander were in the city, and Claiborne suspected them of subversive activity, but there was no revival of the conspiracy.[60]

It had not been difficult for Wilkinson, at the risk of exposing himself, to prove that Clark had been connected with the Mexican Association of New Orleans and with Burr, but it had been equally easy for Clark to prove that the General had been a pensioner of the Spanish Government. Even before a favorably disposed court, things might have gone badly for the great strategist if he had not, as usual, had a trump card up his sleeve. On 16 January he had taken the precaution of writing to his Spanish friends, Folch and Morales, saying that, 'John Randolph and his infamous informer Daniel Clark' had attacked him. Clark, he said, was a member of the Mexican Association and an accomplice of Burr. Power had been compelled by Clark to enter into this combination and had sworn that he was a Spanish officer, although Wilkinson indicated that he had been dismissed several years before. Then the Brigadier added,

> The monies received [by me] from Louisiana after the year 1790 and subsequent with [*sic*] the termination of my trade to that Province was reported to me by Philip Nolan, my agent, & certified by Don Gilberto [Leonard], as the proceeds of a quantity of tobacco, which had been

[59] Same to same, 9 Jan. 1808, ibid. 60–61.

[60] Wilkinson to citizens of Orleans, *Louisiana Gazette*, 8 Mar. 1808; Claiborne to Madison, 17 Mar. 1808, Rowland, *Claiborne*, IV, 167; *Courier de la Louisiane*, 24 June 1808.

condemned, for being in bad condition and was afterwards received by the Crown; but I have lost or mislaid the accounts. I think the quantity was 220,000 pounds weight, for which I received $4000 by Mr. Lacassagne $6000 by Captn. Collins, & $9000 by Nolan to whom it was delivered by Capt. Power, leaving a ballance in my favor. Certified Statements of this [*sic*] transactions, would enable me to repel Clark's calumnies . . .[61]

The Spanish governor was evidently equal to the emergency and later wrote to Wilkinson:

My dear friend: I believe that you are already well convinced that I have worked as befits a faithful servant of the honorable monarchy of Spain, and that I have sincerely fulfilled the duties that friendship imposes on me. I have done still more, since I have sent to the Archives of Havana all that pertains to the old story, sure that before the United States will be in a state to conquer that capital, You, I, Jefferson, Madison, with all the secretaries of the different departments, and even Prophet Daniel himself will have made many marches on the trip to the other world.

In a note to Someruelos, Captain-General of Cuba and Folch's superior officer, he commented that, 'this is D[on] Daniel Clark, the same who made the noisy accusation against Wilkinson in last year's session of Congress, as a result of which the accused was judged, and absolved through the favor I did him in his defense, believing it my duty . . .' [62] On 25 August 1808, Wilkinson wrote to Folch and thanked him for his kindness in obtaining Collins' affidavit.[63]

The Spanish Government had become much concerned over the charges relating to Wilkinson's pension, and Cevallos asked Casa Calvo to clarify the matter. This he did, but the ministry experienced considerable difficulty in locating the papers which Folch had sent to Havana.[64]

On 24 and 25 June, Wilkinson appeared before the court and

[61] Wilkinson to Folch and Morales, 16 Jan. 1808, A.G.I., Papeles de Cuba, leg. 2375, no. 113; Wilkinson to Folch, same date, ibid. no. 112.

[62] Folch to Wilkinson, n.d., A.H.N., Est. leg. 5550, exp. 2, 124–9.

[63] Wilkinson to Folch, 25 Aug. 1808, A.G.I., leg. 2375, no. 121.

[64] Casa Calvo to Cevallos, 2 Apr. 1808, A.H.N., Est., leg. 5545, exp. 15, 432–6; Foronda to Cevallos, 20 Jan. 1808, ibid. 579–81; Yrujo to Cevallos, 15 Jan. 1808, ibid. 492–507; Foronda to Cevallos, 24 Jan. 1808, ibid. 582–4; Cevallos to Casa Calvo, 29 Mar. 1808, ibid. 437–8.

summed up his charges against Clark, Power, Harper, and others.[65] On 28 June this tribunal handed down its decision:

> It has been proved to the satisfaction of this court that Brigadier General James Wilkinson had been engaged in a Tobacco Trade with Governor Miro of New Orleans, before he entered the American Army in the year 1791, that he received large sums of money for tobacco delivered in New Orleans in the year 1789 & that a large quantity of tobacco belonging to him was condemned and stored in New Orleans in that year. But it has not been proved — that he received any money from the Spanish Government or any of its officers since 1791, —. It has been stated by the General, that after his damaged tobacco had lain some years in store at New Orleans, his agents there received for it & remitted to him the several sums credited in the copy of an account current presented by him — and under the impression that the letters accompanying the said account were written by his said agent Philip Nolan, the Court think it highly probable that this statement is correct. — It is therefore the opinion of this Court that there is no Evidence of Brigadier General James Wilkinson having at any time received a Pension from the Government of Spain, or any of its officers or agents for corrupt purposes, and the Court has no hesitation in saying that as far as his Conduct has been developed by this inquiry, he appears to have discharged the Duties of his Station with honor to himself and fidelity to his Country.

This verdict was signed by H. Burbeck, president, and T. H. Cushing and Jonathan Williams, members of the investigating board, and was approved 2 July 1808, by Thomas Jefferson, President of the United States. Thus the Hero of the Sabine was crowned with another victory.[66]

The Great Conspiracy had ended in a fiasco, and it has usually been looked upon as a minor incident in American history. As far as actual results are concerned, that is a correct view of the affair, but its potentialities were so portentous that it seems reasonable to say that next to the Confederate War it posed the greatest threat of dismemberment which the American Union has ever faced. There were undoubtedly high officials in the Spanish dominions who were prepared to connive at a move to revolutionize Latin America; and there were influential men in New Orleans and

[65] *Louisiana Gazette,* 2 Aug. 1808; Richmond *Enquirer,* 5 July 1808.

[66] National Archives, Office of the Judge Advocate General, R.G. 153, Court-Martial Case Files, 1808–15, box 2, Case of General James Wilkinson, 28 June 1808, 26–7; Wilkinson, *Memoirs,* II, 12; *Louisiana Gazette,* 5 Aug. 1808.

throughout the country ready to co-operate with Burr. The conspirators probably had figured that if they failed, men at the head of a government so recently established by rebels would not be unduly severe on other rebels. Their plot was foiled chiefly because General Wilkinson adhered to his turncoat pattern with chameleon-like consistency. If he had not at the last minute betrayed his friends, it is difficult to estimate what the consequences might have been to the young nation. Aaron Burr went into exile and the Commanding General of the United States Army into a niche of infamy unique in American history.

BIBLIOGRAPHY

MANUSCRIPTS

Alderman Library, University of Virginia.

Adams, Mary, 'Jefferson's Reaction to the Treaty of San Ildefonso,' M.A. thesis, 1951.

Cabell, Joseph C., Notes of evidence in the case of Aaron Burr, June–July 1807.

Luz, Nicia, 'Spanish and French Views of the Burr Conspiracy,' M.A. thesis, 1946.

Smith, Samuel, MSS.

Wickham, John, MSS., Microfilm.

Woodruff, Albert H., 'The Burr Conspiracy and the Press,' M.A. thesis, 1949.

Chicago Historical Society.

Wilkinson Papers.

Graff, Everett D., 38 South Dearborn Street, Chicago, Illinois.

Burr Conspiracy MSS.

Historical and Philosophical Society of Ohio, Cincinnati.

Papers in the Defense of John Smith of Ohio.

Library of Congress.

Archives du Ministère des Affaires Étrangères, Paris, Correspondance Politique, États Unis. Photostats.

Archivo del Ministerio de Estado, Madrid, legajo 215.

Archivo General de Indias, Seville, Papeles de Cuba, legajo 2375. Photostats.

Archivo General de Indias, Seville, Audiencia de Guadalajara, 296. Photostats.

Archivo General de la Nación, Mexico City, Provincias Internas, tomo 239; Marina, tomo 218: 1805–8.

Archivo Histórico Nacional, Madrid, Estado, legajos 5539, 5542, 5543, 5545, 5546, 5548, 5632, 5633. Photostats.
Burr Conspiracy MSS.
Innes, Harry, MSS.
Jefferson, Thomas, Papers.
Madison, James, Papers.
McKee, John, MSS.
Wilkinson, James, Correspondence.

Louisiana Historical Museum, New Orleans.
Miscellaneous MSS.

Museum of New Mexico, Santa Fe.
Spanish Archives. Photostats.

National Archives.
Office of the Judge Advocate General, R.G. 153, Court-Martial Case Files, 1808–15, box 2, Case of General James Wilkinson, 26–7.
Records of the United States Court for the Southern District of Ohio, Record group 21, Affidavits relating to the proposed trial of Aaron Burr, 1807.

New York Historical Society.
Miscellaneous MSS.

New York Public Library.
Burr MSS.

Pennsylvania Historical Society, Philadelphia.
Autograph Collection.

United States District Court, Richmond, Virginia.
Papers relating to the trial of Aaron Burr.

PUBLIC DOCUMENTS

American State Papers: Documents, Legislative and Executive (Washington, 1832–61). 38 vols.

Bacon, E., Chairman, *Report of the Committee Appointed to Inquire into the Conduct of General Wilkinson, February 26, 1811* (Washington, 1811).

Biographical Directory of the American Congress, 1774–1927 (Washington, 1928).

Carter, Clarence Edwin (ed.), *The Territorial Papers of the United States, The Territory of Mississippi*, 1798–1817, vols. v, vi (Washington, 1937, 1938), *The Territory of Orleans*, 1803–1812, vol. ix (Washington, 1940).

Clark, Daniel, *Deposition of Daniel Clark in Relation to the Conduct of General James Wilkinson* (Washington, 1808).

Coombs, J. J., *The Trial of Aaron Burr for Treason* (Washington, 1864).

Cranch, William (ed.), *Reports of Cases Argued and Adjudicated in the Supreme Court of the United States*, vol. IV (New York, 1812).

Heitman, Francis B. (ed.), *Historical Register and Dictionary of the United States Army* (Washington, 1903).

[Hening, W. W. and Munford, Wm. (eds.)], *The Examination of Col. Aaron Burr before the Chief Justice of the United States, upon the Charges of High Misdemeanor, and of Treason against the United States* (Richmond, 1807).

Lloyd, Thomas (ed.), *The Trials of William S. Smith and Samuel G. Ogden, for Misdemeanor, had in the Circuit Court of the United States for the New York District* (New York, 1807).

Ohio, *Supplementary Journal of — The First Session of the Fifth General Assembly of the State of Ohio, December*, 1806. Photostat in the Alderman Library, University of Virginia, from collection of the Western Reserve Historical Society.

Orleans, *Debate in the House of Representatives of the Territory of Orleans on a Memorial to Congress, Respecting the Illegal Conduct of General Wilkinson* (New Orleans, 1807).

Poore, Ben. Perley (ed.), *The Federal and State Constitutions, Colonial Charters, and other Organic Laws of the United States* (Washington, 1872). 2 vols.

Richardson, James D. (ed.), *A Compilation of the Messages and Papers of the Presidents* (New York, 1897–1922). 20 vols.

Robertson, David (ed.), *Report of the Trials of Colonel Aaron Burr* (New York, 1875). 2 vols.

Rowland, Dunbar (ed.), *Official Letter Books of W. C. C. Claiborne, 1801–1816* (Jackson, Miss., 1917). 6 vols.

United States Senate

Annals of Congress, Tenth Congress, First Session, Trial of Aaron Burr (Washington, 1852).

Queries Addressed by the Committee, 9 *December*, 1807, *to Mr. Smith, with his Answers, as Finally Given, Senate Documents, Tenth Congress, First Session* (Washington, 1807). Pamphlet, L. of C.

Report of the Committee Appointed to Inquire into the Facts Relating to the Conduct of John Smith — An Alleged Associate of Aaron Burr (Washington, 1807). Pamphlet, U. Va.

MISCELLANEOUS DOCUMENTS

[Alston, Joseph], *A Short Review of the Late Proceedings at New Orleans — in two Letters to the Printer, by Agrestis* (South Carolina, 1807). L. of C., Miscellaneous pamphlets, vol. 922, no. 8.

Bay, W. V. N., *Reminiscences of the Bench and Bar of Missouri* (St. Louis, 1878).

Biddle, Charles, *Autobiography* (Philadelphia, 1883).

Bolton, Herbert E. (ed.), 'Papers of Zebulon M. Pike, 1806–1807,' *American Historical Review*, XIII (July 1908), 798–827.

Brown, Everett Somerville (ed.), *William Plumer's Memorandum of Proceedings in the United States Senate*, 1803–1807 (New York, 1923).

Brown, Jeremiah, *A Short Letter to a Member of Congress Concerning the Territory of Orleans* (Washington, 1806). Pamphlet, L. of C.

Clark, Daniel, *Proofs of the Corruption of Gen. James Wilkinson, and of his Connexion with Aaron Burr* (Philadelphia, 1809).

Coues, Elliott (ed.), *The Expeditions of Zebulon Montgomery Pike* (New York, 1895). 3 vols.

Daveiss, J. H., *A View of the President's Conduct Concerning the Conspiracy of* 1806 (Frankfort, Ky., 1807). Reprinted in *Quarterly Publications of the Historical and Philosophical Society of Ohio*, XII (1917), nos. 2 & 3, I. J. Cox and Helen A. Swineford (eds.).

Eberstadt, Edward and Sons, New York, *Catalogue no.* 129.

Ellicott, Andrew, *The Journal of Andrew Ellicott* (Philadelphia, 1803).

Ford, Paul Leicester (ed.), *The Writings of Thomas Jefferson* (New York, 1892–9). 10 vols.

Ford, Worthington C. (ed.), *Some Papers of Aaron Burr* (Worcester, Mass., 1920). Reprinted from the *Proceedings of the American Antiquarian Society*, Apr. 1919.

Garrett, Julia Kathryn (ed.), 'Doctor John Sibley and the Louisiana-Texas Frontier, 1803–1814,' *Southwestern Historical Quarterly*, XLV (Jan., Apr. 1942).

Gratz, Simon (ed.), 'Thomas Rodney' (letters), *Pennsylvania Magazine of History and Biography*, XLIV (1920).

Henshaw, Leslie (ed.), 'Burr-Blennerhassett Documents,' *Quarterly Publications of the Historical and Philosophical Society of Ohio*, IX (1914).

'A Kentuckian,' *A Plain Tale Supported by Authentic Documents Justifying the Character of General Wilkinson* (New York, 1807). L. of C., Political Pamphlets, vol. 105, no. 16.

Lipscomb, A. A. and Bergh, A. E. (eds.), *The Writings of Thomas Jefferson*, (Memorial ed., Washington, 1903–4). 20 vols.

Littell, William, *Reprints of Littell's Political Transactions in and Concerning Kentucky and Letter of George Nicholas to his Friend in Virginia. Also General Wilkinson's Memorial, with an Introduction by Témple Bodley* (Louisville, 1926). *Filson Club Publications*, no. 31.

[Livingston, Edward?], *Faithful Picture of the Political Situation of New Orleans at the Close of the Last and the Beginning of the Present Year*, 1807 (Boston, 1808, reprinted from the original New Orleans ed.). *Louisiana Historical Quarterly*, XI (July 1928).

Louisiana. *Esquisse de la Situation Politique et Civile de la Louisiane, depuis* *le* 30 *Novembre* 1803, *jusqu'au ler Octobre*, 1804, *par un Louisianais* (New Orleans, 1804). Pamphlet, L. of C.

Memorial Presented by the Inhabitants of Louisiana to the Congress of the United States in Senate and House of Representatives Convened (Washington, 1804). Pamphlet, L. of C.

Reflections on the Cause of the Louisianians, Respectfully Submitted by their Agents (n.p., n.d.). Pamphlet, L. of C.

Madison, James, *Letters and Other Writings of James Madison* (Congress ed., Philadelphia, 1865). 4 vols.

Nolan, Philip, 'Letters Concerning Philip Nolan,' *Texas Historical Association Quarterly*, VII (1903–4).

Padgett, James A. (ed.), 'Letters of James Taylor,' Kentucky State Historical Society, *Register*, XXXIV (1936).

Rowland, Dunbar (ed.), Department of Archives and History of the State of Mississippi, *Third Annual Report*, 1903–4 (Nashville, 1905).

Safford, William Harrison (ed.), *The Blennerhassett Papers* (Cincinnati, 1861).

Seybert, Adam (ed.), *Statistical Annals — of the United States of America* (Philadelphia, 1818).

Thomson, William, *Compendious View of the Trial of Aaron Burr — Charged with High-Treason: Together with Biographical Sketches of Several Eminent Characters* (Press of the *Holston Intelligencer*, 1807). L. of C., Political Pamphlets, vol. 105, no. 15.

Thwaites, Reuben Gold (ed.), *Early Western Travels*, IV, *Cuming's Tour to the Western Country* (Cleveland, 1904).

Tinling, Marion and Davies, Godfrey (eds.), *The Western Country in* 1793, *Reports on Kentucky and Virginia by Harry Toulmin* (San Marino, 1948).

Van Doren, Mark (ed.), *Correspondence of Aaron Burr and his Daughter Theodosia* (New York, 1929).

Whitaker, Arthur Preston (ed.), 'Documents Relating to the Commercial Policy of Spain in the Floridas,' *Publications of the Florida State Historical Society*, no. 10 (De Land, Fla., 1931).

Wilkinson, James, *Memoirs of my Own Times* (Philadelphia, 1816). 3 vols. *Wilkinson-Randolph Correspondence* (n.p., n.d., circa 1808). Pamphlet. L. of C.

Wilson, Samuel M. (ed.), 'The Court Proceedings of 1806 in Kentucky against Aaron Burr and John Adair,' *The Filson Club Historical Quarterly*, X (Jan. 1936).

Wirt, William, *The Two Principal Arguments of William Wirt, Esquire, on the Trial of Aaron Burr for High Treason and on the Motion to Commit Aaron Burr and others for Trial in Kentucky* (Richmond, 1808).

Wood, John, *A Full Statement of the Trial and Acquittal of Aaron Burr, Esq.* (Alexandria, Va., 1807).

Trial of Aaron Burr before the Federal Court at Frankfort, Ky., Nov. 25, 1806 (Alexandria, Va., 1807). Pamphlet, Va. State Library.

Workman, James, Esq., late Judge of the County of Orleans, *A Letter to the Respectable Citizens, Inhabitants of the County of Orleans,—Relative to the Extraordinary Measures lately Pursued in this Territory* (New Orleans, 1807).

NEWSPAPERS

American Citizen, New York City.
Charleston Courier, Charleston, South Carolina.
Courier de la Louisiane, New Orleans.
The Enquirer, Richmond, Virginia.
Georgia Republican, Savannah, Georgia.
The Kentucky Gazette, Lexington, Kentucky.
The Lancaster Intelligencer, Lancaster, Pennsylvania.
The Louisiana Gazette, New Orleans.
The Louisiana Gazette and New Orleans Daily Advertiser, New Orleans.
The Minerva, Raleigh, North Carolina.
National Intelligencer, Washington, D.C.
The Aurora, Philadelphia.
Raleigh Register and North Carolina State Gazette, Raleigh, North Carolina.
The Republican and Savannah Evening Ledger, Savannah, Georgia.
United States' Gazette, Philadelphia.

SECONDARY WORKS

Abernethy, Thomas P., 'Aaron Burr in Mississippi,' *Journal of Southern History*, xv (1949), 9–21.
The Formative Period in Alabama (Montgomery, 1922).
Western Lands and the American Revolution (New York, 1937).

Adams, Henry, *History of the United States of America* (New York, 1890–91). 9 vols.

Alessio, Robles, Vito, *Coahuila y Texas, desde la Consumación de la Independencia hasta el Tratado de Paz de Guadalupe Hidalgo* (Mexico City, 1945–6). 2 vols.

Anderson, Dice Robins, *William Branch Giles; a Study in the Politics of Virginia and the Nation from 1790 to 1830* (Menasha, Wis., 1914).

Arthur, Stanley Clisby, *The Story of the West Florida Rebellion* (St. Francisville, La., 1935).

Ballesteros y Beretta, Antonio, *Historia de España y su Influencia en la Historia Universal*, v (Barcelona, 1918).

Bemis, Samuel Flagg, *A Diplomatic History of the United States* (New York, 1936).

Beveridge, Albert J., *The Life of John Marshall*, III (Boston, 1919).

Bierck, Harold A., Jr., 'Dr. John Hamilton Robinson,' *The Louisiana Historical Quarterly*, xxv (July 1942).

Bowers, Claude G., *Jefferson in Power* (Boston, 1936).

Brady, Joseph P., *The Trial of Aaron Burr* (New York, 1913).

Bruce, William Cabell, *John Randolph of Roanoke*, 1773–1833 (New York, 1922). 2 vols.

Cabell, James Alston, *The Trial of Aaron Burr* (Albany, 1900).

Castañeda, Carlos E., *The Mission Era: The End of the Spanish Régime*, 1780–1810, vol. V of Gibbons, James P. (ed.), *Our Catholic Heritage in Texas*, 1519–1936 (Austin, Tex., 1942).

Chadwick, French E., *The Relations of the United States and Spain, Diplomacy* (New York, 1909).

Channing, Edward, *A History of the United States*, IV (New York, 1917).

Claiborne, J. F. H., *Mississippi as Province, Territory and State* (Jackson, Miss., 1880).

Clark, Thomas D., *A History of Kentucky* (New York, 1937).

Cox, Isaac Joslin, 'The Burr Conspiracy in Indiana,' *Indiana Magazine of History*, xxv (Dec. 1929).

'General Wilkinson and his Later Intrigues with the Spaniards,' *American Historical Review*, XIX (July 1914).

'Hispanic-American Phases of the Burr Conspiracy,' *Hispanic-American Historical Review*, XII (May 1932).

'The Louisiana-Texas Frontier,' pt. 1, 'The Franco-Spanish Regime,' reprint from the *Quarterly of the Texas State Historical Association*, x, no. 1 (July 1906); pt. 2, reprint from the *Quarterly of the Southwestern Historical Association*, XVI, nos. 1 & 2 (July and Oct. 1913).

'Opening the Santa Fe Trail,' *The Missouri Historical Review*, xxv (Oct. 1930).

'Western Reaction to the Burr Conspiracy,' *Transactions of the Illinois State Historical Society*, 1928 (Springfield, 1928).

The West Florida Controversy, 1798–1813 (Baltimore, 1918).

Davis, Matthew L., *Memoirs of Aaron Burr, with a Miscellaneous Selection from His Correspondence* (New York, 1852).

Fisher, Lillian Estelle, *The Background of the Revolution for Mexican Independence* (Boston, 1934).

Franklin, Francis, *The Rise of the American Nation*, 1789–1824 (New York, 1943).

Gayarré, Charles, *History of Louisiana*, III & IV (New Orleans, 1879, 1885).

Green, James A., *William Henry Harrison, His Life and Times* (Richmond, 1941).

Hamilton, Peter J., *Colonial Mobile* (Boston, 1897).

Hatcher, Mattie Austin, *The Opening of Texas to Foreign Settlement*, 1801–1821, *University of Texas Bulletin*, no. 2714 (Austin, 1927).

Hay, Thomas Robson, 'Charles Williamson and the Burr Conspiracy,' *Journal of Southern History*, II (May 1936).

Henshaw, Leslie, 'The Aaron Burr Conspiracy in the Ohio Valley,' *Ohio Archaeological and Historical Publications*, XXIV (1915).

Hollon, W. Eugene, *The Lost Pathfinder, Zebulon Montgomery Pike* (Norman, Okla., 1949).

Jacobs, James Ripley, *Tarnished Warrior, Major-General James Wilkinson* (New York, 1938).

James, Marquis, *Andrew Jackson, the Border Captain* (Indianapolis, 1933). *The Life of Andrew Jackson* (Indianapolis, 1938).

Jillson, Willard Rouse, *Henry Clay's Defense of Aaron Burr in* 1806 (n.p., 1943). Pamphlet, New York Public Library.

Johnson, Allen and Malone, Dumas (eds.), *Dictionary of American Biography* (New York, 1928–37). 20 vols.

Kennedy, John P., *Memoirs of the Life of William Wirt* (Philadelphia, 1850). 2 vols.

King, Grace, *New Orleans, the Place and the People* (New York, 1899).

Lafuente Ferrari, Enrique, *El Virrey Iturrigaray y los Orígenes de la Independencia de Méjico* (Madrid, 1941).

Little, John P., *History of Richmond* (Richmond, 1933).

McCaleb, Walter F., *The Aaron Burr Conspiracy* (New York, 1936). *The Conquest of the West* (New York, 1947).

Marshall, Humphrey, *The History of Kentucky* (Frankfort, Ky., 1824). 2 vols.

Mayo, Bernard, *Henry Clay, Spokesman of the New West* (Boston, 1937).

Mitchell, Jennie O'Kelly, and Calhoun, Robert Dabney, 'The Marquis de Maison Rouge, the Baron de Bastrop, and Colonel Abraham Morhouse. Three Ouachita Valley Soldiers of Fortune,' *Louisiana Historical Quarterly*, XX (1937).

Moores, Merrill, 'Edward Livingston,' *Louisiana Historical Quarterly*, III (Oct. 1920).

Mordecai, Samuel, *Richmond in By-gone Days* (Richmond, 1946).

Nott, G. William, *A Tour of the Vieux Carré* (New Orleans, 1928).

Owen, Thomas M., *History of Alabama and Dictionary of Alabama Biography* (Chicago, 1921). 4 vols.

Parton, James, *The Life and Times of Aaron Burr* (New York, 1858). *Life of Andrew Jackson* (Boston, 1866). 2 vols.

Pickett, Albert James, *History of Alabama and Incidentally of Georgia and Mississippi* (Birmingham, 1900).

[Prentiss, Charles], *The Life of the late General William Eaton* (Brookfield, Mass., 1813).

Robertson, William Spence, *The Life of Miranda* (Chapel Hill, 1929). 2 vols.

Rowland, *History of Mississippi, the Heart of the South* (Chicago, 1925). 2 vols.

Rydjord, John, *Foreign Interest in the Independence of New Spain* (Durham, N.C., 1935).

Savelle, Max, *George Morgan, Colony Builder* (New York, 1932).

Schachner, Nathan, *Aaron Burr* (New York, 1937).

Shreve, Royal O., *The Finished Scoundrel* (Indianapolis, 1933).

Silver, James W., 'Edmund Pendleton Gaines and Frontier Problems, 1801–1849,' *Journal of Southern History*, I (Aug. 1935).

Simpson, Albert F., 'The Political Significance of Slave Representation, 1787–1821,' *Journal of Southern History*, VII (Aug. 1941).

Stanton, Elizabeth Brandon, *Colonel Aaron Burr* (n.p., 1939). Pamphlet, New York Public Library.

Wandell, Samuel H. and Minnigerode, Meade, *Aaron Burr* (New York, 1925). 2 vols.

Wright, Louis B. and Macleod, Julia H., 'William Eaton's Relations with Aaron Burr,' *Mississippi Valley Historical Review*, XXXI (Mar. 1945).

Yoakum, Henderson K., *History of Texas from its First Settlement in 1685 to its Annexation to the United States in 1846*, I (New York, 1855).

INDEX

68- 69244

Abernethy, Thomas Perkins, 1890–
The Burr Conspiracy. Gloucester, Mass., P. Smith, 1968 [c1954]

xi, 301 p. maps (on lining papers), port. 21 cm.

Bibliography: p. 276–284.

1. Burr Conspiracy, 1805–1807. 2. Burr, Aaron, 1756–1836.

E334.A6 1968 973.4′8 68–3511

Library of Congress [2]

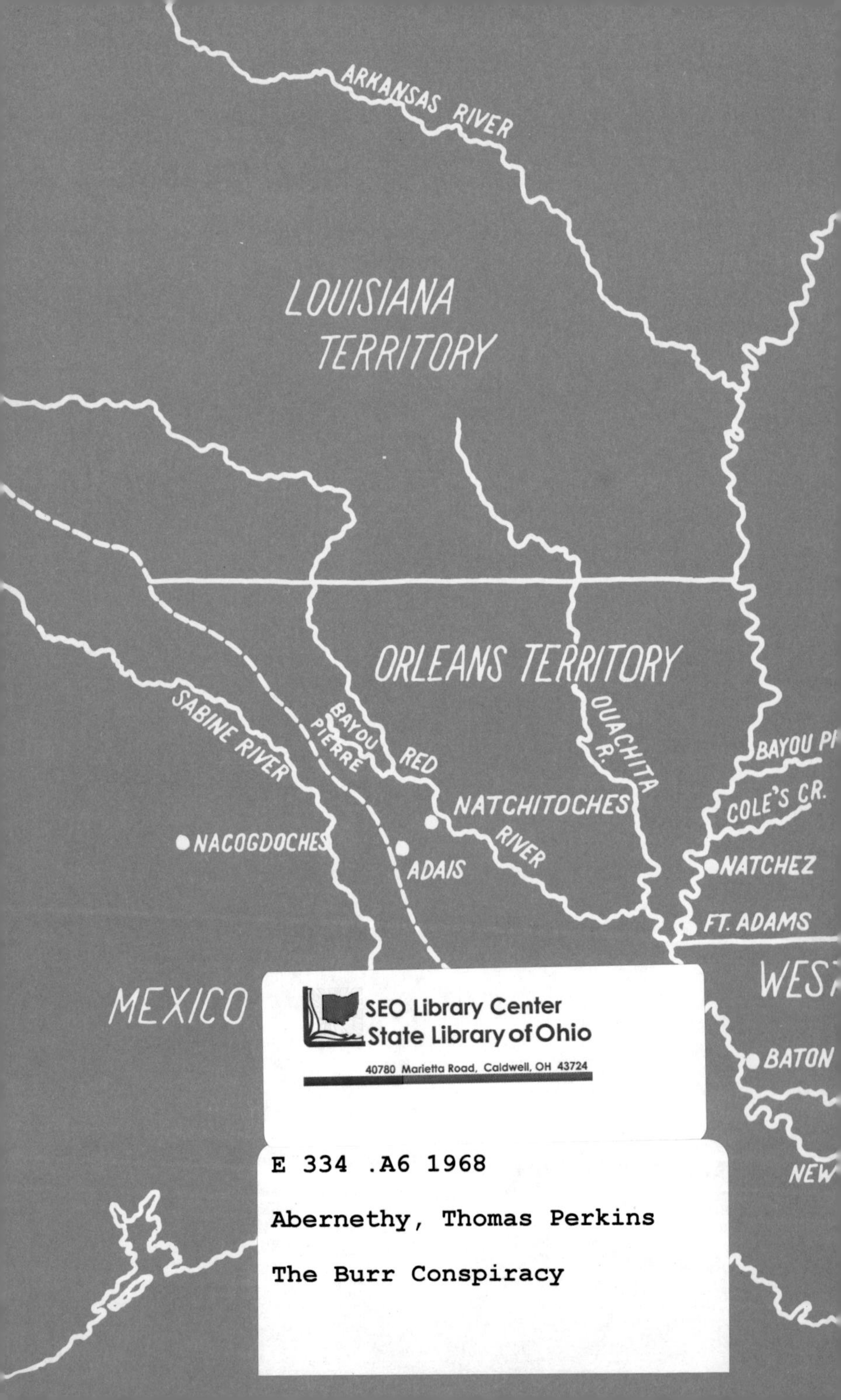
ARKANSAS RIVER
LOUISIANA TERRITORY
ORLEANS TERRITORY
SABINE RIVER
BAYOU PIERRE
RED
NATCHITOCHES
RIVER
QUACHITA R.
BAYOU PI
COLE'S CR.
NATCHEZ
FT. ADAMS
NACOGDOCHES
ADAIS
MEXICO
WEST
BATON
NEW